T0214053

Communications
in Computer and Information Science 1446

More information about this series at http://www.springer.com/series/7899

Slimane Hammoudi · Christoph Quix ·
Jorge Bernardino (Eds.)

Data Management Technologies and Applications

9th International Conference, DATA 2020
Virtual Event, July 7–9, 2020
Revised Selected Papers

 Springer

Editors
Slimane Hammoudi
MODESTE/ESEO
Angers, France

Christoph Quix
Fraunhofer FIT and RWTH Aachen
University
Aachen, Germany

Jorge Bernardino
University of Coimbra
Coimbra, Portugal

ISSN 1865-0929   ISSN 1865-0937 (electronic)
Communications in Computer and Information Science
ISBN 978-3-030-83013-7   ISBN 978-3-030-83014-4 (eBook)
https://doi.org/10.1007/978-3-030-83014-4

This Springer imprint is published by the registered company Springer Nature Switzerland AG
The registered company address is: Gewerbestrasse 11, 6330 Cham, Switzerland

Preface

The present book includes extended and revised versions of a set of selected papers from the 9th International Conference on Data Science, Technology and Applications (DATA 2020), exceptionally held as a web-based event, due to the COVID-19 pandemic, during July 7–9, 2020.

DATA 2020 received 70 paper submissions from 31 countries, of which 20% were included in this book. The papers were selected by the event chairs and their selection is based on a number of criteria that include the classifications and comments provided by the Program Committee members, the session chairs' assessment and also the program chairs' global view of all papers included in the technical program. The authors of selected papers were then invited to submit a revised and extended version of their papers having at least 30% innovative material.

The purpose of the 9th International Conference on Data Science, Technology and Applications (DATA) was to bring together researchers, engineers and practitioners interested in databases, big data, data mining, data management, data security and other aspects of information systems and technology involving advanced applications of data.

The papers selected to be included in this book contribute to the understanding of relevant trends of current research on data science, technology and applications, especially of approaches required to tackle current and future challenges in data science and data management. Thus, this book covers diverse but complementary topics such as data management and quality, new computational models for big data, big data search and mining, statistics exploratory data analysis, predictive modelling, big data infrastructure and architecture, data privacy and security, data and big data in Industry 4.0.

We would like to thank all the authors for their contributions and all the reviewers who have helped ensure the quality of this publication.

July 2020

Slimane Hammoudi
Christoph Quix
Jorge Bernardino

Organization

Conference Chair

Jorge Bernardino   Polytechnic of Coimbra - ISEC, Portugal

Program Co-chairs

Slimane Hammoudi   ESEO, France
Christoph Quix   Hochschule Niederrhein, University of Applied Sciences/Fraunhofer FIT, Germany

Program Committee

Maha Amami   University of Milan-Bicocca, Italy
Christos Anagnostopoulos University of Glasgow, UK
Gustavo Arroyo-Figueroa   Instituto Nacional de Electricidad y Energías Limpias, Mexico
Karim Benouaret   Université Claude Bernard Lyon 1, France
Jan Bohacik   University of Zilina, Slovak Republic
Gloria Bordogna   ICAR-CNR, Italy
Nieves R. Brisaboa   University of A Coruña, Spain
Cinzia Cappiello   Politecnico di Milano, Italy
Paola Carrara   IREA-CNR, Italy
Richard Chbeir   Université de Pau et des Pays de l'Adour, France
Antonio Corral   University of Almeria, Spain
Gianni Costa   ICAR-CNR, Italy
Shruti Daggumati   University of Nebraska-Lincoln, USA
Theodore Dalamagas   Athena Research and Innovation Center, Greece
Bruno Defude   Institut Mines Telecom, France
Steven Demurjian   University of Connecticut, USA
Martin Drlik   Constantine the Philosopher University in Nitra, Slovak Republic
Fabien Duchateau   Université Claude Bernard Lyon 1/LIRIS, France
John Easton   University of Birmingham, UK
Markus Endres   University of Augsburg, Germany
Francesco Folino   ICAR-CNR, Italy
Pedro Furtado   University of Coimbra, Portugal
Jérôme Gensel   Université Grenoble Alpes, France
Paola Giannini   University of Piemonte Orientale, Italy
John Gibson   Telecom SudParis, France
Janis Grabis   Riga Technical University, Latvia

Iulian Sandu Popa	University of Versailles Saint-Quentin-en-Yvelines/Inria, France
Diego Seco	University of Concepción, Chile
Nematollaah Shiri	Concordia University, Canada
Marius Silaghi	Florida Institute of Technology, USA
Stavros Simou	University of the Aegean, Greece
Spiros Skiadopoulos	University of the Peloponnese, Greece
Cosmin Stoica	Romania
Sergey Stupnikov	IPI RAN, Russia
Zbigniew Suraj	University of Rzeszow, Poland
George Tambouratzis	Institute for Language and Speech Processing, Greece
Tatiana Tambouratzis	University of Piraeus, Greece
Horia-Nicolai Teodorescu	Gheorghe Asachi Technical University of Iasi, Romania
Catarci Tiziana	Università degli Studi di Roma La Sapienza, Italy
Maurice van Keulen	University of Twente, The Netherlands
Michael Vassilakopoulos	University of Thessaly, Greece
Thanasis Vergoulis	Athena Research and Innovation Center, Greece
Marco Villani	University of Modena and Reggio Emilia, Italy
Gianluigi Viscusi	EPFL Lausanne, Switzerland
Zeev Volkovich	Ort Braude College, Israel
Leandro Wives	Universidade Federal do Rio Grande do Sul, Brazil
Shengkun Xie	Ryerson University, Canada
Filip Zavoral	Charles University in Prague, Czech Republic
Jiakui Zhao	State Grid Big Data Center of China, China

Additional Reviewers

Michele A. Brandão	IFMG, Brazil
Karam Bou Chaaya	Spider Research Group, France
Athanasios Davvetas	University of the Peloponnese, Greece
Abbas Javadtalab	Concordia University, Canada
Susana Ladra Gonzalez	University of A Coruña, Spain
Stavros Maroulis	Athena Research and Innovation Center, Greece

Invited Speakers

| Wil van der Aalst | RWTH Aachen University, Germany |
| Ioana Manolescu | Inria, France |

Contents

Removing Operational Friction Using Process Mining: Challenges Provided by the Internet of Production (IoP)

Wil M. P. van der Aalst[1,2(✉)], Tobias Brockhoff[1],
Anahita Farhang Ghahfarokhi[1], Mahsa Pourbafrani[1], Merih Seran Uysal[1],
and Sebastiaan J. van Zelst[1,2]

[1] Process and Data Science (Informatik 9), RWTH Aachen University,
Aachen, Germany
wvdaalst@rwth-aachen.de
[2] Fraunhofer-Institut für Angewandte Informationstechnik,
Sankt Augustin, Germany

Abstract. Operational processes in production, logistics, material handling, maintenance, etc., are supported by cyber-physical systems combining hardware and software components. As a result, the digital and the physical world are closely aligned, and it is possible to track operational processes in detail (e.g., using sensors). The abundance of event data generated by today's operational processes provides opportunities and challenges for process mining techniques supporting process discovery, performance analysis, and conformance checking. Using existing process mining tools, it is already possible to automatically discover process models and uncover performance and compliance problems. In the DFG-funded Cluster of Excellence "Internet of Production" (IoP), process mining is used to create "digital shadows" to improve a wide variety of operational processes. However, operational processes are dynamic, distributed, and complex. Driven by the challenges identified in the IoP cluster, we work on novel techniques for *comparative* process mining (comparing process variants for different products at different locations at different times), *object-centric* process mining (to handle processes involving different types of objects that interact), and *forward-looking* process mining (to explore "What if?" questions). By addressing these challenges, we aim to develop valuable "digital shadows" that can be used to remove operational friction.

Keywords: Process mining · Internet of Production · Operations management

1 Introduction

Data are collected about anything, at any time, and at any place. Of course, operational processes in production, logistics, material handling, and maintenance are no exception. In [5] the term *Internet of Events* (IoE) was introduced

© Springer Nature Switzerland AG 2021
S. Hammoudi et al. (Eds.): DATA 2020, CCIS 1446, pp. 1–31, 2021.
https://doi.org/10.1007/978-3-030-83014-4_1

to reflect that machines, products, vehicles, customers, workers, and organizations are increasingly connected to the internet and that our capabilities to track and monitor these entities advanced in a spectacular manner. Notions such as the *Internet of Things* (i.e., all physical objects that are able to connect to each other and exchange data) and *Industry 4.0* (i.e., the fourth industrial revolution enabled by smart interconnected machines and processes), reflect our abilities to monitor operational processes.

The DFG-funded Cluster of Excellence "Internet of Production" (IoP) joins the efforts of over 200 engineers and computer scientists with the goal to fundamentally transform the way industrial production takes place by using data-driven techniques (www.iop.rwth-aachen.de). A key concept within IoP is the notion of a *digital shadow*, i.e., automatically generated models that can be used to control and improve production processes. Although IoP also considers novel production technologies and materials science and engineering, the lion's share of IoP activities is devoted to improving production processes. This position paper focuses on *operational processes* that involve *physical objects* (products, machines, etc.) and have *discrete* process steps. One of the main goals of IoP is to remove *operational friction* in such processes. Much like physical friction, operational friction refers to phenomena that consume additional effort and energy and lead to less-than-optimal results. Examples of operational friction are unnecessary rework, delays, waste, deviations, fraud, missing products, unresponsiveness, and communication loops.

Process Mining can be used to remove operational friction by making conformance and performance problems visible in such a way that it becomes clear what the root-causes of such problems are [5]. Starting point for process mining are the event data mentioned before. Events may take place inside a production facility, inside a transportation system, inside a product, or inside an enterprise information system. Events may be triggered by people, machines, or organizations. *Process Discovery* techniques use event data to create process models describing the operational processes in terms of their key activities. These process models reveal the actual processes and can be extended to show bottlenecks and outlier behavior. *Conformance Checking* techniques compare observed behavior (i.e., event data) with modeled behavior (i.e., process models). These techniques can be used to show deviations, i.e., behaviors different from what is expected or desired. Process models may also include probabilities, time distributions, and business rules. Therefore, process mining also includes a range of techniques enabling *predictive and prescriptive analytics*.

The process models created and used by process mining techniques form the *digital shadows* that are intended to manage, control, and improve operational processes. The notion of a digital shadow is at the core of IoP. The notion of a digital shadow is closely related to the notion of a *digital twin* [30]. Digital twins are complex models providing digital counterparts to physical production artifacts (i.e., the physical twins), e.g., detailed simulation models that update and change as their physical counterparts change. The digital shadow concept is broader and includes the traces of the actual production processes, i.e., *digital shadows based on process mining include both process models and actual event data*. For example, when analyzing a bottleneck, it is possible to use the process model to drill-down into event data that caused the problem. Moreover, the process model and event data can be used to predict the trajectory of current process instances and antici-pate the effect of interventions. This makes process mining a key ingredient of IoP.

The process mining discipline emerged around 20 years ago [5], and today there are over 35 commercial process mining tools (e.g., Celonis, Disco, UiPath/ProcessGold, myInvenio, PAFnow, Minit, QPR, Mehrwerk, Puzzledata, LanaLabs, StereoLogic, Everflow, TimelinePI, Signavio, and Logpickr). Many of the larger organizations (especially in Europe) have adopted this technology. For example, within Siemens over 6000 employees are using Celonis Process Mining to remove operational friction and increase automation. Despite the widespread adoption of process mining and the availability of easy-to-use commercial tools, the process mining discipline is relatively young and there are still many open challenges. In this position paper, we focus on three questions particularly rele-vant for IoP:

- *How to Compare Different Process Variants (over time, over locations, over different case types)?* The same production process may be performed at different locations. It is valuable to understand why operational friction is less at some of these locations. Also, the performance may not be constant over time and we may see drifts, e.g., bottlenecks are shifting. Therefore, we need to support comparative process mining [2,3,17,25]
- *How to Deal with Processes Involving Different Interacting Objects?* Tradi-tionally, each event refers to a single case (e.g., an order). This is made pos-sible by flattening event data. This may lead to convergence and divergence problems. The same event may be replicated for multiple cases or unrelated events may appear to be related. This leads to misleading diagnostics. More-over, depending on the question at hand, the event data need to be extracted differently from systems such as SAP, Oracle, and Microsoft Dynamics. There-fore, we need to support *object-centric* process mining techniques that are able to handle different types of objects (i.e., case notions) in one model [7].
- *How to Improve the Process using Forward-looking Techniques?* The initial focus of process mining was on diagnosing historical event data. However, the ultimate goal is to improve processes and remove operational friction. Therefore, we need process mining techniques that are *forward-looking* and that provide *actionable* results, e.g., automated alerts, interventions, recon-figurations, policy changes, and redesign. To anticipate the effect of process interventions, a tighter integration with simulation is needed [1,6,39,46].

The remainder of this position paper is organized as follows. Section 2 intro-duces an overview of process mining techniques. Section 3 introduces a running example based on which we discuss the potentials and challenges of applying process mining to operational processes from a research and process owner's perspective. Section 4 uses the running example to illustrate the capabilities of existing process mining tools. Section 5 discusses the need for comparative process mining and presents some of the initial capabilities to support process cubes, concept drift, and process comparison using advanced concepts such as the earth mover's distance. Section 6 presents the problems related to convergence and divergence in processes due to events that refer to multiple objects. Initial support for object-centric process mining techniques based on process cubes is presented. In Sect. 7, we advocate a shift from backward-looking process mining to more forward-looking forms of analysis combining simulation and process mining. Next to traditional discrete event simulation with models generated from event data, we also need simulation approaches operating at a higher abstraction level. For this purpose, we propose to combine process mining and system dynamics. Section 8 concludes the paper.

2   Process Mining: Removing Friction in Operational Processes

To help organization to remove operational friction, process mining reveals unnecessary rework, delays, waste, deviations, fraud, missing products, lost responses, etc. This is not so easy. As an example, take the Order-to-Cash (O2C) process of a large multinational that processes over 30 million ordered items per year. These 30 million cases (i.e., instances of the O2C process) generate over 300 million events per year. Over 60 different activities may occur. Although the O2C process is fairly standard, over 900,000 process variants can be observed in one year! These variants describe different ways of executing this process. In such processes, often 80% of all cases are described by just 20% of the process variants. However, the remaining 20% of the cases generate 80% of the process variants and are often responsible

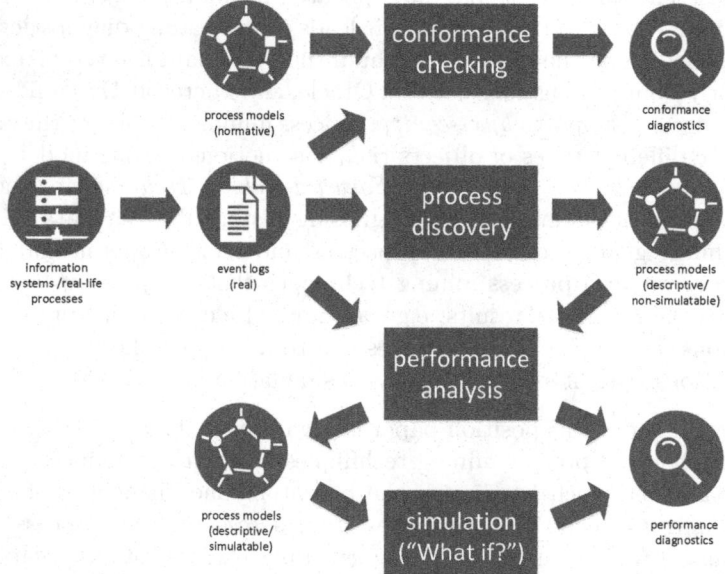

Fig. 1. An overview of process mining showing how event logs, process models, and diagnostics relate.

for a disproportional part of an organization's operational friction. Such problems cannot be tackled by traditional process modeling or workshops, because these focus on the dominant 20% of the process variants. Process mining aims to provide insights into real-life operational processes using the event data at hand.

The starting point for traditional process mining is an *event log* extracted from the information system(s). Each *event* in such a log refers to an *activity* possibly executed by a *resource* at a particular *time* and for a particular *case* [5]. An event may have many more attributes, e.g., transactional information (e.g., start, complete, and abort), costs, customer, location, and unit. Typical challenges are *data quality* and finding a *suitable case notion*. A typical data quality problem is the granularity of the timestamps in the event log. Some events may only have a date (e.g., 29-9-2020) and are manually recorded, whereas other events may have a millisecond precision (e.g., 29-9-2020:15.36.45.567) and are captured fully automatic. As a result, the precise ordering is unknown or uncertain. Events are grouped into traces using the selected case notion. However, as detailed in Sect. 6, this is not always easy. One event may refer to one order, ten parts, two machines, one person, and a location. Different events may share objects and one event may refer to many objects.

As Fig. 1 shows, event data are used for process discovery, conformance analysis, and performance analysis [5]. *Process Discovery* techniques automatically learn process models based on an event log. A process model can be represented using different modeling languages, e.g., Petri nets, BPMN models, UML activity diagrams, DFGs, automata, and process trees. Such a process model specifies how a case can be handled. The simplest model is a so-called Directly Follows Graph (DFG). The nodes in such a model are the activities and two special nodes: the start and end of the process. The arcs describe how the process transitions from one node to another. Arcs can be decorated with frequencies and mean durations. For example, 500 times activity "send invoice" was followed by activity "make payment" and the average time between both activities was 2.45 days. DFGs are simple and can be constructed efficiently, also for huge events logs. However, DFGs fail to capture concurrency and often lead to spaghetti-like underfitting models. Petri nets, BPMN models, UML activity diagrams, and process trees are able to express concurrency and there are many process discovery algorithms to discover such models. Here, we abstract from the actual representation of process models and focus on the more general concepts.

Conformance checking techniques take as input both a process model and an event log. The event log is replayed on the model to uncover discrepancies between the observed and modeled behavior. It may be the case that an activity occurs although this is not possible according to the model, or an activity should have occurred according to the model, but did not happen in reality. It is also possible to see that behavior allowed by the process model never happens. If the process model is extended with temporal or resource constraints, conformance checking may reveal that something takes too long or is performed by the wrong person.

By replaying the event data on the model, it is also possible to show performance problems. Since events have timestamps, it is possible to measure delays, next to routing probabilities. Even when the event data do not completely fit the

Fig. 2. Different research directions relevant for the improvement of operational processes: *comparative* process mining, *object-centric* process mining, and *forward-looking* process mining.

model, it is possible to "squeeze" the data into to model using alignment computations. Process models with performance information can be used to analyze bottlenecks and other performance problems. Moreover, by combining stochastic models learned from historic event data with event data from running cases, it is possible to predict performance and compliance problems. Although existing process mining techniques and tools have proven to be a powerful means to remove operational friction, several challenges remain. In the context of our Cluster of Excellence "Internet of Production" (IoP), we address the three challenges already mentioned in the introduction. Figure 2 sketches these challenges and corresponding solution directions. To compare different process variants (over time, over locations, over different case types) we use process cubes and novel techniques to compare subsets of events (see Sect. 5). Process cubes store event data using any number of dimensions. Novel techniques based on the Earth Mover's Distance (EMD) notion are used to compare two different event logs (or a log and model) while also considering time and resources (also detailed in Sect. 5). To deal with processes involving different interacting objects, we use object-centric event logs and corresponding process mining techniques (detailed in Sect. 6). Traditional process mining techniques require the selection of a single case notion and each event refers to precisely one case. However, for the types of processes we have in mind, this is often too restrictive. Each event may refer to any number of objects and the case notion is just a view on the process. Objects may refer to physical products (raw materials, end products, intermediate products, etc.), resources, or information. Resources include machines, people, space, etc. To make process mining more forward-looking, we support different types of simulation. This allows us to anticipate the effects of process interventions and use process models as highly informative digital shadows. Next to traditional Discrete Event Simulation (DES), we also support System Dynamics (SD) techniques that view the process at a higher aggregation level (see Sect. 7). For SD models, we do not simulate the individual events, but use aggregated steps representing different time periods (e.g., days or weeks).

3   Running Example

Various types of operational processes can be found in industry. Automotive production lines are a common type of production lines that are used to

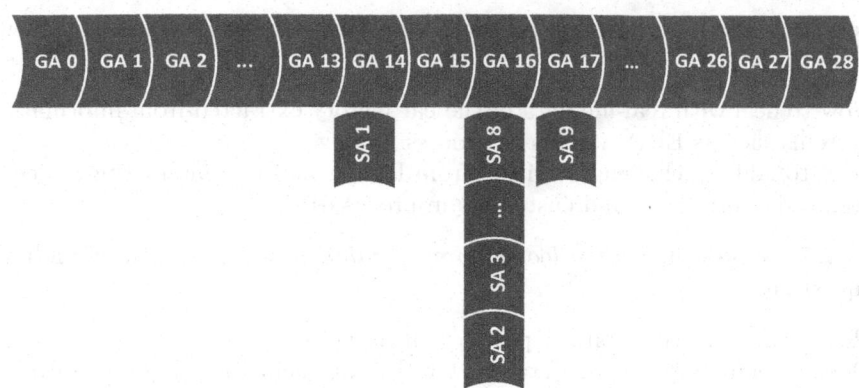

Fig. 3. A part of the simulated model of the production line, used for designing the simulation model. The production line includes one general assembly line with 28 stations and 33 sub-assembly stations.

execute operational processes. Automotive production lines are highly structured and activities therein are tightly coupled. In a simple production line, multiple assembly lines are coordinated in order to join in a single major assembly line. Due to the variability of activities in the automotive production lines and the strong dependencies between them, they are suitable for process mining analysis. Therefore, in order to illustrate process mining techniques for operational processes, this section introduces an extendable automotive production line model. The model is based on a production line at e.GO Mobile AG, a local car manufacturer located in Aachen. Due to reasons of confidentiality, we resort to simulated data and present our results without utilizing the real data of e.Go. A fragment of the simulated model is shown in Fig. 3. It shows the production line is built around a sequence of general assembly stations where some stations depend on additional sequential sub-assembly stations. For example, the station *SA9* is a prerequisite for the general assembly station *GA17*. Each station can have at most one car at a time, during which the human operators execute specific tasks before the car proceeds to the next station. A car can only move along the general assembly line if the subsequent station is empty. We consider 28 stations in the general assembly line and 33 stations in the sub-assembly line. Several activities are executed at one station and most of the time the order of activities at the stations does not matter. The production line is active between 8:00–17:00 o'clock and 5 days a week. In the following sections we demonstrate how process mining is able to help a company to steer and evolve their operational process. To this end, we extend the basic model in order to illustrate the challenges mentioned in the introduction. In Sect. 5, we present *comparative process mining* techniques to answer the following questions:

- How to compare performance-related factors of two different factories in two different locations?
- How to investigate resource allocation in two different factories?

In Sect. 6, we discuss *object-centric process mining* approaches to answer following questions:

- How to deal with real-life data of the car factory extracted from information systems such as ERP systems in process mining?
- How to address challenges arising from having multiple interacting objects, e.g., order, products, and customers in processes?

In Sect. 7, we present *forward-looking process mining* methods to answer following questions:

- How to increase the monthly production rate of cars?
- Does a temporary queuing station for the cars help to increase the overall production rate?

Whereas the emphasis of this paper is on advanced process mining techniques, we first present a few common process mining techniques, e.g., basic approaches for process discovery and conformance checking. These examples diagnostics also help us to obtain an overview of the process used throughout this paper.

4   Applying Existing Process Mining Techniques

Process mining provides a wide variety of techniques for process analysis [5]. Examples of process mining techniques include process discovery algorithms that are able to find process models that describe the event log, conformance checking algorithms that compare process models with the event logs, and model enhancement algorithms that enrich the process model with additional information extracted from the event log. To gain more insights about the process, we apply standard process mining techniques (see [5] for a comprehensive introduction). First, in Sect. 4.1, we perform an explorative analysis by means of process visualization techniques, i.e., the dotted chart. In Sect. 4.2, we discover a process model of the generated data. In Sect. 4.3, we highlight deviations between the discovered process model and the event log by applying conformance checking techniques. In Sect. 4.4, we address the performance problems in the production line through bottleneck analysis.

4.1   Exploring Event Data

Explorative process analysis is a common starting point in order to obtain an overview of the execution of the process. A widely adopted tool that interactively visualizes multiple perspectives of an event log is the dotted chart [49]. Figure 4 presents the dotted chart for the generated data where each event is shown by a dot, colored according to the station it originated from. The x-axis and y-axis show time and the car id respectively. There are different ways of sorting the events in the dotted chart. However, in this dotted chart, events are sorted based on the case duration. As indicated in the figure, there are gaps between events that show the period in which no event occurs such as nights and weekends.

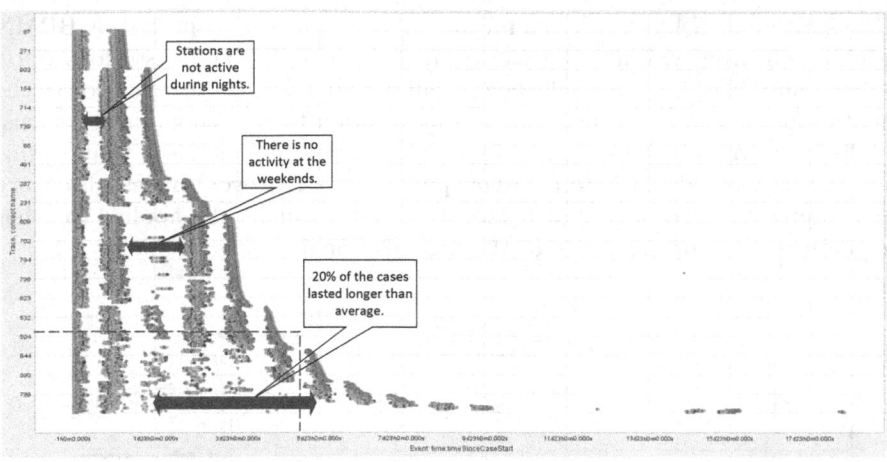

Fig. 4. Dotted chart for the generated event log. Working hours and working days are demonstrated in the dotted chart. Besides, we observe a big gap between events in 20% of the cases, lasted longer than normal.

We can observe 80/20 rule, also known as the Pareto principle in the dotted chart. Approximately 20% of the cases last exceptionally long. Following the Pareto principle, 80% of the performance problems (e.g., delay in the production line) are caused by 20% of the cases. Clearly, these 20% of all the process instances are interesting cases for further analysis.

Even though process visualization by means of a dotted chart helps the analysis, most of the analysis by using the dotted chart is empirical and not quantified. Thus, other process mining techniques such as process discovery and conformance checking techniques are required to find actionable results for improving operational processes.

4.2   Process Discovery

Although the visualization approach, discussed in Sect. 4.1, provides an overview of the event data, it does not show the relationship between different activities. Process discovery techniques take an event log as an input and generate a process model that captures the relation between activities and abstracts the observed behavior in the event log.

There are various techniques for process discovery, e.g., the Alpha-algorithm [12], the Inductive Miner [26], Region-based approaches [5], and the Heuristics Miner [51]. For the resulting models, there are multiple different notations, e.g., Petri nets [14], BPMN [21], YAWL [24], UML [11], etc. Figure 5 shows a fragment of the BPMN model for the example log by applying Inductive Miner. As the model shows, the general assembly stations are sequential and some of them have prerequisites, i.e., sub-assembly stations. For example, we start triggering the execution of activities at the station *GA14*, when execution of activities at the stations *SA1* and *GA13* have been finished. Another aspect, captured by BPMN model, is concurrency. While the execution of the activities at the stations *GA0*, *GA1*, ..., and *GA13* is sequential, they are all in parallel with the execution of the activities at the station *SA1*. Therefore, in addition to the sequential relations, this discovery reveals the concurrency in activity executions. Note that in this discovery, we focused on the control-flow perspective. However, process discovery is not limited to the control flow perspective and it can also be applied to other perspectives of the process, such as the organizational perspective [5].

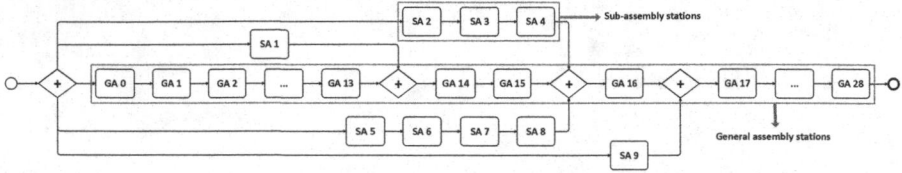

Fig. 5. An example process model of the production line using BPMN notation [21]. The flow of activities for cars during the production line is shown. Activities at general assembly stations are always executed in a sequence. Also, activities at sub-assembly stations, required for a specific general assembly station, are executed sequentially.

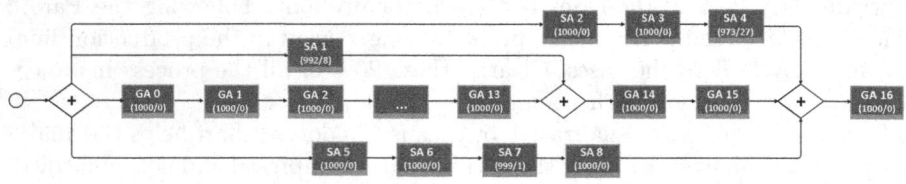

Fig. 6. A part of the detected deviations in the process. Activities with red square show deviations while activities with green square show that there was no deviation in that activity. (Color figure online)

4.3   Conformance Checking

Given a process model, conformance checking assesses the similarity of the behavior described by the model and the real behavior as recorded in the event log. Therefore, conformance checking techniques [13] are used to identify deviations of the production plan. Since the event data used originate from an idealized simulation model, there are no deviations in the initial setting. However, we manipulate the simulation model such that for some stations deliberately deviations are injected. One of the common techniques, used in conformance checking, are alignments. In alignments, we check the synchronization between the behavior in the event log and behavior according to the model [8]. An example of alignments is depicted in Fig. 6 which shows a fragment of the mined BPMN model with the results of conformance checking. As this figure shows, using conformance checking, deviations of the example process from the previously mined model are easily detected and visualized. Two numbers in parenthesis, below the name of the station, clarify the number of deviations. For instance, for 27 cars, activities at the station *SA4* have not been executed before activities at the station *GA16* and after the activities at the station *SA3*. These cars have skipped the station *SA4* and they may cause quality problems after the production. Accordingly, identifying these types of deviations in the production line can help the production line managers to control the quality and steps of the process accurately.

Figure 7 shows the results of conformance checking using the alignments-based technique. In alignments, we check for a car, whether the behavior of the model and the behavior of the events related to that car match with each other or not. We have two types of misalignment which are model move and log move. In model move, a move in the log cannot be mimicked by a move in the model. In Fig. 7, there are two model moves (purple color). For example, based on the model, we need the station *SA7* in the event log between the stations *SA6* and *SA8*. However, it is missed in this case. In log move, a move in the model cannot be mimicked by a move in the log. In Fig. 7, there is a log move (yellow color). Based on the event log, this car moves from the station *GA21* to the station *SA7* and from the station *SA7* to the station *GA22*. However, it cannot happen according to the model. Typically, by capturing such misstatements, we can discover the deviations that affect the quality of the final product. However, in order to increase the performance of the production line we need to analyze the performance of the stations to find the bottlenecks.

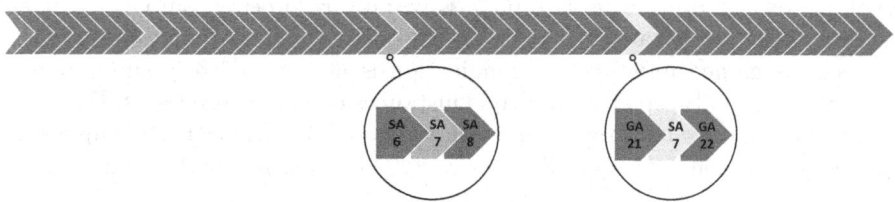

Fig. 7. An alignment for a specific car. A car ideally passes 61 stations. However, there are mismatches between the discovered model and the event log, captured in the alignment by different colors. (Color figure online)

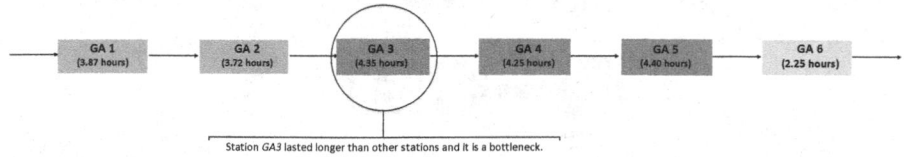

Fig. 8. Snapshot of the performance view of the general assembly line. The average service times of the stations are shown. (Color figure online)

4.4   Performance Analysis

The performance of production lines is one of the important metrics which needs to be observed and improved continuously [8]. After verifying the suitability of the given model using conformance checking, this section assesses the performance of the process by means of bottleneck analysis. In Fig. 8, we depict a projection of performance diagnostics, on top of the discovered process model. Within the figure, the darker colors of the stations show performance problems and bottlenecks in the process. For instance, the dark red color of the stations *GA3*, *GA4*, and *GA5* indicates the long service times at these stations (i.e., the time actually worked on the car). Most of the time, improving the performance of bottlenecks such as the station *GA6* improves the overall performance of the process. In general, process mining bottleneck analysis reveals this kind of problems and subsequent actions can be taken accordingly. In this performance analysis, we considered service time of the stations. However, it is possible to analyze the performance based on the waiting times for the different stations (i.e., the time that a car is waiting for the station to become available).

5   Comparative Process Mining

The techniques presented in Sect. 4 capture the current state of the process using the complete event log. In this analysis, we do not consider variability in the processes which can be derived from the heterogeneity of demand in different seasons. In order to isolate process variations, process comparison, which systematically investigates the presence and absence of systematic differences, has recently gained interest. The application is not limited to a single process instance but can also consider multiple instances of similar processes. For example, suppose that we have two car factories in two different locations, implementing the production lines described in Sect. 3. Comparing performance-related

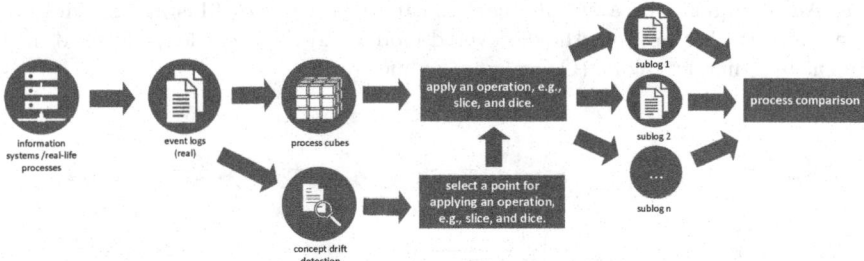

Fig. 9. Process cubes are built on the event logs extracted from information systems. We detect the change point in the regular patterns of the process by concept drift detection. Therefore, based on the change point, we apply process cube operations such as *slice*. The output of such process cube operations are sublogs, used for process comparison.

metrics of these two factories with each other or even comparing the performance metrics of a single company in different time windows of a year is valuable from the business perspective. Characteristics related to the performance, such as the duration of the underlying production process for the comparison of the two factories, are of importance in operational management. This comparison can be addressed by splitting event data into process variants by using existing process mining approaches in a way that differences between variants are exposed (Fig. 9). To provide better insights into current approaches for process comparison, we first show how event data can be organized considering different dimensions of variability, which enables basic process comparison in Sect. 5.1. While the former method assumes prior knowledge about the expected variability, Sect. 5.2 assesses how this can naturally be complemented by process change detection approaches and the emerging challenges for operational processes. Finally, in Sect. 5.3, given the methods to organize the data, we introduce a challenging process comparison scenario, which motivates further research on performance-oriented operational process comparison.

5.1 Process Cubes

Classical process mining techniques focus on analyzing a process through processing its corresponding event log as a whole. However, there may exist variability in the process. To consider this variability in the process, we use process cubes which isolate the different processes. As shown in Fig. 10, a process cube consists of multiple dimensions that refer to the properties of the event log, e.g., time, color, and location. Each cell in this process cube refers to all events related to the cars with a specific color, in a specific region, and in a particular time window. To gain more insights about the specific cell, process mining techniques, e.g., process discovery and conformance checking techniques can be applied to a collection of events extracted from the cells of the process cube [17]. The notion of process cubes is inspired by application of Online Analytical Processing (OLAP) in process mining [44]. OLAP is a well-known concept in Business

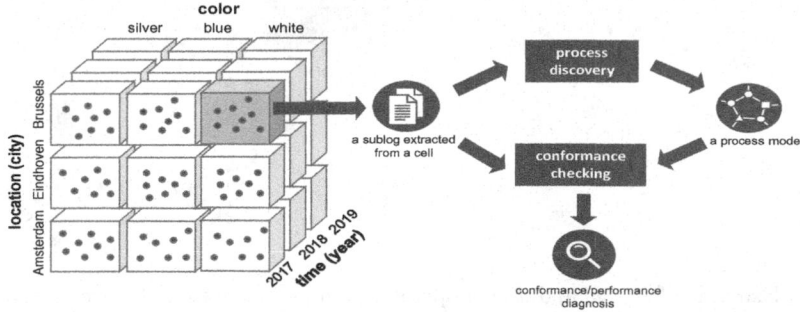

Fig. 10. An example of a three-dimensional process cube. The selected cell contains all events related to white cars produced in Brussels in 2017.

Intelligence (BI) that facilitates data discovery and management reporting. First, OLAP considers simple numerical analysis, e.g., plotting car production duration in a factory against the months of the year. In [20,29,31], OLAP operations, i.e., *slice, dice, drill-down*, and *roll-up* were also applied to non-numerical data. Although the idea of the process cube is related to OLAP, there are significant differences between OLAP and process cubes. We can not use OLAP for process data directly, because, for example, as a design choice in a process cube, cells are associated with both process models and event data. In a process cube, event data and process models are directly related. We can discover models from event data extracted from cells of the cube and compare observed and modeled behavior [2]. Different implementations of process cubes are provided in [16,33]. In these implementations, we can apply OLAP operations such as *slice, dice, roll-up*, and *drill-down* on the event data. Assume we are interested in discovering the model of cars produced in the years *2017* and *2018*. As shown in Fig. 11, we can slice the cube for the *time* dimension, for the years *2017* and *2018* and find the process model of the remaining events. In fact, through *slicing* the cube, we zoom into a *slice* of the data and remove that dimension from the cube. However, by *dicing*, we apply a filter on multiple dimensions. Assume we are interested in discovering the model for cars with white and blue color produced in years *2017* and *2018*. As shown in Fig. 11, we can dice the cube for dimensions *color*, and *time* and discover the model of the remained events.

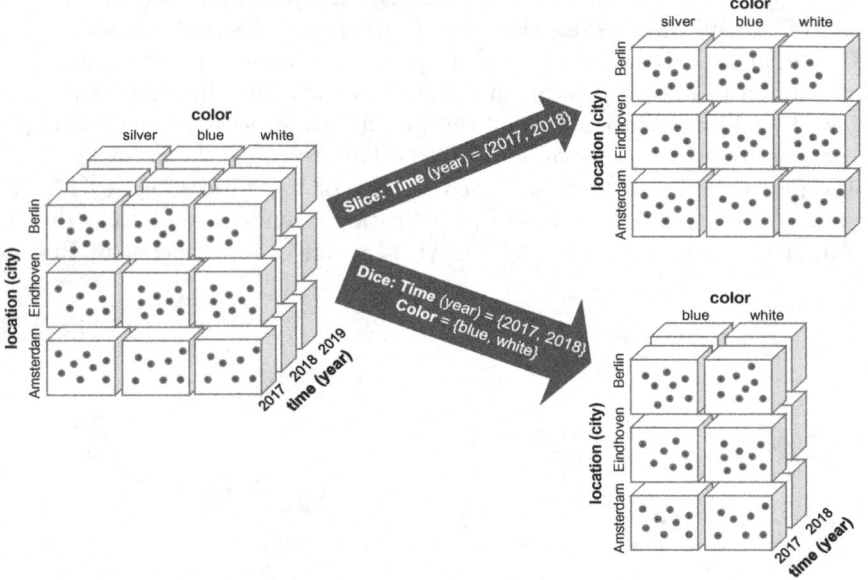

Fig. 11. Example of *slicing* and *dicing* operations in process cubes. A *slice* of the cube for the *time* dimension and *dice* of the cube for the *time* and *color* dimensions are shown. (Color figure online)

Roll-up and *drill-down* operations, show the cube with different levels of granularity. An example is shown in Fig. 12. We can drill down the *location* dimension from *country* to *city*. *Roll-up* is the opposite of *drill-down* operation. It performs aggregation on a dimension. As shown in Fig. 12, we can roll up the *location* dimension from *city* to *country*.

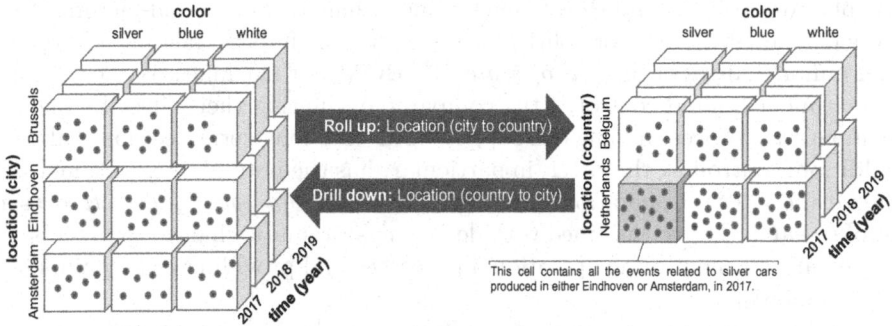

Fig. 12. Example of *rolling up* and *drilling down* operations in process cubes.

A brief example of the application of process cube operations for the generated data is shown in Fig. 13. In this figure, the models of two different *slices* corresponding to two different seasons of a year are compared to each other. We can compare performance of the stations with each other through performance analysis. As indicated in the figure, the average time of execution of activities at the station *GA5* has increased in the second season of the year.

Although there are several implementations of process cubes, some challenges remain. In OLAP, we reduce a set of values into a single summarized value such as the average. However, process cubes deal with event data and we cannot simply reduce many events into one event. The ways that are used for summarizing the events affect the performance of the process cube. Consequently, defining a way for summarizing the events in the process cube with high performance is an open issue.

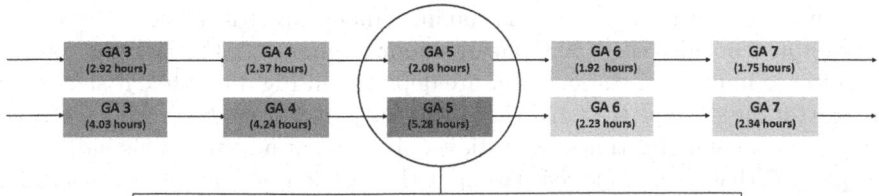

Fig. 13. Example of comparing the company in two different time windows.

5.2   Concept Drift

Even though operational processes should ideally be stable, complex internal and external dependencies will typically lead to continuous changes of the process. The resulting variability is, on the one hand, problematic for traditional process mining techniques, which implicitly assume steady behavior. On the other hand, changes can also require an immediate adaptation by the process managers. In principle, we can attribute the aforementioned changes to external factors, e.g., suppliers, market demand, or political regulations, and internal factors, e.g., operators, minor changes of the *Bill-of-Material* (BOM), or machines. While the former are under limited control of the company, evaluating their effect by means of comparative process mining can support mid- and long-term decision making. In addition, controlling the latter, in particular, has the potential to continuously improve and steer the operational process. Therefore, *concept drift detection*, as a field of research that is concerned with detecting systematic changes in processes, is important for monitoring operational processes and providing entry points for further analysis.

A general challenge for methods that systematically assess changes in the execution of a process arises from the different natures of occurrence and duration [18]. For example, *sudden drifts* are caused by rapid process changes and might require instant action while *gradual drifts* describe slowly changing processes where different behaviors overlap. Concerning the long-term development of the process, sequences of multiple changes, i.e., *incremental drifts* and *recurring drifts*, which describe periodical behavior changes, can be distinguished. On the one hand, detecting them is essential in order to understand the overall process evolution. On the other hand, being aware of recurring, e.g., seasonal changes enable process owners to anticipate and adapt while also setting the context for additional analyses.

While existing work focuses on the data [25] and especially the control-flow perspective [18,19,32], it neglects time, such as waiting times or activity service times, as a factor of major concern in operational processes. As in many operational processes activities are highly structured and tightly coupled, the impact of small delays can accumulate causing a significant decrease in the overall performance. For instance, in our running example delays at sub-assembly stations can temporarily stop significant parts of the entire production line. However, changes such as a battery shortage do not change the ground truth control flow but increase the sojourn times at affected stations making time-aware drift detection essential. For example, consider the rolling mean sojourn times over the last ten vehicles for a selected number of stations that are depicted in Fig. 14. While it shows two increases for the stations $GA4$ and $GA5$ after the first 350 and 600 vehicles, respectively, the mean sojourn times for station $GA6$ are not affected. This indicates a concept drift that worsens the situation at the bottleneck station $GA5$ blocking the preceding stations and, therefore, increasing their sojourn times. Using additional background knowledge, this drift can be attributed to problems with the battery supply and, later on, a severe battery shortage. In general, detecting time drift and its causes becomes especially challenging if changes are not local to a station but distributed over the production line.

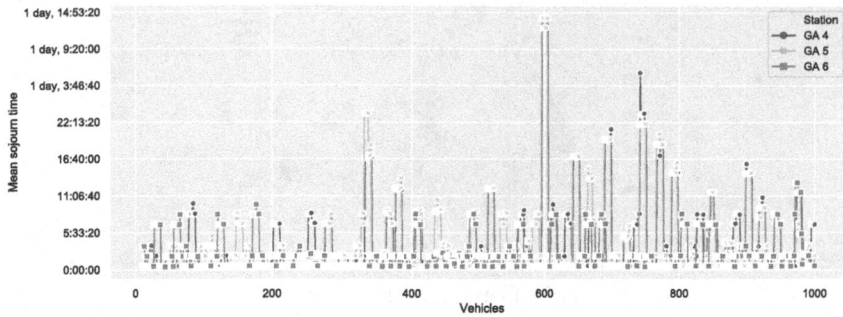

Fig. 14. Mean sojourn time for stations *GA4*, *GA5*, and *GA6* over the last ten vehicles. It shows two drifts for *GA4* and *GA5* after 350 and 600 cars, respectively.

In addition to the time perspective, change point detection methods that generally allow for different perspectives on the operational process are essential in order to incorporate domain knowledge, e.g., from the BOM. Consequently, this enables the user to focus the sensitivity of the detection method on specific parts of the process while reducing the sensitivity for irrelevant changes. For example, the user might focus on changes of important quality metrics and changing impacts of preceding production steps on the former instead of detecting changes in operator-dependent activity orderings. Apart from the change identification, a good visualization showing the nature of the change [18] is crucial to make changes actionable. While change characterization of the control flow has been addressed in [36,37], change characterization of operational processes should acknowledge additional perspectives.

Consequently, in order to address these challenges and unravel the process dynamics, holistic and especially time-aware change point detection approaches with a multi-perspective view on the operational process are needed.

5.3 Comparison

Applying the concepts from Sects. 5.1 and 5.2, allows us to organize the data into process cubes, potentially refined by concept drift detection results. Subsequently, this organization provides us a framework and entry points for process comparison along the dimensions of variability which can be challenging even in case of a stable control flow. Depending on the inter-activity dependencies, pairwise activity comparison between two process variants can be insufficient and activity relations, i.e., the process knowledge need to be incorporated.

In order to illustrate the challenges for time-centered process comparison introduced by inter-activity dependencies, we complement the baseline model by a human factor, which expresses in operator-dependent service times, and compare two factories of the same car manufacturing company at different locations. Similar to the workforce assignment in the underlying real-world process of the electric vehicle manufacturer, we divide the production pipeline into multiple sections. Each section has a separate pool of operators from which free

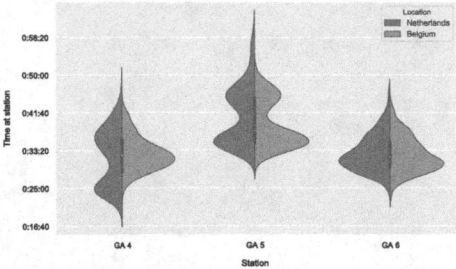

(a) Activity-wise comparison.

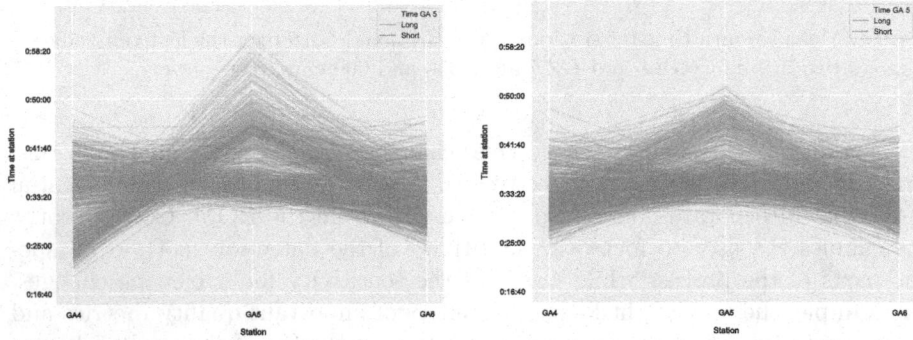

(b) Relations between the station durations in the Netherlands.

(c) Relations between the station durations in Belgium.

Fig. 15. A comparative analysis of the times spent in the different stations in both the Netherlands and Belgium.

operators are assigned to the manufacturing tasks. Moreover, we also model operator preferences for certain stations. Accordingly, when a vehicle arrives at an assembly station, a free operator is randomly assigned based on the current list of preferences in the pool. We generate events for two factories located in the Netherlands and in Belgium and store them in a process cube.

The process owner is interested in comparing the two implementations of his manufacturing process in order to identify possibilities for improvement. To this end, we first *slice* and *dice* the process cube in order to generate a sublog for each location. As we show next, comparison methods should consider the inter-activity dependencies in order to provide a holistic analysis to the company. Activity-wise comparison, as depicted in Fig. 15a, yields that the station duration distributions for the station *GA6* are similar to each other, while the distributions differ for the stations *GA4* and *GA5*. For the station *GA5*, the station duration distribution has a longer tail in the Dutch factory, which indicates inefficiencies for the Dutch location. Considering station *GA4*, the distribution for the Netherlands has two peaks(but not for the location in Belgium) suggesting that it is possible to considerably improve processing times at this station.

However, a process-oriented view, as shown in Figs. 15b and 15c, that considers additional context information, yields a different conclusion. The figures show the relations between subsequent stations where traces are colored according to their time at the station *GA5*. Figure 15b shows that the time improvement for the station *GA4* correlates with an increased duration at the station *GA5*. Quick but imprecise work at this station that requires additional rework increases the overall effort. Process comparison reveals this process insight and the absence of this relation in the Belgian factory. Furthermore, the modes of station *GA5* in the Belgian factory seem to be uncorrelated with the time for station *GA4* suggesting the existence of an additional latent variable. Comparison with Fig. 15b and the absence of a corresponding pattern in Fig. 15c, further suggest that this latent variable is not inherent in the baseline process, but related to the location. For example, different operators working at different speeds could cause this behavior rather than imprecisely fitting parts, causing problems in the next step.

This example shows that, although simple comparison approaches can provide insights into the differences between the processes, they might not consider all the relevant context information. This motivates the use of flexible comparison methods such as the *Earth Mover's Distance* (EMD) [23,47]. On the one hand, these methods should be sensitive to the frequency of the occurring patterns and thus to their relevance. On the other hand, they should also allow for different perspectives on the process.

By considering the car as the case identifier, we examined the process using general process mining techniques (e.g., process discovery, and conformance checking) and process comparison approaches. However, in reality, the data extracted from the information system of a car factory contains other case identifiers, e.g., orders, and customers. Therefore, in our analysis, we need to provide a more holistic vision of the process by considering multiple case notions, as is discussed next.

6   Object-Centric Process Mining

Object-centric process mining is an emerging branch of process mining aiming to apply process mining techniques on event logs which are closer to the data extracted from information systems. Multiple objects such as customers, orders, and deliveries are involved in the car factory, described in Sect. 3. Analyzing the processes covering all these aspects is addressed in object-centric process mining.

Companies record their information in information systems such as the ERP (Enterprise Resource Planning) systems of SAP, which do not have the structure of traditional event logs. In traditional event logs, each event refers to a single case notion (i.e., a process instance), an activity, a timestamp, and any number of additional attributes (e.g., costs, resources, etc.). However, in operational processes with many interactions (i.e., an event is related to multiple objects), it may be problematic to create and analyze traditional event logs with a single case notion [7]. Information systems that support production, such as SAP, store information in the related tables of a database. In the production planning module of SAP, multiple objects (e.g., planned order, supplier, product, component, and delivery) are involved. Each planned order consists of many products, each comprising a range of components (e.g., based on the BOM a car is composed of the frame, engine, battery, etc.). Accordingly, we are able to study the process from multiple different angles and dimensions. Extracted event logs from SAP systems usually suffer from *convergence* and *divergence* [7]. These two problems are of high importance to discuss, because they cause challenges in applying process mining techniques, e.g., process discovery, on these event logs. To illustrate these two problems, as an example, consider the simplified process of production planning shown in Fig. 16 with three case notions (i.e., planned order, component, and product) and three activities (i.e., *place order, confirm products, check the inventory*), respectively. The mentioned problems in this process are:

- *Convergence*: Events referring to multiple objects of the selected type are replicated, possibly leading to unintentional duplication [7]. For example, an order may contain many products and each product may contain different components. Assume that there is an order comprising 10 products, e.g., cars. In order to apply classical process mining techniques, we need to flatten the event data by picking a case notion. If we select the product as a case notion, then this leads to 10 replications of the same *place order* event. The duplication of events for different cases may lead to an explosion of the number of events. Moreover, when time and costs are associated to events, this may lead to very misleading insights In object-centric event logs, an event may contain references to many objects of the same case notion, thus avoiding the duplication problem.
- *Divergence*: Events referring to different objects of a type not selected as the case notion are considered to be causally related but are executed independently [7]. Assume that we pick order as a case notion (to avoid convergence problems). A single order may contain multiple products and each product may contain different components. However, there are activities executed for a single product or a single component, e.g., *check inventory*. Many *check inventory* events may refer to the same order although they actually independent and refer to different objects. Since we picked order as a case notion, these events cannot be disentangled, typically leading to Spaghetti models. Things that happen in a strict order for both components and products become blurred when using a coarser case notion.

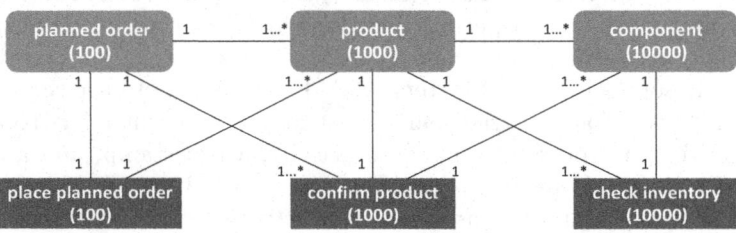

Fig. 16. Overview of the relationship among case notions (i.e., *planned order, product,* and *component*) and activities (i.e., *place planned order, confirm product,* and *check inventory*). For example, there is one-to-one relationship between *planned order* and *place planned order* and one-to-many relationship between *planned order* and *product*.

Object-centric process mining aims to provide a solution for the aforementioned challenges. The interest in this subdiscipline is rapidly increasing, because organizations are in need of a more holistic way to interact with event logs extracted from information systems [15,28,34]. Several techniques were developed to deal with object-centric event logs for process analysis:

- Extracting object-centric event logs from information systems: This includes several contributions related to the storage format and some work on the extraction from SAP logs or ERP systems in general [15,34,48].

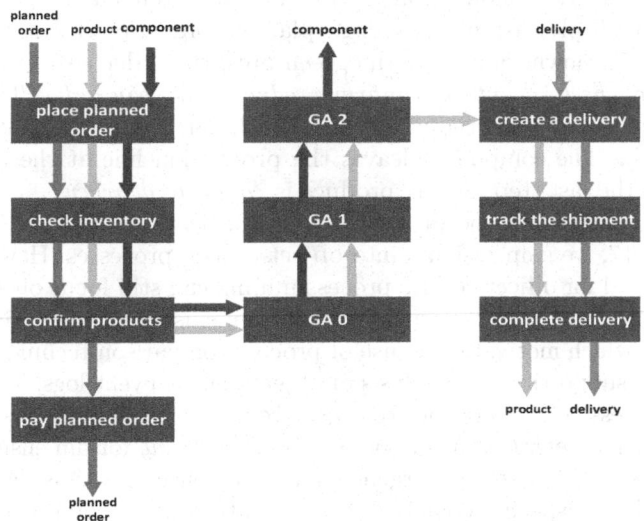

Fig. 17. Directly-Follows Multigraph for the case notions order, product, component, and delivery. A fragment of the production line is captured that consists of the stations *GA1*, *GA2*, and *GA3*. (Color figure online)

- Discovering process models from object-centric event logs: Artifact-centric modeling is an approach to model processes with multiple case notions by combining process and data [22,35]. The techniques proposed based on the artifact-centric process modeling do not show the process as a whole. Therefore, in [27] a discovery algorithm was proposed to discover Object-Centric Behavioral Constraints (OCBC) models from object-centric event logs. These models show interactions between the data and behavioral perspectives on the attribute level in one diagram. The main challenge of OCBC is scalability and complexity, which led to the development of MVP (Multiple Viewpoint) Models. MVP models are Directly-Follows Graphs (DFG) with colored arcs annotated by frequency and performance information. MVP models show the process model without omitting any of the case notions [15]. MVP models cannot capture concurrency well and the diagnostics may be misleading. This led to the development of techniques to discovered colored Petri nets. Object-centric Petri nets are another type of object-centric process models that can be extracted from object-centric event logs and provide the execution semantics [9].

A baseline discovery model for object-centric processes is the Directly-Follows Multigraph, inspired by DFGs [7]. DFGs are graphs where the nodes represent activities or events in the event log. Nodes are connected through edges if there is at least one case in the event log where the source event or activity is followed by the target event or activity [5]. For generating Directly-Follows Multigraph, we merge the DFGs that are generated for each case notion into an overall DFG where the arcs with different colors correspond to different case notions. In Fig. 17, a Directly-Follows Multigraph for the extended model of the car factory with multiple case notions (e.g., planned order, products, component, and delivery), is shown. Following the green arcs, the order goes through *place planned order*, *check inventory*, *confirm products*, and *pay order*. The product and component enter the production line which consists of the stations *GA0*, *GA1*, and *GA2*. The component leaves the production line at the last station (*GA2*), while the last step for any product is *complete delivery*.

Using object-centric process models such as Directly-Follows Multigraph shown in Fig. 17, we gain insights into object-centric processes. However, techniques developed for object-centric process mining can still focus on single location, time period, or process variant. There may exist multiple variants of the same process, which motivates the use of process comparison techniques such as process cubes, supporting the analysis of object-centric event logs. To adapt the concept of process cube operations to object-centric process mining is not trivial since an event may refer to any number of objects. *Slicing* for dimensions related to case notions may lead to convergence and divergence problems. For example, events related to a specific component also contain other components. *Dicing* suffers from the same problem. Therefore, traditional process cubes cannot handle object-centric event logs and it is worthwhile to bridge the gap between process comparison approaches and object-centric process mining. This needed to compare the processes in a more holistic setting.

7   Forward-Looking Process Mining

The value of process mining in analyzing the past is clear and widely accepted. However, just diagnosing the past is not a goal in itself. The actual goal is to continuously improve processes and respond to changes. Operational processes are subject to many changes, e.g., a sudden increase in the number of orders, and therefore the managers require an extended vision of the future in order to deal with changes in the process. Due to the high cost of operational processes, in the face of deliberate changes in order to improve the operational processes performance or unexpected changes, having the ability to look forward is of paramount importance. Simulation is capable of enabling process mining to look forward. At the same time, data-driven support provided by process mining, e.g., past executions of the process and process model, can make the simulation models more realistic. In order to answer forward-looking questions regarding the future of processes using process mining, the first step is to demonstrate how process mining and simulation can complement each other. The knowledge gained about the process (including the discovered process model and the current performance of the process) can be used to predict future states of the running cases (e.g., the remaining flow time) under the assumption of a stable process, i.e., no changes in the process. However, process mining is backward looking and cannot be used for "What if?" questions. Hence, process mining and simulation perfectly complement each other [6]. Among the different simulation techniques, we consider two different approaches: discrete event simulation or system dynamics simulation. These techniques are both able to model the operational processes at different levels of detail by capturing process events and variables.

7.1 Discrete Event Simulation

One of the well-known simulation techniques which can be used for simulating operational processes is Discrete Event Simulation (DES). DES uses predefined rules according to which the simulation process generates events. Whenever an event occurs, the state of the system changes and the new state is recorded. Each state enables new events. Each possible way is described by a simulation run which shows the result of the play-out of the model [6]. Tools such as Coloured Petri Nets (CPNs) can be used for simulating a process including all the details of a process, e.g., number of resources for each activity and duration of each activity [43]. Predefined key performance indicators such as average waiting time for each process instance can be calculated and compared in different situations by redesigning the simulation models and experiments [6]. Despite the capable simulation tools along with the provided forward-looking approaches, the real-life application of simulation is limited [4]. Detailed simulation models like DES may be very time-consuming to build. Interpreting simulation results is not an easy task and often models need to be tuned to behave similar to the real process (coffee breaks, visits to the toilet, holidays, illness, etc. lead to lower performance than expected based on the initial simulation model). Furthermore, simulation models tend to capture only some aspects of a process or use an oversimplified model of reality [1]. Therefore, organizations try to use the evidence-based approaches in which the previously captured state of the organization can be used for more accurate simulation models [6]. In order to achieve more realistic results using simulation techniques, different approaches have been proposed [45, 46].

Discrete Event Simulation (DES) requires considerable domain knowledge of the process. For instance, to answer the forward-looking question for our example production line, we need to implement all the details of the production line to see the effect of inventory options for one of the stations on the overall production line. Also, it is not easy to consider the context in which the simulation is running [10]. Incorporating effects of external factors in the models, e.g., human behaviors or environmental variables are other aspects that are missing from current simulation techniques in processes [39]. Moreover, selecting the right level of abstraction and avoiding too much detail are other important aspects of creating a simulation model and performing simulation. Unfortunately, the inherently required level of detail in these types of approaches does not allow for high-level modeling and long-term predictions. As opposed to the existing simulation techniques, System Dynamics (SD) allows us to assess the impact of changes in the process from a global perspective as well as the effects of external factors. Using different levels of granularity in the modeling, we can address the major drawbacks of discrete event simulation techniques. Therefore, the goal is to assess and predict the future behavior of operational processes including the effects of potential changes as well as the roles of external factors, e.g., human behavior at an aggregated level.

7.2   System Dynamics

System Dynamics (SD) techniques are used to model dynamic systems and their relations with their environment. Using system dynamics, the factors affecting a system's behavior are captured [50]. Stocks, flows and variables are fundamental elements in modeling a system as a stock-flow diagram, i.e., one of the main system dynamics diagrams. Figure 18 shows a simple stock-flow diagram for the running example in which *arrival rate* and *production rate* as flows add/remove

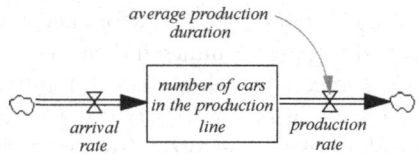

Fig. 18. A sample stock-flow diagram for the running example. The value of the stock *number of cars in the production line* is calculated from the value of *arrival rate* and *production rate* as flows per time step, e.g., per day. Also, the value of the *production rate* is affected by the value of *average production duration*.

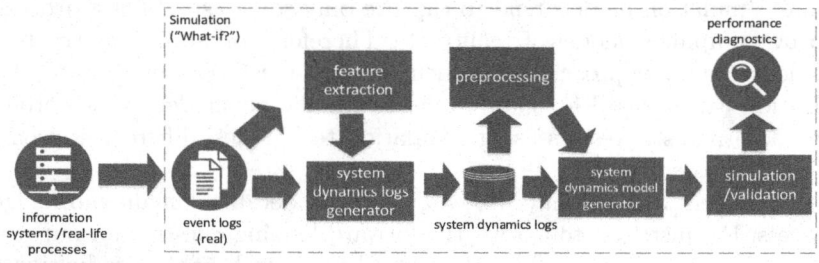

Fig. 19. A general framework for using process mining and simulation for improving operational processes. Using event logs and transforming them to System Dynamics logs (SD-logs) along investigating the relations between different parameters in the process over time, the simulation regarding answering "What if?" questions is possible.

to/from the values of *number of cars in the production line* as stock, also, *average production duration* (a variable) affects *production rate*. System dynamics provide the opportunity to add exogenous factors, e.g., variables in stock-flow diagrams as well to capture the hidden relationships among the players in the operational processes [39]. As shown in Fig. 1, different executions of operational processes that are stored in the information systems can be captured in the form of event logs. The provided event logs for operational processes can be transformed in other formats to be used as inputs for simulation techniques. These transformed event logs include the performance metrics of the processes over different time steps, e.g., arrival rate, average service time and the number of waiting items over steps of time in the process [41].

The authors in [42] exploit the general proposed approach in [39], i.e., a simulation approach for the business process using system dynamics and process mining techniques, which is designed for the specific purpose of simulating the production lines w.r.t performance metrics. Therefore, as shown in Fig. 19, for operational processes, the simulation model in the form of a system dynamics model using trained variables based on event logs can be generated. We use system dynamics and process mining together to answer "What if?" questions, e.g., what will happen if we add one more resource to one of the stations? We transform the generated event log into a *System Dynamics log* (SD-Log) which describes the values of a collection of variables of the process over time using the time window selection technique in [40]. Then, we use the calculated values of the variables to detect the relationships between metrics and generating a stock-flow diagram which is used for simulation [41] (Fig. 20).

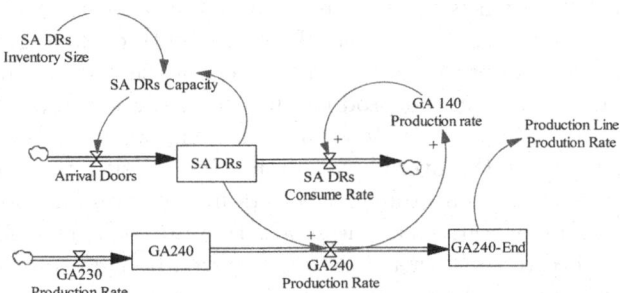

Fig. 20. A sample stock-flow diagram generated based on the production line event log. The purpose of the model is to simulate the effect of adding an inventory option to the doors sub-assembly on the final production rate of the production line at an aggregated level, e.g., per month.

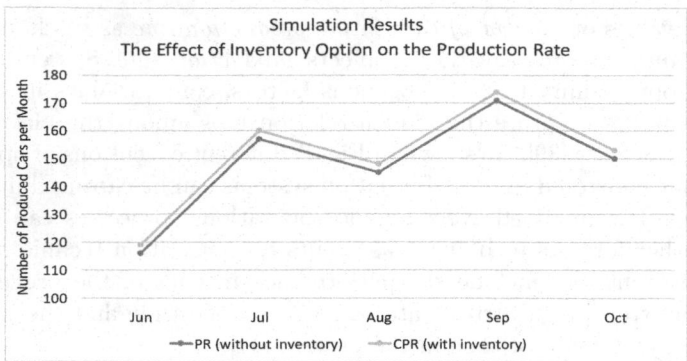

Fig. 21. A comparison between the actual production rate (PR) and the simulated PR using our approach along actually changed production rate (CPR) and simulated CPR for adding an inventory to the doors sub-assembly, e.g., in August 3 more cars will be produced.

7.3   Forward-Looking in Production Lines

As indicated in Sect. 3, the stations in the base model do not have an inventory or queuing option. As a simplified example, consider the station $GA24$, at which the cars at this station require the doors prepared in $SA7$, i.e., a door preparation sub-assembly station. Therefore, in the production line, there can be situations in which a car is at the station $GA24$ and cannot leave the station because it is waiting for the doors to be prepared. One of the scenarios to improve the above-mentioned situation is to prepare the doors for each car beforehand and keep them at the sub-assembly station. The possibility of having a temporary queue, especially for sub-assembly stations, is one of the possible actions which potentially leads to an improved production rate of the whole production line. The question to be answered is: How does the temporary queue for the door assembly stations affect the overall production line? Using the approach presented in [38], we can measure the effect of adding an inventory option to only one of the sub-assembly stations at the production rate of the whole production line. We do not need to consider the details required by DES approaches.

We also populate the generated simulation model, i.e., the stock-flow diagram, with the values generated from the event log of the current status of the production line. We use the data generated in a regular situation in which there is no inventory option for the sub-assembly station, and after transforming it to the system dynamic log, we generate the model using the proposed approach in Fig. 19. The result of simulation after adding the inventory option is shown in Fig. 21. As expected, the whole production rate has increased and the production line manager can decide whether to invest in adding the possibility to keep inventory for the door preparation sub-assembly station. The described scenario shows the potential of using a combination of process mining and SD-based simulation in order to improve operational processes. Using process mining and simulation techniques we are able to answer "What if?" questions in the operational processes.

8   Conclusion

In this paper, we discussed how process mining can be used to remove *operational friction* (e.g., rework, delays, waste, and deviations). We discussed the capabilities provided by existing tools and highlighted some of the main challenges addressed in the DFG-funded Cluster of Excellence "Internet of Production" (IoP). Process mining is widely used to improve standard processes like the Order-to-Cash (O2C) and the Purchase-to-Pay (P2P). However, in other areas (e.g., in production, materials handling, and logistics) process mining is not yet widely used. We believe that by addressing the challenges discussed in this paper, adoption can be accelerated.

We highlighted three important research directions: comparative process mining, object-centric process mining, and forward-looking process mining.

Comparative Process Mining aims to visualize and show root causes for differences over time or between different organizational units (e.g., two factories producing the same or similar products). It is valuable to identify differences and generate insights. These may help to detect problems early (e.g., using concept-drift detection) and establish so-called "best practices" (i.e., routines that are considered to be correct or most effective).

Object-centric Process Mining addresses one of the main limitations of today's process mining tools. In many applications it is not reasonable to assume a single case notion. Consider for example the Bill of Materials (BOM) in an assembly process. A single car has about 2000 parts (or even up to 50,000 parts, counting every part down to the smallest screws). When an engine is produced it may not be clear in what type of car it will end up. Both the car and the engine have unique identifiers are related somewhere in the process. This example shows that assuming a single case notion automatically leads to a particular view on the process. Such views are valuable, but at the same time incomplete and potentially misleading. Object-centric process mining can be used to provide a more holistic view, also avoiding the convergence and divergence problems described.

Forward-looking Process Mining techniques aim to not only diagnose performance and compliance problems in the past, but to predict and change processes. We are particularly interested in answering "What if?" questions. Therefore, simulation plays an important role. Next to traditional Discrete Event Simulation (DES), we also proposed the use of System Dynamics (SD). SD tools simulate the process at a higher abstraction level (i.e., the steps are days or weeks rather than individual events). To learn SD models we need to convert traditional event logs to SD-Logs. This is far from trivial, but allows extending the model with contextual factors that are not directly related to individual events.

We strongly believe that progress in comparative process mining, object-centric process mining, and forward-looking process mining will assist in the creation of realistic *digital shadows* that can be used to manage, control, and improve operational processes. Digital shadows based on process mining include both process models and actual event data. The combination of process models and actual event data allows us to drill-down into the actual process when a problem emerges, predict the trajectory of current process instances, and anticipate the effects of interventions (e.g., adding resources or reordering production steps).

Acknowledgment. Funded by the Deutsche Forschungsgemeinschaft (DFG, German Research Foundation) under Germany's Excellence Strategy–EXC-2023 Internet of Production – 390621612. We also thank the Alexander von Humboldt (AvH) Stiftung for supporting our research.

References

1. van der Aalst, W.M.P.: Business process simulation revisited. In: Barjis, J. (ed.) EOMAS 2010. LNBIP, vol. 63, pp. 1–14. Springer, Heidelberg (2010). https://doi.org/10.1007/978-3-642-15723-3_1
2. van der Aalst, W.M.P.: Process cubes: slicing, dicing, rolling up and drilling down event data for process mining. In: Song, M., Wynn, M.T., Liu, J. (eds.) AP-BPM 2013. LNBIP, vol. 159, pp. 1–22. Springer, Cham (2013). https://doi.org/10.1007/978-3-319-02922-1_1
3. van der Aalst, W.M.P.: How people really (like to) work. In: Sauer, S., Bogdan, C., Forbrig, P., Bernhaupt, R., Winckler, M. (eds.) HCSE 2014. LNCS, vol. 8742, pp. 317–321. Springer, Heidelberg (2014). https://doi.org/10.1007/978-3-662-44811-3_25
4. van der Aalst, W.M.P.: Business process simulation survival guide. In: vom Brocke, J., Rosemann, M. (eds.) Handbook on Business Process Management 1. IHIS, pp. 337–370. Springer, Heidelberg (2015). https://doi.org/10.1007/978-3-642-45100-3_15
5. van der Aalst, W.M.P.: Process Mining, 2nd edn. Springer, Heidelberg (2016). https://doi.org/10.1007/978-3-662-49851-4
6. van der Aalst, W.M.P.: Process mining and simulation: a match made in heaven! In: Proceedings of the 50th Computer Simulation Conference, SummerSim 2018, pp. 4:1–4:12. Society for Computer Simulation International, San Diego (2018). http://dl.acm.org/citation.cfm?id=3275386
7. van der Aalst, W.M.P.: Object-centric process mining: dealing with divergence and convergence in event data. In: Ölveczky, P.C., Salaün, G. (eds.) SEFM 2019. LNCS, vol. 11724, pp. 3–25. Springer, Cham (2019). https://doi.org/10.1007/978-3-030-30446-1_1
8. van der Aalst, W.M.P., Adriansyah, A., van Dongen, B.F.: Replaying history on process models for conformance checking and performance analysis. WIREs Data Min. Knowl. Discov. **2**(2), 182–192 (2012). https://doi.org/10.1002/widm.1045
9. van der Aalst, W.M.P., Berti, A.: Discovering object-centric Petri nets. Fund. Inform. **175**(1–4), 1–40 (2020). https://doi.org/10.3233/FI-2020-1946
10. van der Aalst, W.M.P., Dustdar, S.: Process mining put into context. IEEE Internet Comput. **16**(1), 82–86 (2012)

11. van der Aalst, W.M.P., Kumar, A., Verbeek, H.: Organizational modeling in UML and XML in the context of workflow systems. In: Haddad, H., Papadopoulos, G. (eds.) SAC 2003: Proceedings of the 2003 ACM Symposium on Applied Computing, pp. 603–608. Association for Computing Machinery, New York (2003)

12. van der Aalst, W.M.P., Weijters, T., Maruster, L.: Workflow mining: discovering process models from event logs. IEEE Trans. Knowl. Data Eng. **16**(9), 1128–1142 (2004). https://doi.org/10.1109/TKDE.2004.47

13. Adriansyah, A., van Dongen, B.F., van der Aalst, W.M.P.: Towards robust conformance checking. In: zur Muehlen, M., Su, J. (eds.) BPM 2010. LNBIP, vol. 66, pp. 122–133. Springer, Heidelberg (2011). https://doi.org/10.1007/978-3-642-20511-8_11

14. Badouel, E., Bernardinello, L., Darondeau, P.: Petri Net Synthesis. Texts in Theoretical Computer Science. An EATCS Series, Springer, Heidelberg (2015). https://doi.org/10.1007/978-3-662-47967-4

15. Berti, A., van der Aalst, W.: Extracting multiple viewpoint models from relational databases. In: Ceravolo, P., van Keulen, M., Gómez-López, M.T. (eds.) SIMPDA 2018-2019. LNBIP, vol. 379, pp. 24–51. Springer, Cham (2020). https://doi.org/10.1007/978-3-030-46633-6_2

16. Bolt, A., van der Aalst, W.M.P.: Multidimensional process mining using process cubes. In: Gaaloul, K., Schmidt, R., Nurcan, S., Guerreiro, S., Ma, Q. (eds.) CAISE 2015. LNBIP, vol. 214, pp. 102–116. Springer, Cham (2015). https://doi.org/10.1007/978-3-319-19237-6_7

17. Bolt, A., de Leoni, M., van der Aalst, W.M.P., Gorissen, P.: Exploiting process cubes, analytic workflows and process mining for business process reporting: a case study in education. In: Ceravolo, P., Rinderle-Ma, S. (eds.) Data-Driven Process Discovery and Analysis. CEUR Workshop Proceedings, vol. 1527, pp. 33–47. CEUR-WS.org (2015). http://ceur-ws.org/Vol-1527/paper3.pdf

18. Bose, R.P.J.C., van der Aalst, W.M.P., Žliobaitė, I., Pechenizkiy, M.: Handling concept drift in process mining. In: Mouratidis, H., Rolland, C. (eds.) CAiSE 2011. LNCS, vol. 6741, pp. 391–405. Springer, Heidelberg (2011). https://doi.org/10.1007/978-3-642-21640-4_30

19. Bose, R.P.J.C., van der Aalst, W.M.P., Zliobaite, I., Pechenizkiy, M.: Dealing with concept drifts in process mining. IEEE Trans. Neural Netw. Learn. Syst. **25**(1), 154–171 (2014). https://doi.org/10.1109/TNNLS.2013.2278313

20. Chen, C., Yan, X., Zhu, F., Han, J., Yu, P.S.: Graph OLAP: a multi-dimensional framework for graph data analysis. Knowl. Inf. Syst. **21**(1), 41–63 (2009). https://doi.org/10.1007/s10115-009-0228-9

21. Chinosi, M., Trombetta, A.: BPMN: an introduction to the standard. Comput. Stand. Interfaces **34**(1), 124–134 (2012). https://doi.org/10.1016/j.csi.2011.06.002

22. Cohn, D., Hull, R.: Business artifacts: a data-centric approach to modeling business operations and processes. IEEE Data Eng. Bull. **32**(3), 3–9 (2009). http://sites.computer.org/debull/A09sept/david.pdf

23. Dobrushin, R.L.: Definition of a system of random variables by conditional distributions. Teoriya Veroyatnostei i ee Primeneniya **15**, 469–497 (1970)

24. van der Aalst, W., Adams, M., ter Hofstede, A., Russell, N.: Introduction. In: ter Hofstede, A., van der Aalst, W., Adams, M., Russell, N. (eds.) Modern Business Process Automation, pp. 3–19. Springer, Heidelberg (2010). https://doi.org/10.1007/978-3-642-03121-2_1 http://www.yawlbook.com/home/

25. Hompes, B., Buijs, J.C.A.M., van der Aalst, W.M.P., Dixit, P.M., Buurman, H.: Detecting change in processes using comparative trace clustering. In: Ceravolo, P., Rinderle-Ma, S. (eds.) Data-Driven Process Discovery and Analysis. CEUR Workshop Proceedings, vol. 1527, pp. 95–108. CEUR-WS.org (2015). http://ceur-ws.org/Vol-1527/paper7.pdf

26. Leemans, S.J.J., Fahland, D., van der Aalst, W.M.P.: Discovering block-structured process models from incomplete event logs. In: Ciardo, G., Kindler, E. (eds.) PETRI NETS 2014. LNCS, vol. 8489, pp. 91–110. Springer, Cham (2014). https://doi.org/10.1007/978-3-319-07734-5_6

27. Li, G., de Carvalho, R.M., van der Aalst, W.M.P.: Object-centric behavioral constraint models: a hybrid model for behavioral and data perspectives. In: Hung, C., Papadopoulos, G.A. (eds.) Proceedings of the 34th ACM/SIGAPP Symposium on Applied Computing, SAC 2019, pp. 48–56. Association for Computing Machinery, New York (2019). https://doi.org/10.1145/3297280.3297287

28. Li, G., de Murillas, E.G.L., de Carvalho, R.M., van der Aalst, W.M.P.: Extracting object-centric event logs to support process mining on databases. In: Mendling, J., Mouratidis, H. (eds.) CAiSE 2018. LNBIP, vol. 317, pp. 182–199. Springer, Cham (2018). https://doi.org/10.1007/978-3-319-92901-9_16

29. Li, X., Han, J.: Mining approximate top-k subspace anomalies in multi-dimensional time-series data. In: Proceedings of the 33rd International Conference on Very Large Data Bases, VLDB 2007, pp. 447–458. VLDB Endowment (2007)

30. Liebenberg, M., Jarke, M.: Information systems engineering with digital shadows: concept and case studies. In: Dustdar, S., Yu, E., Salinesi, C., Rieu, D., Pant, V. (eds.) CAiSE 2020. LNCS, vol. 12127, pp. 70–84. Springer, Cham (2020). https://doi.org/10.1007/978-3-030-49435-3_5

31. Liu, M., et al.: E-Cube: multi-dimensional event sequence processing using concept and pattern hierarchies. In: Li, F., et al. (eds.) IEEE 26th International Conference on Data Engineering, pp. 1097–1100. IEEE Computer Society (2010). https://doi.org/10.1109/ICDE.2010.5447886

32. Maaradji, A., Dumas, M., La Rosa, M., Ostovar, A.: Fast and accurate business process drift detection. In: Motahari-Nezhad, H.R., Recker, J., Weidlich, M. (eds.) BPM 2015. LNCS, vol. 9253, pp. 406–422. Springer, Cham (2015). https://doi.org/10.1007/978-3-319-23063-4_27

33. Mamaliga, T.: Realizing a process cube allowing for the comparison of event data. Master's thesis, Eindhoven University of Technology, Eindhoven (2013)

34. de Murillas, E.G.L., Reijers, H.A., van der Aalst, W.M.P.: Case notion discovery and recommendation: automated event log building on databases. Knowl. Inf. Syst. **62**(7), 2539–2575 (2020). https://doi.org/10.1007/s10115-019-01430-6

35. Narendra, N.C., Badr, Y., Thiran, P., Maamar, Z.: Towards a unified approach for business process modeling using context-based artifacts and web services. In: 2009 IEEE International Conference on Services Computing, pp. 332–339. IEEE Computer Society (2009). https://doi.org/10.1109/SCC.2009.14

36. Ostovar, A., Leemans, S.J.J., Rosa, M.L.: Robust drift characterization from event streams of business processes. ACM Trans. Knowl. Discov. Data **14**(3), 30:1–30:57 (2020). https://doi.org/10.1145/3375398

37. Ostovar, A., Maaradji, A., La Rosa, M., ter Hofstede, A.H.M.: Characterizing drift from event streams of business processes. In: Dubois, E., Pohl, K. (eds.) CAiSE 2017. LNCS, vol. 10253, pp. 210–228. Springer, Cham (2017). https://doi.org/10.1007/978-3-319-59536-8_14

38. Pourbafrani, M., van der Aalst, W.M.P.: PMSD: data-driven simulation using system dynamics and process mining. In: BPM 2020 Best Dissertation Award, Doctoral Consortium, and Demonstration & Resources Track, pp. 77–81. CEUR-WS.org (2020). http://ceur-ws.org/Vol-2673/paperDR03.pdf
39. Pourbafrani, M., van Zelst, S.J., van der Aalst, W.M.P.: Scenario-based prediction of business processes using system dynamics. In: Panetto, H., Debruyne, C., Hepp, M., Lewis, D., Ardagna, C.A., Meersman, R. (eds.) OTM 2019. LNCS, vol. 11877, pp. 422–439. Springer, Cham (2019). https://doi.org/10.1007/978-3-030-33246-4_27
40. Pourbafrani, M., van Zelst, S.J., van der Aalst, W.M.P.: Semi-automated time-granularity detection for data-driven simulation using process mining and system dynamics. In: Dobbie, G., Frank, U., Kappel, G., Liddle, S.W., Mayr, H.C. (eds.) ER 2020. LNCS, vol. 12400, pp. 77–91. Springer, Cham (2020). https://doi.org/10.1007/978-3-030-62522-1_6
41. Pourbafrani, M., van Zelst, S.J., van der Aalst, W.M.P.: Supporting automatic system dynamics model generation for simulation in the context of process mining. In: Abramowicz, W., Klein, G. (eds.) BIS 2020. LNBIP, vol. 389, pp. 249–263. Springer, Cham (2020). https://doi.org/10.1007/978-3-030-53337-3_19
42. Pourbafrani, M., van Zelst, S.J., van der Aalst, W.M.P.: Supporting decisions in production line processes by combining process mining and system dynamics. In: Ahram, T., Karwowski, W., Vergnano, A., Leali, F., Taiar, R. (eds.) IHSI 2020. AISC, vol. 1131, pp. 461–467. Springer, Cham (2020). https://doi.org/10.1007/978-3-030-39512-4_72
43. Ratzer, A.V., et al.: CPN tools for editing, simulating, and analysing coloured Petri nets. In: van der Aalst, W.M.P., Best, E. (eds.) ICATPN 2003. LNCS, vol. 2679, pp. 450–462. Springer, Heidelberg (2003). https://doi.org/10.1007/3-540-44919-1_28
44. Ribeiro, J.T.S., Weijters, A.J.M.M.: Event cube: another perspective on business processes. In: Meersman, R., et al. (eds.) OTM 2011. LNCS, vol. 7044, pp. 274–283. Springer, Heidelberg (2011). https://doi.org/10.1007/978-3-642-25109-2_18
45. Rozinat, A., Mans, R.S., Song, M., van der Aalst, W.M.P.: Discovering simulation models. Inf. Syst. **34**(3), 305–327 (2009)
46. Rozinat, A., Wynn, M.T., van der Aalst, W.M.P., ter Hofstede, A.H.M., Fidge, C.J.: Workflow simulation for operational decision support. Data Knowl. Eng. **68**(9), 834–850 (2009)
47. Rubner, Y., Tomasi, C., Guibas, L.J.: The earth mover's distance as a metric for image retrieval. Int. J. Comput. Vis. **40**(2), 99–121 (2000). https://doi.org/10.1023/A:1026543900054
48. Simović, A.P., Babarogić, S., Pantelić, O.: A domain-specific language for supporting event log extraction from ERP systems. In: 7th International Conference on Computers Communications and Control, pp. 12–16. IEEE (2018)
49. Song, M., van der Aalst, W.M.P.: Supporting process mining by showing events at a glance. In: Chari, K., Kumar, A. (eds.) WITS 2007 - Proceedings of the 17th Annual Workshop on Information Technologies and Systems, Montreal, Canada, pp. 139–145, December 2007
50. Sterman, J.D.: Business Dynamics. McGraw-Hill, New York (2002)
51. Weijters, A.J.M.M., van der Aalst, W.M.P.: Rediscovering workflow models from event-based data using little thumb. Integr. Comput.-Aided Eng. **10**(2), 151–162 (2003)

Efficient Scheduling of Scientific Workflow Actions in the Cloud Based on Required Capabilities

Michel Krämer[1,2](✉) [iD]

[1] Fraunhofer Institute for Computer Graphics Research IGD, Fraunhoferstr. 5,
64283 Darmstadt, Germany
michel.kraemer@igd.fraunhofer.de
[2] Technical University of Darmstadt, 64289 Darmstadt, Germany

Abstract. Distributed scientific workflow management systems processing large data sets in the Cloud face the following challenges: (a) workflow tasks require different capabilities from the machines on which they run, but at the same time, the infrastructure is highly heterogeneous, (b) the environment is dynamic and new resources can be added and removed at any time, (c) scientific workflows can become very large with hundreds of thousands of tasks, (d) faults can happen at any time in a distributed system. In this paper, we present a software architecture and a capability-based scheduling algorithm that cover all these challenges in one design. Our architecture consists of loosely coupled components that can run on separate virtual machines and communicate with each other over an event bus and through a database. The scheduling algorithm matches capabilities required by the tasks (e.g. software, CPU power, main memory, graphics processing unit) with those offered by the available virtual machines and assigns them accordingly for processing. Our approach utilises heuristics to distribute the tasks evenly in the Cloud. This reduces the overall run time of workflows and makes efficient use of available resources. Our scheduling algorithm also implements optimisations to achieve a high scalability. We perform a thorough evaluation based on four experiments and test if our approach meets the challenges mentioned above. The paper finishes with a discussion, conclusions, and future research opportunities. An implementation of our algorithm and software architecture is publicly available with the open-source workflow management system "Steep".

Keywords: Scientific workflow management systems · Cloud computing · Distributed systems · Task scheduling

1 Introduction

With the growing amount of global data, it becomes more and more necessary to automate data processing and analysis. Specialised task automation systems are used in areas such as Bioinformatics [31], Geology [18], Geoinformatics [25], and Astronomy [5] to transform data and to extract or derive knowledge. A special kind of those task automation systems are scientific workflow management systems. They focus on

S. Hammoudi et al. (Eds.): DATA 2020, CCIS 1446, pp. 32–55, 2021.
https://doi.org/10.1007/978-3-030-83014-4_2

data-driven scientific workflows, which are typically represented by directed acyclic graphs that describe in what order processing tasks need to be applied to a given input data set to produce a desired outcome. Scientific workflows can become very large with *hundreds up to several thousands of tasks* processing data volumes ranging from gigabytes to terabytes.

Modern scientific workflow management systems operate in a distributed manner. They can utilize resources of computing infrastructures such as the Grid [14] or the Cloud [29] to horizontally scale out. This not only speeds up workflow execution but also allows data sets of arbitrary size exceeding the storage capabilities of single computers (Big Data) to be processed. To accomplish this, distributed infrastructures combine the computational power and storage resources of a large number of independent machines. This imposes a challenge on scientific workflow management systems: *How can workflow tasks be assigned to these machines in a smart way to make best use of available resources?*

The general task scheduling problem is known to be NP-complete [23,38] and of high interest to the research community. Several approaches with varying aims and requirements have been published to find practical solutions for the Grid and the Cloud [20,34]. In this paper, we present a *distributed task scheduling algorithm* and a *corresponding software architecture* for a scientific workflow management system that specifically targets the Cloud. The main challenges that need to be covered in this respect are, on the one hand, that machines are highly heterogeneous in terms of hardware, number of virtual CPUs, main memory, and available storage, but also with regard to installed software, drivers, and operating systems. On the other hand, the different tasks in a scientific workflow also have requirements. A compute-intensive task might need a minimum number of CPUs or even a graphics processing unit (GPU), whereas another task might require a large amount of main memory, and a third one needs a specific software to be installed. In other words, *machines have certain capabilities* and *tasks have requirements regarding these capabilities* (or *required capabilities*). This has to be considered during task scheduling. As shown in Sect. 2, this concept has not been fully covered by existing approaches yet.

In addition to the heterogeneity of machines, the topology of a Cloud is *highly dynamic*. New compute and storage resources can be added on demand and removed at any time. This property is often used to scale a distributed application up when needed (e.g. to manage peak load or to speed up processing) and later down again to save resources and, in consequence, money. Of course, scaling up only makes sense if work can actually be distributed, which is typically the case when a workflow is very large and contains many tasks that could potentially be executed in parallel.

As mentioned above, workflow tasks should be assigned to machines in a smart way in order to optimise resource usage, reduce the total time it takes to complete a workflow, and, in consequence, save money by freeing up resources as soon as possible. However, in a distributed environment whose topology changes dynamically and that is used by multiple tenants at the same time, it is impossible to calculate an optimal task-to-machine mapping in advance to achieve the "perfect" run time. Instead, task scheduling has to be performed during workflow execution and needs to be able to adapt dynamically to changing conditions.

It is further known that in a distributed environment (and in a Cloud in particular), *faults* such as crashed machines, network timeouts, or missing messages can happen at any time [10]. This highly affects the execution of scientific workflows, which often take several hours or even days to complete.

1.1 Challenges and Requirements

To summarise the above, a scientific workflow management system running in the Cloud has to deal with at least the following major challenges:

Capability-based Scheduling
Workflow tasks require different capabilities from the machines but, in contrast, the infrastructure is highly heterogeneous.

Dynamic Environment
The execution environment is highly dynamic and new compute resources can be added and removed on demand.

Scalability
Scientific workflows can become very large and may contain hundreds of thousands of tasks.

Fault Tolerance
In a distributed system, faults such as crashes or network errors can occur at any time.

From these challenges, we derive specific requirements that our scheduling algorithm and software architecture should meet:

REQ 1. The algorithm should be able to assign tasks to heterogeneous machines, while matching the capabilities the tasks need with the capabilities the machines provide.

REQ 2. Tasks should be assigned to parallel machines in an optimised manner so that the overall run time of the workflow is reduced.

REQ 3. Our system should not assume a static number of machines. It should horizontally scale the workflow execution to new machines added to the cluster and be able to handle machines being removed (be it because a user or a service destroyed the machine or because of a fault).

REQ 4. If necessary, the execution of workflow tasks that require capabilities currently not available in the cluster should be postponed. The overall workflow execution should not be blocked. The algorithm should continue with the remaining tasks and reschedule the postponed ones as soon as machines with the required capabilities become available.

REQ 5. The system should support rapid elasticity. This means it should automatically trigger the acquisition of new machines on demand (e.g. during peak load or when capabilities are missing).

REQ 6. The system should be scalable so it can manage both a large number of tasks as well as a large number of machines.

REQ 7. As faults can happen at any time in a distributed environment, our system should be able to recover from those faults and automatically continue executing workflows.

1.2   Contributions

In the scientific community, dynamically changing environments, very large workflows, and fault tolerance are considered major challenges for modern distributed scientific workflow management systems, but they have not been fully covered by existing approaches yet and therefore offer many research opportunities [11]. In the previous section, we discussed these challenges and added another major one, namely that tasks in a scientific workflow need certain capabilities from the machines but the Cloud is highly heterogeneous.

A system that addresses all four of these challenges needs to be designed from the ground up with them in mind. To the best of our knowledge, none of the existing approaches, algorithms, and systems cover all of them in one design (see also our comparison with related work in Sect. 2). *In this paper, we present such an algorithm as well as the software architecture of a scientific workflow management system in which the algorithm is embedded.*

Our scheduling algorithm is able to assign workflow tasks to heterogeneous machines in the Cloud based on required capability sets. The software architecture consists of a set of components that communicate with each other through an event bus and a database to perform task scheduling in an efficient, scalable, and fault-tolerant manner.

A full implementation of our approach is publicly available with the *Steep Workflow Management System*, which has been released under an open-source licence on GitHub: https://steep-wms.github.io/.

1.3 Differences to the Conference Paper

This paper is a significant extension of our conference paper presented at DATA 2020 [26]. In the previous work, we introduced a first version of our algorithm and software architecture. In the meantime, we were able to explore new research aspects and, as a result of this, to significantly improve our approach. In summary, the extended paper covers the following additional topics:

- We *improved our scheduling algorithm to use heuristics* (Sect. 5.3) in order to distribute tasks more evenly to machines. Our old approach did not fully use available resources. We therefore added a new requirement regarding optimised allocation of tasks to machines (REQ 2). Our new approach *significantly reduces the overall run time of workflows*.
- In addition, we implemented several optimisations to improve the scalability of our approach, not only in terms of amount of work it can handle but also *to support thousands of machines running in parallel* (Sects. 5.4 and 5.5).
- We conducted a *completely new evaluation* to test our new approach and to show how it compares with our old one (Sect. 7). The evaluation now also *measures the performance of our scheduling algorithm* (Sect. 7.2).
- We improved our software architecture so *multiple agents can be started on a single virtual machine* (Sect. 4). We make use of this new feature in our scalability experiment.
- Sect. 4.1 now describes *virtual machine setups*, which are an integral part of our architecture to create virtual machines with given capabilities.
- We added more details about our scheduling algorithm (Sect. 5) and an illustrative example (Sect. 6).

1.4 Structure of the Paper

The remainder of this paper is structured as follows. We first analyse the state of the art in Sect. 2. Then, we introduce an approach to map scientific workflow graphs dynamically to individual *process chains* (i.e. linear sequences of workflow tasks), which can be treated independently by our scheduling algorithm (Sect. 3). We describe the software architecture in Sect. 4 and finally our main contribution, the scheduling algorithm, in Sect. 5. An illustrative example in Sect. 6 demonstrates how our system works in practise. We also present the results of four experiments we conducted to evaluate if our approach meets the challenges and requirements defined above (Sect. 7). We finish the paper in Sect. 8 with conclusions and future research opportunities.

2 Related Work

There are various algorithms performing task scheduling. Their aims vary from each other but most of them try to optimise resource usage and to reduce the *makespan*, i.e. the time passed between the start of the first task in a sequence and the end of the last one. For this, they implement heuristics. Min-Min and Max-Min [15,22], for example, iterate through all tasks in the sequence and calculate their earliest completion time on all machines. Min-Min schedules the task with the minimum earliest completion time while Max-Min selects the task with the maximum one. This process continues until all tasks have been processed.

In contrast, the Sufferage algorithm reassigns a task from machine M to another one if there is a second task that would achieve better performance on M [28]. As an extension to this approach, Casanova et al. present a heuristic called XSufferage, which also considers data transfer costs [9]. The authors claim their approach leads to a shorter makespan because of possible file reuse. Gherega and Pupezescu improve this algorithm even further and present DXSufferage, which is based on the multi-agent paradigm [16]. Their approach prevents the heuristic itself from becoming a bottleneck in the scheduling process. For increased flexibility, Nayak and Padhi present an approach that first analyses all tasks to be scheduled and then, based on the current situation, selects from different heuristics to achieve the best performance [30].

Our approach is also based on heuristics. Since it is very hard to analyse tasks and to predict their earliest completion time on heterogeneous virtual machines in a dynamic environment like the Cloud, our approach uses the remaining number of workflow tasks for a certain set of required capabilities to evenly distribute work to machines and to adapt to changing conditions during run time.

Other dynamic approaches are based on genetic algorithms (GA), which mimics the process of natural evolution by using historical information. A GA selects the best mapping of tasks to machines. Good results with this type of algorithms were achieved by Hamad and Omara who use Tournament Selection [19] or by Page and Naughton whose algorithm does not make assumptions about the characteristics of tasks or machines [32].

Applying behaviour known from nature to task scheduling is an idea that has lead to other noteworthy approaches: Ant colony optimisation [27,35] tries to dynamically adapt scheduling strategies to changing environments. Thennarasu et al. present a scheduler that mimics the behaviour of humpback whales to maximize work completion and to meet deadline and budget constraints [36].

The algorithms mentioned above can be used to schedule individual tasks. In contrast, there are more complex approaches that consider the interdependencies in the directed acyclic graphs of scientific workflows. Blythe et al. investigate the difference between task-based and workflow-based approaches [7]. They conclude that data-intensive applications benefit from workflow-based approaches because the workflow system can start to transfer data before it is used by the tasks, which leads to optimised resource usage. Binato et al. present such a workflow-based approach using a greedy randomized adaptive search procedure (GRASP) [6]. Their algorithm creates multiple scheduling solutions iteratively and then selects the one that is expected to perform best. Topcuoglu et al. present two algorithms: HEFT and CPOP [37]. HEFT traverses the complete workflow graph and calculates priorities for individual tasks based on the number of successors, average communication costs, and average computation costs. CPOP extends this and prioritises critical paths in workflow graphs.

Scientific workflow management systems such as *Pegasus* [12], *Kepler* [1], *Taverna* [21], *Galaxy* [17], *Argo* [3], *Airflow* [2], and *Nextflow* [13] typically implement one or more of the algorithms mentioned above. There are other frameworks to process large data sets in the Cloud. Most noteworthy systems are Spark [39] and Flink [8]. They are not workflow management systems but follow a similar approach and also need to schedule tasks from a directed graph.

There are some similarities between our approach and existing ones. DXSufferage, for example, uses the multi-agent paradigm [16]. Similar to agents, our components are independent and communicate with each other through an event bus. There can be multiple schedulers sharing work and processing the same workflow. In addition, we convert workflow graphs to process chains, which group tasks with the same required capabilities and common input/output data. Just like in XSufferage [9], this can potentially lead to better file reuse.

Note that our approach is not directly comparable to workflow-based scheduling algorithms that consider the graph in total. Instead, we employ a hybrid strategy that first splits the graph into process chains and then schedules these instead of individual tasks.

3   Traversing Scientific Workflow Graphs

Fig. 1a shows an example of a scientific workflow represented by a directed graph. An input file (the circle with the dot) is first consumed by task A, which produces two output files. These files are then processed independently (and possibly in parallel) by tasks B and D. The result of B is further transformed by task C. The results of C and D

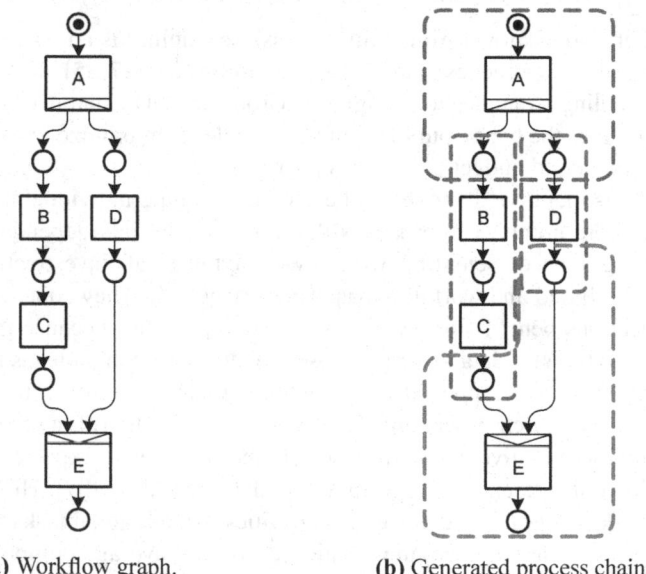

(a) Workflow graph.   (b) Generated process chains.

Fig. 1. A workflow is split into four individual process chains [26].

are consumed by a task E, which produces the final outcome of the workflow. The figure uses the extended Petri Net notation proposed by van der Aalst and van Hee (2004).

Our scientific workflow management system transforms such workflow graphs into individual executable units called *process chains*. These are linear sequential lists of tasks (without branches and loops) that can be scheduled independently on virtual machines in the Cloud. In order to find process chains, our system traverses the graph and looks for tasks that require the same capabilities from the machines. On each junction (i.e. when a task creates more outputs than it consumes inputs; or the other way around), the system creates a new process chain. For the example in Fig. 1a, the system creates a process chain for task A, then two chains (one containing B and C, and another one containing only D), and a final one for task E. The chains with B/C and D can be assigned to separate virtual machines and executed in parallel according to our algorithm presented in Sect. 5.

In our implementation, capabilities are user-defined strings. For example, the set {*Ubuntu, GPU*} might mean that a task depends on the Linux distribution Ubuntu as well as the presence of a graphics processing unit. In the following, we call the union of the required capabilities of all tasks in a process chain a *required capability set*.

4   Software Architecture

Our scientific workflow management system consists of four main components: the HTTP server, the controller, the scheduler, the agent, and the cloud manager (see Fig. 2). Typically, one instance of our system will be deployed to exactly one virtual machine in the Cloud. If necessary, it is possible to run multiple instances on the same machine.

Each component can be enabled or disabled in a given instance. In a cluster, there can be one primary instance, for example, that has only the controller and scheduler enabled, and multiple secondary instances each running one agent. In addition to that, the agent can be spawned more than once inside a single instance. This allows this instance to run multiple workflow tasks in parallel and to make best use of available

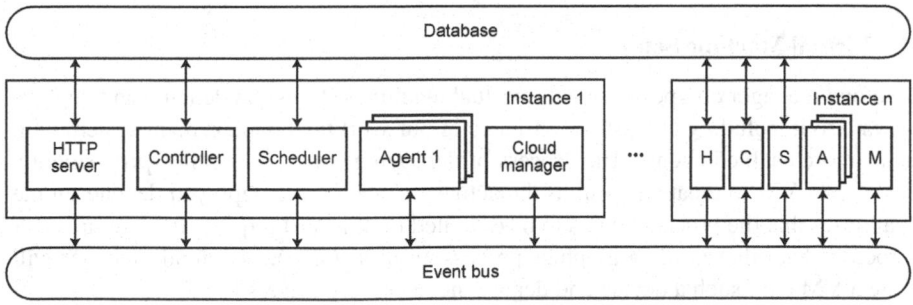

Fig. 2. An overview of the components in our scientific workflow management system and how they communicate with each other.

resources (for example, if each workflow task only requires one CPU core or a limited amount of memory).

The system contains an event bus that is used by all components of all instances to communicate with each other. Moreover, the HTTP server, the controller, and the scheduler are connected to a shared database where they manage workflows and process chains. In the following, we describe the roles and responsibilities of each component.

The HTTP server is the main entry point to our system. It provides information about scheduled, running, and finished workflows to clients. If the HTTP server receives a new workflow from a client, it stores the workflow in the database and sends a message to one of the instances of the controller.

The controller receives this message, loads the workflow from the database, and starts transforming it iteratively to process chains as described in Sect. 3. Whenever it has generated new process chains, it puts them into the database and sends a message to all instances of the scheduler.

The schedulers then apply our algorithm (see Sect. 5) and select agents to execute the process chains. They load the process chains from the database, send them via the event bus to the selected agents for execution. Upon completion, they write the results into the database. The schedulers also send a message back to the controller so it can continue with the next iteration and generate more process chains until the workflow has been completely transformed.

In case a scheduler does not find an agent suitable for the execution of a process chain, it sends a message to the cloud manager. This component interacts with the API of the Cloud infrastructure, creates new virtual machines on demand, and deploys agents to them. This is based on so-called *virtual machine setups*, which are described in Sect. 4.1.

Note that messages between the HTTP server, the controller, and scheduler may get lost (e.g. because of network failures). Due to this, the controller and the scheduler also check the database for new workflows and process chains respectively at a regular interval. We found 20 s to be a sensible value in practise, but in our implementation, this is configurable. This approach decouples the components from each other and increases fault tolerance.

4.1 Virtual Machine Setups

The cloud manager component creates virtual machines (VMs) on demand and deploys software to it including at least one instance of our workflow management system with one or more enabled agents. The process of deploying software is called *provisioning*. The kind of VM to create as well as the actual software to be deployed depend on the capabilities that the process chains to be executed on this VM require. For example, for a process chain that needs a graphics processing unit (GPU), the cloud manager will create a VM with such a device and deploy the necessary drivers to it.

The behaviour of the cloud manager is configurable. The mapping between required capabilities and VM types (sometimes called *flavors* or *instance types*; depending on the Cloud provider) is specified in a configuration file, and the software is deployed by provisioning templates. These templates are shell scripts that the cloud manager executes on the virtual machines right after they have been created. The last step in each set of provisioning templates always starts an instance of our system, so the cloud manager knows when the provisioning process has completed and the new agents can be used for scheduling.

Each set of provisioning templates and the corresponding mapping from required capabilities to VM types is called a *virtual machine setup* in our system.

5 Capability-Based Scheduling Algorithm

This section introduces the capability-based scheduling algorithm that is executed in our scheduler component. First, the main scheduling function (Sect. 5.1) is described as well as how our algorithm selects candidate agents (Sect. 5.2) based on heuristics (Sect. 5.3). After that, database queries (Sect. 5.4) and optimisations for improved scalability (Sect. 5.5) are discussed.

5.1 Main Scheduling Function

As mentioned above, the scheduler runs at regular intervals and immediately after new process chains have been added to the database. Listing 1.1 shows the main function of our algorithm that assigns process chains to agents.

Our algorithm first calls the function *findRequiredCapabilitySets()*, which performs a database query to retrieve all distinct sets of capabilities required to execute the process chains not scheduled yet. In other words, given a capability set $R_i = \{c_1, ..., c_n\}$ for a process chain pc_i, the result of *findRequiredCapabilitySets()* is a set $S = \{R_1, ..., R_m\}$ of distinct required capability sets.

From line 3 on, our algorithm performs up to *maxLookups* scheduling operations. After the regular interval or when new process chains have been added, the function will be called with *maxLookups* set to infinity. The main idea is that the algorithm will try to schedule as many process chains as possible until it reaches a *break* statement. There is only one of these statements in line 12. It is reached when all agents indicate they are not available (see details below).

Inside the main for loop, the function first selects a set of candidate agents that are able to execute at least one of the given required capability sets from S (line 4) by calling the function *selectCandidates()*. This function is described in detail in Sect. 5.2. In short, it returns a list of pairs of a candidate agent and the required capability set R it can execute.

If this list is empty (line 5), all agents are currently busy or there is no agent that would be able to execute at least one $R \in S$ (i.e. none of them is available). In this case, the function iterates over all required capability sets (line 8) and checks if there actually is a corresponding process chain in the database (line 9). This is necessary because all process chains with a certain required capability set may have already been processed since *findRequiredCapabilitySets()* was called (e.g. by another scheduler instance or in a preceding iteration of the outer for loop). If there is a process chain, the function *requestAgent* will be called, which asks the cloud manager component (see Sect. 4) to create a new VM with an agent that has the given required capabilities (line 11). We

```
1   function lookup(maxLookups):
2     S = findRequiredCapabilitySets()

3     for i ∈ [0, maxLookups):
4       candidates = selectCandidates(S)

5       if candidates == ∅:
6         /* All agents are busy or none of them
7            have the required capabilities. */
8         for R ∈ S:
9           if existsProcessChain(R):
10            launch:
11              requestAgent(R)
12        break

13      for (candidate, R) ∈ candidates:
14        pc = findProcessChain(R)
15        if pc == undefined:
16          /* All process chains with R were
17             executed in the meantime. */
18          continue

19        agent = allocate(candidate)
20        if agent == undefined:
21          /* Agent is not available any more. */
22          continue

23        /* Execute process chain
24           asynchronously. */
25        launch:
26          executeProcessChain(pc, agent)
27          deallocate(agent)

28          /* Agent is has become available.
29             Trigger next lookup. */
30          lookup(1)
```

Listing 1.1. The main function of our algorithm checks what capabilities are required at the moment and if there are available agents that can execute process chains with these capabilities. If so, it retrieves such process chains from the database and schedules their execution [26].

use the keyword *launch* here to indicate that the call to *requestAgent* is asynchronous, meaning the algorithm does not wait for an answer.

The algorithm then leaves the outer for loop because it is unnecessary to perform any more scheduling operations while none of the agents can execute process chains (line 12). Process chains with required capabilities none of the agents can provide will essentially be postponed. As soon as the cloud manager has created a new agent with the missing capabilities, the *lookup* function will be called again and any postponed process chains can be scheduled.

If there are agents available that can execute process chains with any of the required capability sets from *S*, the algorithm iterates over the result of *selectCandidates()* in line 13. For each pair of a candidate agent and the corresponding required capability set *R* it can execute, the algorithm tries to find a matching registered process chain with

R in the database. If there is none, it assumes that all process chains with this required capability set have already been executed in the meantime (line 15). Otherwise, it tries to allocate the candidate agent, which means it asks it to prepare itself for the execution of a process chain and to not accept other requests anymore (line 19). If the agent cannot be allocated, it was probably allocated by another scheduler instance in the meantime since *selectCandidates* was called (line 20).

Otherwise, the algorithm launches the execution of the process chain in the background and continues with the next scheduling operation. The code block from line 25 to line 30 runs asynchronously in a separate thread and does not block the outer for loop. As soon as the process chain has been executed completely in this thread, our algorithm deallocates the agent in line 27 so it becomes available again. It then calls the *lookup* function and passes 1 for *maxLookups* because exactly one agent has become available and therefore only one process chain has to be scheduled.

5.2 Selecting Candidate Agents

The function *selectCandidates* takes a set $S = \{R_1, ..., R_n\}$ of required capability sets and returns a list $L = \{P_1, ..., P_m\}$ of pairs $P = (a, R_i)$ of an agent a and matching required capability set R_i. Listing 1.2 shows the pseudo code.

The function uses the event bus to send all required capability sets to each agent. The agents analyse the required capability sets based on defined heuristics (see Sect. 5.3) and then reply whether they are available and which set they support best. The function collects all responses in a set of *candidates*. Finally, it selects exactly one agent for each required capability set.

Note that some or all agents might not be available, in which case the result of *selectCandidates* contains less required capability sets than S or is even empty.

```
1   function selectCandidates(S):
2       candidates = ∅

3       for a ∈ Agents:
4           send S to a and wait for response
5           if a is available:
6               get best Rᵢ ∈ S from response
7               P = (a, Rᵢ)
8               candidates = candidates ∪ {P}

9       L = all P ∈ candidates with best a for each Rᵢ

10      return L
```

Listing 1.2. Pseudo code of the function that selects agents based on their capabilities [26].

5.3 Scheduling Heuristics

An agent receives required capability sets from the scheduler and matches them against the capabilities it actually has. For example, let us assume one of these sets is $\{Ubuntu,$

GPU} (as described in Sect. 3, capabilities are user-defined strings). The agent will only consider this set if it actually runs on Ubuntu and has a GPU (as specified in its VM setup; see Sect. 4.1).

After the agent has selected all required capability sets it generally supports, it chooses one set for which it would like to receive process chains to execute. In Listing 1.2, this is called the "best" $R_i \in S$.

In our previous work, we only had one heuristic that selected the best agent for a certain required capability set based on the longest idle time [26]. In practise, this has proven to achieve good throughput and, at the same time, to prevent starvation because every agent was selected eventually.

Our new approach extends the existing heuristic. When selecting the best capability set, the agent now also considers the number of remaining process chains in the database for each $R_i \in S$. If two or more capability sets are supported similarly well, the agent selects the one with the highest number of remaining process chains. This makes sure process chains are distributed more evenly to agents supporting similar capabilities (see our evaluation results in Sect. 7).

5.4 Caching Database Queries

The function *findRequiredCapabilitySets* performs a database query to look for distinct required capability sets. Queries for distinct values are complex and can take quite some time, especially for very large collections. The only way to find all distinct values is to perform a sequential scan on the collection. Most DBMS even have to sort the collection first. There are approaches to find approximations of distinct values [4,24] but our algorithm needs exact results.

Such a query should not be performed too often as it can drastically impact the throughout of the scheduler. As an optimisation, we use a cache to keep distinct required capability sets in memory until the next regular scheduling interval. This can lead to inconsistencies if multiple schedulers access the database and their caches become outdated. In the worst case, two things can happen:

- The cache may still contain required capability sets of process chains that have already been executed. In this case, the algorithm will not find a matching process chain in the database (line 15) and just continue with the next candidate agent and required capability set. This means, there may be unnecessary queries per scheduling operation, but these queries are negligibly fast because they can be implemented with simple SELECT-WHERE statements that make use of an index.
- One or more required capability sets may be missing from the cache. This can only happen if new process chains are added to the database while a scheduling operation is currently running. Adding new process chains will, however, trigger a cache update, so the next scheduling operation will use all required capability sets.

In any case, the cache will be updated at the regular interval, which will eliminate unnecessary queries and trigger the scheduling of remaining process chains.

5.5 Optimisations for Improved Scalability

Another possible bottleneck of our algorithm besides database queries is the *selectCandidates* function, which sends required capability sets to all agents. Even though all capability sets can be sent together in one message, in a setup with n process chains and m agents, $n \times m$ messages need to be sent per workflow execution. Since these messages are sent over the event bus and possibly through a slow network, the execution of *selectCandidates* can significantly affect the time it takes to schedule a single process chain and, as a consequence, the run time of the whole workflow.

In addition to caching database queries, we therefore implemented two other optimisations. First, each scheduler instance caches the capabilities supported by the individual agents. This allows it to skip those agents that definitely do not support a certain required capability set. Second, the scheduler also keeps track of which agents are currently executing process chains (i.e. to which of them it has sent a process chain and has not received a result yet). Those agents can also be skipped as they would respond that they are unavailable anyhow. In the best case, when all agents are busy except one, the scheduler only needs to ask this agent and can skip the others.

6 Illustrative Example

Fig. 3 shows an example of how our scheduling algorithm works in practise. Note that it represents one specific case (other control flows are possible) but covers almost all aspects of our algorithm and architecture.

At the beginning, there are 500 process chains in the database to be scheduled. Some of them require "Docker" to be installed on the virtual machine on which they will be executed, others require "TF" (TensorFlow) and "Python", and a third group requires the VM to have a graphics processing unit ("GPU"). Two agents are currently running in the Cloud. One supports "C++" applications and the other one has "Docker" installed but is currently busy.

In the first scheduling step (Fig. 3a), the scheduler fetches distinct required capability sets from the database ❶. It gets $\{Docker\}$, $\{TF, Python\}$, and $\{GPU\}$ ❷. The scheduler then sends these sets to all agents ❸. Agent $A1$ responds that it does not support any of these capabilities, and agent $A2$ indicates that it is currently busy. Since there are no agents available, the scheduler sends the required capabilities to the cloud manager and tells it to create new VMs ❹. The first scheduling step stops at this point.

After the cloud manager has created new VMs and deployed agents to it (Fig. 3b), the next scheduling step starts. The scheduler fetches distinct required capability sets from the database again ❺ and sends them to all agents ❻ (except $A1$ because it knows it does not support the capabilities). This time, the new agents $A3$, $A4$, and $A5$ respond that they are available and which capability sets they support.

Once the scheduler has received all answers (Fig. 3c), it fetches a process chain for the capability set $\{Docker\}$ from the database and assigns it to agent $A3$ ❼. This process repeats for $\{TF, Python\}$ and $\{GPU\}$, which are assigned to $A4$ and $A5$, respectively ❽❾.

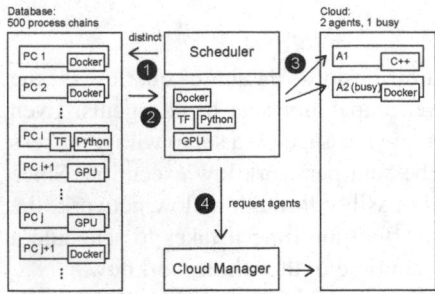

(a) The scheduler accesses the database, the agents, and the cloud manager.

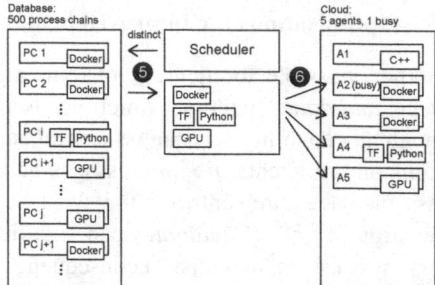

(b) The second scheduling step utilises the newly created agents.

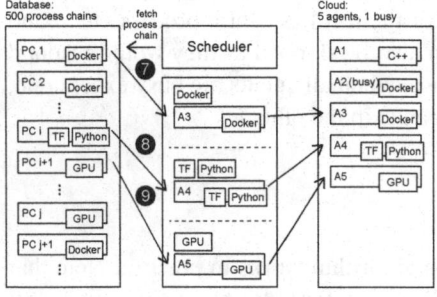

(c) Process chains are assigned to the new agents one by one.

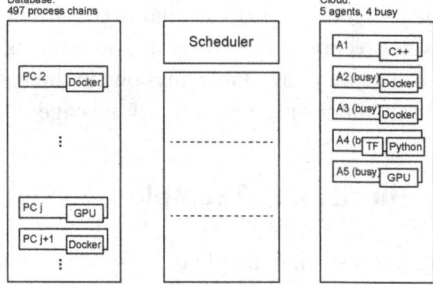

(d) At the end, the new agents are busy executing process chains.

Fig. 3. Illustrative scheduling example.

At the end of the second scheduling step (Fig. 3d), all new agents are busy. As soon as one of them becomes available again, a next step will be triggered to schedule the remaining process chains in the database.

7   Evaluation

In order to evaluate if our scheduling algorithm and our software architecture meet the challenges and requirements defined in Sect. 1.1, we conducted four practical experiments (one for each challenge). This section presents the results of these experiments and discusses benefits and drawbacks of our approach.

All experiments were performed in the same environment (a private OpenStack Cloud). We set up our system so that it had access to the API of the OpenStack Cloud and was able to create virtual machines on demand. We deployed the full stack of components presented in Sect. 4 to each virtual machine. All components communicated with each other through a distributed event bus. We also deployed a MongoDB database on a separate virtual machine to which the components had access.

We defined four VM setups for virtual machines and agents with the capability sets $R1$, $R2$, $R3$, and $R4$ respectively, as well as fifth one with both capability sets $R3$ and $R4$.

To simulate a heterogeneous environment, we configured a maximum number of virtual machines that our system was allowed to create per required capability set. Table 1 shows the settings we chose for the individual experiments. Note that in experiment 1, 2, and 4, we deployed one agent per virtual machine. In experiment 3 where we tested the scalability of our system, we deployed 125 agents per virtual machine resulting in a total number of 1 000 agents.

Table 1. Maximum number of virtual machines configured for each required capability set.

Required capability set	Maximum number of virtual machines
$R1$	2
$R2$	2
$R3$	1
$R4$	1
$R3 + R4$	2
Total	**8**

For each experiment, we collected all log files of all instances of our system and converted them to graphs. Figure 4 shows the results of experiments 1 and 2 including a legend. Each sub-figure—which we discuss in detail in the following sections—depicts a timeline of a workflow run. The lanes (from left to right) represent individual agents and indicate when they were busy executing process chains. All required capability sets have different colours (see legend in Fig. 4e). The colour of the agents and the process chains specifies what capabilities they offered or required respectively. A process chain has a start (emphasized by a darker shade of the colour) and an end. In experiment 4, we also killed agents on purpose. The point in time when the fault was induced is marked by a black X (see Fig. 5b).

7.1 Experiments

Experiment 1: Capability-Based Scheduling
(Requirements covered: REQ 1–2)

Fig. 4a shows the results of our first experiment. One of our goals in this paper was to create a scheduling algorithm that is able to assign workflow tasks to distributed machines based on required and offered capabilities. The results show that this goal was reached.

We deployed a static number of eight agents with different capability sets and sent a workflow consisting of 100 process chains to one of the instances of our system. As soon as the workflow was saved in the database, all scheduler instances started assigning process chains to the individual agents. The colours in the figure show that all process chains were correctly assigned. Agents $A6$ and $A7$ were able to execute process chains requiring both $R3$ and $R4$, which is indicated by alternating colours. The workflow took 11 min and 48 s to complete in total.

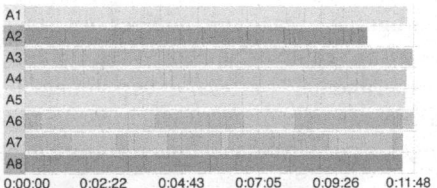

(a) 100 process chains are distributed to agents with the correct capabilities.

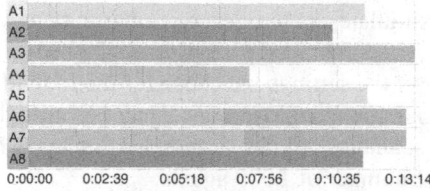

(b) Results of experiment 1 from our earlier work for comparison [26].

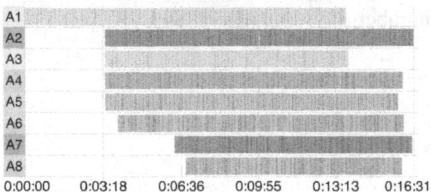

(c) The system creates agents with capabilities required by 1 000 process chains.

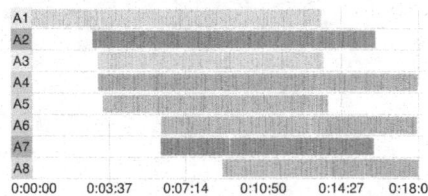

(d) Results of experiment 2 from our earlier work for comparison [26].

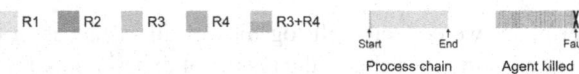

(e) Legend: colours for required capability sets, start and end of a process chain, and time when an agent was killed.

Fig. 4. Results of experiments 1 and 2.

Note that these results also show a significant improvement of our algorithm compared to our earlier work [26]. This is mostly due to the new scheduling heuristics presented in Sect. 5.3. Previously, as shown in Fig. 4b, agents $A6$ and $A7$ preferred to accept process chains with $R3$ first before they continued with $R4$. This resulted in an inefficient use of resources. Agent $A4$ was not used completely during the workflow run and too much work was allocated to $A3$, $A6$, and $A7$. The workflow took 13 min and 14 s. Our improved algorithm is about one and a half minutes faster and distributes work much more evenly.

Experiment 2: Dynamic Environment
(Requirements covered: REQ 1–5)

Our second experiment started with only one agent supporting capability set $R1$. We executed a workflow with 1 000 process chains. Figure 4c shows the timeline of the workflow run.

According to our algorithm, the scheduler first looked for available agents to which to assign process chains. Since there was only one agent running, it assigned process chains to it but also asked the cloud manager component to create new agents for the other capability sets. Starting a virtual machine and deploying itself to it took our system almost three minutes. Process chains requiring missing capabilities were postponed but the scheduler continued assigning the ones with $R1$. As soon as the new agents had started, process chains were assigned to them.

Note that we configured our system to only create one virtual machine of a certain capability set at a time. Also, as described earlier, we limited the number of virtual machines per capability set. These are the reasons why only four new agents appear at about minute 3, one more between minutes 3 and 4, and two other ones around 6:30.

The experiment shows that our system can create new virtual machines on demand and that the schedulers make use of new resources as soon as they become available. Similarly to experiment 1, we compared the results with those from our earlier work [26]. The workflow now took 16 min and 31 s and was more than one and a half minutes faster than the previous 18 min and 4 s. Workflow tasks were again distributed much more evenly to the agents and resources were used reasonably.

Experiment 3: Scalability
(Requirements covered: REQ 1–6)

In order to show the scalability of our system, we launched a workflow with 300 000 process chains. Similar to the second experiment, we started with one virtual machine. The other ones were automatically created by our system on demand. However, this time we increased the number of agents per virtual machine to 125 resulting in a total number of 1 000 agents.

Figure 5a shows the timeline of the workflow over more than six and a half hours. Note that we sorted the agents in this graph by capability set for better legibility. Again,

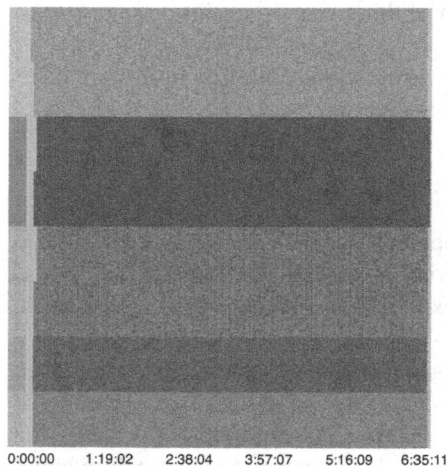

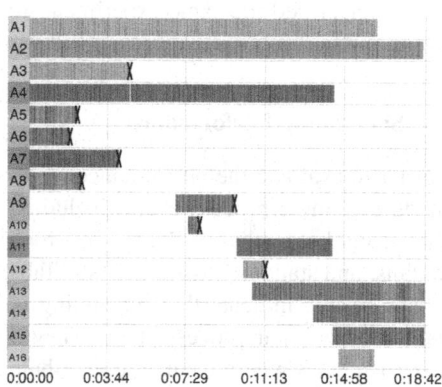

(a) The system is able to handle 300 000 process chains running on 1 000 agents (sorted by capability set for better legibility).

(b) The system is able to recover from faults and to still finish all 1 000 process chains from the current workflow.

Fig. 5. Results of experiments 3 and 4.

all process chains were assigned to the correct machines. Although the number of process chains the system had to manage was very large, it did not crash and kept being responsive the whole time. Also, the system was able to handle the large number of agents without interruptions. There are no gaps in the graph, which means new process chains were scheduled immediately when an agent became available. This shows that our optimisations described in Sect. 5.5 worked as expected. All agents also finished their work almost at the same time, which means our scheduler distributed the work evenly (based on the heuristics described in Sect. 5.3).

In our previous work, we performed a similar experiment but with only 150 000 process chains and 8 agents [26]. At that time, our system was not able to manage 1 000 agents. Our improved approach is much more scalable now.

Experiment 4: Fault Tolerance
(Requirements covered: all)

In our final experiment, we tested if our system can manage faults during a workflow run. Figure 5b shows the timeline. We started with eight agents and executed the same workflow as in experiment 2 with 1 000 process chains. Between minutes 2 and 3, we started to randomly kill agents by sending them a SIGKILL signal (indicated in the figure by a black X).

We killed eight agents during the workflow run. The figure shows that each time, the system was able to recover from the faults. It created new agents with the missing required capabilities and started assigning process chains to them as soon as they became available. Between minutes 3 and 7, approximately, there was no agent able to execute process chains with $R3$. The execution of these process chains was postponed and resumed later.

We performed the same experiment in our earlier work [26]. The results are quite similar and our improved approach still works as expected.

7.2 Scheduling Performance

In order to evaluate the performance of our approach, we measured the time it took to schedule a single process chain (including asking all agents and fetching the process chain from the database). We did this for all experiments and calculated the averages, medians, and standard deviations (see Table 2).

The results indicate that scheduling is in general very fast and does not produce much overhead per process chain. They also show that our system is scalable. Even in experiment 3 where we had to distribute 300 000 process chains to 1 000 agents, the performance was not slower than in experiment 100. It also stayed consistent throughout the whole workflow run. This is mostly due to the optimisations described in Sects. 5.4 and 5.5. Note that the performance in experiment 3 was actually slightly better than in experiment 1 (on average by about 1–1.5 ms), which is most likely due to the fact that our implementation runs on the Java Virtual Machine, and the longer it runs, the better the just-in-time compiler can optimise the code.

Table 2. Measured performance of the scheduler component for each experiment (values are per process chain).

Experiment	Average	Median	Std. deviation
1	16.3 ms	16 ms	2.1 ms
2	16.8 ms	16 ms	4.9 ms
3	15.1 ms	15 ms	3.9 ms
4	16.5 ms	16 ms	6.9 ms

7.3 Discussion

The results of our experiments show that our system meets all challenges and requirements for the management of scientific workflows in the Cloud defined in Sect. 1.1.

To assign process chains to the correct machines with matching capabilities, our scheduler asks each agent whether it wants to execute a process chain with a given capability set or not. An alternative approach would be to let the agents fetch the process chains themselves whenever they are ready to execute something. However, in this case, it would not be possible to create agents on demand. If there is no agent fetching process chains, nothing can be executed. Our scheduler, on the other hand, has an overview of all required capability sets and can acquire new resources when necessary.

In our previous work [26], the scheduler only chose between multiple available agents by comparing their idle time. This was not very efficient and led to unnecessary long workflow runs and unused resources. Our new approach with improved heuristics and caching not only reduces the overall time of workflow runs but also makes the system more scalable. Our previous experiments also revealed small gaps in the workflow run, which could be traced back to the unoptimised scheduling algorithm. We did not observe these gaps anymore with the new approach.

According to our evaluation results, the heuristics presented in Sect. 5.3 are quite effective. Nevertheless, more sophisticated approaches also considering the expected run time of individual process chains [15, 22] or even the dependencies between process chains in the workflow graph [6, 37] are conceivable. However, in a distributed environment, it is very hard to predict the run time of a single task without additional knowledge, so this topic remains for future work.

The fact that we use a database to store process chains has many benefits. First, this out-of-core approach reduces the number of process chains that need to be kept in memory at a time. This allows the scheduler to process hundreds of thousands of process chains without any issue. Second, multiple scheduler instances can access the database and work in parallel on different virtual machines. Due to this, the total time it takes to schedule all process chains of a workflow can be reduced and the values presented in Sect. 7.2 become negligible compared to the whole workflow run. Lastly, since the database holds the remaining process chains to execute, it essentially keeps the current state of the overall workflow execution. This enables fault tolerance: if one scheduler instance crashes, another one can take over. Our open-source implementation even supports resuming workflows if all schedulers have crashed after a restart of the whole cluster.

Nevertheless, the database can be considered a single point of failure. If it becomes unavailable, workflow execution cannot continue. In practise, this is, however, not a problem because as soon as it is up again, our scheduling algorithm can proceed and no information will be lost.

There are still places where our system could be improved. At the moment, our cloud manager creates only one virtual machine per capability set at a time. This could be parallelised in the future to further reduce the overall run time of workflows. However, this requires a clever heuristic so that the cloud manager does not create more virtual machines than actually necessary. This heuristic should be based on the number of remaining process chains in the database for a given capability set, which can change while the virtual machines are being created. This optimisation remains for future work.

8   Conclusion

Distributed scientific workflow management systems running in the Cloud face the challenges of capability-based scheduling, a dynamic environment, scalability, and fault tolerance (see Sect. 1.1). In this paper, we presented a software architecture and a scheduling algorithm addressing these challenges. Our work contributes to the scientific community as the challenges have not been fully addressed in literature yet.

The *Steep Workflow Management System*, which has been released under an open-source licence, implements our approach. Steep is used in various projects. One of them, for example, deals with the processing of large point clouds and panorama images that have been acquired with a mobile mapping system in urban environments. The data often covers whole cities, which makes the workflows particularly large with thousands of process chains. The point clouds are processed by a service using artificial intelligence (AI) to classify points and to detect façades, street surfaces, etc. Since this is a time-consuming task and the workflows often take several days to execute, the scalability and fault tolerance of Steep are fundamental in this project.

The AI service requires a GPU, which is a limited resource in the Cloud and particularly expensive. The capability-based scheduling algorithm we proposed in this paper helps in this respect by distributing workflow tasks to the correct machines. As our system supports elasticity and a dynamic number of machines, it can scale up and down on demand. It only creates GPU machines when needed and releases them as soon as possible. In other words, in this project, our approach saves time and money.

There is a range of opportunities for future research. For example, the approach to transform workflow graphs to process chains introduced in Sect. 3 is implemented in an iterative way and allows very complex workflows to be processed. It supports workflows *without a priori design-time knowledge* [33], which means the system does not need to know the complete workflow structure before the execution starts. As the number of instances of a process chain can depend on the results of a preceding one, this property allows the system to dynamically change the workflow structure during run time. This approach is also suitable to execute workflows *without a priori run-time knowledge*, meaning that the number of instances of a certain process chain may even change *while* the process chain is running. This enables cycles and recursion. Details on this will be the subject of a future publication on which we are currently working.

References

1. Altintas, I., Berkley, C., Jaeger, E., Jones, M., Ludascher, B., Mock, S.: Kepler: an extensible system for design and execution of scientific workflows. In: Proceedings. 16th International Conference on Scientific and Statistical Database Management, 2004, pp. 423–424. IEEE (2004)
2. Apache Airflow: Apache Airflow Website (2020). https://airflow.apache.org/. Accessed 14 Apr 2020
3. Argo Workflows: Argo Website (2020). https://argoproj.github.io/. Accessed 21 Oct 2020
4. Bar-Yossef, Z., Jayram, T.S., Kumar, R., Sivakumar, D., Trevisan, L.: Counting distinct elements in a data stream. In: Rolim, J.D.P., Vadhan, S. (eds.) RANDOM 2002. LNCS, vol. 2483, pp. 1–10. Springer, Heidelberg (2002). https://doi.org/10.1007/3-540-45726-7_1
5. Berriman, G.B., et al.: Montage: a grid-enabled engine for delivering custom science-grade mosaics on demand. In: Optimizing Scientific Return for Astronomy through Information Technologies, vol. 5493, pp. 221–233. International Society for Optics and Photonics (2004)
6. Binato, S., Hery, W.J., Loewenstern, D.M., Resende, M.G.C.: A Grasp for Job Shop Scheduling, pp. 59–79. Springer, Boston (2002). https://doi.org/10.1007/978-1-4615-1507-4_3
7. Blythe, J., et al.: Task scheduling strategies for workflow-based applications in grids. In: Proceedings of the IEEE International Symposium on Cluster Computing and the Grid (CCGrid), pp. 759–767 (2005). https://doi.org/10.1109/CCGRID.2005.1558639
8. Carbone, P., Katsifodimos, A., Ewen, S., Markl, V., Haridi, S., Tzoumas, K.: Apache Flink: stream and batch processing in a single engine. Bull. IEEE Comput. Soc. Tech. Committee Data Eng. 36(4), 28–38 (2015)
9. Casanova, H., Legrand, A., Zagorodnov, D., Berman, F.: Heuristics for scheduling parameter sweep applications in grid environments. In: Proceedings of the 9th Heterogeneous Computing Workshop HCW, pp. 349–363 (2000). https://doi.org/10.1109/HCW.2000.843757
10. Chircu, V.: Understanding the 8 fallacies of distributed systems (2018). https://dzone.com/articles/understanding-the-8-fallacies-of-distributed-syste. Accessed 18 Feb 2020
11. Deelman, E., et al.: The future of scientific workflows. Int. J. High Perform. Comput. Appl. 32(1), 159–175 (2018)
12. Deelman, E., et al.: Pegasus: a workflow management system for science automation. Future Gener. Comput. Syst. 46, 17–35 (2015). https://doi.org/10.1016/j.future.2014.10.008
13. Di Tommaso, P., Chatzou, M., Floden, E.W., Barja, P.P., Palumbo, E., Notredame, C.: Nextflow enables reproducible computational workflows. Nat. Biotechnol. 35(4), 316–319 (2017). https://doi.org/10.1038/nbt.3820
14. Foster, I., Kesselman, C. (eds.): The Grid: Blueprint for a New Computing Infrastructure. Morgan Kaufmann Publishers Inc., San Francisco (1998)
15. Freund, R.F., et al.: Scheduling resources in multi-user heterogeneous computing environments with SmartNet. The NPS Institutional Archive, Calhoun (1998)
16. Gherega, A., Pupezescu, V.: Multi-agent resource allocation algorithm based on the XSufferage heuristic for distributed systems. In: Proceedings of the 13th International Symposium on Symbolic and Numeric Algorithms for Scientific Computing, pp. 313–320 (2011). https://doi.org/10.1109/SYNASC.2011.37
17. Giardine, B., et al.: Galaxy: a platform for interactive large-scale genome analysis. Genome Res. 15(10), 1451–1455 (2005). https://doi.org/10.1101/gr.4086505
18. Graves, R., et al.: CyberShake: a physics-based seismic hazard model for southern California. Pure Appl. Geophys. 168(3), 367–381 (2011). https://doi.org/10.1007/s00024-010-0161-6
19. Hamad, S.A., Omara, F.A.: Genetic-based task scheduling algorithm in cloud computing environment. Int. J. Adv. Comput. Sci. Appl. 7(4), 550–556 (2016). https://doi.org/10.14569/IJACSA.2016.070471

20. Hemamalini, M.: Review on grid task scheduling in distributed heterogeneous environment. Int. J. Comput. Appl. **40**(2), 24–30 (2012)
21. Hull, D., Wolstencroft, K., Stevens, R., Goble, C., Pocock, M.R., Li, P., Oinn, T.: Taverna: a tool for building and running workflows of services. Nucl. Acids Res. **34**, W729–W732 (2006)
22. Ibarra, O.H., Kim, C.E.: Heuristic algorithms for scheduling independent tasks on nonidentical processors. J. ACM **24**(2), 280–289 (1977). https://doi.org/10.1145/322003.322011
23. Johnson, D.S., Garey, M.R.: Computers and Intractability: A Guide to the Theory of NP-Completeness. WH Freeman (1979)
24. Kane, D.M., Nelson, J., Woodruff, D.P.: An optimal algorithm for the distinct elements problem. In: Proceedings of the 29th ACM SIGMOD-SIGACT-SIGART Symposium on Principles of Database Systems, PODS 2010, pp. 41–52. Association for Computing Machinery (2010). https://doi.org/10.1145/1807085.1807094
25. Krämer, M.: A microservice architecture for the processing of large geospatial data in the cloud. Ph.D. thesis, Technische Universität Darmstadt (2018). https://doi.org/10.13140/RG.2.2.30034.66248
26. Krämer, M.: Capability-based scheduling of scientific workflows in the cloud. In: Proceedings of the 9th International Conference on Data Science, Technology, and Applications DATA, pp. 43–54. INSTICC, SciTePress (2020). https://doi.org/10.5220/0009805400430054
27. Li, K., Xu, G., Zhao, G., Dong, Y., Wang, D.: Cloud task scheduling based on load balancing ant colony optimization. In: Proceedings of the 6th Annual Chinagrid Conference, pp. 3–9 (2011). https://doi.org/10.1109/ChinaGrid.2011.17
28. Maheswaran, M., Ali, S., Siegal, H.J., Hensgen, D., Freund, R.F.: Dynamic matching and scheduling of a class of independent tasks onto heterogeneous computing systems. In: Proceedings. Eighth Heterogeneous Computing Workshop (HCW 1999), pp. 30–44, April 1999. https://doi.org/10.1109/HCW.1999.765094
29. Mell, P.M., Grance, T.: The NIST definition of cloud computing. Technical report, National Institute of Standards & Technology, Gaithersburg, MD, USA (2011)
30. Nayak, B., Padhi, S.K.: Mapping of independent tasks in the cloud computing environment. Int. J. Adv. Comput. Sci. Appl. **10**(8), 314–318 (2019)
31. Oinn, T., et al.: Taverna: a tool for the composition and enactment of bioinformatics workflows. Bioinformatics **20**(17), 3045–3054 (2004). https://doi.org/10.1093/bioinformatics/bth361
32. Page, A.J., Naughton, T.J.: Dynamic task scheduling using genetic algorithms for heterogeneous distributed computing. In: Proceedings of the 19th IEEE International Parallel and Distributed Processing Symposium (2005). https://doi.org/10.1109/IPDPS.2005.184
33. Russell, N., van van der Aalst, W.M., ter Hofstede, A.H.M. : Workflow Patterns: The Definitive Guide. MIT Press, Cambridge (2016)
34. Singh, S., Chana, I.: A survey on resource scheduling in cloud computing: issues and challenges. J. Grid Comput. **14**, 217–264 (2016). https://doi.org/10.1007/s10723-015-9359-2
35. Tawfeek, M.A., El-Sisi, A., Keshk, A.E., Torkey, F.A.: Cloud task scheduling based on ant colony optimization. In: Proceedings of the 8th International Conference on Computer Engineering Systems (ICCES), pp. 64–69 (2013). https://doi.org/10.1109/ICCES.2013.6707172
36. Thennarasu, S., Selvam, M., Srihari, K.: A new whale optimizer for workflow scheduling in cloud computing environment. J. Ambient Intell. Humanized Comput. (2020). https://doi.org/10.1007/s12652-020-01678-9
37. Topcuoglu, H., Hariri, S., Wu, M.-Y.: Performance-effective and low-complexity task scheduling for heterogeneous computing. IEEE Trans. Parallel Distrib. Syst. **13**(3), 260–274 (2002). https://doi.org/10.1109/71.993206

38. Ullman, J.: NP-complete scheduling problems. J. Comput. Syst. Sci. **10**(3), 384–393 (1975). https://doi.org/10.1016/S0022-0000(75)80008-0
39. Zaharia, M., Chowdhury, M., Franklin, M.J., Shenker, S., Stoica, I.: Spark: cluster computing with working sets. In: Proceedings of the 2nd USENIX Conference on Hot Topics in Cloud Computing. USENIX Association (2010)

iTLM-Q: A Constraint-Based Q-Learning Approach for Intelligent Traffic Light Management

Christian Roth$^{(\boxtimes)}$ (ID), Lukas Stöger, Mirja Nitschke (ID), Matthias Hörmann,
and Dogan Kesdogan

University of Regensburg, Regensburg, Germany
{christian.roth,lukas.stoger,mirja.nitschke,matthias.hormann,
dogan.kesdogan}@ur.de

Abstract. Vehicle-to-everything (V2X) interconnects participants in vehicular environments to exchange information. This enables a broad range of new opportunities. For instance, crowdsourced information from vehicles can be used as input for self-learning systems. In this paper, we propose *iTLM-Q* based on our previous work *iTLM* to optimize traffic light management in a privacy-friendly manner. We aim to reduce the overall waiting time and contribute to a smoother traffic flow and travel experience. *iTLM-Q* uses Q-learning and is constraint-based in such a way that no manual traffic light cycles need to be defined in advance, hence, being able to always find an optimal solution. Our simulation-based on real-world data shows that it can quickly adapt to changing traffic situations and vastly decrease waiting time at traffic lights eventually reducing CO2 emissions. A privacy analysis shows that our approach provides a significant level of k-anonymity even in low traffic scenarios.

Keywords: Traffic light · V2X · Privacy · Reinforcement learning · Q-learning

1 Introduction

Confronted by the climate change nowadays, there is an urgent need to reduce CO2 emissions produced by vehicles. Particularly in cities, the pollution is severe because of frequent stop-and-go traffic. One reason may lie in rather inflexible cyber-physical systems, i.e. traffic lights, unable to quickly adapt to changing situations. Therefore, the field of traffic control requires new economic approaches to optimize the efficiency of existing infrastructure, ultimately protecting the environment by reducing pollutants. In this paper, we investigate an intelligent traffic light management (TLM) using crowdsourced user input in a privacy-friendly manner to achieve this goal.

With an increasing number of vehicles having the ability to communicate with other cars (V2V) or infrastructure (V2I) without additional costs, vehicle-to-everything (V2X) communication is finally reaching the mass market [1].

© Springer Nature Switzerland AG 2021
S. Hammoudi et al. (Eds.): DATA 2020, CCIS 1446, pp. 56–79, 2021.
https://doi.org/10.1007/978-3-030-83014-4_3

V2X can be considered to be an enabler for real-time TLM because it is now possible to cheaply distribute the needed information using V2X. This facilitates the mostly academic field of self-learning, self-optimizing traffic light scheduling to become applied in real environments. To present an applicable approach, we assume a mixed environment with some vehicles not being enabled for V2X. With our approach, it is conceivable that such participants could also (although not necessarily) be integrated using a smartphone-based solution.

In our previous work [15], we already proposed an intelligent traffic light management system called *iTLM* which takes into account the various, challenging requirements in this scenario. It considers the many security implications in the open, loosely-connected V2X environment. In particular, in guarantees integrity to provide a safe environment by relying on a state-of-the-art privacy-enhanced attribute-based credential (privacy-ABC) called ABC4Trust [16]. It also takes benefit from the connected participants to feed an learning algorithm which can decide when to switch traffic light based on manually defined strategies. However, the approach is limited in complex, quickly changing traffic scenarios due to the small amount of actions available.

Hence, in this paper we try to overcame that disadvantage by removing the need for manual definition of strategies. In fact, we use a constraint-based modelling approach where an intelligent, self-learning system can derive the best strategy almost immediately for a specific traffic situation. It uses the same information also available to *iTLM*, but uses Q-learning to exploit the situation even more. Consequently, we call the approach proposed in this paper *iTLM-Q* (Intelligent Traffic Light Management with Q-learning).

1.1 Contribution

This paper is an extension of [15]. However, it is includes multiple new sections by overcoming drawbacks identified in previous work. In particular, the light cycles applied by the more advanced approaches called *iTLM-Free* and *iTLM-Q* are tailored specifically for heterogeneous situations identified during live application. The system derives them as-is based only on three simple constraints. In particular, we contribute with

1. a communication protocol for V2X traffic light management based on the ABC4Trust platform,
2. a self-learning traffic light management algorithm called *iTLM-Q* based on Q-Learning to derive strategies to best control an intersection using user input, and
3. a simulation using SUMO based on real-world data to evaluate the performance of our approach in comparison to our previous *iTLM* which has already proven to perform superior to standard, widely applied models, and
4. a study of the contradicting requirements of privacy and integrity.

1.2 Structure

Section 2 briefly presents different approaches for traffic light systems w.r.t. privacy. It also briefly introduces ABC4Trust. Subsequently, Sect. 3 presents the scenario including all participants as well as attacks common in the given scenario. Section 4 sums up *iTLM* [15] and then discusses drawbacks of the previous approach. Afterwards, Sect. 5 presents the extension based on Q-learning and constraint-based modelling. Section 6 thoroughly evaluates the approach in terms of performance and discusses the impacts of the privacy enhancing techniques (PETs) as well emissions reduced by shorter waiting times. Section 7 pointedly concludes the paper.

Table 1. Comparison of different approaches for traffic light scheduling [15].

	Method	Pros & Cons	Properties
Static	Different predefined light cycle schedules (optionally time dependent)	+ Common + Easy to deploy − Not dynamic at all	High privacy: no sensors at all; not dynamic
Actuated	1–2 inductive loops per lane detect presence of vehicles to control the length of green phases (e.g. [5])	+ Can adjust to traffic density − High traffic density cannot be handled very well − Short-term information	High privacy: no personal data; limited dynamic
Camera	Cameras per lane detect (number of) vehicles to control the length of green phases (e.g. [12,14,21])	+ Can adjust to traffic density + Fair system gives every lane green time − Short-term information	Medium privacy: license plate allows tracking; limited dynamic
V2X	Virtual traffic lights communicate directly with cars and receive information of arrival time to model actual traffic flow (e.g. [7,19])	+ Very dynamic + No physical traffic lights needed + Can find optimal solution − Requires all participants to be enabled for V2X communication	Poor privacy: assignable communication allows tracking; full dynamic
RL	Fusion of multiple input sources give feedback for decisions, optionally connected to other TLCSs, tries to predict traffic flow (e.g. [2,11,18])	+ Dynamic + Constantly optimizing − Seems to be an academic solution − Needs to know trajectory of cars	Poor privacy: moving pattern allows tracking; full dynamic

2 Related Work

Traffic light control systems (TLCS) can be organized in static or dynamic approaches [10]. Table 1 presents an overview of methods for traffic light control. It specifies for every method not only the pros and cons, but also reviews the privacy friendliness of the approaches and discusses if the method can respond to dynamic traffic flows.

We shortly focus on recent developments of reinforcement learning (RL) approaches which try to model the actual traffic conditions to provide highly dynamic traffic light schedules. It does so by predicting the number of cars for each (waiting) lane with basic approaches, e.g. by relying on actuated or camera inputs [2]. Other superior approaches are more privacy-invasive as they use the car's current position and speed to predict arrival times [6,11]. Interconnecting multiple traffic lights optimizes the traffic light schedules [18] by overcoming the limited area of view of camera-based systems. However, as already mentioned, many of these systems use data provided by cameras or environmental sensors to track individual cars and to derive decisions.

A holistic approach must ensure that the privacy of each individual is protected while taking into account the open and untrusted environment of V2X scenarios (i.e. smart traffic light scheduling) due to its contradicting requirements [4]. Typical pseudonym-based approaches are not feasible in V2X networks [20]. Pseudonyms may also be critical when they are shared across multiple messages. Such messages can be linked together to form a location trajectory of such a car. [17] describes concrete requirements for vehicular communication systems which are currently not achieved in any RL-based traffic light approach. We cherry-picked the advantages of RL-based approaches and V2X benefits and overcome the drawbacks. That given, we propose a system combining the dynamics of RL and V2X with privacy properties of conventional methods. Furthermore, for the first time, everything is poured into a new privacy-friendly protocol based on the robust ABC4Trust platform [16].

Other approaches such as Traffic Light Assistants are considered passive as they only provide information of the light cycle [3,8,9]. Even if they are widely used, they are not focused in this paper.

ABC4Trust. [16] is a EU funded privacy enhanced attribute-based credential (privacy-ABC) system. It allows to build trustworthy applications which combine contradicting goals such as reliability, integrity and privacy. A common architecture abstracts the specific implementation of the ABC system, enabling one to build complex yet secure applications. ABC4Trust defines five different roles, i.e. *User, Verifier, Issuer, Inspector* and *Revocator*. Furthermore, it defines **credentials** as containers for **attributes** which are defined either by a user or issuer, (blindly) confirmed by an issuer and owned by a user. Knowing and owning a signed credential can then be used to gain access to a remote system protected by a Verifier. In addition, a **pseudonym** is a (temporary) identity of a user and allows (limited) linkability if needed and prevents replay attacks which is explicitly relevant in our use case since Sybil attacks are an omnipresent risk in

V2X environments. Both elements can be bound to a secret only known to a user, adding an additional layer of authenticity. It is a viable foundation for securing communication in our privacy-friendly cyber-physical system architecture.

3   Definition of the Scenario

According to our scenario, vehicles try to find the fastest route to a destination using static (road network) and dynamic (traffic congestion) information. However, travel duration is often impacted by the waiting time t^w at traffic lights. To allow a traffic light (TL) to intelligently optimize the light schedule, it needs additional information, e.g. the time of arrival of a vehicle. This information may be sent by vehicles to a traffic light long before arrival. By aggregating the information from multiple vehicles, the traffic light can find the optimal light schedule which globally minimizes the overall waiting time $(\sum t^w)$ at a junction.

The proposed architecture takes the special conditions in V2X environments into account. The protocol is based on an attribute-based credential system to provide privacy. At the same time, the system was designed to handle the open nature of V2X environments with untrustful participants. Thus, integrity protecting mechanisms are needed.

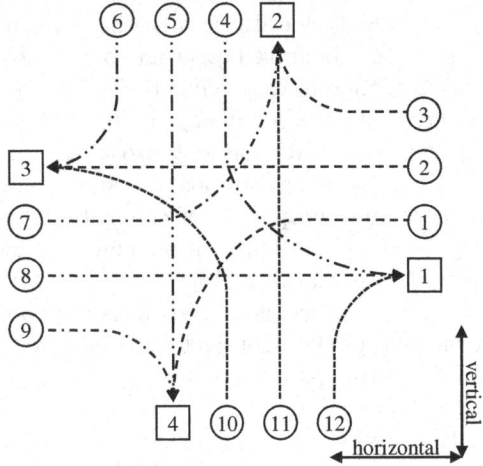

Fig. 1. Architecture of an junction throughout the paper.

Both contradicting goals can be achieved using ABC4Trust [16] which provides the needed building blocks.

3.1   System Model

We now describe the system of our scenario which is mainly taken from Roth et al. [15].

Junction. The given environment throughout this paper is a junction where a traffic light controls all waiting lanes $\mathcal{WL}$. A typical junction in our scenario has 12 waiting (3 per incoming direction) and 4 outgoing lanes. Each waiting lane $wl \in \mathcal{WL}$ has a dedicated outgoing orientation of north (n), west (w), south (s) or east (e) resulting in $|\mathcal{WL}| = 12$ per junction. Hence, a waiting lane is a combination of two orientations.

Participants. Communication in the system is kept minimal to take into account the limited communication range and unstable connections in V2X environments. We distinguish between V2X communication using one of the existing standards (e.g. WAVE) and Out-of-Band (OoB) communication happening in special conditions (c.f. Fig. 2).

User. The first participant, the *User*, is a *Vehicle* (V) equipped with an On-Board-Unit (OBU) including a unique ID and cryptographic material enabling it to exchange data in the V2X network. OoB communication is also possible. A vehicle is considered to know both its current position and its route (including travel duration) to a destination at any time. In addition, the V uses a scope-exclusive pseudonym P for a specific scope. The scope can be publicly known. We use a scope artifact $ScopeString = \mathcal{H}(id(TL)\|\,TimeWindow)$ and derive a scope-exclusive pseudonym P with a constant, publicly distributed value $id(TL)$ for the traffic light, thus the V uses for every TL another pseudonym to allow limited linkability [13]. Additionally the granularity of the dynamic part $TimeWindow$ controls how long a TL can track a V via its unique P, e.g. it can be one day in a year. In this case, a V appears to change his identity towards a single TL once every day.

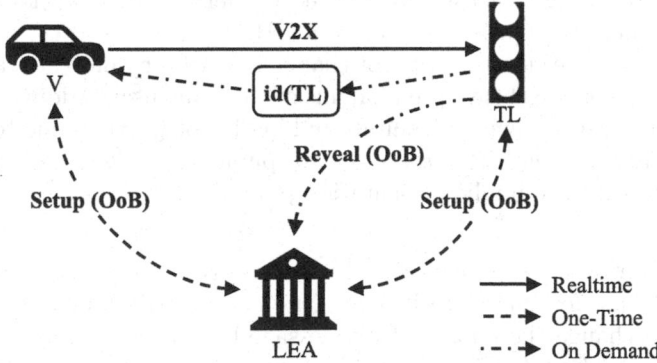

Fig. 2. Minimal communication overhead of participants [15].

Traffic Light System. The *Traffic Light System* (TL) is a cyber-physical system attached to a communication network, able to communicate via V2X, but also via OoB communication. It controls a real-world traffic light so that traffic can be controlled not only by autonomously driving cars levels 3 and 4 (cooperative driving), but also by non-connected vehicles. TL is also a *Verifier* since it checks incoming messages from Vs for validity.

Law Enforcement Agency. To provide a robust system in terms of integrity and revocability, a *Law Enforcement Agency* (LEA) is introduced. It knows the real identities of all vehicles in the system. LEA itself is not included in traffic control operations but manages the users which are able to participate (therefore called *Issuer*). Thus, she does not need to know the location of any car at any time. She is a semi trusted entity since all participants in the system trust digital signatures issued by her. In situations of fraud, she can reveal the identity of a V once it is requested by a TL and then exclude vehicles (making LEA also an *Inspector* and *Revocator* in terms of ABC4Trust).

3.2   Attacks and Abuses

As in most V2X scenarios, two main security threats arise, namely for privacy and integrity.

Traffic Light System. We assume that a traffic light performs only passive attacks and is not actively manipulating traffic in a bad way (e.g. red light for all $\mathcal{WL}$). The main objective is to track Vs passing a junction controlled by the TL. It can therefore record any received message and derive individual movement patterns. This threat becomes more severe when multiple TLs start exchanging information about seen cars, allowing them to create location trajectories. Precisely, the location privacy of a user is threatened if (one or cooperating) TLs are able to find a list $\mathcal{T} = (TL_1, \ldots, TL_n)$ with $n > 1$ of traffic lights passed during a trip. Knowing that list may be used to identify a TL without the need for an unique identifier (such as the ID of a OBU).

Section 6.3 provides empirical proof that it is hard for different traffic lights to link multiple scope-exclusive pseudonyms of the same user. Adding additional information to a pseudonym to facilitate linking is not possible due to protocol design: the $id(TL)$, *TimeWindow*, and $\mathcal{H}$ are public knowledge. Other manipulation conflicts with the public presentation policy.

Vehicle. In contrast, Vs are considered untrustworthy and thus try to actively influence a TL i.a. for their own benefit. One can identify four different goals. First, a V can change the impact of its message by trying to appear towards a TL as multiple vehicles (sybil attack). Furthermore, it is possible to send either a wrong time of arrival t^a or a wrong wl, both potentially resulting in inaccurate calculation of the traffic light schedule eventually downgrading service quality. Furthermore, in the context of reinforced learning (see Sect. 5.3), not providing feedback to a TL also may impact service quality. Sybil attacks are prevented by a combination of key bound credentials and scope exclusive pseudonyms, which are indirectly also key bound.

Absolute privacy contradicts the integrity of the system since vehicles can lie without fearing any consequences, ultimately resulting in poor service quality. Therefore, privacy-ABC systems introduce an (trusted) inspector (i.e. LEA) who can reveal a V's identity under well defined conditions (i.e. policy conditions L) on request of a TL. The inspection grounds are clear for all included parties since they are signed into the presentation token in a tamperproof way, protecting against malicious TL.

Law Enforcement Agency. LEA has no knowledge about package flow and payload because she is not involved in the actual traffic light calculation procedure. Furthermore she does not participate in V2X communication. She is bound to the inspection policy which every participant in the system agrees on. As a consequence she is unable to illegitimately reveal the identity of a V. Therefore, she has to use pseudonyms in the same way cooperating TL do and does not have additional knowledge.

External Eavesdropper. Like TLs, external entities can also have an interest in deriving individual movement patterns. However, similar to LEA, external eavesdroppers need to link pseudonyms in order to derive a location trajectory.

Furthermore, the system allows revoking a specific set of attribute values without revealing the actual values. The revocation process can be triggered either by a V or a TL. For example, revocation can be used by a car owner if his V gets stolen.

4 Assumption-Based Approach for Dynamic Control of Traffic Lights

This section presents the first stage of development of the proposal already discussed in the previous paper [15]. Based on the rather simple approach, potential limitations are illuminated and discussed.

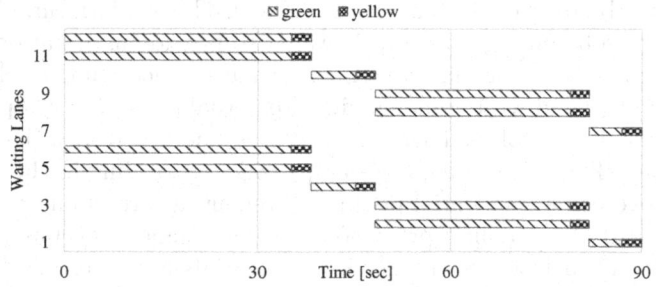

Fig. 3. Example of a traffic light cycle for the given intersection.

4.1   Main Idea

The first development of a system for dynamic traffic light control is based on several assumptions to achieve the highest possible throughput.

For example, it is assumed that the flow of vehicles through a green phase is approximately constant. This assumption is generally true as long as vehicles move in the system in a traceable and similar manner (e.g. speed, starting and braking behavior) and no external influences affect the traffic system.

Furthermore, the system distributes the duration of the green phases according to predefined switching patterns. These are based on the well-known and widespread procedure of differentiating between horizontal and vertical lanes. The traffic light switching is divided into iterations. In each iteration, all lanes have exactly one green light so that they can drive freely. If turning left, the green arrow, which is common in most countries, is used. It legitimates left turners to drive freely, while other, colliding lanes have to stand. *iTLM* now distributes a certain amount of time so that as many vehicles as possible can pass the traffic light globally across all lanes. This means that the green phases are distributed accordingly along the vertical and horizontal axes. Yellow phases are included as well. Figure 3 shows a potential light cycle for an intersection where all lanes have green exactly once.

4.2   Traffic Cycle Protocol

Setup. The setup phase is performed once. It is desirable to include as many operations as possible in this static one-time phase to take into account the highly dynamic, low-latency, and loosely-connected nature of V2X environments. During the setup phase the V and TL exchange with the LEA all (cryptography) information and policies needed for participation.

Announcement of Arrival (TranVT). To allow a TL to calculate feasible traffic light schedules, it requires information from Vs. However, to use this information, a V has to prove that it is a valid member of the network by 1) having a valid OBU and 2) is still allowed to participate. To guarantee that, one can use the key binding credentials from the ABC4Trust platform. Credentials are guaranteed to be unforgeable. If a V wants to provide information to a TL, it has to select a specific amount of verified credentials according to the (static) presentation policy and wrap it along with the actual $arr = (wl, t^a)$ payload, in a so-called presentation token. Then the package is encrypted with the addressed TL's public key. This allows tamper proof package forwarding in the V2X environment. To overcome "credential pooling", credentials are bound to a specific OBU of a V using an implicit proof-of-knowledge (called key binding). Once a presentation token provides the needed credentials and confirms the agreed presentation policy, the TL buffers arr for further calculation.

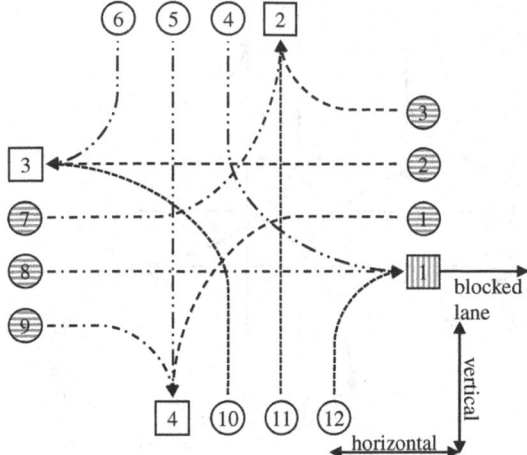

Fig. 4. External impacts might alter traffic flow within an intersection.

Calculation of Traffic Light Schedule (TLLC). We consider that the traffic lights of our junction use a simple four-phase-model. That means that every light cycle consists of 4 traffic flows. In one phase the vehicles in one direction driving straight ahead and turning right have green, then those in the other direction. The same applies to left-turning vehicles. We calculate the duration of the corresponding green ΔT^g and yellow Δt_{wl}^y periods in the next light cycle. The TL uses all buffered $arr \in \mathcal{A}rr$ where the timestamp of arrival lies before the timestamp of starting the new traffic light schedule and where no feedback messages arrived. The algorithm also considers the specified length of the whole light cycle Δt^{Cycle}, the total length of the green period for all straight and right lanes Δt_{sr}^g, and the total length of the green period for all left lanes Δt_l^g. In the first step the traffic intensity per wl is calculated. Then, according to the intensities, the green periods are calculated. In the end, the yellow periods of the waiting lanes are calculated according to the given speed limits.

4.3 Drawbacks of Predefined Light Patterns

Although it was shown in Roth et al. [15] that the dynamic distribution of green phases has advantages compared to existing systems like traffic lights based on induction loops or even static circuits, it has obvious disadvantages in certain scenarios.

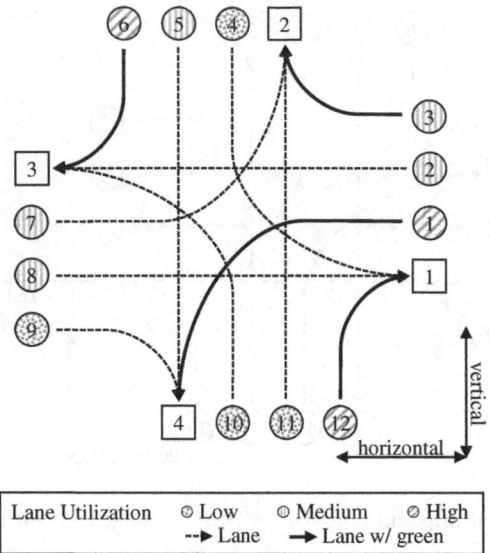

Fig. 5. There are situations where more sophisticated strategies allow better traffic flow.

External Impacts. Figure 4 illustrates that unpredictable events degrade the flow rate of a lane. Consequently, the assumptions with which the traffic light works are no longer valid. In the example, vehicles can no longer leave the intersection system through exit 1, which can lead to tailbacks at input 8. The arrival time calculated by vehicles and communicated to the traffic light loses reliability and the data situation deteriorates. If vehicles are also unable to leave the intersection, they potentially block other lanes, such as input 4 or 12. This situation can be avoided by transmitting feedback.

Static Strategies. Another drawback of the current solution is the static green light pattern limited to horizontal or vertical strategies. However, there are multiple situations where a more dynamic portfolio of strategies is more efficient. As seen in Fig. 5, input lanes 1, 6, 12 are highly utilized, i.e. many vehicles are arriving in a time frame. *iTLM* will now select the horizontal lane to have a longer green period since the utilization of 1 lane is high, 4 are medium and only 1 is low, in contrast to vertical where in total 3 are low. However, an intelligent algorithm should take into account the weight of all lanes to globally optimize the intersection. Thus, there might exist a strategy that is superior to direction-based switching. One can see, that traffic of all highly utilized lanes can flow without interference applying a correct light schedule (bold arrows).

5   Introduction of the Constraint-Based *iTLM* Extension

Motivated by the fact that additional knowledge allows better traffic flow by including multiple parameters in a decision to derive light cycles, this section presents our next iteration of *iTLM*. This is a two-fold approach. First, we give up the st right horizontal-vertical strategy yielding *iTLM-Free*. Then, we try to further optimize our approach by including vehicle feedback to overcome the second drawback of the more basic *iTLM*. We therefore use Q-learning to find the best combination of lanes to set green. We call our final model *iTLM-Q*.

5.1   Exploiting Strategies

As shown the flexibility of horizontal-vertical strategy is strongly limited, giving away much potential. Hence, *iTLM-Free* completely detaches itself from predefined traffic light cycles. The traffic light control system continuously analyzes the current traffic situation based on the received messages *arr* and decides individually the best strategy or desired state at that time for the next phase. The whole system is dependent on traffic. The algorithm is careful to choose a light cycle with the best possible result in every traffic situation. The duration of the phases is determined in advance since the focus is on the dynamic design of the lane clearance.

Each phase consists of an interaction of twelve different red-green values. All lanes of the traffic light system are considered separately and switched individually, resulting in one specific state $\sigma = \{0, 1\}^{12}$ with binary settings for each $wl_{1,...,12}$. Σ is the set of all valid states, totaling $|\Sigma| = 112$. However, lanes can interfere which is prohibited to provide a safe environment. A σ can only contain binary situations, i.e. red or green light. For instance, $\sigma = \{001001001001\}$ gives green lights for turning right while all others lanes have to wait. Thus, we derive the following logic.

Consequently, in a system with twelve lanes many dependencies must be taken into account to ensure collision-free passage. The exclusion criterion here is the free passage possibility. This means that only lanes that do not cross or obstruct each other within the traffic light are released. Waiting left turns, as they are often found in real traffic, are not allowed to guarantee a deterministic situation. The following constraints are defined.

Straight Lanes. block left lanes on the opposite, all lanes on its right side and left as well as straight lanes on its left side. Hence, in total straight lanes block 6 other lanes, only allowing three more green lights.

Left-turning Lanes. are similar to straight lanes, blocking 6 other lanes. Only two left-turning lanes can have green at the same time.

Right-turning Lanes. interfere only with two other lanes, i.e. the straight lane on its left side and the left lane on the opposite side. This is the cheapest.

From all 112 possibilities, ω with the highest throughput in the given traffic situation must be selected.

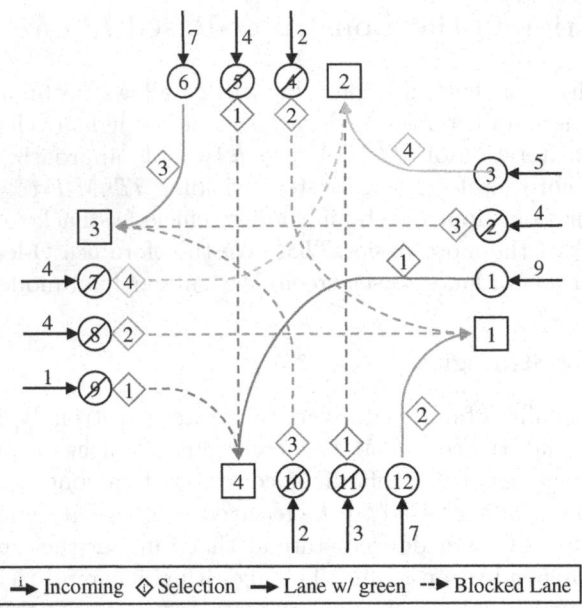

Fig. 6. Example of desired state identification process for a traffic light phase.

To select the best desired state, a greedy algorithm is used which optimizes the total amount of vehicles that are able to pass an intersection. Figure 6 shows the selection of a sample state $\sigma_t = \{101001000001\}$ for time frame t. After TL collected all incoming vehicles for i, one can see, that input lane 1 is leading with 9 vehicles which like to leave the intersection via output 4. Hence, it is obvious that such a strategy is likely to be selected which turns lane 1 green. This results in blocking lanes 4 and 9 since they will conflict with the said restrictions. Next, lane 12 allows 7 vehicles to pass the intersection and is therefore selected, however, this results in lanes 8 and 2 not being selectable anymore. The process is greedy in such a way that the maximum number of vehicles for an intersection is considered, thus it can be more meaningful to not select the top lane with the most cars but the combination of lanes with the highest throughput. Compared to *iTLM*, *iTLM-Free* is able to process 28 vehicles while the former can either allow 21 (vertical) or 14 (horizontal) cars to pass the intersection with a green light (hence, left-turning lanes have to be excluded).

5.2   Adding Yellow Phases

To complete the traffic light system, the necessary yellow phases of Δt_{wl}^y still have to be implemented. Two yellow phases are required for each green phase. The first phase initiates the release of the lanes, the second phase ties up the respective green phase. As a result, one cycle of the fully dynamic system now consists of the phase duration plus $2 * \Delta t_{wl}^y$ for the two safety phases. In this period, no cars are able to pass an intersection, hence the number of yellow phases should be minimized. Considering that yellow phases are intermediate steps between the selection of two strategies, they might be obsolete in some cases: whenever a lane is green in two successive phases, a green phase is not required, so in some cases it is better to leave one lane green than to give a supposedly better priority to one. In this case a theoretical flow time for vehicles is used.

5.3 Optimising Using Feedback

We now present the final iteration called $iTLM$-Q which has access to the same 112 different strategies Ω. It is based on Reinforcement Learning (RL), more specifically Q-learning.

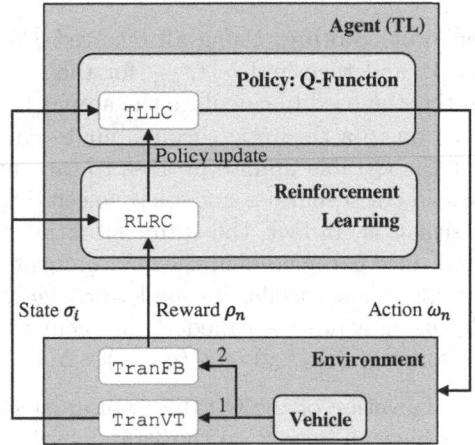

Fig. 7. Architecture of reinforcement learning in an $iTLM$-Q.

To further optimize the time of loss at a junction, the traffic light requires feedback from vehicles. Thus Vs are constraint to send the TL a feedback message fb including wl and their actual time of departure t^d. Using the same pseudonym P as before the traffic light can match fb to arr. This feedback process (TranFB) is similar to TranVT, only the input payload is obviously different.

Reinforcement Learning. Reinforcement learning is an approach to maximize a reward ρ while interacting with a complex environment via specific actions ω, i.e. enforcing strategies $\sigma \in \Sigma$. However, the ρ_t for ω_t is not known in advance. One reinforcement learning circle t in our environment is one light cycle, i.e. one selected strategy for a specific duration.

At the beginning and due to missing knowledge, the TL assumes that all waiting lanes provide an equal throughput. This is information is stored in a

(112 × 112) matrix named Q-table Q. Q holds every possible combination of $\omega_{t,t+1} : \sigma_t \rightarrow \sigma_{t+1}$, which describe a transition ω from one traffic light setting (σ_t) to another (σ_{t+1}), along with a reward ρ specifically for this action. Hence, Q is a matrix. The more vehicles can pass the intersection within one light cycle t, the higher ρ and hence, the better the chosen transition ω. We therefore define $Q(\sigma_t, \omega_t) \leftarrow Q(\sigma_t, \omega_t) + \alpha(\rho_{t+1} + \gamma * \max_\omega Q(\sigma_{t+1}, \omega) - Q(\sigma_t, \omega_t))$ where α is the learning rate, i.e. how much the new situation influences older ones, and γ as the discount rate defines how much earlier rewards should be taken into account.

TL uses `TranVT` messages to select a specific action via its selection `TLLC` introduced in the previous section (c.f. Fig. 7). However, some lanes might be less efficient compared with others. For example, some may perform worse for some time periods due to tailbacks. Using our smart `iTLS-Q`, one can adapt to these complex and highly dynamic situations. Using a Q-network and information from `TranFB`, the TL will learn over time which lanes are favorable.

Including Q for Decision Making. Using all received fbs, TL can first calculate the actual t_j^w of V_j and then find $\sum t_{t,wl_k}^w$ for the t-th traffic light cycle and wl_k. The sum can then be used to calculate the actual V throughput per ω, and putting this in relation to a theoretic throughput to calculate a reward ρ. Furthermore, we adapt the Q-table update process to take into account a proportional reward since ω in our scenario is not solely selected based on Q but also on the current traffic situation. In fact, the traffic situation prescribes majorly which ω is to be selected since parameters in the environment are quickly changing - a scenario Q-learning is not specifically made for. We therefore denote an update to the Q-table (using a process called Reinforcement Learning Reward Calculation (`RLRC`)) as follows: $Q(\sigma_t, \omega_t) \leftarrow Q(\sigma_t, \omega_t) + \alpha(\rho_{t+1} - Q(\sigma_t, \omega_t))$.

Initializing Q. The initialization of the Q-table is of great interest when using Q-learning because they have an impact on the strategy selection process. Basically, there are two possible approaches:

Nullify. Initializing with zeros does not lead to any learning behavior when using our `RLRC`). By using exclusively positive rewards, after performing a certain action in a state once, the respective value becomes positive and immediately represents the optimal action in this state.

Randomise. Using random values to initialize the Q-table is a more meaningful approach. Still, the traffic situation remains the main impact factor for the decision, however, it is now possible to overrule the traffic-related optimal solution by exploring different ω. This allows to take into account external events such as a tailback. Hence, this approach should be superior to *iTLM-Free* depending on the traffic situation.

6   Evaluation

We now present an evaluation of our proposed traffic light management system. A performance evaluation against our previous work and a discussion on privacy are part of this section.

6.1   Simulation

Setup. We evaluated our approach using SUMO, which is a microscopic simulator for urban mobility. Our testbed is a standard 4-arm intersection with $|\mathcal{WL}| = 12$ according to our system model (see Fig. 1). Traffic light switching schedules can be controlled in SUMO using *tlLogic* elements with states G,g,y,r applied[1]. Each simulation was run for 900 simulation seconds. Vehicles Vs were set to a maximum speed of 50 kph, however, their top speed fluctuates around 20% to simulate a more realistic driving behavior. The simulation environment, i.e. our road network, was designed in such a way that vehicles can reach their top speed. Listing 1 shows the vehicle definition as used in the simulation.

```
<vType id="typeNormal" accel="2.6" decel="4.5" sigma="0.5" length="5"
    minGap="2.5" maxSpeed="50" guiShape="passenger"/>
```

List. 1. XML definition of a SUMO vehicle.

The evaluation is accomplished with real-world data from the City of Hamburg[2] in Germany. The traffic counts of three years illustrate the traffic densities of all roads in the annual average weekday traffic that was broken down to provide a realistic simulation and come up with feasible results.

The general administrative regulation to the road traffic order prescribes a yellow phase duration of three seconds for a traffic light system in an environment with a permissible maximum speed of 50 kph[3]. Consequently, we set $\Delta t^{y}_{wl} = 3$ s.

All data are collected over a simulation time of 900 s. Thus, 15-minute intervals are always considered. *iTLM-Free* uses 30 s for each green light phases, thus achieving the best results for the procedure. To evaluate *iTLM-Q*, four consecutive intervals are considered, each of which passes its extended Q-table to the next interval. The learning rate α for *iTLM-Q* was set to 0.5.

Metrics. In order to evaluate the performance, we focus on the waiting time of Vs and the related traffic density. The waiting time defines the overhead of time spent during the simulation because of waiting periods at the junction (i.e. red lights). The composition of the road network ensures that only the intersection and the associated traffic lights influence the travel time of a vehicle. In addition, there is also the time loss during which a vehicle is moving slowly with under 0.1 kph. Both metrics are closely related with time loss including the former.

---

[1] https://sumo.dlr.de/docs/Simulation/Traffic_Lights.html.
[2] https://www.hamburg.de/bwvi/verkehrsbelastung/.
[3] VwV-StVO zu §37, Randnummer 17, Punkt IX).

We consider different logics for traffic lights. As a benchmark, we rerun experiments from our previous paper [15], namely the fixed time (*STA*) approach with time-based light cycles and our *iTLM* approach. In addition, we also present results from *iTLM-Free* and *iTLM-Q*.

Scenarios. For the sake of comparison, we formulate the same three hypotheses (H1-3) as in our preceding paper [15] which are evaluated in six traffic scenarios, all based on the densities as in the dataset of the city of Hamburg. Figure 8 illustrates the spawn frequency of vehicles/sec in relation to the simulation cycle. Exit lanes are selected with a static distribution.

Hypothesis 1 (H1). *TLL is capable to quickly adapt the green light phase to alternating traffic flow intensities.*

Hypothesis 2 (H2). *TLL is capable of detecting and monitoring the rush direction while adapting to changing intensities.*

Hypothesis 3 (H3). *TLL is capable of reacting to asymmetric incoming lanes and prefers the major arteries.*

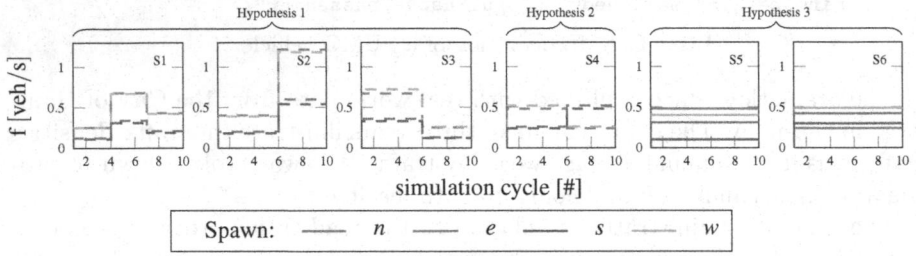

Fig. 8. Overview of all scenarios used to verify our hypotheses [15].

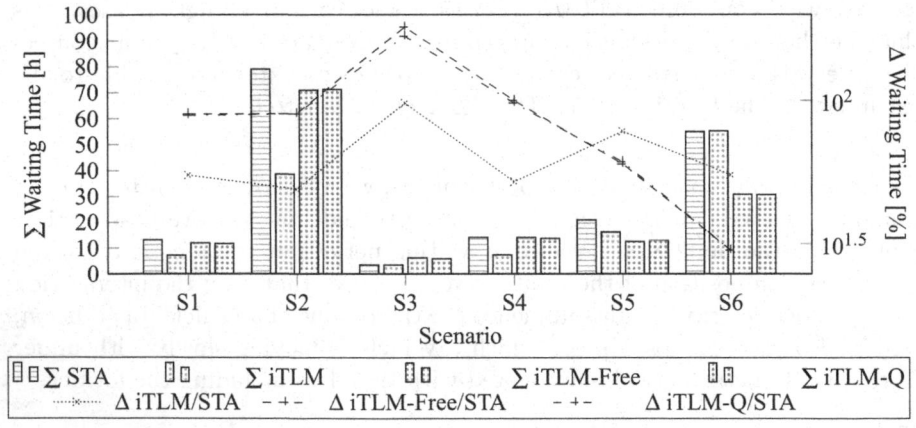

Fig. 9. Overview of performance for all approaches across all scenarios.

6.2   Performance

Figure 9 shows an overview of all waiting times for each scenario using every available logic to calculate green phases. It can be seen that the procedures offer a wide range in terms of reducing waiting times for the vehicles. Both the accumulated waiting time across all vehicles and the percentage change compared to a standard traffic light are shown. It should be noted that the number of vehicles that occurred per scenario can vary greatly due to the different spawn rates. This of course has an impact on the total amounts of the waiting time, hence, they are not comparable across scenarios. In the following, the three hypotheses will be examined more closely to identify the strengths and weaknesses of the different logics.

H1. Figure 10 gives insight into the most basic scenario S1. At the beginning, there is not much difference in the performance because the road network is slowly filling up with cars. Though, it can be seen that with a rapidly increasing number of vehicles during rush hour after 20% of the simulation, *iTLM* can adapt to this situation and is able to convey the increasing number of cars resulting in a lower increase in waiting time and lower overall density in the system. *iTLM-free* however performs similar to a *STA* light schedule, showing that dynamically composing light cycles is not needed in such a basic horizontal-vertical scenario where only one artery has major traffic densities.

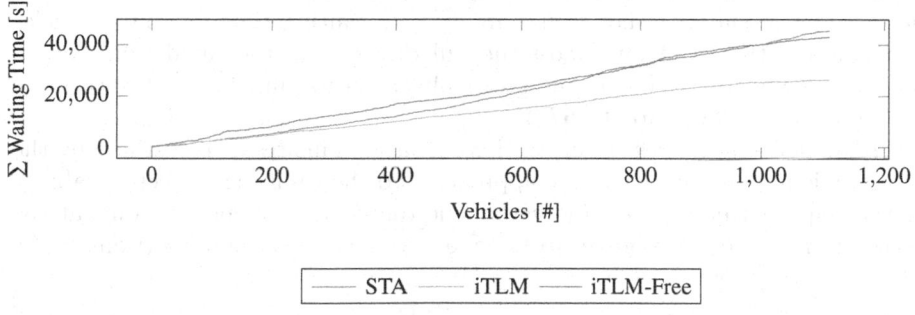

Fig. 10. Progression of the waiting time with increasing number of vehicles in the simulation (S2).

The results of S2 and S3 illustrate a major deficit of the classical methods. In fact, from our simulation, we can conclude that the standard traffic light system with fixed durations is not able to handle dynamically changing situations with rush hour elements at all. *iTLM* on the contrast can handle the huge amounts of vehicles spawning in S2. *iTLM-Free* and *iTLM-Q* seem to find some inefficient light cycles and are unable to detect the best ω for a rush hour situation. Figure 11 can explain this situation and shows that almost 50% of all vehicles do not wait at all. *iTLM-Free* and *iTLM-Q* are not fair, i.e. they prefer the lanes where most cars arrive. In contrast to *STA* and *iTLM* which both distribute a light cycle interval between all lanes, thus, every lane has green for one time, our dynamic approaches always try to keep the number of vehicles at an intersection low. As a consequence, some lanes never get a green light if only a few vehicles are waiting and it is not meaningful to let these cars pass. This explains the long-accumulated waiting time in S2 and S3 for *iTLM-Free* and *iTLM-Q*. H1 is hereby confirmed.

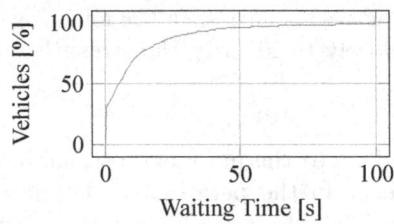

Fig. 11. Correlation of vehicles and their stopping time in S3 of *iTLM-Free*.

H2. To confirm H2 we use S4. We can see from Fig. 12 that *iTLM* detects the change of the major traffic axes, and thus intelligently optimizes the green-light periods. This results in less waiting times at red lights. However, the more dynamic approaches *iTLM-Free* and *iTLM-Q* suffer the same drawbacks as in the previous scenarios of not being fair. Hence, waiting time for some vehicles increases and they wait for almost the full duration of the simulation. Nevertheless, dynamically changing the green phases is meaningful as it lowers the waiting time in comparison to *STA*.

iTLM delivers the best result in this scenario. This result is justified by the algorithmic implementation of the approach and the resulting perfect suitability for the requirements of the hypothesis. The distribution algorithm aims at the distribution of the green phases to the axes. It calculates the proportions of the

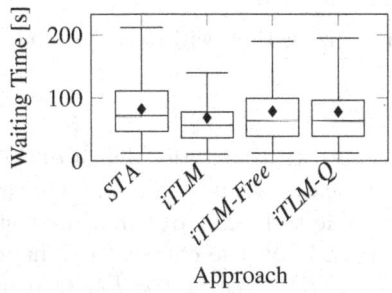

Fig. 12. Box plot of all four approaches showing the respective waiting times per vehicle (S4).

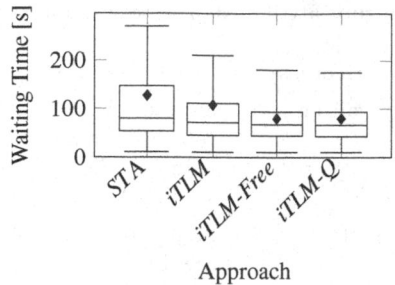

Fig. 13. Box plot of all four approaches showing the respective waiting times per vehicle (S5).

total green phase duration based on the distribution of the traffic on the two axes. Thus, the stronger axis is weighted with a longer green phase duration. In this way, the system automatically adapts to the change in direction of the main traffic flow.

H3. H3 assumes that the traffic light system is adaptable to asymmetrical distributions of traffic. As expected, for the complex and realistic scenarios S5 and S6, the dynamic approach in the form of *iTLM-Free* and *iTLM-Q* shows the best results and can even beat the basis model *iTLM*. *iTLM* is able to calculate the distribution of all lane combinations. Hence it is able to correctly prioritize lanes e, n, w in S5, resulting in much shorter waiting times compared to *STA* (see Fig. 9). In fact, Fig. 13 illustrates that the more dynamic approaches can minimize the waiting time on average even more. If a vehicle has to stop at the traffic light, the standing phase is reduced as well in comparison to other, less dynamic approaches.

Further looking at S6, we can see from Table 2 that the average waiting time is near half as long as with our previous approach *iTLM*. *iTLM-Free* and *iTLM-Q* achieve similar results. This may be due to the fact that our simulation does not include any external events such as a road closures or traffic jams after the intersection majorly reducing throughput on a specific lane. As a consequence, adapting Q does not bring much advantage here, though, results are promising. Finally, we can confirm H3.

Table 2. Overview of waiting time and time loss for S6.

		$\sum$ WT[a]	WT/V	$\sum$ TL[b]	TL/V
Approach	*STA*	195033	148	357772	272
	iTLM	196591	149	353279	268
	iTLM-Free	110284	83	188697	143
	iTLM-Q	109740	83	187428	142

[a]Waiting time in seconds
[b]Time loss in seconds

Table 3. Corrupt attributes of V to TL and the effects.

Attribute	Form of incorrectness	Effect on TLLC
wl	Send other waiting lane	Falsifies the actual number of vehicles per waiting lane, similar as reducing the number of participants, see Fig. 14
t^a	Send t^a of earlier TL-cycle	Might influence calculation, see Fig. 14
	Send t^a of later TL-cycle	Might influence calculation, see Fig. 14
—	No data received at all (equals not participating vehicles)	Might influence calculation, see Fig. 14

iTLM-Q. The results of the Q-learning based approach do not differ to a large extent from those of the procedure that only takes into account traffic events. This is largely due to the design of the simulation, which makes simplified assumptions. However, it is expected that in real-world environments, *iTLM-Q* will be superior to *iTLM-Free* and, in particular, *iTLM*. Attempts to form Q over a longer period (24 h) show that the quality and performance of *iTLM-Q* deteriorates. It is therefore advisable to revise RLRC so that it does not stiffen to certain ωs. This would lock the approach in a local and not the global optimum.

Our experiments have shown that only a few of the 12544 possible Ω are chosen to derive a decision. Across all experiments, only 2.78% of the possible state transitions were considered. However, it is not advisable to reduce Ω and exclude candidates from the outset, since they are strongly related to the scenario. No clear ωs could be found between the scenarios, which are less meaningful. The intelligent approach is basically able to avoid less optimal states for the respective situation and does not need such a manual simplification.

6.3 Impact of PET

We now discuss some important privacy impacts of our system as it was designed to enable privacy-by-design. In particular, we want to find out how robust the system is in terms of integrity and anonymity. The communication layer is not focused since it is based on ABC4Trust.

Of interest when talking about integrity are the two transmitted parameters wl and t^a by a V. Table 3 lists the impact of each attribute on the system.

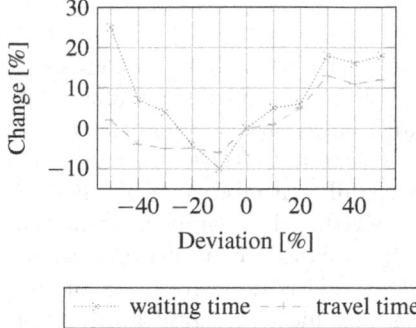

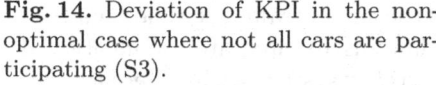

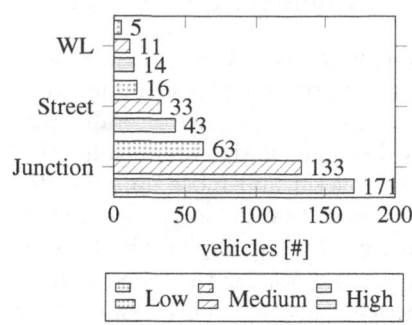

Fig. 14. Deviation of KPI in the non-optimal case where not all cars are participating (S3).

Fig. 15. k-anonymity at traffic light for different vehicle densities (one light cycle).

Figure 14 shows that the calculation is, of course, influenced when corruption happens, although the system can handle inaccuracies regarding transmitted information. If the inaccuracies are similarly distributed as the occurrences of the vehicles, TLL distributes 90 s of a light cycle accordingly, resulting in a feasible light schedule. If this is not the case, TL can rely on fb to gain information about that current distribution to update its internal policy. In this manner, targeted denial of service attacks can be identified and handled appropriately.

From Fig. 15 one can see that even with low traffic, on average, five vehicles pass a junction on a single waiting line. Therefore, these five vehicles form a k-anonymity set of 5 as long as nobody can derive in which order they arrive at and leave the junction. Although the presentation tokens are generally cryptographically unlinkable and untraceable, conclusions could be drawn from the content or time of transmission. Therefore, it is necessary that V communicate independently of their location with TL and that the arrival time is not exact to the second, but should be given in buckets of e.g. 5 s. The independence from the location can be achieved by sending the messages to the traffic light with a random delay.

6.4 Emissions

By optimizing the traffic light cycle, emissions could be reduced significantly. For instance in S1, the total CO_2 emissions as simulated by SUMO of all vehicles was 619 kg for STA, 634 kg for ACT and only 603 kg for TLL, equalling a reduction of around 5% for the same number of vehicles and driven distance. Similar results exist for the noise level. This is related to how TLL optimizes the light cycle. By trying to reduce the travel time, the number of restarts of a car after stopping, and giving it a clear lane, the environmental impact of vehicles can be downscaled. The reduction of emissions scales with Δ Waiting Time.

7   Conclusion

Here, we extended our previous approach for intelligent traffic light management using crowdsourced user input transferred via V2X to optimize the traffic light cycle and thus reduce overall waiting time and emissions. We identified and tackled some major limitations of *iTLM* and present *iTLM-Q* which can react even quicker and more appropriate to complex traffic situations. A simulation has shown that up to 70% of waiting time can be reduced in complex situations with vastly changing traffic flows. Therefore, the emissions can also be lowered by around 5% for the same number of vehicles. This is done by i.a. avoiding unnecessary stops. Furthermore, our approach still achieves a significant level of privacy by adapting ABC4Trust to our needs.

For future work, we want to analyze the structure of traffic scenarios that can be optimized with *iTLM-Q*. Hence, we are planning to integrate the mentioned external factors. Also an even more diverse traffic system with different vehicles and characteristics is to be examined. Furthermore, we plan to analyze the potential of our approach by extending the range of information available, i.e. interconnecting the traffic light network, allowing two or more traffic lights to exchange information and knowledge. However, the impact of privacy for vehicles has to be taken into account. Our existing k-anonymity results only allow a specific level of interconnection, which is of further interest.

References

1. Abuelsamid, S.: Volkswagen Adds 'Vehicle-To-Everything' Communications to Revamped Golf with NXP Chips (2019)
2. Arel, I., Liu, C., Urbanik, T., Kohls, A.G.: Reinforcement learning-based multi-agent system for network traffic signal control. IET Intell. Transp. Syst. **4**(2), 128–135 (2010)
3. Bauer, T., Jingtao, M., Offermann, F.: An online prediction system of traffic signal status for assisted driving on urban streets. Technical report (2015)
4. Blumberg, A.J., Keeler, L.S., Shelat, A.: Automated traffic enforcement which respects "driver privacy". In: IEEE Conference on Intelligent Transportation Systems, Proceedings, ITSC 2005 (2005)
5. Darroch, J.N., Newell, G.F., Morris, R.W.J.: Queues for a vehicle-actuated traffic light. Oper. Res. **12**(6), 882–895 (1964)
6. Gao, J., Shen, Y., Liu, J., Ito, M., Shiratori, N.: Adaptive traffic signal control: deep reinforcement learning algorithm with experience replay and target network. Technical report (2017)
7. Gao, K., Han, F., Wen, M., Du, R., Li, S., Zhou, F.: J. Central South Univ. **26**(9), 2516–2527 (2019). https://doi.org/10.1007/s11771-019-4191-7
8. Katsaros, K., Kernchen, R., Dianati, M., Rieck, D.: Performance study of a green light optimized speed advisory (GLOSA) application using an integrated cooperative ITS simulation platform. In: IWCMC 2011–7th International Wireless Communications and Mobile Computing Conference (2011)
9. Koukoumidis, E., Peh, L.S., Martonosi, M.R.: SignalGuru: leveraging mobile phones for collaborative traffic signal schedule advisory. In: MobiSys 2011 - Compilation Proceedings of the 9th International Conference on Mobile Systems, Applications and Services and Co-located Workshops (2011)

10. Li, Y.: Netzweite Lichtsignalsteuerung auf Basis Rekurrenter Neuronaler Netze. Dissertation, Technische Universität München (2012)
11. Liang, X., Du, X., Wang, G., Han, Z.: A deep reinforcement learning network for traffic light cycle control. IEEE Trans. Veh. Technol. **68**(2), 1243–1253 (2019)
12. Nirmani, A., Thilakarathne, L., Wickramasinghe, A., Senanayake, S., Haddela, P.S.: Google map and camera based fuzzified adaptive networked traffic light handling model. In: 2018 3rd International Conference on Information Technology Research, ICITR 2018. Institute of Electrical and Electronics Engineers Inc. (2018)
13. Bezzi, M., Duquenoy, P., Fischer-Hübner, S., Hansen, M., Zhang, G. (eds.): Privacy and Identity 2009. IAICT, vol. 320. Springer, Heidelberg (2010). https://doi.org/10.1007/978-3-642-14282-6
14. Rachmadi, M.F., et al.: Adaptive traffic signal control system using camera sensor and embedded system. In: TENCON 2011–2011 IEEE Region 10 Conference. IEEE (2011)
15. Roth., C., Nitschke., M., Hörmann., M., Kesdoğan., D.: ITLM: a privacy friendly crowdsourcing architecture for intelligent traffic light management. In: Proceedings of the 9th International Conference on Data Science, Technology and Applications - DATA, INSTICC. SciTePress (2020)
16. Sabouri, A., Krontiris, I., Rannenberg, K.: Attribute-based Credentials for Trust. Springer, Cham (2015). https://doi.org/10.1007/978-3-319-14439-9
17. Schaub, F., Ma, Z., Kargl, F.: Privacy requirements in vehicular communication systems. In: Proceedings - 12th IEEE International Conference on Computational Science and Engineering, CSE 2009, vol. 3 (2009)
18. Steingröver, M., Steingröver, M., Schouten, R., Peelen, S., Nijhuis, E., Bakker, B.: Reinforcement learning of traffic light controllers adapting to traffic congestion. In: Benelux Conference on Artificial Intelligence, BNAIC 2005 (2005)
19. Varga, N., Bokor, L., Takacs, A., Kovacs, J., Virag, L.: An architecture proposal for V2X communication-centric traffic light controller systems. In: Proceedings of 2017 15th International Conference on ITS Telecommunications, ITST 2017. Institute of Electrical and Electronics Engineers Inc. (2017)
20. Wiedersheim, B., Ma, Z., Kargl, F., Papadimitratos, P.: Privacy in inter-vehicular networks: Why simple pseudonym change is not enough. In: WONS 2010–7th International Conference on Wireless On-demand Network Systems and Services (2010)
21. Xing, S.Y., Lian, G.L., Yan, D.Y., Cao, J.Y.: Traffic signal light optimization control based on fuzzy control and CCD camera technology. DEStech Trans. Comput. Sci. Eng. (CMSMS) (2018)

Open Data in the Enterprise Context: Assessing Open Corporate Data's Readiness for Use

Pavel Krasikov(✉) ⓘ, Timo Obrecht, Christine Legner ⓘ, and Markus Eurich ⓘ

Faculty of Business and Economics (HEC), University of Lausanne, 1015 Lausanne, Switzerland
{pavel.krasikov,timo.obrecht,christine.legner,
markus.eurich}@unil.ch

Abstract. Open data initiatives have long focused on motivating governmental bodies to open up their data. Although governments and other organizations make their data increasingly available, open data consumers are reluctant or experience difficulties with using open data. Prior studies have therefore set the focus on open data portals and open data quality, but only few have examined enterprises as consumers of open data. To close this gap, we aim at assessing whether open data is ready for use by enterprises. We focus our efforts on open corporate data, i.e., data on companies provided by business registers, which has confirmed reuse potential. Our assessment of 30 business registers confirms that the heterogeneity of access, licensing, publishing conditions, and content in open corporate datasets hinder their reuse in a business context. Only half of analyzed registers provide companies' full legal addresses, only 20% mention their complete organizational information, while contact details are fully available in 13% of all the cases. We find that open data's readiness for use from an enterprise perspective is highly dependent on the concrete use case.

Keywords: Open data · Corporate registers · Open corporate data · Usability · Data quality · Open data assessment

1 Introduction

Open data can be defined as "data that is freely available, and can be used as well as republished by everyone without restrictions from copyright or patents" [1]. It holds great business potential, with global economic value estimated as from $3.2 to $5.4 trillion annually [2], as well as forecasted cost savings of 1.7 billion EUR for the EU28+ countries [3]. Open data initiatives have long focused on motivating governments to open their data [4]. However, although the number of open datasets is growing steadily, their adoption is lagging behind [5]. In the first wave, application developers were the main users of open data, achieving only modest success [6]. In the current second wave, authorities as well as national and European initiatives are pushing open data's wider adoption and using it to create added value [7]. It is widely believed that multiple industry sectors could significantly benefit from open data, among them transportation, consumer products, electricity, oil and gas, healthcare, consumer finance, agriculture, urban development,

© Springer Nature Switzerland AG 2021
S. Hammoudi et al. (Eds.): DATA 2020, CCIS 1446, pp. 80–100, 2021.
https://doi.org/10.1007/978-3-030-83014-4_4

and the social sector [2, 5, 8–10]. Despite the significant business potential, enterprises are far from leveraging the available open data resources and most of them are reluctant to even try [8, 11]. This is due to a lack of transparency, unknown quality, and unclear licensing unsettling challenges [12, 13].

In this study, we assess whether open data is ready for use in the enterprise context. We focus on one of the most important segments of open government data: open corporate data (OCD). OCD can be defined as data on companies that corporate registers (also known as business registers), in keeping with local laws, usually collect. This data is transparent and interoperable, and has a confirmed reuse potential [15]. Our study extends our earlier conference paper [14] which provided an initial analysis of OCD provided by business registers from different countries. It addresses the following research questions:

- *To which extent is open corporate data ready for use by enterprises?*
- *Does open corporate data satisfy the requirements of typical enterprise use cases?*

Compared to [14], we improve and refine the use case-driven analysis of OCD. The suggested approach (see Fig. 1) extends beyond metadata and schema analysis and incorporates the "ready for use" assessment. This additional step (see Sect. 4.4) comprises the mapping of required business concepts with OCD attributes and is demonstrated in four typical use cases. In addition, we revisited the originally considered business registers, updated the metadata and content analysis as of October 2020, and added 10 new corporate registers.

In total, we analyze data from 30 open corporate registers: first, by assessing the provided metadata and, second, by examining the content of these corporate registers. To assess whether open corporate data is ready for use, we compare the datasets' content with the common data objects that typical use cases require. Our findings confirm that the heterogeneity of access, licensing, publishing conditions, and content in open corporate datasets hinder their reuse in a business context. In addition, our study shows that only half of analyzed registers provide companies' full legal addresses, only 20% mention their complete organizational information, while contact details are fully available in 13% of all the cases. For four typical use cases (master data management, fraud prevention, intelligence and analytics, and marketing), we conclude that open corporate data has only limited use due to its lacking coverage of relevant business concepts. Our study thereby underlines shortcomings in business registers, but also draws attention to the need for domain-specific semantic models that make open data more usable for enterprises.

The remainder of the paper is organized as follows: In Sect. 2, we examine relevant literature on open data adoption barriers and assessment techniques, which clarifies the research gap. In the section that follows, we explain our research methodology. In Sect. 4 we thoroughly describe this study's results. Finally, we present our concluding remarks, discuss the study's limitations, and provide suggestions for future research.

2 Related Work

While governments and other organizations make their data increasingly available, open data consumers are reluctant or experience difficulties with using open data. In this section, we will review research on the barriers to open data adoption from both providers' and consumers' perspective and analyze various assessment methods, which have been proposed in prior literature.

2.1 Barriers to Open Data Adoption

Prior studies on the barriers to open data adoption differentiate between open data consumption and supply (see Table 1). Although the barriers are associated with either consumption or supply, there is a strong interdependency between the two: the way the data is published impacts how it is used [4]. Consequently, most studies investigate both consumption and supply.

When it comes to data provisioning, these studies identify several common issues: the risk of excessive costs, an unclear purpose, as well as litigation and differing licensing standards and documentation complicating open data suppliers' release process [13, 16–18]. Studies addressing consumption barriers emphasize that the setbacks are not strictly technical [4, 13, 18], but also concern the broader context of data use. The absence of information describing an open dataset is often associated with poor metadata documentation [4]. The latter generally refers to technical barriers, demonstrating the interdependence of the impediments' consumption and supply sides. In addition, a lack of understanding of the contents and insufficient domain knowledge commonly hinder open data use [4, 12, 18]. As underlined by [14], three challenges prevail in using open data: first, there is a lack of transparency about datasets' availability and their usefulness for the end user [12]. Second, open datasets' heterogeneity in terms of licensing conditions, available formats, and access to information complicates the integration efforts [13]. Third, the quality of open data remains unknown and uncertain in terms of typical assessment criteria [4].

Finally, it is worthwhile noting that many of the existing studies do not consider any specific use context, and only two studies examined enterprises as consumers of open data. This underpins the lack of research on open data use in the enterprise context.

Table 1. Barriers to open data adoption based on [14].

Source and topic	Method	Adoption barriers	Open data
Janssen et al. 2012 [12] Gap between the benefits of and barriers to open data adoption	Group session (n = 9), findings were discussed during interviews(n = 14)	6 categories: institutional, task complexity, use and participation, legislation, information quality, technical. Categories are exemplified by a total of 57 examples of barriers	Generic consumption Supply

(continued)

Table 1. (*continued*)

Source and topic	Method	Adoption barriers	Open data
Zuiderwijk et al. 2012 [4] Open data users' perspective on identified impediments	Literature review (n = 37) Interviews (n = 6) Workshops (n = 4)	A total of 118 socio-technical impediments in 3 categories: data access, data use, and data deposition 10 sub-categories: availability and access, findability, usability, understandability, quality, linking and combining data, comparability and compatibility, metadata, interaction with data provider, and opening and uploading	Generic consumption Supply
Zuiderwijk et al. 2012 [4] Open data users' perspective on identified impediments	Literature review (n = 37) Interviews (n = 6) Workshops (n = 4)	A total of 118 socio-technical impediments in 3 categories: data access, data use, and data deposition 10 sub-categories: availability and access, findability, usability, understandability, quality, linking and combining data, comparability and compatibility, metadata, interaction with data provider, and opening and uploading	Generic consumption Supply
Martin et al. 2013 [13] Risks for re-users of public data differ from those for open data providers	Analysis of open data platforms (n = 3)	Typology of barriers comprising 7 categories: governance, economic issues, licenses and legal frameworks, data characteristics, metadata, access, and skills	Business consumption Supply
Conradie and Choenni 2014 [17] Release processes of government open data	Participatory action research: Exploratory workshop (n = 5). Questionnaire answered by a consortium (n = 14). Questionnaire answered by other civil servants (n = 50) In-depth interviews (n = 18). Workshop with data users (n = 8). Plenary session discussion (n = 21). Follow-up meeting with decision makers (n = 2). Experiences with data release (n = 4)	4 categories of barriers: fear of false conclusions, financial effects, opaque ownership and unknown data locations, and priority	Supply
Barry and Bannister 2014 [16] Implications of opening up the data	Case studies (n = 2), inductive approach to the analysis of collected data	6 types of barriers: economic, technical, cultural, legal, administrative, and task related. A total of 20 barriers to open data's release	Supply
Beno et al. 2017 [18] Practitioners using and providing open data in Austria	Literature review (n = 17) Survey (n = 110)	3 major groups: user specific, provider specific, and both users and providers with a total of 54 barriers	Consumption by enterprises, academia, and public sector Supply

2.2 Open Data Assessment

Since open data portals play an important role in publishing open data, researchers have set their focus on their assessment. Table 2 summarizes the scope of prior studies and the ways they assessed open data. It sheds light on two crucial aspects in open data assessment studies: (1) whether the unit of analysis was the metadata or the dataset content as well, and (2) the methods used. We find that prior research almost exclusively focuses on the metadata quality. Although "poor data quality can be widespread, and potentially hamper an efficient reuse of open data" [19], only three studies analyze the contents of the underlying datasets. Interestingly, these studies build on generic quality assessment methods according to typical data quality dimensions, such as completeness, accuracy, or timeliness. They neither consider specific data requirements nor the use contexts, although data quality is commonly defined as "fitness for use" from the data consumers' perspective [20]. This means that the reviewed literature largely ignores the actual user's perspective and the data domain knowledge, which has found to be crucial for overcoming the barriers (Sect. 2.1).

As a final point, open data's usefulness is only addressed by Osagie et al. [21], who take a very specific focus on the usability of open data platforms' features for specific use cases.

Table 2. Open data assessments.

Source	Scope	Unit of analysis	Assessment approach
Bogdanović-Dinić et al. 2014 [22]	7 open data portals	Metadata	"Data openness score" based on eight open data principles [23]
Reiche et al. 2014 [24]	10 open government dataportals	Metadata	Ranking of open data repositories with the average score computed by means of quality metrics
Umbrich et al. 2015 [25]	82 CKAN portals	Metadata	Open data quality and monitoring assessment framework with 6 quality dimensions
Neumaier et al. 2016 [26]	260 open data portals	Metadata	Metadata quality assessment framework
Vetrò et al. 2016 [19]	11 datasets	Metadata and dataset	Quality framework supported by data quality models from the literature, 6 dimensions and 14 metrics
Máchová and Lněnička 2017 [27]	67 open data portals	Metadata	Benchmarking framework for evaluating open data portals' quality
Welle Donker and van Loenen 2017 [28]	20 "most wanted" datasets in Netherlands	Metadata	Holistic open data assessment framework with 3 main levels: open data supply, open data governance, and open data user characteristics
Osagie et al. 2017 [21]	5 datasets	Platform features	Usability evaluation with ROUTE-TO-PA and QUIN criteria. (12 usability criteria)

(*continued*)

Table 2. (*continued*)

Source	Scope	Unit of analysis	Assessment approach
Bicevskis et al. 2018 [29]	4 company registers for 11 attributes	Dataset	Three-part data quality model (syntax analysis): definition of a data object, data object quality specifications, and implementation
Kubler et al. 2018 [30]	More than 250 open data portals	Metadata	Open data portal quality (ODPQ) framework with 17 quality dimensions
Stróżyna et al. 2018 [31]	59 data sources	Metadata	Quality-based selection, assessment, and retrieval method. Attribution of quality scores based on "ranking type Delphi" and 6 quality dimensions
Zhang et al. 2019 [32]	20 datasets	Metadata and dataset	Design science research and a systematic approach to repurposed datasets' quality using the LANG approach and according to 10 dimensions

2.3 Research Gap

One of the least addressed barriers in the open data landscape is the "lack of insight into the user's perspective" [12]. This implies understanding the particularities of open data access, publishing, licensing, and content, as well as the extent to which they meet the requirements in a specific use context and business scenario. Existing efforts study barriers mostly on the platform level, rather than on the dataset level [21] or refer to open data supply and its underlying technical impediments evoking users' behavioral intentions [33].

Furthermore, the literature does not specifically cover open data's use in the business context. For instance, governmental directives to open basic data about companies [34] motivate the competent authorities to make this data available. However, this does not necessary mean that the data is also usable [15]. Existing literature often restricts the user's perspective to data availability (the way data is proposed and can be consumed) by considering usability purely in terms of technical specifications [21, 33], such as data format and open data portal's underlying software. We argue for taking a user-centric perspective based on Welle Donker et al.'s [28] definition of open data's usability as "usable for the intended purpose of the user." In fact, being manageable is one of the indicators that the authors introduce in the same work, which implies that a "user should be able to use it (open data) with available resources and for the goal the user had in mind" [28].

The abovementioned gaps motivate our research aimed at answering the question whether open data is ready for use by enterprises.

3 Methodology

In this study, we address the identified research gap by assessing whether open data is ready for use in a specific domain and for the enterprise context. We selected open corporate data (OCD), which is an important segment of open government data. OCD can be defined as data on companies that business registers, in keeping with local laws, usually collect. The resulting data is not only valuable for public authorities, but its high potential for reuse in a business setting has been emphasized by practitioners and researchers [15, 35].

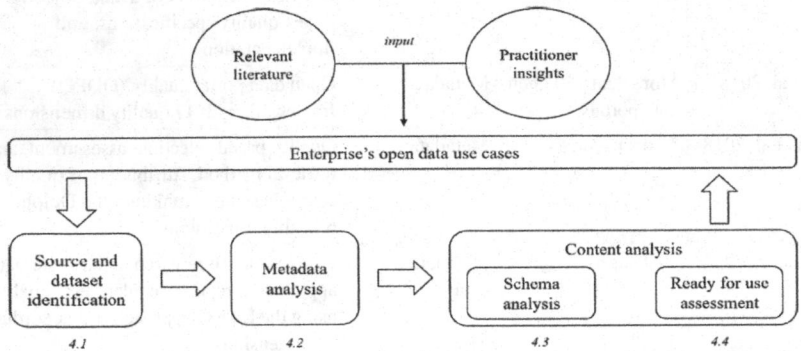

Fig. 1. Research process.

Enterprise's Open Data Use Cases. To discuss and analyze the use context of OCD in enterprises, we formed a focus groups [36, 37] with seven swiss-based data management experts representing transportation, consumer goods, and telecommunication industries (see Table 3). This activity was a part of a broader analysis of open data use cases. all the participants were knowledgeable about open data use cases and had been involved in the generation and documentation processes of OCD scenarios. The focus group first met during a web conference during which it defined three high level use cases based on a structured use case generation framework [38]. Afterwards, the focus group met physically for a workshop that validated open corporate data use cases. additional individual sessions were conducted with the same companies to refine the relevant use cases and obtain further insights. This activity resulted in four concrete use cases and the corresponding business concepts, which could potentially be sourced from OCD datasets (see Sect. 4.4).

Table 3. Focus group composition.

Company	Industry	Size	Key informants	OCD context
A	Public transportation and mobility infrastructure	Revenue: $1B to $50B Employees: ~35 000	Data architect, open data responsible	Data management and business processes improvement
B	Consumer goods	Revenue: $50B to $100B Employees: ~300 000	Data management lead and data method expert	Enhancement of business processes, business intelligence and analytics
C	Telecommunication	Revenue: $1B to $50B Employees: ~20 000	Head of data quality management	Validation, enrichment, and deduplication of internal data

Data Sources and Datasets Identification. Since academic literature on OCD is scarce, we mainly used online sources as providers of insights [39–43]. To date, 737 official corporate registers from 224 countries have been recorded following the Global Legal Entity Identifier Foundation's (GLEIF) accreditation process [44]. However, only a small number of these officially confirmed registers are available as open sources. In our analysis we considered 30 corporate registers provided by official government agencies that have their data available in full open access [31]. We have extended and updated the previous list [14] by adding the leading countries in the open data initiatives in EU [5] and world leading economies with recognized open data initiatives [41–43]. Our selection covers corporate registers of United States, Europe, and other countries, and considers different geographical granularity. Many registers claim their data to be provided with an open license, whereas the real access is restrained by registration, forms submissions, or even blocked by fees for downloads or API calls. Even though we initially wanted to consider registers that provide strictly full access to the data (such as bulk download or API), we realized, during the course of the analysis, that some claiming to have an open license only allow partial access to the datasets, for example, the Austrian, Belgian, Danish, Indian, Swiss etc. (see Table 4) business registers.

Metadata Analysis. As seen in Sect. 2.2, most of the open data assessment methods focus on metadata. In fact, the primary insights into whether the desired data is usable or not are obtained through the metadata published at the source. We relied on previous literature (see Table 1) when dealing with corporate registers and collected five categories of open data information: its identification, access, licensing, publisher, and basic information about the underlying datasets' content (see Appendix 1, Source Information). Two researchers collected and reconciled the metadata of the selected 30 corporate registers (see Appendix 2).

Schema Analysis. Following the research process, a comprehensive content analysis of the corporate registers was undertaken to assess its readiness for use (see Sect. 4.3). Two researchers conducted a bottom-up analysis to understand the similarities between the attributes that the registers provide. Based on the focus group participants' input, we examined the corporate registers to ascertain the presence of attributes related to the use cases' relevant business concepts. Moreover, we took existing efforts regarding the OCD semantics' standardization into consideration for this analysis. We derived 21 typically used attributes (see Appendix 1, Content Information), based on the analysis of the selected business registers. Furthermore, we have assessed the presence of these attributes within the 30 selected registers.

Ready for Use Assessment. Finally, we investigate OCD's readiness for use in a business setting, by determining the presence of required business concepts within the analyzed corporate registers. We specifically analyzed four use cases analyzed in the first step, i.e., master data management, fraud prevention, intelligence and analytics, and marketing. For these scenarios, the participants of the focus group helped to identify relevant data objects, which we then compared to the business concepts typically found in corporate registers. Section 4.4 elaborates on our findings regarding the usability of OCD for the given usage scenarios.

4 Findings

This section summarizes our findings along the different steps in the research process, i.e., identification of relevant datasets provided by the corporate registers (4.1), their assessment in terms of metadata documentation (4.2), schema analysis (4.3), and ready for use assessment with presence of business concepts required for the identified use cases (4.4).

4.1 Data Sources Identification

Corporate registers are usually assigned to a country or an administrative area and cover local business entities that need to undergo a local registration procedure. Aggregated unofficial lists of existing company registers are available online per country [40], although there is no assessment process that confirms this sources' accuracy. The above-mentioned GLEIF has an attribution procedure by means of a legal entity identifier (LEI), and maintains a catalogue with accredited official business registers, which provides initial insights into the available OCD [39]. The register's presence on this list does not guarantee that the provided data is open. For instance, the Austrian corporate register maintained by the Federal Ministry of Justice [14], is currently available only at a fee. For this reason, we have selected an open Austrian business register provided by a different publisher.

For our analysis, we have selected 30 sources, i.e., corporate registers covering United States, Europe, and other countries worldwide with advanced open data initiatives, as listed in Table 4.

Table 4. Analyzed corporate registers with GLEIF identifier.

Alaska Business Entity Register (RA000594)	Norway Register of Business Enterprises (RA000472)
Argentinian National Registry of Companies (RA000010)	Oregon Business Entity Register (RA000631)
Australian Business Register (RA000013)	Russian Register of Legal Entities (RA000499)
Bulgarian Commercial Register (RA000065)	Singapore ACRA Register (RA000523)
Canada Corporate Register (RA000072)	UK Companies House (RA000585)
Colorado Business Entity Register (RA000599)	Ukrainian State Register Service (RA000567)
Finnish Business Information System (RA000188)	Washington Business Entity Register (RA000641)
Florida Business Entity Register (RA000603)	Wyoming Business Entity Register (RA000644)
France Register of Companies (RA000189)	Austrian Corporate Register (RA000687)*
Iowa Business Entity Register (RA000606)	Central Belgium Company Database (RA000025)*
Ireland Companies Register (RA000402)	Cyprus Companies Section (RA000161)*
Japanese National Tax Agency (RA000413)	Danish Company Register CVR (RA000170)*
Latvian Register of Enterprises (RA000423)	Indian Business Register (RA000394)*
Moldova State Register of Legal Entities (RA000451)	New Zealand Company Register (RA000466)*
New York Business Entity Register (RA000628)	Swiss UID-Register (RA000548)*

*Corporate registers provide full access to the data, except for the ones marked with * (restricted access)*

4.2 Metadata Analysis

The analysis of the collected metadata provides first insights into the sources. Appendix 2 (Fig. 4, Fig. 5, and Fig. 6) summarize the metadata documentation for the business registers and present identification information regarding the relevant countries and GLEIF registry codes, which allows to identify the webpage for each dataset.

Metadata regarding access revealed some interesting insights. Registers, which provided bulk download option, most frequently relied on such machine readable and suitable for processing file formats as CSV, JSON, and XML. A growing number of registers (11) started to offer APIs as an access point to the data. Five registers required a login procedure in order to obtain a full access to the data, but still offering the possibility of a lookup service with limited access. Moreover, with the exception of one, all of the registers provided a free lookup service to query the register. In terms of licensing, vast majority of registers operated under an open license, a Creative Commons one or a national equivalent, whereas seven registers provided access to the data without any license specification. More than a half (16) of the business registers noted a publishing date, which was after 2013. The data's update frequency varied from daily or weekly to monthly or even yearly. Finally, these attributes' importance should not be underestimated [45] as they are an integral part of the enterprises' specific needs (see Sect. 4.4).

Metadata regarding the content reveals an important difference between the registers' sizes, which ranged from 82,902 to 21,059,740 entry points. Their geographical coverage explains this, as larger registers cover the national level of granularity (France, Australia, and UK), while smaller ones are restricted to states (US) or administrative areas. We also notice that the revisited registers are not static and continue to grow compared to our previous analysis [14]. Almost all the registers are available in English, even though the country of origin has a different national language or more than one, which demonstrates the efforts taken to make data available for an international audience. While this information allows first insights into the data, we provide a thorough analysis of the contents and mapping to the identified use cases in the following sections.

4.3 Schema Analysis

Upon the identification and documentation of the corporate registers, we analyzed the presence of common attributes and compared the schemas. Figure 2 summarizes the attributes' presence in the open corporate registers' datasets.

Companies' address information and their identification concepts are present in the majority of the assessed corporate registers. Nevertheless, certain attributes of these categories, such as "Tax Number", "Premise" and "Postal Delivery Point" appear seldomly. Organizational information from the business registers in vast majority of the cases provides insights about the incorporation status, date, and companies' legal form, but largely ignores further details about the legal structure and financial statements. Ultimately, such contact detail as "Website", "Phone Number", and "E-mail" are only available for 5 to 7 corporate datasets respectively.

With a total of 21 attributes, where all of them appear at least once across the datasets, no corporate register is complete. Similar to our previous findings, on average, 12 of the

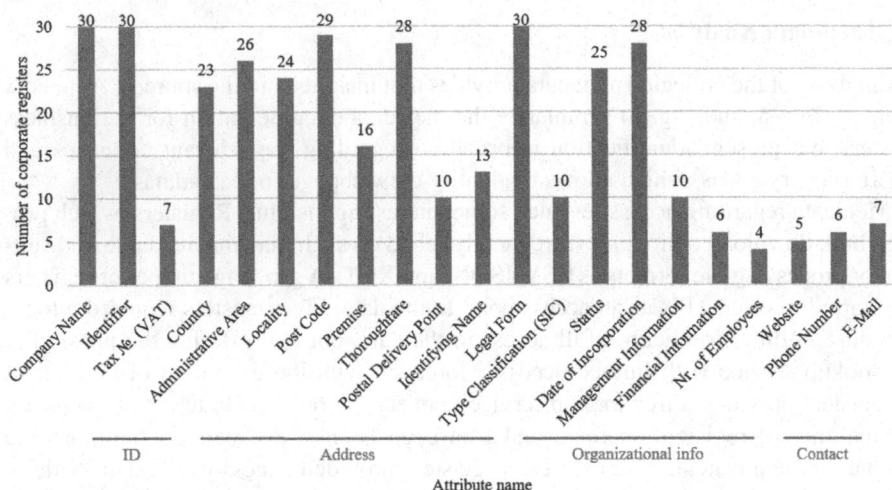

Fig. 2. Schema analysis: presence of attributes across the analyzed registers.

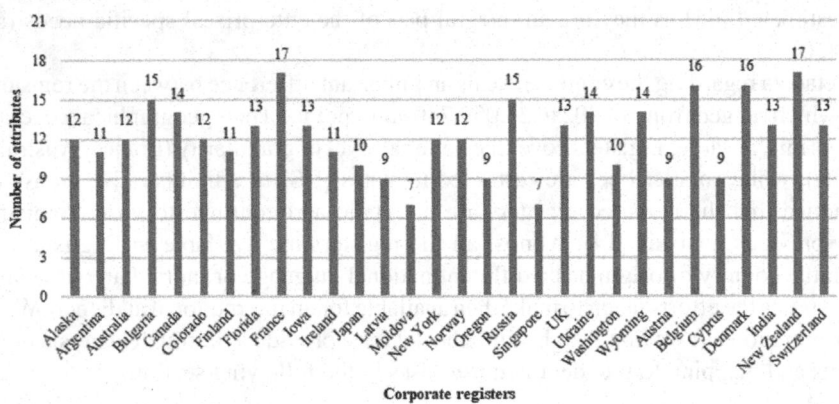

Fig. 3. Schema analysis: presence of attributes per corporate register.

21 identified attributes were present per register. Figure 3 reveals that the French register accompanied by the New Zealand register have 17 attributes, which is the best result. Belgian and Danish registers show 16 attributes present, followed by Bulgarian and Russian registers. Interestingly the US state registers do not provide the same attributes although they are part of the same country. Business registers of Moldova and Singapore ended up with the least available attributes, yet their data is fully accessible and is published in machine-readable formats (i.e., XLSX and CSV respectively).

4.4 Ready for Use Assessment

The working sessions described in Sect. 3 provided practitioners' insights into how OCD can be used in the business environment. These sessions helped us identifying, discussing and validating four concrete use cases, and allowed us to link each attribute to the relevant business concept (see Tables 5, 6, 7, 8). For each of the collected use cases, we have marked with an underscore the business concepts which are frequently available in OCD (more than in 80% of the analyzed corporate registers). This allows us to understand if the data currently available in OCD offers the necessary information for the feasibility of the use cases.

Master Data Management. The maintenance of business partner data (customers and/or vendors) within a company's IT systems is the most popular OCD use case. This use case supports master data management and aims at maintaining the most accurate version of the data in the company's internal systems, most prominently for addresses and companies' names. OCD can help to ensure the data quality by removing duplicates, reconciling concepts representing the same real-world object, enriching the data with new entries, and ensuring its completeness and accuracy by adding up-to-date information from authoritative sources.

This use case, even with an obvious lack of the "Contact" information across corporate registers, is feasible and demonstrates the highest maturity (see Table 5). This is mainly due to the fact that "Identification" and "Address" information are widely present in the registers and are commonly required to be published by the governmental bodies.

Table 5. Analysis of master data management use case.

Use case benefits	Internal data objects	Attributes from business registers	
		Group	Name
• Data quality improvement • Validation of existing records • Duplicate removal • Enrichment with new data • Update and automatic maintenance of data	• Customer master data (ID, address, legal status,contact details) • Vendor master data (ID, address, legal status) • Business partner master data (ID, address, legal status)	Identification	Company Name, Identifier, Tax Number. (VAT)
		Address	Country, Administrative area, Locality, Post Code, Premise, Thoroughfare, Postal Delivery Point
		Organizational Information	Date of Incorporation, Incorporation Status, Legal Form
		Contact	Website, Phone Number, E-mail

Fraud Prevention. OCD can help with the identification of fraudulent business partner. This can be achieved by validating if the business partner counterpart is officially listed in a corporate register. Additionally, in case a register provides details regarding the directors, it can be helpful to verify if the company owner is not present in a sanctions list. OCD can also support investigations into corruption, abuse of power, and violations of cartel laws [15].

Similar to the previous use case, the presence of "Identification" and "Address" data already allows to identify if the analyzed data entry corresponds to the information provided by the business registers. However, the largely missing "Organizational information" complicates the process of identification of black-listed business partners. The trustworthiness of the data coming from official corporate registers plays a key role for a potential success of this usage scenario, making it a viable use case. Another attribute which would have improved the fraud identification process are banking details, such as SWIFT or IBAN numbers, related to a particular company. This information was not identified among the assessed corporate registers.

Table 6. Analysis of fraud prevention use case.

Use case benefits	Internal data objects	Attributes from business registers	
		Group	Name
• Reduce fraud risk • Decrease financial losses related to fraud cases • Establish trustworthy relations with business partners	• Busines partner master data (ID, VAT, name, address) • Current suppliers and praospects • Banking details, financial structure	Identification	Company Name, Identifier, Tax Number. (VAT)
		Address	Country, Administrative area, Locality, Post Code, Premise, Thoroughfare, Postal Delivery Point, Identifying name
		Organizational Information	Management Information

Intelligence and Analytics. OCD can be used to gain insights into customers, partners, and competitors. Moreover, it is possible to identify a particular enterprise with a unique identifier, which helps prevent confusion due to similar company names.

In this regard, companies seek to use more sophisticated information for analytics, which goes beyond the "Address" details. Even though several registers do contain management (33%) and financial information (20%), this is too little to be useful. For instance, only the registers of Denmark and France provide the full set of attributes in this category. We can conclude that this lack of information complicates the feasibility of the Intelligence and Analytics. Consequently, companies willing to pursue this usage scenario are pushed to search for the missing attributes, for instance among specialized data vendors or data marketplaces.

Table 7. Analysis of intelligence and analytics use case.

Use case benefits	Internal data objects	Attributes from business registers	
		Group	Name
• Improved competitive advantage • Insights about customers, partners, and competitors • Optimization of operational efficiency	• Business partner master data (ID, address, legal status) • Financial structures • Customer contact details	Identification	Company Name, Identifier
		Organizational Information	Legal Form, Incorporation Status, Date of Incorporation, Number of Employees
		Address	Country, Post Code, Thoroughfare, Identifying Name
		Management Information	Financial Statement. Organizational structure, Number of Employees, Legal Form, Industry Classification Type, Incorporation Status

Marketing. OCD helps to identify potential clients in particular industries and to target marketing campaigns at them. In this case, it is crucial to have up-to-date information about their activities and their initial contact information.

Even though "Company Name" and "Incorporation Status" are among the most available attributes, the rest of the necessary business concepts are far less common. Marketing-related use cases, i.e., marketing campaigns, suffer from a lack of contact information, which is also relatively scarce in all of the corporate registers. "Contact" category is fully covered in the corporate registers of Bulgaria, Russia, Ukraine, and New Zealand. In this regard, this use case is more difficult to implement in an enterprise setting.

Table 8. Analysis of marketing use case.

Use case benefits	Internal data objects	Attributes from business registers	
		Group	Name
• Reduction of operational costs • Acceleration of procurement activities • Improved analytics	• Business partner master data (ID, address, status, contact details) • Product master data (shipping, tracking, status reports)	Identification	Company Name
		Organizational Information	Incorporation Status, Industry Classification
		Contact	Website, Postal Delivery Point, PhoneNumber, email

It is interesting that "Address" is an overarching concept in all the use cases, while other concepts (identification numbers, organizational information, and contact details) are only relevant for selected use cases. It is widely available in all of the registers, but not all of the attributes are equally present across the datasets. For instance, the complete scope of "Address" information is covered in certain US state registers (Florida, Iowa, New York, and Wyoming) and the business register of Belgium, although important attributes ("Locality", "Post Code" and "Thoroughfare") are mostly present. The corporate registers present "Organizational information" only infrequently, with "Contact" details appearing least.

5   Conclusion

Despite governments, NGOs, and companies' enormous efforts to open their data and the open data movement's decade of evolution, the adoption of open data stays generally behind expectations. This is particularly the case for enterprises, which are reluctant to even try open data. Our study contributes to the emerging stream of research on the use of open data and addresses the "lack of insight into the user's perspective" [12]. More specifically, we assess to what extent open corporate data is ready for use in four typical enterprise use cases.

The main contribution of our study is a use case-driven analysis of open corporate registers, which considers both the metadata and the dataset content. Our analysis of 30 corporate registers reveals that open corporate datasets have limited use for typical use cases. On the one hand, the heterogeneity of access, licensing, publishing conditions, and content in open corporate datasets hinder their reuse in a business context. On the other hand, the presence of required business concepts differs per use case. For instance, legally required information about companies, such as their addresses and identification, is mostly available, but not always complete, while many other attributes are only partially available. Therefore, the most interesting insights from our study are the ready for use assessments for four specific use cases. We find that master data management can already benefit from OCD, whereas the other use cases lack the required business concepts. To the best of our knowledge, the conducted analysis is one of the first to provide insights into open data's readiness for use from an enterprise perspective.

Beyond the assessment of OCD, our study provides a methodological contribution by proposing a use case-driven approach comprising four steps: (1) the identification of the open data sources, (2) a metadata analysis, (3) a schema analysis of the datasets, and (4) a ready for use assessment based on a comparison to relevant business concepts in the selected use case. This approach goes beyond the existing assessment approaches of open data quality (see Sect. 2.2) by integrating the use context and business scenario.

A limitation of this work is that our analysis focusses on selected registers in countries that are considered as advanced with regard to open data provision [5]. Given the total number of existing business registers, our sample does not allow us to draw conclusions about the domain as a whole. In addition, our assessment relies on four use cases identified by the focus group, but others could be potentially discovered.

An implication from our study is that the proposed open data assessment methods require amendments to integrate the user's perspective. Future research needs to put more emphasis on domain- and use case-specific analysis to complement these methods in order to assess open data's usability. We also see opportunities to further develop the proposed approach to cover other open data domains. This could result in developing a general approach to usability assessment for open data from the enterprise perspective. From a theoretical perspective the concept of open data quality should be revisited with regard to usability [19, 29]. In order to thoroughly address the data quality aspects, future research could embed the assessment techniques with metrics along the data quality dimensions in the content analysis part (e.g., timeliness, accuracy, and completeness).

Our study also underlines the need for domain ontologies, such as the euBusiness-Graph [46] common semantic model for company data, which could be a basis to provide more consistent and compatible open datasets across different open data portals and providers.

Appendix 1

See Table 9.

Table 9. Definition of attributes [14].

Source Information

ID	Registry Code	Unique identification of legal entities by GLEIF [39].
	Country	Defines a country to which the register refers.
Access	Resource Format	Describes the format of the published data, e.g., XML, JSON, CSV.
	Access Login	Mentions whether access to the dataset requires an account.
	Free Lookup Service	Indicates whether the register has a free company lookup service.
	License	License under which the data is provisioned.
Publisher	Publisher	Entity responsible for providing the data.
	Publishing Date	Date when the register originally published the dataset.
	Update Cycle	Describes the frequency of the data update in days.
Content	Resource Language	Mentions the language(s) in which the data is published.
	Geographic Coverage	Defines the scope of the publishing institution, either on a state or national level.
	# of Diverse Attributes	Counts the different attributes that the register reports.
	#of Records	Estimate of the total number of entries in a register.

Content Information

ID	Company Name	Defines the entity's name in a local language.
	Identifier	A unique identifier assigned to the relevant register.
	Tax № (VAT)	The tax number of the entity (VAT).
Address	Country	A geopolitical area, typically a nation.
	Administrative Area	A top-level geographical or political area division in a country.
	Locality	A more granular level of an administrative area's geographical division.
	Post Code	A country-specific code for a certain address component.
	Premise	An area of land and its adjacent buildings.
	Thoroughfare	A form of the access route of the address: a street, road, avenue, etc.
	Postal Delivery Point	A single mailbox or other place at which postal mail is delivered.
	Identifying Name	A name assigned to an address, e.g., the legal representative.
	Legal Form	The type of entity with respect to the local corporate law.
	Type Classification (SIC)	Classification of entities and their respective industries.

(continued)

Table 9. (*continued*)

		Content Information
Organizational information	Status	The entity's status, e.g., active, bankrupt.
	Date of Incorporation	Date of the entry in the register.
	Management Information	Information about the company's organizational structure and legal ownership.
	Financial Information	Usually financial reports on corporate figures.
	Number of Employees	The entity's number of employees.
Contact	Website	The entity's website.
	Phone Number	The entity's phone number.
	E-Mail	The e-mail address of the entity.

Appendix 2

See Figs. 4, 5, 6

		Alaska 1	Argentina 2	Australia 3	Bulgaria 4	Canada 5	Colorado 6	Finland 7	Florida 8	France 9	Iowa 10
ID	Registry Code	RA000594	RA000010	RA000013	RA000065	RA000072	RA000599	RA000188	RA000603	RA000189	RA000606
	Country	United States	Argentina	Australia	Bulgaria	Canada	United States	Finland	United States	France	United States
Access	Resource Format	CSV	CSV	XML, SOAP API	XML, JSON	XML, API	CSV, RDF, RSS, TSV, XML, REST	JSON, API, HTTP	TXT	CSV, API	CSV, RDF, RSS, TSV, XML, SODA API
	Access Login Free	no	no	no	no	no	no	no	no	no	no
	Lookup Service	available	available	available	available	available	available	available	available	not available	available
License	License	Open Government License	Creative Commons Attribution 4.0	Creative Commons Attribution 3.0 Australia	Open License	Open Government License - Canada	Public Domain	Creative Commons Attribution 4.0	N/A	Open License V2.0	Creative Commons Attribution 4.0
Publisher	Publisher	State of Alaska Department of commerce	Argentinian Ministry of Justice and Human Rights	Australian Business Register	Bulgarian Ministry of Justice Registry Agency	Innovation, Science and Development Canada	Colorado Department of State	Finnish Patent and Registration Office	Division of Corporation Florida	National Institute of Statistics and Economic Studies	Secretary of State Iowa
	Publishing Date	N/A	19 Sep 2016	05 Sep 2014	N/A	18 Feb 2014	19 Mar 2014	N/A	N/A	24 Aug 2018	10 Nov 2014
	Update Cycle	N/A	30d	1d	N/A	7d	1d	N/A	1d	1d	30d
Content	Resource Language	English	Spanish	English	Bulgarian	English, French	English	English, Finnish	English	French, English	English
	Geographic Coverage	State	National	National	National	National	State	National	State	National	State
	# of Records	82,902	N/A	18,000,000	972,362	995,900	2,043,641	874,382	8,948,976	21,059,740	260,522
	#of Diverse Attributes	35	26	22	11	25	35	86	45	118	19

Fig. 4. Metadata analysis of corporate registers 1 to 10.

		Ireland 11	Japan 12	Latvia 13	Moldova 14	New York 15	Norway 16	Oregon 17	Russia 18	Singapore 19	UK 20
ID	Registry Code	RA 000402	RA 000413	RA 000423	RA 000451	RA 000628	RA 000472	RA 000631	RA 000499	RA 000523	RA 000585
	Country	Ireland	Japan	Latvia	Moldova	United States	Norway	United States	Russia	Argentina	United Kingdom
Access	Resource Format	REST API	XML, CSV (Shift_JIS), CSV(Unicode)	CSV, XLSX	XLSX	CSV, RDF, RSS, TSV, XML	CSV, JSON, XML, REST API	CSV, RDF, RSS, JSON, XML, SODA API	XML	CSV	CSV, REST
	Access Login Free	no	no	no	no	no	no	no	no	no	no
	Lookup Service	available	available	available	available	available	available	available	available	available	available
License	License	Open License	Open License	N/A	N/A	Open Government License	Norwegian Open License	N/A	Open License	Singapore Open Data License	Free, Open Government License v3.0
Publisher	Publisher	Companies Registration Office Ireland	Financial Service Agency	Register of Enterprises of the Republic of Latvia	Moldavian State Chamber of Registration	New York Department of State	The Central Coordinating Register for Legal Entities	Secretary of State Oregon	Russian Federal Tax Service	Singapore Accounting and Corporate Regulatory Authority	Companies House UK
	Publishing Date	N/A	N/A	10 Mar 2014	N/A	14 Feb 2013	N/A	19 May 2016	01 Aug 2016	12 Dec 2016	11 Dec 2013
	Update Cycle	N/A	30d	N/A	30d	30d	N/A	7d	7d	Ad-hoc	7d
Content	Resource Language	English	Japanese, English	Latvian	Romanian	English	Norwegian	English	Russian	English	English
	Geographic Coverage	National	National	National	National	State	National	State	National	National	National
	# of Records	N/A	4,937,210	425,637	223,841	2,944,438	1,823,057	397,816	N/A	1,613,261	12,649,839
	#of Diverse Attributes	18	19	21	10	30	42	18	115	8	55

Fig. 5. Metadata analysis of corporate registers 11 to 20.

		Ukraine 21	Washington 22	Wyoming 23	Austria 24	Belgium 25	Cyprus 26	Denmark 27	India 28	New Zealand 29	Switzerland 30
ID	Registry Code	RA 000567	RA 000641	RA 000644	RA 000687	RA 000025	RA 000161	RA 000170	RA 000394	RA 000466	RA 000548
	Country	Ukraine	United States	United States	Austria	Belgium	Cyprus	Denmark	India	New Zealand	Switzerland
Access	Resource Format	XML	XML, JSON, TXT	CSV	PDF	PDF	WebGUI	REST API	CSV	XML, JSON, API	WebGUI
	Access Login Free	no	no	no	yes	yes	yes	yes	yes	yes	no
	Lookup Service	not available	available	available	available	available	available	available	not available	available	available
License	License	Open License	N/A	N/A	restricted access	restricted to queries	Open License	N/A	National License	Creative Commons Attribution 4.0	restricted to queries
Publisher	Publisher	Ukrainian National Information Systems	Secretary of State Washington	Secretary of State Wyoming	Federal Ministry Republic of Austria Digital and Economic Affairs	Ministry of Economy Belgium	Cyprus Department of Registrar of Companies and Official Receiver	Danish Business Authority	Ministry of Corporate Affairs India	Ministry of Business Innovation and Employment of New Zealand	Swiss Federal Statistical Office
	Publishing Date	12 Dec 2016	N/A	19 Mar 2014	N/A	N/A	N/A	10 Jun 2015	N/A	N/A	11 Dec 2013
	Update Cycle	5d	1d	N/A	N/A	7d	N/A	1d	365d	N/A	1d
Content	Resource Language	Ukrainian	English	English	German, English	English, French, Dutch, German	English, Greek, Turkish	Danish, English, Kalaallisut	English	English	English, French, Italian, German
	Geographic Coverage	National	State	State	National	National	National	National	State	National	National
	# of Records	1,743,903	1,381,897	522,691	N/A	1,235,529	425,060	N/A	N/A	N/A	N/A
	#of Diverse Attributes	131	20	87	14	22	11	35	17	50	25

Fig. 6. Metadata analysis of corporate registers 21 to 30.

References

1. Braunschweig, K., Eberius, J., Thiele, M., Lehner, W.: The state of open data. Limits of current open data platforms. In: Proceedings of 21st World Wide Web Conference 2012, pp. 1–6. ACM (2012)

2. Manyika, J., Chui, M., Groves, P., Farrell, D., Van Kuiken, S., Doshi, E.A.: Open data: Unlocking innovation and performance with liquid information. McKinsey Global Institute (2013)
3. European Commission. Directorate General for the Information Society and Media, Capgemini Consulting, Intrasoft International, Fraunhofer Fokus, con.terra, Sogeti. Open Data Institute, Time.lex, University of Southampton.: Creating value through open data: study on the impact of re-use of public data resources. European Union (2015)
4. Zuiderwijk, A., Janssen, M., Choenni, S., Meijer, R., Alibaks, R.S.: Socio-technical Impediments of Open Data, vol. 10, p. 17 (2012)
5. Publications Office of the EU: Open data maturity report 2019 (2020)
6. Bizer, C., Heath, T., Berners-Lee, T.: Linked data - The story so far. Int. J. Semant. Web Inf. Syst. **5**, 1–22 (2009)
7. Puha, A., Rinciog, O., Posea, V.: Enhancing open data knowledge by extracting tabular data from text images. In: Proceedings of the 7th International Conference on Data Science, Technology and Applications, pp. 220–228. SCITEPRESS - Science and Technology Publications, Porto, Portugal (2018)
8. Davies, T., Walker, S., Rubenstien, M., Perini, F. (eds.): The state of open data: histories and horizons. In: African Minds and International Development Research Centre (2019)
9. Deloitte Analytics: Open Data – Driving Growth, Ingenuity and Innovation. https://www2.deloitte.com/content/dam/Deloitte/uk/Documents/deloitte-analytics/open-data-driving-gro wth-ingenuity-and-innovation.pdf. Accessed 09 July 2019
10. Dinter, B., Kollwitz, C.: Towards a framework for open data related innovation contests. In: Proceedings of the 2016 Pre-ICIS SIGDSA/IFIP WG8.3 Symposium: Innovations in Data Analytics, p. 13 (2016)
11. Oliveira, M.I.S., de Oliveira, L.E.R., Lima, G., de Fatima, A.B., Lóscio, B.F.: Enabling a unified view of open data catalogs. In: Proceedings of the 18th International Conference on Enterprise Information Systems, pp. 230–239. SCITEPRESS - Science and and Technology Publications, Rome, Italy (2016)
12. Janssen, M., Charalabidis, Y., Zuiderwijk, A.: Benefits, adoption barriers and myths of open data and open government. Inf. Syst. Manag. **29**, 258–268 (2012)
13. Martin, S., Foulonneau, M., Turki, S., Ihadjadene, M.: Risk analysis to overcome barriers to open data. Electron. J. e-Government **11**, 348–359 (2013)
14. Krasikov, P., Obrecht, T., Legner, C., Eurich, M.: Is open data ready for use by enterprises? Learnings from corporate registers. In: Proceedings of the 9th International Conference on Data Science, Technology and Applications, pp. 109–120. SCITEPRESS - Science and Technology Publications, Lieusaint - Paris, France (2020)
15. Varytimou, A., Loutas, N., Peristeras, V.: Towards linked open business registers: the application of the registered organization vocabulary in Greece. Int. J. Semant. Web Inf. Syst. **11**, 66–92 (2015)
16. Barry, E., Bannister, F.: Barriers to open data release: a view from the top. IP **19**, 129–152 (2014)
17. Conradie, P., Choenni, S.: On the barriers for local government releasing open data. Gov. Inf. Q. **31**, S10–S17 (2014)
18. Beno, M., Figl, K., Umbrich, J., Polleres, A.: Open data hopes and fears: determining the barriers of open data. In: 2017 Conference for E-Democracy and Open Government (CeDEM), pp. 69–81. IEEE, Krems, Austria (2017)
19. Vetrò, A., Canova, L., Torchiano, M., Minotas, C.O., Iemma, R., Morando, F.: Open data quality measurement framework: definition and application to Open Government Data. Gov. Inf. Q. **33**, 325–337 (2016)
20. Wang, R., Strong, D.: Beyond accuracy: what data quality means to data consumers. J. Manag. Inf. Syst. **12**, 5–33 (1996)

21. Osagie, E., Waqar, M., Adebayo, S., Stasiewicz, A., Porwol, L., Ojo, A.: Usability evaluation of an open data platform. In: Proceedings of the 18th Annual International Conference on Digital Government Research, pp. 495–504. ACM, New York, NY, USA (2017)
22. Bogdanović-Dinić, S., Veljković, N., Stoimenov, L.: How open are public government data? An assessment of seven open data portals. In: Rodríguez-Bolívar, M.P. (ed.) Measuring E-government Efficiency. PAIT, vol. 5, pp. 25–44. Springer, New York (2014). https://doi.org/10.1007/978-1-4614-9982-4_3
23. Open Government Working Group: The 8 Principles of Open Government Data. https://opengovdata.org/. Accessed 23 July 2019
24. Reiche, K.J., Höfig, E., Schieferdecker, I.: Assessment and visualization of metadata quality for open government data. In: Conference for E-Democracy and Open Government, pp. 335–346. Donau-Universität (2014)
25. Umbrich, J., Neumaier, S., Polleres, A.: Quality assessment and evolution of open data portals. In: 2015 3rd International Conference on Future Internet of Things and Cloud, pp. 404–411. IEEE, Rome, Italy (2015)
26. Neumaier, S., Umbrich, J., Polleres, A.: Automated quality assessment of metadata across open data portals. J. Data Inf. Qual. **8**, 1–29 (2016)
27. Máchová, R., Lněnička, M.: Evaluating the quality of open data portals on the national level. J. Theor. Appl. Electron. Commer. Res. **12**, 21–41 (2017)
28. Welle Donker, F., van Loenen, B.: How to assess the success of the open data ecosystem? Int. J. Digital Earth. **10**, 284–306 (2017)
29. Bicevskis, J., Bicevska, Z., Nikiforova, A., Oditis, I.: Data quality evaluation: a comparative analysis of company registers' open data in four European countries. In: Presented at the 2018 Federated Conference on Computer Science and Information Systems (2018)
30. Kubler, S., Robert, J., Neumaier, S., Umbrich, J., Le Traon, Y.: Comparison of metadata quality in open data portals using the Analytic Hierarchy Process. Gov. Inf. Q. **35**, 13–29 (2018)
31. Stróżyna, M., Eiden, G., Abramowicz, W., Filipiak, D., Małyszko, J., Węcel, K.: A framework for the quality-based selection and retrieval of open data - a use case from the maritime domain. Electron. Mark. **28**(2), 219–233 (2017). https://doi.org/10.1007/s12525-017-0277-y
32. Zhang, R., Indulska, M., Sadiq, S.: Discovering data quality problems: the case of repurposed data. Bus. Inf. Syst. Eng. **61**, 575–593 (2019)
33. Weerakkody, V., Irani, Z., Kapoor, K., Sivarajah, U., Dwivedi, Y.K.: Open data and its usability: an empirical view from the Citizen's perspective. Inf. Syst. Front. **19**(2), 285–300 (2016). https://doi.org/10.1007/s10796-016-9679-1
34. Directive 2012/17/EU of the European Parliament and of the Council of 13 June 2012 amending Council Directive 89/666/EEC and Directives 2005/56/EC and 2009/101/EC of the European Parliament and of the Council as regards the interconnection of central, commercial and companies registers Text with EEA relevance (2012)
35. Koznov, D., Andreeva, O., Nikula, U., Maglyas, A., Muromtsev, D., Radchenko, I.: A survey of open government data in Russian Federation: In: Proceedings of the 8th International Joint Conference on Knowledge Discovery, Knowledge Engineering and Knowledge Management. SCITEPRESS - Science and Technology Publications, Porto, Portugal, pp. 173–180 (2016)
36. Bryman, A., Bell, E.: Business Research Methods. Oxford University Press, Oxford (2007)
37. Creswell, J.W.: Research Design: Qualitative, Quantitative, and Mixed Methods Approaches. Sage Publications, Thousand Oaks (2009)
38. Krasikov, P., Harbich, M., Legner, C., Eurich, M.: Open data use cases: Framework for the generation and documentation of open data use cases (2019). https://www.cc-cdq.ch/system/files/Open_data_use_cases_working_report_2019.pdf
39. GLEIF: Registration Authorities List. https://www.gleif.org/en/about-lei/code-lists/gleif-registration-authorities-list. Accessed 26 Oct 2020

40. List of company, tax and statistical business registers (2020). https://en.wikipedia.org/w/index.php?title=List_of_company,_tax_and_statistical_business_registers&oldid=985324530
41. OpenDataBarometer, World Wide Web Foundation: Open Data Barometer. https://opendatabarometer.org/?_year=2017&indicator=ODB. Accessed 26 Oct 2020
42. Global Open Data Index: Company Register. https://index.okfn.org/dataset/companies/. Accessed 26 Oct 2020
43. OpenCorporates: Open Company Data Index. http://registries.opencorporates.com/. Accessed 27 Oct 2020
44. GLEIF: Accreditation Process. https://www.gleif.org/en/about-lei/gleif-accreditation-of-lei-issuers/accreditation-process. Accessed 16 Nov 2019
45. Kampars, J., Zdravkovic, J., Stirna, J., Grabis, J.: Extending organizational capabilities with Open Data to support sustainable and dynamic business ecosystems. Softw. Syst. Model. 19(2), 371–398 (2019). https://doi.org/10.1007/s10270-019-00756-7
46. euBusinessGraph: Ontology for Company Data. https://www.eubusinessgraph.eu/eubusinessgraph-ontology-for-company-data/. Accessed 15 Nov 2019

A Data Science Approach to Explain a Complex Team Ball Game

Friedemann Schwenkreis

DHBW Stuttgart, Paulinenstr. 50, 70565 Stuttgart, Germany
`friedemann.schwenkreis@dhbw-stuttgart.de`

Abstract. Only a few attempts have been made to come up with models to explain the mechanisms of team handball based on measured indicators. CoCoAnDa is a project located at the Baden-Wuerttemberg Cooperative State University that addresses this gap. This paper will describe the results of the analysis of available data collected as part of the match organization of matches of the first and second German team handball league, HBL. Furthermore, the data of more than 170 games of national teams, the first league, and the third league have been manually collected using the apps developed on behalf of the CoCoAnDa project. We will show the structure of the data and the techniques used to extract knowledge regarding the "mechanics" of the game.

Keywords: Information model · Team handball · Statistics · Applied data science

1 Introduction

As described in [1], team handball is a complex team sport that is still "dominated" by the intuition of coaches. Furthermore, due to the complexity of the game there exists no model that explains the game so far, which is also the reason for the absence of successful computer games covering that sport.

The project CoCoAnDa [2] has started in 2016 to fill this gap by using methods of data science to extract the "patterns of team handball". However, there was not enough data available and it has taken three years to build tools that allowed to collect enough data for the application of data science methods. In this article we will present our approach for the analysis and some insights which have been discovered as part of the project.

In the following we will not present any details regarding the sport itself. Readers are referred to [1] for a brief introduction and [3] for the official game rules. Section 2 describes the sources of the data that were used for the analysis. In Sect. 3 the "process" of data understanding is introduced. It is of particular importance because it will also explain the mapping of application-level questions onto the analysis level. Section 4 will present insights based on the application of statistical methods, while Sect. 5 will focus on the application of data mining methods. The article will be concluded by Sect. 6 containing a summary and an outlook on future work.

© Springer Nature Switzerland AG 2021
S. Hammoudi et al. (Eds.): DATA 2020, CCIS 1446, pp. 101–114, 2021.
https://doi.org/10.1007/978-3-030-83014-4_5

In comparison to [1], this article will provide a detailed view of the data that was used for the analysis. Furthermore, details regarding analysis results will be explained, that have only been introduced briefly in the previously mentioned paper.

2 Data Collection

Team handball is a very traditional sport and the regulations have been very restrictive until recently. For instance, the first German league [4] waited until the season 2019/2020 to automatically collect data using sensors, and the International Handball Federation just recently decided to allow to use information from outside the field of play for coaching purposes during a match. Hence, there is not much data available about team handball matches. Even worse, the available data that has been collected in the past, like data that has been collected by Sportradar [5] for betting purposes, do not have the needed quality for in-depth analysis in the context of research projects. For instance, simple checks for the balanced number of attacks during a match reveal significant discrepancies. Furthermore, there are errors and missing data, for example due to network outages during the recording. Consequently, the CoCoAnDa project [2] had to develop its own data gathering mechanisms first, in order to collect enough data with sufficient quality as a basis for applying analytics.

2.1 Specialized Mobile Apps for Data Collection

One of the major challenges to collect data in case of team handball are the limited budgets of the teams (even in the first league). When looking at options to collect data during matches, the teams usually need solutions that can be used when playing at home as well as abroad. Thus, fixed solutions in the arenas do only make sense if all teams of a league agree to equip their sports hall with that solution and to share the collected data. In general, we are still far from such a uniform infrastructure (and its use) in the halls. Thus, CoCoAnDa decided to build mobile apps that support the manual collection of information which can be digitally processed later. Currently, we use two apps to collect information and one app to provide a near real-time visualization to the coaches.

The Scouting App. The so-called Scouting App (see Fig. 1) was developed to record the team handball specific events during a match. It has been developed with a main emphasis on the efficient recording of events with a minimum risk of errors. The app is based on the Ionic™ framework [6], runs on Android™ tablets, and allows to record the following events:

- Attempts to score with their location, involved players and outcome.
- Scoring goals including the targeted area of the goal
- Technical errors including the involved players.
- Sanctioned fouls and penalties including the involved players (as well as temporary suspensions).
- Saves including the targeted area of the goal and misses.

- Blocked attempts including the involved player.
- Replacing the goalkeeper by an additional field player.

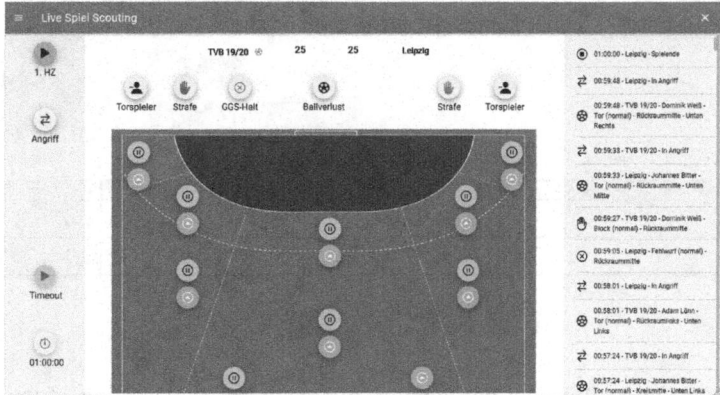

Fig. 1. The Scouting App.

The Scouting App is installed on a scouting tablet and is a very lightweight and highly portable solution [7]. It can be used without any support of the sport halls of a match, even when it is used in combination with the near real-time monitoring app: The Coaching App.

Using the Scouting App, we have recorded the game events of 89 first league matches and 52 matches of the 3rd and the 4th league, the national women's team, and the national junior teams.

The PassCounter App. The PassCounter App (see Fig. 2) is an additional stand-alone app that has been developed to "record" a team handball match based on passes rather than time and game events. Since more than 1500 passes happen during the 60 min of a team handball match, the PassCounter App has been particularly designed to support the efficient recording of passes and to cope with errors.

With the PassCounter App we record the number of passes, the number of fouls, and the number of technical errors during an attack as well as misses. Since the recording person needs to react very fast to events on the field, there is a high probability of errors. Two features help to minimize the number of errors in the result generated by the PassCounter App:

- A large button for recording passes.
- An Undo button to compensate for errors.

Up to this point we have recorded the information of 145 first league matches and of 22 matches of lower leagues, the women's national team and the EHF Champions League using the PassCounter App.

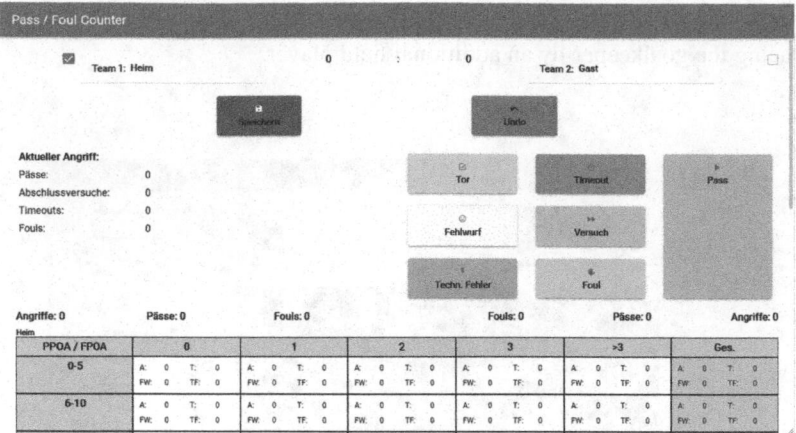

Fig. 2. The PassCounter App.

Sensor-Based Data. With the introduction of sensor-based recording of the players' location in the first league, we have now access to the precise positions of players and their movement traces (with a time resolution of 20 positions per second). This will allow us to automatically detect tactics and trigger actions in the future [8], and by combining this information with the collected game events we will be able to analyze the success of certain tactics. furthermore, we can calculate a sophisticated player contribution index based on the position data [9]. However, this is just at its beginning and we cannot present results, yet.

2.2 Publicly Available Data

As mentioned before, there is some publicly available data, that is collected by the German Bundesliga [4]. Although its overall quality is questionable (e.g., we detected huge differences in the number of attacks per team in a single match), some information can still be used, as for example the sequence of scored goals. Since the HBL cooperates with the CoCoAnDa project, we have received the collected data of almost four seasons of the first (1190 matches) and the second (1559 matches) German team handball leagues.

3 Data Understanding

3.1 Match Data

All sources that were used to collect data create so-called event data. Event data represents information regarding a particular event during a match. Basically, an event can be described by the time when it occurred, the location where it occurred, the type of event that occurred and the participating or affected players. Additionally, events of a team handball match happen in a context. In the context different types of attacks are differentiated (for instance fast breaks versus positional attacks), and the defense performance is provided (for instance a free attempt versus an attempt with a very good defense). The event sources differ regarding the provided event types and the supported context information.

It might be trivial but important to keep in mind that a single event is not sufficient to "explain" a team handball match. It is always an aggregated set of events that needs to be considered. While recording the events in matches of the season 2019 and 2020, approximately 260 events have been recorded per match. This is not a huge number from a computer science perspective, but a from a human perspective. Humans, and particularly team handball coaches, are overwhelmed with remembering or even processing these events.

3.2 Data on Passes, Fouls, and (Non-)Success

Rather than just focusing on the sequence of events in game, we extended our work by a more attack-oriented view. Since a team handball match consists of more than 100 attacks, the probability of attack-success (i.e., scoring a goal) is highly correlated with winning the game.

Thus, we investigated the properties of attacks by collecting the detail data using the PassCounter App in addition to the event data collected by the Scouting App. Up to now, the pass data of 168 matches of the first league have been recorded (plus 20 other matches). This allows first insights based on 16,651 attacks consisting of approximately 222,000 passes and 9,470 sanctioned fouls of the first league, and 2,540 attacks of the other matches consisting of approximately 30,000 passes and 1,280 sanctioned fouls.

Since this is work that just has recently been started, the detailed results have not been verified yet, due to the relatively small amount of data (at the point in time this paper was written). The recently introduced sensors in the HBL [10] will help to collect pass data automatically if the match balls are equipped with the sensors in addition to the players. However, the quality of that recording needs to be proven first, for instance, based on the data that we collect using the PassCounter App.

3.3 Decision Support Versus Explanation

Tightly coupled with data understanding is to understand the questions of the application level that we want to answer with data science [11]. In case of team handball two categories of questions need to be distinguished:

1. Questions that need to be answered to understand team handball in general.
2. Questions that need to be answered in order to win a match.

While the first category is interesting for sport sciences, education and probably team development, the latter category is important for coaches during a match. A simple example question of the second category is "Will we win?". As the question indicates, time is an important factor in this case. If we answer the question after the match, it will not help the coach anymore (from the point of view of category 2 questions). If we can explain the answer that we give after the match, then the coach can at least derive some helpful insights, with respect to future matches, from the explanation.

Since our project aims to support coaches during matches, it is crucial to derive insights at the earliest possible point in time of match. Thus, we had to introduce a special approach to process our data.

3.4 The Goal Clock

The concept of time is simple and somehow complicated. It is simple because everyone understands it but complicated because its granularity arbitrary. Given our application area we have 3600 s but only around 260 events. Even worse, trying to help coaches based on rules that are just valid in a particular second will not really help. Minutes on the other are too coarse grained, given that we observe more than 4 events per minute.

As a solution, an application specific clock has been introduced. It ticks whenever the nth goal is scored first (the so-called *goal clock tick* or *GCT*). To give some examples:

- When a team scores the first goal the clock ticks the first time: 1:0 or 0:1 (GCT 1).
- Whenever a goal is scored and the maximum of the number of goals of the two teams changes, then the clock ticks again:
  1:1 – clock does not tick; 1:2 – clock ticks the second time (GCT 2); 1:3 clock ticks the third time (GCT 3); 2:3 – clock does not tick.

Mathematically this might seem somehow complicated as well, but for coaches as well as handball players it is very easy to observe the goal clock. Furthermore, a "responsible" team can be associated with goal clock ticks: the team that has caused the goal clock to tick.

3.5 The Team Match View Record

There are some data science or data mining methods that can directly process event streams, but these methods do either not allow to process complex events, or they recognize patterns without providing an explanation which allows to derive actions. Hence, the event streams are transformed into a record format that represents the status of a match at the time of the last event of the transformed stream from the point of view of one team.

A team match view consists currently of 27 team performance related attributes that are calculated from the event stream for each team which are all of numeric type. Thus, the overall match status is described by the records of the two teams. For instance, the team match view consists of the number of scored goals, the number of turnovers and such.

4   Advanced Statistics

4.1   Basic Observations

According to our observations, a match of the first German league consists in average of approximately 49 (between 40 and 60) attacks per team. Each team performs 40 attempts, out of which 14 (between 5 and 22) are misses or opponent saves and 26 (between 15 and 40) result in goals. Thus, the defense effectiveness is almost identical with the goalkeeper effectiveness. In average the goalkeepers have approximately 9 saves (between 3 and 19) per game, which means that 5 of the 14 misses are attempts that effectively miss the goal. In average, 10 (between 3 and 16) attacks are finished with a technical error. Blocked attempts ending an attack are rare in matches and in average there is a single blocked ball in two games.

From the collected pass data of the HBL it can be derived that a match consists in average of approximately 1,300 passes and 56 sanctioned fouls (which is about 1 sanctioned foul every second attack). In terms of relative indicators, an average team of the HBL has (you might want to check [1] for a definition of the performance indicators):

- An attack effectiveness of approximately 53% and a zone independent attempt effectiveness of approximately 65%.
- A technical error rate of approximately 20%.
- A goalkeeper effectiveness of approximately 23%.

4.2   General Properties of Team Handball

The Baseline. When applying predictive modelling there needs to be a baseline regarding probabilities in order to evaluate the quality of results. A very simple starting point is to look at the random case first. in case of matches that would correspond with throwing a coin to determine the winner of the match- which means that the probability of winning a match is 50% in the pure random case (ignoring ties).

A typical question in case of team ball sports is whether there is a significant advantage of playing at home rather than playing abroad. In case of our observation there is an advantage of being the home team: In approximately 73% of the cases the home team does not lose.

Another question that came up was, whether the outcome of a match can be derived from the current rank of the teams in the league. It turned out that having a better or equal rank than the opponent team (before the match) results in a 71% "probability" of not losing the game.

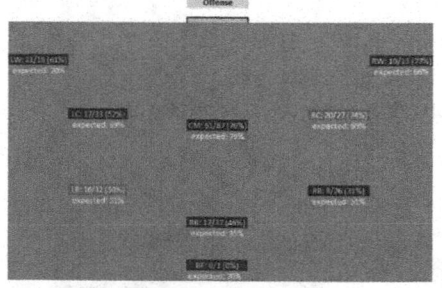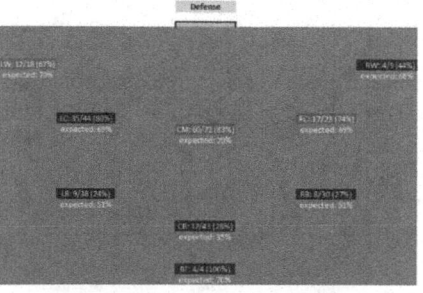

Fig. 3. Field zone specific attempt effectivity.

The first three baseline "predictions" are completely independent from the actual match or any property of the players. Thus, they cannot be consciously influenced by the coaches or the players. Finally, we looked at the halftime results and whether the outcome of the match can be derived from them. We found, that in 72% the cases, a team does not lose, if the team was not behind at halftime. This means that, if your team is behind at halftime, there is only a 28% chance that your team will not be losing in the end.

Zone-Specific Insights. Collecting match information using the Scouting App has increased the data quality and enhanced the information with additional data compared to the HBL data. based on the attack information of 384 team specific views of matches (correspond with 192 matches), we were able to analyze 13,656 attempts.

According to our observations, an average team in the first German league has an attempt effectiveness of approximately 42% from the far distance (9 m and beyond), a near-zone attempt effectiveness of approximately 75%, and an attempt effectiveness from the wing positions of approximately 66%, which adds up to an overall attempt effectiveness of 58%.

Overall, goalkeepers reach in average approximately an effectiveness of 49% from the far zone, 20% from the near zone and 28% from the wings (which adds up to 25% in total).

We have compared these numbers with indicators collected during 52 games of a team playing 3rd league in one season and 4th league in a second season. While the lower leagues have a 4% higher attempt effectiveness from the far zone, and similar effectiveness from the near zone, the attempt effectiveness from the wings is 6% lower. The overall effectiveness is 57%. The zone-specific goalkeeper effectiveness numbers in the lower leagues are 7% lower regarding the far zone, similar in the near zone and 12% better from the wings.

Figure 3 shows an example of how we use these numbers as expected performance in our visualizations of the performance of a team. The coloring of the fields with the current values show whether the team performs in the expected range or whether it is under- or overperforming.

Goal Area Specific Insights. The Scouting App has been extended with the ability to record the goal area that has been targeted by an attempt which reaches the goal. The goal has been divided into nine areas for that purpose (see Fig. 4).

- Three areas in the top section: top left, top mid, and top right
- Three areas in the middle section: mid left, mid mid, mid right
- Three areas in the bottom section: bottom left, bottom right, bottom right

Attempts			Defended		
28/31(90%)	6/11(55%)	14/19(74%)	8/27(30%)	8/17(47%)	8/27(30%)
exp.: 83%	exp.: 64%	exp.: 79%	exp.: 17%	exp.: 36%	exp.: 21%
9/16(56%)	1/8(13%)	9/15(60%)	12/26(46%)	3/5(60%)	12/26(46%)
exp.: 42%	exp.: 30%	exp.: 53%	exp.: 58%	exp.: 70%	exp.: 47%
50/68(74%)	8/17(47%)	42/56(75%)	16/44(36%)	7/29(24%)	16/44(36%)
exp.: 77%	exp.: 71%	exp.: 81%	exp.: 23%	exp.: 29%	exp.: 19%

Fig. 4. Attempt and goalkeeper performance. (Color figure online)

Whenever a goal is scored or a save happens, the targeted goal area is recorded from the attacker's point of view. Thus, the zones are mirrored from a goalkeeper's perspective. Furthermore, we do not actually record the goal area where the ball passes the goal line but rather the area where the ball passes the goalkeeper or where the goalkeeper saves the ball. Hence, the collected information is intended to answer questions like "Where are the strong/weak areas of a goalkeeper?", "Is there an area which should be better covered by the blocking players to help the goalkeeper?", or "Has an attacker a certain "sweet area" when attempting?".

The recording of the goal areas in case of saves by goalkeepers has been added rather recently. Thus, we currently have only data of 92 HBL games with 7105 attempts. Most attempts are targeted at the bottom section of the goal (approximately 52%). Less than a quarter of the attempts (22%) are targeted at the top section, even though the summarized attempt effectiveness numbers are very similar (77% at the bottom and 77% at the top respectively). Only about one fifth of the attempts are targeted at the middle section, which shows a significantly lower attempt effectiveness of only 44%. The goalkeeper's effectiveness can simply be calculated by subtracting the attempt effectiveness from 100%.

Again, the numbers have been compared to the data collected in the 4th league. We were able to use 23 matches) including 2,015 attempts. The distribution of the attempts across goal areas is almost the same as in case of the HBL (with a maximum difference of 2% in each section). However, in case of the lower league we have a lower attempt effectiveness of 74% in the top section, a significantly higher effectiveness of 59% in the middle section, and 74% in the bottom section.

As in case of the field zones, the numbers are used to create colored visualizations of the attempt performance and the goalkeeper's performance, respectively. Figure 4 shows an example visualization of a performance summary of 6 matches of a team of the HBL. The blue color indicates a "normal" performance, while the orange color indicates a performance below the expected values. Green indicates a performance that is better than the expected number.

4.3 Using the Goal Clock

While considering the question whether the outcome of a match can be predicted significantly before the end of a match based on the team's performance, we looked at the most prominent indicator: the number of goals. several hypotheses have been investigated and one showed a surprising result: "The team that is associated with the nth goal clock tick, will not lose the match".

We compared the "prediction quality" of different GCTs (the n) ranging from 10 up to 28 based on 98 matches of the first league. Below the investigated range, the accuracy decreases. Above the GCT 24 the accuracy does also decrease because the number of matches in which less than the required number of goals are scored, increases (we have in average of approximately 25 goals per match and team in the set of observed matches).

Two results are particularly interesting. There is a peak (local maximum) around GCT 16 (92.9%) after which the accuracy decreases. Furthermore, there is a second peak (the global maximum) around GCT 20 and GCT 21 (95.9%).

We have verified these patterns with the data from 52 matches of the lower leagues. We have found the same two peaks, the first one at GCT 16 (85.4%) and the second one at GCT 26 (100%). However, the average number of goals per match is significantly higher (approx. 29) compared to the matches of the first league.

Since the publicly available HBL data has sufficient quality regarding the sequence of goals, we also verified the "two peak finding" using long-term data (almost 4 seasons) of 1190 first league matches and of 1559 second league matches. The two peaks do not exist in long-term data. However, at GCT 16 we find an accuracy of 86.6% in the first league and 83.2% in the second league. The maximum accuracy is at GCT 21 in the first league (91.3%) and GCT 22 in the second league (88.9%). If we just look at the 306 matches of the last season of the first league, we find the two peaks at GCT 17 (89.5%) and at GCT 20 (91.5%). Based on 379 second league matches of the last season we found the first peak at GCT 16 (85%) and the maximum at GCT 21 (91%).

5 Data Mining

5.1 Applying Classification

The prediction of the winner of matches is a typical classification task [11]. The business questions "behind" the classification is: "Which (minimal) combination of indicators that we measure can be used to predict the outcome of a match". Since we are measuring the indicators while the match is played, and we want to have an indication during the match whether we need to intervene, it is useless to train models using the absolute numbers of finished matches.

Data Mining and its methods are completely new to team handball coaches. Thus, it is very important that the results can be explained in terms which can be understood by the coaches. That is why we started by using tree classification as our data mining method. Tree classification models can be explained as a set of rules based on the measured indicators, which makes them easily understandable.

Regarding the computation parameters, we found that the information gain criterion was the best split criterion and using pruning and pre-pruning avoids overfitting of the model (while reducing the prediction accuracy just a bit). The (CART-)tree model we have found has a prediction accuracy (of the training data) of approximately 94% and seems to be a logical extension of the basic observations:

If the attempt effectiveness is 65% or better, and the defense effectiveness is 26% or better, and the penalty (seven meter) ratio is higher than 56% the game will be won. Even if the penalty ratio is lower, this can be compensated with faster attacks (average attack time less than 36 s).

- If our attempt effectiveness is 65% or better, but our defense effectiveness is less than 26%, the low defense effectiveness can be compensated by a very high attempt effectiveness (greater than 77%).
- If the attempt effectiveness is less than 65%, we can compensate for that by a defense effectiveness of 34% or higher. Otherwise, it is likely that we will lose the game.

As an alternative to the tree classification method, we have used the support vector machines (SVMs) technique [12]. Based on the radial kernel the resulting model reached a prediction accuracy (of the training data) of approximately 99%. Unfortunately, SVM models cannot be described by a simple set of rules as in case of the tree classifier. SVM models are partially described in terms of weights of the measured indicators. The basic insight is slightly different compared to the tree classification model:

- The defense effectiveness is most important, then attempt effectiveness follows and the goalkeeper effectiveness is ranked third in terms of their weight.
- With a significant distance, the previous indicators are followed by the penalty success ratio and the fast break success ratio.
- Finally, it is beneficial to have a low average attack time.

Besides trying to find a combination of indicators that can be used to predict the outcome of matches, we also looked at further questions:

- "Can we predict the outcome of a game based on the zone-specific attempt effectiveness?"
  No significant patterns were found while analyzing the zone-specific effectiveness. It seems that the zone-specific effectiveness of the teams varies too much.
- "Can we predict the final rank class of a team after a season based on the performance indicators of a team?"
  The rank class of a team splits the league table into multiple sections like "champions league", "EHF cup", "mid-range", and "declassification range".

Unfortunately, we do not have enough data with sufficient quality to derive accurate patterns for these questions at this point.

5.2   Using Co-occurrence Grouping

Motivation. Given that our main objective is to help coaches with patterns that can be directly used to support decisions regarding actions during matches, the overall model to predict the outcome of games in all cases is not our main focus [13]. We rather want to identify patterns with a high confidence, even if they are not observed in very many matches. Tree classification models are only of limited value because they optimize on a model with a single check (the root in the tree) that is contained in all the rules that are expressed by the tree model. However, there are patterns with a high confidence which do not contain this root check which will not find, when using tree classification.

Since we need the explainable rules in order to able translate the rules into actions of a coach, while avoiding the single root check problem, co-occurrence grouping was identified as an alternative. Basically, co-occurrence grouping, also called "mining for association rules" [14], generates all rules and filters the "interesting" rules based on selectable criteria. In case of the analysis of match data for coaches the most important selection criterion is the confidence while the support of a rule is secondary.

Rules and the Clock. An important criterion to identify "interesting" rules is the time factor. As introduced in Sect. 3, rules identified based on the data of the final goal clock tick do not really help in our context, because no actions can be applied anymore at the point in time when the rule is detected. Furthermore, matches do differ in terms of their final goal clock tick. however, rules "positively developing in confidence over time" are very interesting, because they reflect a "development" in a match that is likely to become a fact in the end.

Besides extracting rules based on the final match status, two goal clock ticks were identified to be most interesting to extract the rules from the match status data: GCT 14 GCT 17, and GCT 22. GCT 17 and GCT 22 are used because of the peaks described in Sect. 3.4 and it was assumed that there will be rules found that have a local confidence optimum. GCT 14 is of specific interest, because it is before or around the halftime break. It allows coaches to communicate decisions on actions that have been derived from recognized patterns.

Data Preparation. Implementations of algorithms to search for association rules are based on so-called transaction data and itemsets [14]. This means that the match status data needs to be converted such that it matches the concept of a set of items that is contained in a transaction. The transaction in our case are the matches but the attributes in a match status correspond with the "number of" the specific item that is represented by an attribute (like the number goals, where goal would be the item). Hence, from an application's perspective the occurrence of an item per se is not the important information but the difference of the number of items between the two teams.

Consequently, the two team match views have been aggregated to a differential match status. This means, that the difference between the attribute values of each attribute is calculated. Furthermore, we categorized the difference in "has more" or not in order to map the data onto the concept of "an item is contained in a transaction or not". We know that this simple approach of differentiating positive and other values might be an oversimplification, but it leads to rules that are easy to understand and recognize by coaches. It will be further investigated whether there is a better approach for the categorization of attribute value differences.

Example Rules. The co-occurrence grouping reveals many rules, and the evaluation of the rules is ongoing. Furthermore, there is still no agreement on the DHB level whether and how much details of the insights should be disclosed. However, there are some results which are interesting examples:

- The team that does not lead will not win (trivial at the end of the match):
  Confidence: End: 100%, GCT 22: 91,6% GCT 17: 82,2%, GCT 14: 81,5%.
  Interpretation: If your team is not associated with GCT 14, then you will probably not win the match.
- The team with more misses will not win:
  Confidence: End: 86,4%, GCT 22: 82,1%, GCT 17: 79,9%, GCT 14: 78,3%.
  Interpretation: If your attempt quality is worse than your opponent's, then you will probably not win the match.

- The team with more misses and more technical errors will not win:
  Confidence: End: 100%, GCT 22: 100%, GCT 17: 91,3%, GCT 14: 90%.
  Interpretation: If your attempt quality is worse than your opponent's and you are losing the ball before attempting more often than the opponent, then you will definitely not win the match.
- The team associated with GCT n and with less passes (see Sect. 3.2) will not lose:
  Confidence: End: 100%, GCT 22: 95,4%, GCT 17: 89,5%, GCT 14: 88,6%.
  Interpretation: If you are in the lead and you have played less passes than the opponent, you are likely to win.

These are all examples for "evolving" rules that are perceived as helpful by coaches.

6 Conclusions

This article reflects the results of approximately 3 years of work. Since there was almost no detailed data of team handball of sufficient quality when the CoCoAnDa project started, mobile apps had to be developed first to generate the data for the later analysis. We are still far from being able to "fully decrypt the DNA of a team handball match", but we found some first patterns and we can explain some characterizing properties of the game. Particularly, we can explain the differences to other games like soccer and why models that have been developed in the context of soccer cannot be applied in case of team handball.

Some coaches of the HBL already use the findings presented in this paper to evaluate the performance of their team and to decide on the need for actions. The Coaching App provides a feature that allows to use the numbers as thresholds which drive the coloring of the graphical representation of the collected data. For instance, if the goalkeeper's effectiveness is significantly below the average of the league, then the indicator is colored in red. Furthermore, we do also provide *team-specific* effectiveness numbers derived from the historical data of the team.

The actual challenge of team handball is the fact that the game is a multi-dimensional problem. All attempts to sufficiently explain the game based on one or two dimensions have proven to be inaccurate. With the availability of multi-dimensional data mining analytics, we now have a chance to bring the insights to the next level, meaning to identify the relevant dimensions that need to be observed.

We will continue to interpret and evaluate the patterns found so far. In particular, the project continues to collect data which is then used to extract rules again. This will be brought to the next stage when automatically recorded position data of players and the ball becomes available, which will then allow to detect tactics [8]. This type of information will significantly enhance the match view data we have today.

Acknowledgements. We would like to thank the DHB for the general support of the project and the DHL for sharing their data. Furthermore, we would like to thank the collaborating teams for their support of the project: the German National teams, MadDogs TSV Neuhausen, Wild Boys TVB Stuttgart, Frisch Auf! Göppingen, SG BBM Bietigheim-Bissingen, and HBW Balingen-Weilstetten. Furthermore, we would like to express our appreciation of the time and expertise contributed by the helping hands who scouted matches (in alphabetical order): Jelena Braun, Stefanie Freytag, Heiko Ruess, Matthias Trautvetter, and Susan Zsoter.

References

1. Schwenkreis, F., Nothdurft, E.: Applied data science: an approach to explain a complex team ball game. In: Proceedings of the 9th International Conference on Data Science, Technology and Applications, DATA 2020, Lieusaint, Paris (2020)
2. Schwenkreis, F.: Coaching support by collecting and analyzing data (CoCoAnDa). In: Opportunities and Challenges for European Projects. Scitepress, pp. 220–225 (2019)
3. IHF- International Handball Federation, IX. Rules of the Game (2016). http://www.ihf.info/files/Uploads/NewsAttachments/0_New-Rules%20of%20the%20Game_GB.pdf
4. HBL: Statistics of the first German team handball league (LiquiMoly HBL) (2019). https://www.liquimoly-hbl.de/en/
5. Sportradar: Handball Scout Admin (HAS) Manual, Sportradar AG (2015)
6. Ionic: What is Ionic Framework (2019). https://ionicframework.com/docs/intro. Zugriff am 18 Nov 2019
7. Schwenkreis, F.: A three component approach to support team handball coaches. In: 23rd Annual Congress of the European College of Sport Science, Dublin (2018)
8. Schwenkreis, F.: An approach to use deep learning to automatically recognize team tactics in team ball games. In: Proceedings of the 7th Conference on Data Science, Technology and Applications, Porto (2018)
9. Schwenkreis, F.: A graded concept of an information model for evaluating performance in team handball. In: Proceedings of the 8th Conference on Data Science, Technology and Applications, Prag (2019)
10. Kinexon: Real-time Performance Analytics, Kinexon (2017)
11. Provost, F., Fawcett, T.: Data Science for Business. O'Reilly and Associates, Sebastopol, CA (2013)
12. Steinwart, I., Christmann, A.: Support Vector Machines. Springer, New York (2008). https://doi.org/10.1007/978-0-387-77242-4
13. Schwenkreis, F.: Why the concept of shopping baskets helps to analyze team-handball. In: Proceedings of the 2020 International Conference on Intelligent Data Science Technologies and Applications (IDSTA), Valencia (2020)
14. Agrawal, R., Srikant, R.: Fast algorithms for mining association rules. In: Proceedings of the 20th VLDB Conference, Santiago, Chile (1994)

Intelligent Public Procurement Monitoring System Powered by Text Mining and Balanced Indicators

Nikola Modrušan[1] (ID), Leo Mršić[2]([✉]) (ID), and Kornelije Rabuzin[3]([✉]) (ID)

[1] Faculty for Information Studies in Novo Mesto, Ljubljanska cesta 31A, Novo Mesto, Slovenia
[2] Algebra University College, Ilica 242, Zagreb, Croatia
`leo.mrsic@algebra.hr`
[3] Faculty of Organization and Informatics, University of Zagreb, Pavlinska 2, Varaždin, Croatia
`krabuzin@foi.hr`

Abstract. Optimising the public procurement process through digitalisation has many benefits. In this regard, text mining and emerging technologies used to create intelligent indicators could potentially be applied throughout the public procurement process. Research is showing that these technologies are not yet firmly established in the public procurement process. However, as presented in this paper, they have the potential to transform this process in various ways, and there is a considerable scope as to how this could be achieved. This paper provides insight into the research and corresponding activities of research teams to establish a prototype of a national public procurement monitoring system that can be used as support for policy makers and for educational purposes, to provide best practices, and/or to improve transparency. As part of our research, we created a system that uses text mining techniques to analyse collected data for more than 60.000 cases over 5 years and use that data sample to identify a total of 56 indicator rules. As addition, lessons learned during the research process were used to propose phase-based development system guidelines and infrastructure planning and management. In the final part, several interesting results are presented as showcases that represent potential usability and the ease of use of the system.

Keywords: Mining · Natural language · Processing · Rule based decision · Knowledge discovery · Public procurement

1 Introduction

The purpose of this paper is to describe an intelligent public procurement monitoring system that allows the detection of anomalies based on indicators obtained by extraction and transformation of data from electronic advertisements further enriched with data from various external sources. The current version is an extended version of the original paper published in the Data 2020 conference [27]. The authors focused their initial research on finding ways to identify anomalies in the public procurement process, especially by using advanced data mining methods over public tender documentation

© Springer Nature Switzerland AG 2021
S. Hammoudi et al. (Eds.): DATA 2020, CCIS 1446, pp. 115–133, 2021.
https://doi.org/10.1007/978-3-030-83014-4_6

content, in which the evaluation criteria are stated and other data that can be found in the public procurement ecosystem as input data. For this purpose, the whole text was extracted, and an improved version of the invention of specific text segments was made [27, 30]. "A model that includes the aforementioned components uses the most common text classification algorithms for the purpose of prediction: naive Bayes, Logistic regression and Support vector machines" [30]. In the mentioned studies, the authors showed that based on the extracted and processed tender documentation context, it is possible to find those public procurement processes that are suspicious. Throughout the process, since we entered in the Big Data area, the problem of creating a system that will be able to process this amount of data and algorithms was raised.

The improvement and the contribution of this extended version is related to the development of an intelligent system that uses text mining techniques and previous study results to analyze collected data and use it to identify total of 56 indicator rules. In addition, the lessons learned during the research process were used to propose a phase-based development system, guidelines, infrastructure planning and management. Moreover, the study focused on detecting the mentioned suspicious tenders over public procurement documentation and presents one part of a robust system that was made during our inquiry.

Public procurement fraud presents a huge problem worldwide. A 2020 study by the Association of Certified Fraud Examiners published a Report on Professional Fraud and Abuse with the results of an analysis of 2,504 cases of professional fraud that occurred in 125 countries worldwide [30]. The most represented sectors among the audited cases include banking and financial services, public administration, and manufacturing. It has been observed that the implementation of fraud detection controls correlates with a reduction in losses and a shortening of fraud detection time. The study stated that companies lose an average of 5% of annual revenue because they do not control potential anomalies (fraud). The reason for such high losses lies in the assessment that, depending on the type of fraud, it takes 14 months on average for fraud to be detected, and an audit reveals only a small fraction of the fraud. In the context of the Republic of Croatia, the value equivalent of the mentioned 5% is around HRK 2.7 billion (2019). The descriptions used in this paper relating to public procurement procedures and intelligent monitoring of these procedures aim to significantly reduce losses due to the current lack of a proactive fraud detection system, both by direct warning of anomalies in real time and by preventive action showing that the public procurement system is continuously and automatically monitored. Electronic public procurement (e-procurement) is a comprehensive name for a public procurement system based on the use of electronic means of communication in public procurement procedures and includes the introduction of electronic tools to support the various stages of the public procurement process.

The central entity of public procurement in the Republic of Croatia is the Electronic Public Procurement Notice. The intelligent public procurement monitoring system is a natural upgrade of the system that adds the functionality of proactive anomaly identification to the electronic advertisement. During the preparation of this study, the current practice was reviewed, the solutions created within the EU were mentioned and described, and public procurement platforms in other countries whose experiences are comparable to those of the Republic of Croatia were analyzed. In particular, the practices of Slovakia, Hungary and Slovenia were analyzed, with the aim of using the current practice for better recommendations in the construction of the system in the Republic of Croatia. According to the European Commission, the Republic of Croatia is among the countries with a high degree of risk of corruption in the public procurement process [31]. So far, a number of proposals and solutions have been developed that aim to raise the quality of procedures such as online catalogues of domestic products to help domestic public procurement companies organized by the Croatian Chamber of Commerce and analysis of selection criteria to introduce the "highest value for money" approach in recent years. Despite to that, it is necessary to improve the supervision during the procedure and during the investment, which often takes too long. A case-based intelligent and automated system of supervision over public procurement procedures is a quality and modern basis that can greatly contribute to reducing the stated risks and efficiency of the described procedures [2].

2 Literature Overview

Detecting quality and essential information is a crucial part of the process in any data analysis, especially when it comes to complex models [27]. Very often, data is presented in an unstructured format, making it challenging to find mechanisms and technology to process this data, especially if an automated process is our goal. There are a different domains, such as web content, reports, public procurement contracts, procedures or entire procurement processes where the data can be found [1, 3, 5–9, 40]. To reduce corruption, but also to help and support government organizations in detecting anomalies in public procurement, a decision support system that works on more than 200 different algorithms was made [2, 35]. What is important to emphasize is that those algorithms take data from different sources and store it in data lakes. Since there are millions of records and 200 algorithms based on data mining, clustering algorithms, anomaly detection, and risk ranking that must be executed, the question of system architecture and using of Big Data technology arises [39]. The challenge is certainly to define and discover which technology and approach to use when digitizing the public procurement process. Thus, a survey was conducted in Nigeria, and a framework was built to define "grey areas that exist in the public procurement process with a view to identifying the appropriate digital solutions available in e-Procurement technologies" [10, 38].

According to a World Bank study there are a few major Technology Trends for Public Sector Fraud and Corruption such as Big Data, Cloud Computing Platforms, Artificial Intelligence/ Machine Learning, Biometrics (ID4D), FinTech Digital money, Distributed Ledger Technology/Blockchains, and Internet of Things (IoT) [21, 22, 37]. Each country has its own electronic public procurement system, which, in the end, may be very different from each other. Tools for monitoring and analyzing the PPP present a part of the electronic public procurement system and are developed as special modules. Namely, there is no comprehensive research that would cover all possible states and systems in them. We will present in this paper only the systems we found in previous studies. It has been observed that the systems are divided into those that are publicly accessible and those that can be accessed by special users, such as monitoring agencies

[13, 40]. To protect financial interests within their borders, the states are financing the development of electronic public procurement systems and promoting the design and definition of different policies [1, 13, 14]. There are also several robust and advanced IT solutions that have been implemented with different methods for detecting corruption, not only in public procurement but also in supply chains in certain large companies [5]. Some of the solutions are described briefly below.

DoZorro is artificial intelligence software based on supervised learning. Thus, it learns to identify the public procurement process or tenders with a high risk of corruption. It is like a part of the national procurement system in Ukraina named ProZorro. Depending on risk indicators, the system automatically finds suspicious tenders using open data and continuous legal support [50]. In the fight against fraud (and irregularities), the European Commission provides a special tool for depth analysis of data under the name ARACHNE to detect projects that might be vulnerable to fraud, conflict of interest and irregularities. It is being developed by the European employment office, social affairs and inclusion and represents a risk assessment tool that can make project selection, controls and audits more effective and can further strengthen the identification, prevention and detection of fraud [25]. PLUTO is an analytical database that contains information about all users and projects funded by DG-CNECT (Directorate-General Communications Networks, Content, and Technology). The European Commission is currently using it to oversee EU funds and provides a visual insight into the connectivity of users, projects, persons, phones, addresses, and other relevant data to detect similar irregularities.

Although currently used only for EU funds, PLUTO has the potential for use in public procurement, with the addition of central database data. It is only used in cases where there is doubt about irregularities in the granting process [13]. The area of development and innovation within the European Commission covers DG-RTD (Directorate-General for Research and Innovation). DG-RTD has developed its own DAISY tool for data mining. The purpose of the tool is to identify links between users of funds from EU funds intended for research projects. DAISY is not an automated tool that performs regular customer checks. It is only used when there is doubt in the specific user of the funds (e.g. identifying different companies from the same address using different EU grants, checking potentially double funding of the same project, etc.) [26]. Tendersure is a decision support tool developed in South Africa that is based on web technology. The main aim is to gain efficiency and improve the public procurement process, and it helps to combat corruption [19]. A red flag system presents warnings that help control public procurement procedures by identifying risks. It is used in the early stage of PPP and was developed and co-financed by the European Commission. This tool is still active and is used a lot, but improvements need to be made [28]. Integrity observer [17] presented a tool for data analysis of the Croatian public procurement process and gathering data on the level of municipalities and cities in the targeted communities in Croatia, collecting legal data, interviews with local stakeholders, and filling in the data in the Public Procurement Database [18]. We did not find any evidence of using any kind of data mining, machine learning, business intelligence algorithms. ERAR is an online service in Slovenia developed for providing information about the public flow of money and insight into operational activities between economic operators and contracting authorities in order to spend public funds efficiently and effectively [16]. Many different systems have been developed to give public analytics and a transparent view of tender procedures. We already stated that each country has their own electronically public procurement system. Through international transparency, we can see that some of them are FYR Macedonia, Georgia, Slovakia, Poland, and others [15].

3 Research

The purpose of this research is to describe a system of public procurement procedures oversight aimed at identifying anomalies using experience from experts in the field of modelling anomaly recognition (fraud management) and their technical references, business, and scientific capacity. The research is divided into six phases: (i) restriction of the area where the analysis is performed (direction); (ii) cataloguing sources, collecting and preparing data (collection); (iii) conversion and enrichment of data and development of a system of recommendations (evaluation); (iv) model evaluation (collation); (v) analysis as a central part of the methodology (analysis); (vi) final product, model (dissemination). The final system contains two basic components, anomaly detection which is described in this paper, and anomaly prevention, which follows as a guideline on how policy makers should act in order to manage procurement processes. In accordance with the initial research idea, the scope of this paper includes the initial part consisting of: (1) preparation of documentation with a description of the elements of the system for monitoring the public procurement process, a description of available data sources and recommendations of potential techniques and models with an explanation of their choice; (2) recommendations for the technical infrastructure of the system, taking into account the protection of existing investments of the system (if any); (3) recommendations of the tools to be used in the data analysis; (4) recommendations for commercialization of the solution; (5) simulations of the case study through a description of the process in the form of PoC presentation with a description of the method/procedure of the application of the selected methods in order to present the expected results of the model as a basis for continuing work in later stages; and (6) presentation of the possibilities, visualization and interpretation of selected data available in the national systems. Given the importance of public procurement as a segment of the economy, the procedures for the implementation of public procurement need to be continuously improved. Regardless of the takeover of business practices and experiences of other EU member states, there is a justified need for an effective system of oversight of public procurement processes.

Therefore, the regulations state as the areas of greatest risk related to the activities of contracting authorities and tenderers within public procurement procedures: (1) planning, preparation and selection of the public procurement procedure; (2) implementation of the public procurement procedure; and (3) realization of the contract. Anomalies are prevented: (1) by collecting information on the market; (2) by choosing the most appropriate procedure: the most open and wide competition; (3) by changing the size and dynamics of concluding contracts; (4) by examining the conditions of ability (using simulations) and the criteria for selecting bids; (5) by strengthening professional ability; (6) by subcontracting; (7) by raising awareness of the dangers of corruption; (8) by searching for opportunities; and (9) by contributions to transparency and fairness. The aim of this paper is to describe the elements and mode of operation of the system of effective supervision of public procurement systems with a special emphasis on anomalies in the procedures being implemented.

4 Understanding the Data

The Intelligent System for Monitoring Public Procurement Processes is a framework of good practices aimed at detecting and preventing undesirable phenomena in the implementation of public procurement procedures. The purpose of the system is to have a centralized monitoring of activities, documents, and events with the aim of timely detection and prevention of anomalies in the public procurement process. In the context of this research, adverse events are viewed from a technical and user point of view. From a technical point of view, inconsistent, incomplete and/or incorrect data in the database are undesirable, while from the user's point of view it is a matter of process anomalies that can result from unintentional omissions but also intentional malversation and abuse of the system. The following are examples of anomaly indicators aggregated into warning categories. The dashboard interface is divided into the following sections: (1) procedure; (2) client; (3) bidder; (4) contract and (5) person.

It is important to emphasize that the indicators and ratings below do not necessarily identify fraud; they only represent the degree of conformity with the defined rules. The overall assessment obtained by summing the individual indicators only indicates a potentially increased probability of irregularities within the observed category, but in no case should it be declared a measure of actual anomaly or irregularity in the procedure directly without expert analysis. Ratings obtained by aggregating indicators are the basis for determining the priority of expert supervision over individual categories of warnings. There is feedback between the results of the expert's supervision and the input indicators of the system, that is, the system learns based on the results of expert supervision and deviations of individual indicators from the average, which, over a longer period of use, allows it to continuously increase the accuracy in evaluating and identifying new and unknown potential anomalies that have not been previously discovered. The following table contains the basic potential causes and indicators of anomalies that are envisaged for implementation in the first production phase of the project. The system is designed to be extensible in the future, with monitoring and continuous improvement by expanding and adapting specific rules for detecting anomalies (Table 1).

The tender documentation represents the basis of any procurement process. The structure of this kind of document includes the quantity of goods, section names, eligible conditions, etc. The content is practically left to the entity to choose, and it is challenging to find relevant content within these documents. In the procurement process, the common name for a set of documents describing the quantities, exclusion conditions, aptitude requirements, and other relevant content is the "tender documents". Nevertheless, the Regulation on Procurement Documents and Offers in Public Procurement Procedures in Croatian law defines the information that the contracting authority must provide when announcing its tender offer [MEEC, 2017]. Research indicates that greater standardization will lead to the reduction of corruption risks in the call for tender documents [12, 13]. The paper highlights the importance of prediction approaches

Table 1. Potential causes and indicators of anomalies, 56 rules/indicators.

Rule no	Potential causes and indicators of anomalies	Warning category				
		Procedure	Client	Bidder	Contract	Person
1	Unusually short deadline between the announcement of the tender and the deadline for submission of bids	•				
2	Time between the announcement of the tender and the signing of the contract	•				
3	High percentage of administratively rejected bids in the procedure	•				
4	Unusually small number of correct bids at the level of the procurement procedure	•				
5	Bid accepted before the deadline for submission of bids	•				
6	High ratio of the value of contracts signed under special conditions in relation to the total value of all contracts of an individual client	•				
7	All providers offer service above the estimated value	•				
8	Price changed after selecting a bidder	•				
9	The procedure was or is being appealed	•				
10	Increased number of inquiries (complaints)	•				
11	Cleavage of procurement items	•				
12	Correct selection of the type of procedure	•				
13	Setting an artificially high budget	•				
14	Overlapping budget allocations between individual departments	•				
15	Very high tender value	•				
16	Extremely large tender volume	•				
17	Terms of reference indicate a preferred supplier	•				

(continued)

Table 1. (*continued*)

Rule no	Potential causes and indicators of anomalies	Warning category				
		Procedure	Client	Bidder	Contract	Person
18	Orientation of the tender towards a specific bidder	•				
19	Unusually large number of contracts signed by one company or group of companies bidding together for a specific procurement item	•				
20	Records of changes in the log database are not in line with the actual state of the database	•				
21	The sequence of steps in the procedure does not correspond to the prescribed sequence of steps	•				
22	There is a pattern of rotation of bidders under different procedures for the same subject of procurement for the same contracting authority	•				
23	Unusually large number of annulled proceedings in relation to the total number of proceedings		•			
24	The client changed the financial data during the procurement process		•			
25	Unusually large number of contracts awarded in accordance with special and special methods (agreement, direct contracting)		•			
26	Accelerated procedure		•			
27	The tender documentation was changed outside the legally established deadlines		•			
28	The client does not respond to inquiries within the legal deadline		•			
29	The potential bidder reacts to the content of the documentation and has not taken over the documentation at all			•		

(*continued*)

Table 1. (*continued*)

Rule no	Potential causes and indicators of anomalies	Warning category				
		Procedure	Client	Bidder	Contract	Person
30	The bidder is a newly established company, without the possibility of checking business capacity on the basis of annual reports			•		
31	The bidder is not registered for the activity required for the realization of the subject of procurement			•		
32	The bid was submitted on behalf of an inactive company			•		
33	The size of the bidder is disproportionate to the value of the procurement			•		
34	The bidder applied for the tender and did not take over the documentation			•		
35	Qualification of the bidder			•		
36	A contract entered into at an unusually early stage of the proceedings				•	
37	Unusually large number of annexes to the contract				•	
38	The annex stipulates an unusually high percentage of the value of the basic contract				•	
39	Subsequent increase in the value of the contracted amount is due to the unrealistically low offered price				•	
40	There is a difference between the offered/contracted/invoiced/paid amount				•	
41	The contractual obligation was paid before the due date				•	
42	The contract is consumed upon expiration				•	
43	The contract was not concluded within the stipulated deadline				•	
44	Change of agreed deadlines after acceptance of the offer				•	

(*continued*)

Table 1. (*continued*)

Rule no	Potential causes and indicators of anomalies	Warning category				
		Procedure	Client	Bidder	Contract	Person
45	An unusually large number of contracts in which the same company is a subcontractor or a member of a consortium				•	
46	Payment is made to a non-contracting company				•	
47	The contract amounts of all contracts of the same contracting authority under the same type of procurement do not follow Benford's law				•	
48	Low bid followed by contracting a changed scope of work				•	
49	Low bid followed by contracting a higher price than offered				•	
50	Low bid followed by contracting longer deadlines than offered				•	
51	Conflict of interest					•
52	The persons mentioned by the bidder for contact are not connected with the bidder					•
53	The persons named by the tenderer do not reside in the place of the tenderer					•
54	The persons specified by the bidder for contact do not have an e-mail address in the domain of the bidder					•
55	The same person appears as a related or contact person of several bidders within the same procedure					•
56	The offer includes multiple contact points					•

based on machine learning methods for validating a broad range of indicators from a methodological point of view [14]. According to this regulation, the tender is divided into several parts, namely the general part, in which the description of the subject of the procurement is discussed; the section where the deadlines are given for the beginning and end of the contract; and a section with the criteria for selecting an economic entity, i.e., the sections that are important for us to extract any content of interest. In particular, it is important to emphasize that the regulation defines the contents that must be included in the tender documentation, but not where this information is to be located, the name of the sections, the serial number, etc. Therefore, this presents a challenge, because it is difficult to define the boundaries and extract the content.

5 System Architecture

Data from external sources is fed into the system in the data ingestion or extraction/transformation (ETL) phase. The method of adjustment depends on the amount, type and other characteristics of the data available from external sources, but its function remains unchanged. The Data Ingestion component performs the transformations needed to structure the data and to build a single data warehouse. Some of the possible transformations include extracting data from the text of documents, extracting data from other sources, transforming that data, and saving it in a suitable form into a future system [20]. The transformed data is ultimately stored in the data warehouse, that is, in the Spark cluster file system. A data ingestion component may include one or more servers of the same or different configurations. The reason for this uncertainty is that the choice of tools and technical infrastructure depends on the characteristics of external sources and their data that are currently unknown (Fig. 1).

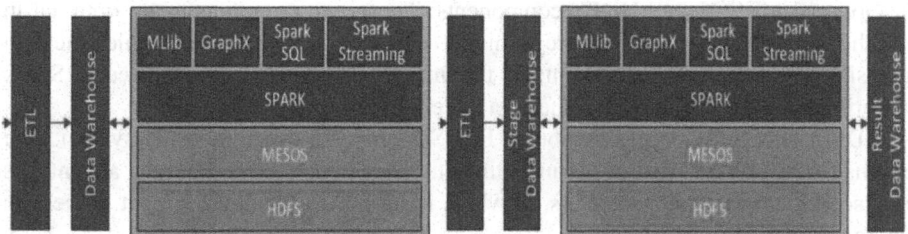

Fig. 1. Architecture for development and production.

5.1 System Components

The architecture of the system through different stages of development and scaling is described below.

File System: This component is listed for complete architecture description. The file management system comes with the operating system, and for high availability and redundancy the system will work in clusters and store data in Parquet format files. Parquet was chosen as the file format for storing data of the future system for a variety of sources. The final data structure will have a relatively large number of columns after enrichment. The Parquet format is column-oriented and works quickly with such data structures. The use of the Parquet format for data storage comes only in the later stages of system scaling, which means that it will only be used in cases where the amount of data becomes too large for the data warehouse.

Apache Spark: Apache Spark is a multi-purpose fast computing system designed to run on a cluster of at least 4 servers. It enables fast processing and analysis of large amounts of data and consists of the following components: Spark SQL, MLlib, GraphX and Spark Streaming, which will be described below. Spark was chosen as the foundation of the future system because it offers the possibility of fast data processing in a horizontally expandable environment; the burden of growing data is solved by adding server resources to the future system as soon as necessary, without the need to make the system available. It has the resources it will need only at some future stage of scaling.

Spark SQL: Spark SQL is a module for processing structured data. Because it can run partially or completely in memory, it is a good choice for a system where low response time is essential. Spark SQL has built-in support for connecting to various types of data sources, which, among other things, includes relational databases and file formats such as Parquet.

MLlib: This module enables the use of scalable machine learning methods and is compatible with other components of this development environment.

GraphX: GraphX is used for analyzing graphs (SNA - Social Network Analysis) or data that have been transformed into a network. Typically, entities such as people or companies are set up for network nodes, and their interrelationships, network statuses and the properties of the entire network are studied.

Spark Streaming: Spark Streaming allows you to work with streaming data. There is no need for this component in the initial phase of the project, and if needed it will enable the expansion of the capabilities of the future real-time data processing system.

Optional MESOS and HDFS components: These two components are optional in case the system stops scaling before coming to Phase D, i.e. the phase in which the data analysis speed becomes insufficient. By the time the D-phase scaling is needed, Spark will primarily read the data from the data warehouse.

HDFS: HDFS (Hadoop Distributed File System) is a distributed file system. The reasons for its use are most pronounced in extremely large clusters, but the advantages are also evident in smaller clusters, in which it simplifies the development process in synergy with MESOS¬.

MEAT: This component enables Spark to treat all cluster resources (disk space, memory, processing power, etc.) as a single pool of resources and not as a series of separate ones. This facilitates the construction and maintenance of the system and possible future expansion.

The architecture of the proposed prototype contains the basic components of the production environment, which are the data warehouse and the Spark cluster. In addition to external data sources independent of the future system, the architecture consists of one logical component: ETL. It is physically located and executed on Spark cluster servers. The architecture of the future system in the development phase contains the basic components of the production environment, which are the data warehouse and the Spark cluster. In addition to external data sources independent of the future system, the architecture consists of one logical component - ETL. It is physically located and executed on Spark cluster servers. The reason why the phases of ETL and data analysis can be performed on the same machines is that these stages of the process are sequentially dependent, and the data analysis is performed strictly after extraction, preparation and storage of fresh data. External data prepared through ETL are stored in the data warehouse or in the form of Parquet files on file servers, and the results of the analysis are stored exclusively in the data warehouse after data processing. Ideally, the development system should remain active even after the future system is put into production. If further development and testing were to be done on the production server, the process of analysis, availability and quality of service to end users would be disrupted. To avoid these problems, development and testing should be carried out on a separate and predetermined system, and in the worst case it would be good to be able to simply start and stop such a system if necessary. In its basic variant, the production system differs from the development system in that they do not use a common data warehouse (StageDW and ResultDW), because we want to maintain the availability and quality of service at the level required by users and at the time the freshly received data is analysed. We expect to need to scale the system in four phases. The following is a description of the phases in the order in which the future increase in the number of external sources is assumed. In case it is determined early enough that the amount of data will be large, there is a possibility that some scaling phases will be skipped.

5.2 Development Phases

Phase A: As more and more different data sources become available, more and more of them will be in StageDW. Given that the minimum size of a Spark cluster is four machines, they will initially be able to withstand the growing needs in the data analysis process.

Phase B: Over time, the data analysis time period in the Spark cluster will increase. This problem will be solved by adding resources to the Spark cluster. StageDW resources will also be increased as needed.

Phase C: In the third phase, to maintain a satisfactory system response speed to the user, the resources of the data warehouse in which the results of the analysis will be located will be increased. Resources for the StageDW and Spark cluster will also increase as needed.

Phase D: There is a possibility that the scaling of the system will also reach its fourth stage if the amount of input data increases beyond the limits that StageDW will support. In this case, the Spark cluster will grow to the level where it will be able to store all input data in the Parquet file format. It is to be expected that ResultDW will never increase to such a level that its integration into the Spark cluster will be required (Fig. 2).

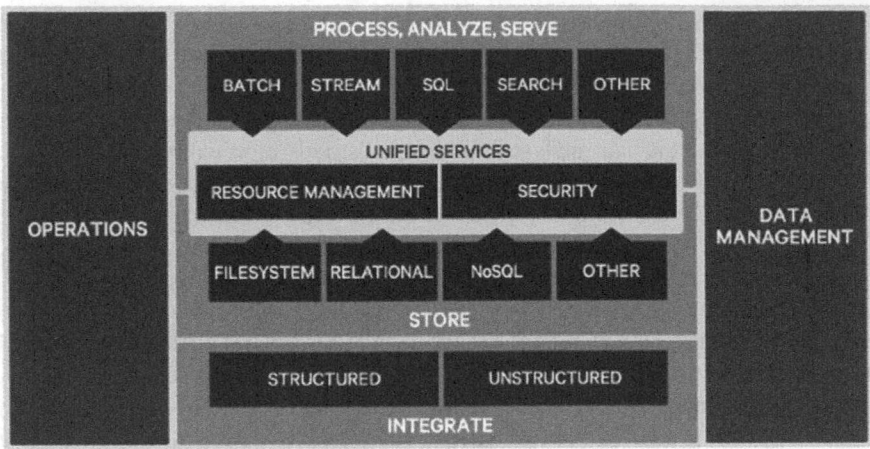

Fig. 2. System components.

6 Results

We established a scraping procedure for public data [27, 30] and created data with 12.213 public procurement cases related to delivery, 32.882 cases related to goods and 19.297 cases related to service, all during the period from January 2016 to November 2020. The share of the number of cases is represented in next figure (Fig. 3).

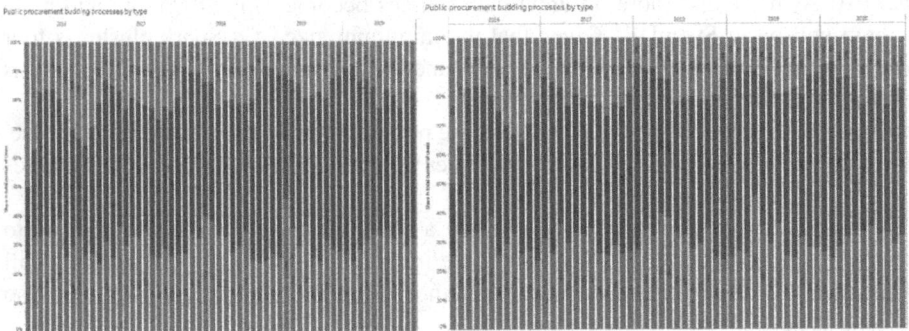

Fig. 3. Share of cases per type and number of cases per type (delivery/orange, goods/blue, services/red). (Color figure online)

We created an anomaly detection prototype based on a ruleset and automated population of indicators dashboard. As an example, the next figure shows the relationship between the total number of days available for the application and number of days before the due date when the bidder has downloaded documents. It indicates that large and complex tenders need enough time for preparation, so very short periods can indicate an anomaly in the process. This does not indicate fraud; however, it is to be examined and put into perspective with guidelines for how much time is needed for a specific case. On the data sample, we executed a simple clustering technique. The clusters are painted in colours (green, orange blue), while the size of the data points represents the total contract value. Values above the line indicate more time for a bidder to prepare documentation, while points near the 45 degrees line indicate a very short time for preparation. As is shown, larger (bigger circles) contracts require more time to be prepared. However, there are many cases where the time between the download and application due date is very short. One realistic explanation is that documents are being shared through specialized services and distributed to bidders without notification on the portal. However, this simple technique shows how efficient this system can be (Fig. 4).

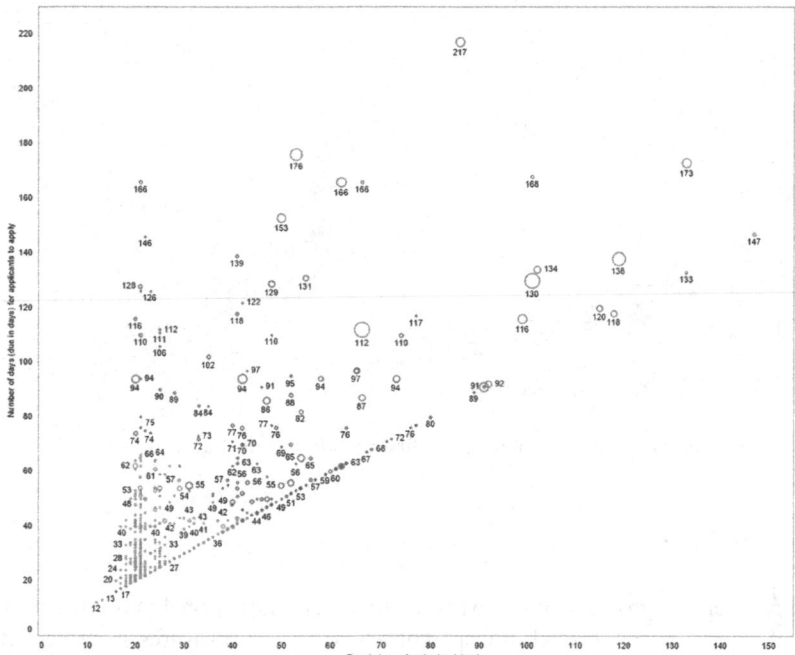

Fig. 4. Number of days for the applicant to apply related to days between download and due date comparison with clustering.

We also applied process mining to analyze the differences between single- and multiple-bid tenders. Process mining has proved that procedures with more than one bid do last longer, and that some single bid tenders lasted for an extremely short period of time. The time difference for a limited data set is presented in the table below (Table 2).

Table 2. Differences in duration; one-bid tenders vs. tenders with more than one bid.

	One bid tenders	Multiple bid tenders	Change (%)
Mean (days)	81,5	107	+31,2%
Median (days)	57,0	71	+24,5%

As a final demonstration, we put the sample data into a Benford rule calculation process, which is commonly used as a first-level notification in the detection of potential fraud [41]. As a comparison to the "fist digit" rule and the "first two digits rule", the results are visualized as indicated below. This technique provides deep insights into relationships beyond a simple "hammer analysis" (where some economies limit public procurement for some groups of goods and services and creates hammer curve when bidders avoid limits by selection either to much lower parts of bidding or group applications into bigger contracts). The visualization represents the anomaly in positive (green) and negative (orange) distance from the expected with different granularities and ability for analysts to interact with the data (Fig. 5).

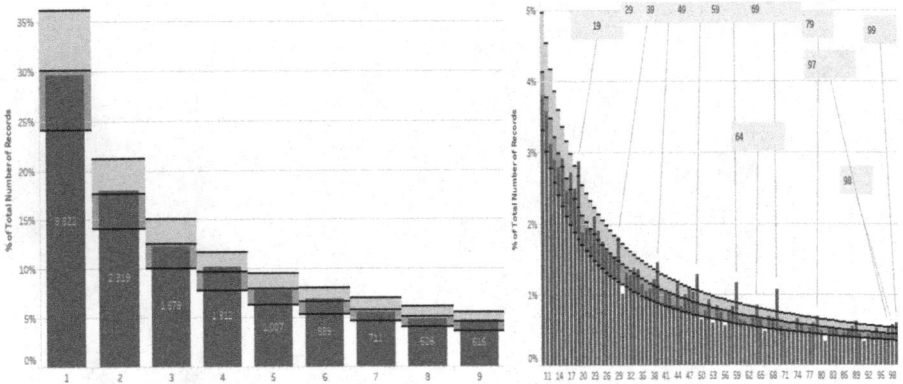

Fig. 5. Benford rule, "first digit" and "first two digits" interactive visualization.

7 Conclusion

Public procurement procedures are expected to ensure the rational and prudent spending of taxpayers' funds through transparent and effective measures to protect public finances. Public procurement is, at the same time, an area of very high risk when it comes to irregularities. It faces fraud and corruption that are manifested in bid rigging, illegal agreements between competitors, conflicts of interest of procurement employees, illegal contracts and other irregularities. The realization of such risks poses a major threat to public institutions, especially given the costly and technologically advanced investments and projects. Fraud prevention and detection professionals and procurement professionals need to be well prepared to identify warning indicators, and the assistance that the Intelligent Public Procurement Monitoring System can provide can be crucial in detecting and preventing illegal activities that would occur without such a comprehensive approach. Data quality is one of the most important features about which the outcome of an analysis or model development depends. An analysis of the literature showed us that scientists have encountered this problem for many years, especially after emerging technologies became a part of everyday life. This analysis found evidence for different challenges, especially in terms of the detection and extraction of the relevant content. One conclusion is that the domain knowledge, which we also used in our case, was indispensable for detecting the necessary terms and sections that we sought within the tender documentation. Numerous applied methods have been detected, specifically the NLP techniques and deep learning. The approaches to the content extraction from structured and unstructured document types are different. Moreover, it is easier to find content in structured document types than in unstructured documents. In our case, we had a challenge because the content could be found in any part of the document structure. We found that more than 90% of the documents had a section called "technical and professional capability", but extracting it did not mean that we covered all of the essential content extraction. Because the procurement documentation is not structured, we had to solve this challenge by determining the boundaries throughout the process of retrieving all of the content. Through interviews with several important public procurement experts, we came up with a list of important terms/words that we used to extract content. Future research should further develop and confirm these initial findings by analyzing the PP process through process mining in order to seek all the connections between the events and the one-bid outcome, or to test the model on a larger dataset, e.g., on the European public procurement portal.

Our system provides a limited but important step in understanding the mechanics and dynamics of public procurement systems with a clear demonstration of the potential of text analytics and interactive visualization in the management of such systems. The proposed architecture covers all important system development parts, including scalability and future rule improvements.

References

1. Red flags projects, New warning system for the identification of red flags in public procurements. https://www.redflags.eu/files/redflags-summary-en.pdf. Accessed 03 Oct 2020
2. Study on up-take of emerging technologies in public procurement DG GROW G.4, Req. No 146 Framework Contract DI/07624 - ABC IV Lot 3 D01.06: Final Report https://joinup.ec.europa.eu/sites/default/files/news/2020-06/D.01.06_Final_report_v3.00.pdf. Accessed 03 Oct 2020
3. Fazekas, M., Kocsis, G.: Uncovering high-level corruption: Cross-national objective corruption risk indicators using public procurement data. Br. J. Polit. Sci. **50**, 155–164 (2017)
4. Afolabi, A., et al.: Digitizing the grey areas in the Nigerian public procurement system using e-Procurement technologies. Int. J. Construct. Manage. 1–10 (2020)
5. Association of Certified Fraud Examiners. https://www.acfe.com/report-to-the-nations/2020/. Accessed 03 Oct 2020
6. Azmi, K.S., Rahman, A.A:. E-procurement: a tool to mitigate public procurement fraud in Malaysia. Electron. J. e-Govern. **13**(2) (2015)
7. Decarolis, F., Cristina, G.: Corruption red flags in public procurement: new evidence from Italian calls for tenders. Questioni di Economia e Finanza, Occasional Papers 544 (2020)
8. DG GROW: Public Procurement Indicators 2017 (2019). https://ec.europa.eu/docsroom/documents/38003/attachments/1/translations/en/renditions/native. Accessed 15 Nov 2019
9. Directorate for the public procurement system (2017). Statistical report for 2017 year. http://www.javnanabava.hr/userdocsimages/Statisticko_izvjesce_JN-2017.pdf. Accessed 15 Oct 2018

10. Domingos, SL., Carvalho, RN., Carvalho, RS., Ramos, GN.: Identifying IT purchases anomalies in the Brazilian government procurement system using deep learning. In: Machine Learning and Applications (ICMLA) (2016)
11. Dragoni, M., Villata, S., Rizzi, W., Governatori, G.: Combining NLP approaches for rule extraction from legal documents. In: 1st Workshop on Mining and REasoning with Legal texts, Sophia Antipolis (2016)
12. Espejo-Garcia, B., Lopez-, F.J., Lacasta, J., Moreno, R.P., Zarazaga, F.J.: End-to-end sequence labeling via deep learning for automatic extraction of agricultural regulations. Comput. Electron. Agric. **162**, 106–111 (2019)
13. European Anti-Fraud Office (OLAF): The OLAF report 2018 (2019). https://ec.europa.eu/anti-fraud/sites/antifraud/files/olaf_report_2018_en.pdf. Accessed 10 Nov 2019
14. European Commission: Javna nabava - Smjernice za praktičare (2015). https://ec.europa.eu/regional_policy/sources/docgener/informat/2014/guidance_public_proc_hr.pdf.   Accessed 15 Jan 2020
15. European Commission, Association of Certified Fraud Examiners. https://ec.europa.eu/info/publications/2020-rule-law-report-communication-and-country-chapters_en. Accessed 05 Oct 2020
16. European Commission, Legal rules and implementation. https://ec.europa.eu/growth/single-market/public-procurement/rules-implementation_en. Accessed 15 Jan 2020
17. Fazekas, M., Kocsis, G.: Uncovering high-level corruption: cross-national objective corruption risk indicators using public procurement data. Br. J. Polit. Sci. **50**, 155–164 (2020)
18. Fazekas, M., Tóth, I.J., King, L.P.: An objective corruption risk index using public procurement data. Eur. J. Crim. Policy Res. **22**(3), 369–397 (2016). https://doi.org/10.1007/s10610-016-9308-z
19. Ferwerda, J., Deleanu, I., Unger, B.: Corruption in public procurement: finding the right indicators. Eur. J. Crim. Policy Res. **23**(2), 245–267 (2016). https://doi.org/10.1007/s10610-016-9312-3
20. Fissette, M.: Text mining to detect indications of fraud in annual reports worldwide. Dissertation, University of Twente (2017)
21. Geetha, S., Mala, G.A.: Extraction of key attributes from natural language requirements specification text. In: IET Chennai Fourth International Conference on Sustainable Energy and Intelligent Systems (2013)
22. Integrityobservers.   http://integrityobservers.eu/UserDocsImages/uvid_u_javnu_nabavu_HR.pdf. Accessed 18 Oct 2020
23. European Social Fund. https://ec.europa.eu/social/main.jsp?catId=325&intPageId=3587&langId=en. Accessed 15 Sept 2020
24. ERAR, Republic of Slovenia. https://erar.si/. Accessed 15 Sept 2020
25. Tendersure,   European   Commission.   https://www.tendersure.co.ke/views/about.php. Accessed 15 Sept 2020
26. Ministry of economy entrepreneurship and crafts (MEEC), Pravilnik o dokumentaciji o nabavi te ponudi u postupcima javne nabave. https://narodne-novine.nn.hr/clanci/sluzbeni/2017_07_65_1534.html. Accessed 15 Sept 2020
27. Modrusan, N., Rabuzin, K., Mrsic, L., Improving Public Sector Efficiency using Advanced Text Mining in the Procurement Process, DATA (2020)
28. Ojokoh, B., Zhang, M., Tang, J.: A trigram hidden Markov model for metadata extraction from heterogeneous references. Information Sciences (2011)
29. OLAF: The OLAF report 2016, The Publications Office of the European Union, Luxembourg (2017)

30. Rabuzin, K., Modrusan, N.: Prediction of public procurement corruption indices using machine learning methods. In: 11th International Conference on Knowledge Management and Information Systems, Vienna (2019)
31. Rabuzin, K., Modrusan, N., Krizanic, S., Kelemen, R., Process Mining in Public Procurement in Croatia (2020)
32. Ratinov, L., Roth, D.: Design challenges and misconceptions in named entity recognition. In Proceedings of the Thirteenth Conference on Computational Natural Language Learning (2009)
33. Tamames, J., de Lorenzo, V.: EnvMine: A textmining system for the automatic extraction of contextual information. BMC Bioinformatics (2010)
34. Torres-Moreno, J.M. (ed.).: Automatic Text Summarization. Wiley, Hoboken (2014)
35. Velasco, R.B., Carpanese, I., Interian, R., Paulo Neto, O.C., Ribeiro, C.C.: A decision support system for fraud detection in public procurement. Int. Trans. Oper. Res. **28**, 27–47 (2021)
36. Wensink, W., Vet, J.M.: Identifying and reducing corruption in public procurement in the EU. PricewaterhouseCoopers (2013)
37. World Bank: Enhancing Government Effectiveness and Transparency: The Fight Against Corruption. World Bank, Kuala Lumpur. © World Bank (2020). https://openknowledge.worldbank.org/handle/10986/34533. License: CC BY 3.0 IGO
38. World Bank: Fraud and Corruption. Awareness Handbook. World Bank, Washington (2009)
39. Yi, L., Yuan, R., Long, S., Xue, L.: Expert information automatic extraction for IOT knowledge base. Procedia Comput. Sci. **147**, 288–294 (2019)
40. Barabesi, L., Cerasa, A., Cerioli, A., Perrotta, D.: Goodness-of-fit testing for the Newcomb-Benford law with application to the detection of customs fraud. J. Bus. Econ. Stat. **36**, 346–358 (2018)
41. Cerioli, A., Barabesi, L., Cerasa, A., Menegatti, M., Perrotta, D.: Newcomb-Benford law and the detection of frauds in international trade. PNAS **116**, 106–115 (2019)

Catalog Integration of Heterogeneous and Volatile Product Data

Oliver Schmidts[1]([✉]), Bodo Kraft[1], Marvin Winkens[1], and Albert Zündorf[2]

[1] FH Aachen, University of Applied Sciences, Jülich, Germany
{schmidts,kraft,winkens}@fh-aachen.de
[2] University of Kassel, Kassel, Germany
zuendorf@uni-kassel.de

Abstract. The integration of frequently changing, volatile product data from different manufacturers into a single catalog is a significant challenge for small and medium-sized e-commerce companies. They rely on timely integrating product data to present them aggregated in an online shop without knowing format specifications, concept understanding of manufacturers, and data quality. Furthermore, format, concepts, and data quality may change at any time. Consequently, integrating product catalogs into a single standardized catalog is often a laborious manual task. Current strategies to streamline or automate catalog integration use techniques based on machine learning, word vectorization, or semantic similarity. However, most approaches struggle with low-quality or real-world data. We propose Attribute Label Ranking (ALR) as a recommendation engine to simplify the integration process of previously unknown, proprietary tabular format into a standardized catalog for practitioners. We evaluate ALR by focusing on the impact of different neural network architectures, language features, and semantic similarity. Additionally, we consider metrics for industrial application and present the impact of ALR in production and its limitations.

Keywords: Catalog integration · Data integration · Data quality · Label prediction · Machine learning · Neural network applications

1 Introduction

E-commerce companies depend on timely integrating new or updated product data from manufacturers into their platform to display and sell their products to customers. However, manufacturers often do not comply with standard product formats like schema.org or a GS1 standard. For some domains - like antibodies - there has been no standard established, and small to medium sized enterprises (SMEs) cannot enforce their standard due to lacking market power. In practice, manufacturers even may change their data structures at any time without notifying the e-commerce company about changes.

This work was supported by the German Federal Ministry for Economic Affairs and Energy (BMWi) within the Central Innovation Programme for SMEs (grant no. 16KN063729) and antibodies-online GmbH.

© Springer Nature Switzerland AG 2021
S. Hammoudi et al. (Eds.): DATA 2020, CCIS 1446, pp. 134–153, 2021.
https://doi.org/10.1007/978-3-030-83014-4_7

Hence, SMEs face the challenge of integrating data in various data formats from different sources and extracting relevant information to display on their platform.

A usual workflow to integrate data from different manufacturers includes steps like data cleaning, format unification, schema matching, and information extraction. Due to these tasks' complexity, data integration usually requires manual corrections since tools frequently fail to automate data pipelines on non-standard or low-quality data.

Our approach aims to simplify the manual integration process by providing recommendations on schema-matches to employees because matching schemas is a critical and time consuming manual task. Enabling employees to identify corresponding attributes in product catalog schemas correctly allows processing complex datasets with reduced effort and domain knowledge. To integrate a product catalog into another, we need to identify related entries in both catalogs, either through attribute names or representatives of an underlying concept.

Due to frequent changes in manufacturers' input schemas, a dictionary or simple similarity-based approach is not feasible. Even if a previously integrated product catalog contains similar attribute names, another manufacturer could use the same naming for a different concept.

We conducted this research in a collaboration project with an e-commerce SME selling antibodies. Therefore, we focus on integrating tabular data from multiple manufacturers into a single product catalog in the antibody product domain. We focus on identifying possible matches in product catalogs by relying only on attribute names and their representatives.

This paper extends the Attribute Label Ranking (ALR) approach, aiming to integrate tabular catalog data. Given unknown column names and column count from different manufacturers, ALR tries to find correspondences between the input schema and the target schema by labeling each representative of an attribute. After labeling each attribute representative, ALR aggregates these predictions to rank among all label candidates of a column. The final result represents a ranking for recommendations to simplify the process of catalog integration for SMEs.

We advance the main contributions of [21] by providing the following extensions:

1. We provide a more generalized model architecture for ALR, allowing to handle attribute name features and attribute instance features separately before concatenation into a combined model. We extend our evaluation, providing convolutional neural networks (CNNs) results compared to simple neural networks applied in ALR.
2. We evaluate the impact of more complex language features than one-hot word vectors. In particular, we evaluate ALR results using specialized FastText embeddings with different model setups.
3. We evaluate the effect of Unicode normalization and data augmentation as preprocessing stages to improve ALR configurations in production. Furthermore, we evaluate all configurations considering dataset imbalances and metrics related closely to the application context.

The remainder of this paper is structured as follows: Sect. 2 provides background information about the challenges and the importance of handling low-quality data in automatic or manually assisted integration approaches for SMEs in e-commerce. Subsequently, Sect. 3 provides an overview of related approaches and recent previous work.

In Sect. 4, we present a more generalized version of ALR as an approach to integrating heterogeneous, noisy data. Based on the dataset for catalog integration of antibody product data[1], we evaluate multiple configurations for ALR in Sect. 5 considering practical relevance, before concluding with a brief summary and outlook in Sect. 6.

2   Background

This section provides background information about antibody product catalog integration, demonstrating the economic importance of automatic integration of heterogeneous, volatile, and low-quality product data, especially for SMEs in e-commerce.

Antibody product data are more complex and challenging to handle than simple product data like smartphones or food for different reasons:

- **Plenties of Attributes:** Antibody products have different numbers of attributes, depending on the product type. The number can range from 14 attributes up to over 100 attributes. Additionally, antibody types may have common attributes (such as description or product name), while other attributes are unique to a specific antibody type.
- **Missing Standards:** Despite the importance of shared standards, antibody product attributes have never been standardized compared to other industries (e.g., GS1 standard for food), although there are open databases for antibodies like UniProt. Missing standards also lead to manufacturers frequently changing their product attribute naming. Even if the input schema is known from a previously integrated catalog, the same (or any other manufacturer) could modify the schema on the next catalog update. Additionally, SMEs cannot force manufacturers to comply with their schema, format, or semantic concept naming due to the lack of market power.
- **Missing Common Concept Understanding:** In addition to missing standards, some attribute names lack a shared conceptual understanding between manufacturers. Hence, manufacturers use the same naming differently, making it impossible to use a dictionary approach for schema matching.
- **The Wordiness of Attribute Representatives:** The content of a single column (attribute representatives) can hold one of three different types of categories: bag of words (BOW), Unstructured Text (UT), or URLs. [21] A BOW column always includes a limited amount of words (e.g., a host is an animal). Hence, we can limit the number of possible attribute names. For example, animals can refer to the host or describe any reactivity. We may find the correct match by combining the attribute name with the content. Content from a BOW mostly refers to 1:1 relations. UT mostly refers to 1:n relations if the content holds more than one concept of a finer-grained schema, despite not mentioning it in the corresponding column name or any other column. It may contain a list of words, sentences, or even paragraphs. Hence, we cannot limit possible matches by a simple lookup. We have to analyze the words or sentences to find possible matches and match them to related attributes in the target schema. In other applications than catalog integration, there might be additional classes, such as IDs or numerical values [18]. However, we handle these cases as

---

[1] https://github.com/oschmi/antibody-catalog-integration-dataset.

Sample Input

Product_Name	Quantity	Host	Reactivity
Hu IRF-3 Pure SL-12.1 100ug	0.1mg	Mouse	Hu

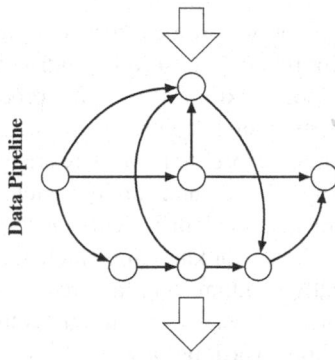

Sample Output

Clone	Quantity	Hosts	Reactivity
SL-12.1	0.1mg	Mouse	Human

Fig. 1. A standard integration workflow for e-commerce data: An industry partner supplies product data in a tabular format, represented by the sample input. After that, a data pipeline with optional manual interaction finally processes these data to integrate the sample output in a webshop [21].

plain text to avoid mistakes based on category confusion because of additional (or missing) symbols or characters.

When integrating these data, employees or automatic data pipelines need to perform multiple tasks to provide products from manufacturers finally to their customers in a web-shop. Figure 1 illustrates a typical integration workflow after format unification. Before this workflow, antibody manufacturers deliver manually edited product data in any format. After format unification, a data pipeline handles integration tasks with or without manual interaction. Typical tasks that require manual actions are (c.f. [21]):

– **Schema Matching:** Often, the first step of an integration pipeline is schema matching. An employee has to find correspondences between an input file to the target schema. If the two schemas are identical or very closely related, automating this task is easy. Regarding the challenges mentioned earlier, automating schema matching becomes a challenging task. Further, manufacturers manually editing product data leading to data quality issues like misspelling or usage of plural (c.f. Fig. 1, *Host* expands to *Hosts*). Different splitting characters, special characters or encoding issues makes schema matching even more challenging in real-world applications. Considering that each manufacturer may use their synonyms and abbreviations in attribute names and representatives, storing transformations once implemented for a single manufacturer in a dictionary seems feasible. However, reality shows that the input schemas change frequently, and a recommendation engine could speed up manual integration tasks.

- **Identifying Additional Information:** Some attribute representatives contain information of a semantic concept relating to a product attribute that misses elsewhere. For example, in Fig. 1, the clone is extracted from the product name since the input schema misses a clone property. Usually, data pipelines can extract these additional concepts (e.g., via unique regular expressions) if they are aware of them. Otherwise, an employee needs to identify, extract, and finally match these concepts manually to the correct attribute. In practice, the latter occurs most of the time due to schema matching issues and data pipelines, not knowing which attribute representative contains which concept. Manually handling this task requires very much time and is error-prone. Again, a recommendation engine simplifies this task significantly.
- **Resolving Synonyms and Abbreviations:** A web-shop needs a consistent vocabulary to display product information. Therefore, synonyms and abbreviations used by different antibody manufacturers to describe their products need to be standardized and resolved to use a consistent vocabulary in the web-shop (c.f. Fig. 1, *Hu* expands to *Human*).
- **Resolving Duplicated Information:** Multiple attribute representatives of different attributes might contain the same information. For example, the input file in Fig. 1 contains the product quantity in separate attributes. The quantity is identical in both attributes, but the measurement unit differs (including a misspelling). In this case, an employee might need to decide which value to use or match to the corresponding attribute in the target schema.

Failing a single task may produce incorrect product data in the web-shop that misleads customers into buying an incorrect product. Hence, highly educated domain specialists review the final integration result manually to guarantee the data quality of products before displaying them to customers. In the worst case, the integration pipeline needs to rerun multiple times until fulfilling quality goals. Avoiding integrating a single file of product data multiple times saves time and money for a SME, depending on the amount of manual work required.

With antibody manufacturers frequently changing their schemas, reducing the manual effort to integrate product data becomes economically relevant. In addition to regular schema changes, some manufacturers try to hide that they resell other manufacturers' products and obfuscate product data.

We improve automatic integration for tabular product data by predicting multiple labels (concepts from a fixed target schema) for each input file's attribute representative. Hence, our approach simplifies schema-matching and identifies additional information through recommendations to streamline tasks with manual interaction in the data integration process.

3   Related Work

Integrating heterogeneous, volatile product catalogs from multiple sources into a single catalog relates to schema matching, schema mapping, column labeling, product or entity matching, and finding related semantic concepts in different datasets.

There are multiple different approaches to tackle schema matching. The majority relies on finding similar attribute names in two or more schemas [8,20]. These approaches are helpful when dealing with noisy data. However, such an approach heavily depends on the used similarity metrics and a proper synonym abbreviation resolution. If we only consider attribute names or table headers, we potentially lose additional information that a web-shop displays to customers.

Other approaches focus on matching schemas through similarities of attribute instances or representatives [3,6,13]. They count on both schemas containing corresponding instances (sometimes in the same order). If one schema does not contain instances, these approaches are not applicable. Concerning catalog integration, we only know instances of the input schema since the input was not integrated into a product data warehouse yet. Hence, we cannot apply pure instance-based approaches.

Major matching frameworks like CUPID [14], COMA++ [2], or ORCHID [9] utilize hybrid approaches, and some further steps like structural information derived from hierarchies (e.g., in XML-Schemas) to provide a general-purpose solution to match or mediate between two schemas [22]. Since catalog integration relies on tabular data in which product attributes are most commonly stored, these approaches show worse performance than a simple approach based on attribute name similarities.

Approaches from the semantic web focus on entity matching to find the same product on different websites or related products in different tabular datasets [4,19]. Foley et al. [11] demonstrate that even low-quality data can enhance a machine learning model behind search engines, thus improving search results. However, entity matching relies on an already unified schema to correctly predict matches. Another strategy by Gu et al. [12] combines schema matching and record matching. They utilize likelihood estimation to find matching entities in different schemas. This approach depends on (at least some) overlapping records and attributes in both tabular datasets. It achieves the best results if one entity from a table matches max. one entity in the other table.

Recent research tries predicting labels or semantic concepts by content analysis [7] or combining attribute names and representatives [17,18]. Chen et al. propose a multi-class classification approach [7] leveraging a deep learning model to predict column labels. This model uses features such as cell length, character ratio, and character unigrams. The prediction result is a column label, where every label represents a single class. Consequently, the model can only predict 1:1 or n:1 relations but ignores 1:n relations. By adapting their approach to a multi-label classification problem, we can apply the model to catalog integration and include 1:n relations to find additional information in columns. They achieve the best results in predicting Bag of Words (BoW) column labels. However, columns concerning product specifications frequently contain text.

Other approaches try to determine similar concepts by analyzing the attribute value distribution through a single column next to other similarity measures [17,18]. Utilizing the value distribution is not possible in catalog integration. For example, a single manufacturer may send two product catalogs to integrate into the web-shop. One catalog contains only products with the host "mouse", while the second catalog contains only products with rabbits as host. Already in this simple case, the value distribution in the same column differs.

4   Catalog Integration

In this section, we propose Attribute Label Ranking (ALR) [21] and provide a more general setup with possible customizations, enabling investigations on features, pre-processing-steps, and neural network architecture impact on matching tabular input files into a fixed target schema.

4.1   Problem Statement

Since we extend ALR, we use the same definition of catalog integration for predicting column labels based on content and attribute name analysis of tabular catalog data as Schmidts et al. [21]: We consider a given product catalog

$$
P^{in} = \begin{bmatrix} L_1^{in} & L_2^{in} & \cdots & L_n^{in} \\ c_{1,1}^{in} & c_{1,2}^{in} & \cdots & c_{1,n}^{in} \\ \vdots & \vdots & \ddots & \vdots \\ c_{m,1}^{in} & c_{m,2}^{in} & \cdots & c_{m,n}^{in} \end{bmatrix}
$$

with the naming conventions:

- **input Schema Labels** (or attribute names): L_i^{in}, where i ($i \in [1, n]$) is the input label index.
- **output Schema Labels:** L_k^{out}, where k ($k \in [1, q]$) is the input label index.
- **input Catalog Content** (or attribute representatives): $c^{in} = [c_{1,1}^{in}, \ldots, c_{m,n}^{in}]$ where $c_{j,i}^{in}$ is a single representative.
- **Column:** $C_i^{in} = [L_i^{in}, c_{1,i}^{in}, \ldots, c_{m,i}^{in}]$.
- **product** (or row): $P_j^{in} = [c_{j,1}^{in}, \ldots, c_{j,n}^{in}]$.

Due to these conventions, catalog integration represents a task trying to integrate product catalogs with unknown schema and content but from the same product domain into the fixed schema L^{out}. The target schema can either originate from another product catalog or a data warehouse. An optimal result would match each column to the correct target schema label [21]. Column labeling [7] corresponds closely to this approach. However, catalog integration leverages multi-label classification labeling instead of multi-class classification to maintain the ability to predict 1:1 and 1:n relations (as [7]) but additionally predicting n:1 associations. Hence, ALR allows to label columns from the input catalog C^{in} with multiple column names L_k^{out} from the target schema.

We use this approach mainly for two reasons: First, we want to find additional information in input columns. After ALR identified all possible labels, we can use extraction tools specialized on these labels and speed up the automatic integration process. Second, we want ALR to assist manual interactions by providing recommendations. Hence, we need to find possible matches, even if the matching-confidence is not perfect.

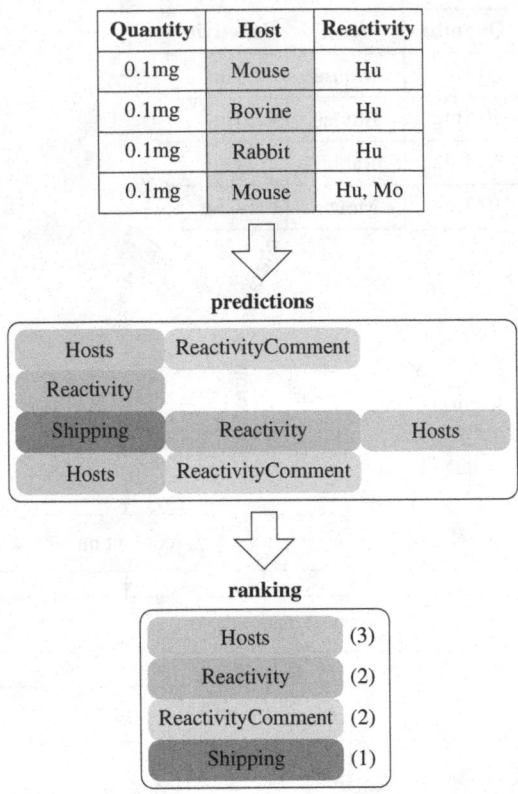

Fig. 3. After predicting labels for each attribute representative, an aggregation function determines the rank of every label. The label with the highest rank becomes the final prediction of ALR. However, ALR returns all predicted labels ordered by rank to provide recommendations. In this example, we use occurrence counting as the aggregation function. *Hosts* is the predicted label for three representatives, thus receiving the highest rank among all predicted labels (c.f. [21]).

(for example, the attribute name) is vectorized individually as additional input for the network. The next section provides more details on vectorization strategies.

After predicting all labels for all attribute representatives of a column, we aggregate label predictions. In Fig. 3 we use counting occurrences in label predictions as the aggregation function. Based on the occurrence count, we build a ranking among all predicted labels. Since the network predicts *Host* as a possible label for three representatives (*Mouse, Rabbit, Mouse*), *Host* receives the highest rank among all labels before *Reactivity* and *ReactivityComment*. With ALR returning a relative ranking score, *Hosts* receives a final score of $\frac{3}{8} = 0.375$ (c.f. [21]).

4.3   Vectorization Strategies

Multiple recent approaches to predicting labels or concepts to tabular data perform well on attributes represented by numerical columns, IDs, or BOW. [7, 18] Besides these attributes, product catalogs contain multiple attributes represented by a textual description. To handle unstructured text in attribute representatives, we use the multiple vectorization techniques based on similarity metrics, language, and attribute content to obtain feature vectors (c.f. Fig. 2) to predict multiple labels for a single attribute representative. Thereby, we need to distinguish between vectorization techniques for attribute names and attribute representatives since attribute names usually contain less than three words, while representatives may contain complete sentences or paragraphs.

- **Similarity Metrics:** Similarity between attribute names indicate matchings between schemas. We utilize the similarity between an input attribute name L_i^{in} and each attribute name from the target schema L_k^{out} as vectorization for an attribute name. The similarity vector could be calculated by any string similarity metric. We use cos-similarity of character bi- and trigrams [21]:

$$cos\_sim(L_i^{in}, L_k^{out})$$

  The resulting feature vector has the length $q = len(L^{out})$. This vectorization is only applicable to attribute names, since we cannot reasonably calculate the similarity of full paragraphs and attribute names (it would be close to zero).

- **Character Features:** Chen et al. provided features that are especially useful when predicting column labels of IDs. These IDs are comparable to antibody names or gene sequences in the context of antibody products. We employ the character count, limited to a maximum of 1024 characters per representative, and normalize the value to [0, 1]. Further, we employ the ratios of numeric, alphabetic, and symbolic characters of an attribute representative. Character features only apply to attribute instances or representatives but not attribute names since names contain mostly characters. A counterexample here is the attribute name *Storage C*. However, this particular case is too rare to handle it as a feature.

- **Language Features:** Modern word vectorization techniques like Bert [10] and Elmo [16] include sentence context to improve results in natural language processing (NLP) tasks like named entity recognition or text labeling. Furthermore, they are trained on generally available text, such as Wikipedia, where antibody product content misses. Customizing these pre-trained vectors cost too much compute power for SMEs. Nevertheless, we can produce specialized word embeddings by applying FastText [5] to improve results on labeling text attributes. Additionally, we investigate the effectiveness of simple one-hot word vectors and character n-grams of word tokens (sub-word n-grams). We evaluate and compare both vectorization approaches in our evaluation of theoretical and applied performance on catalog integration. Language features could be used for both attribute names and attribute representatives. However, we only apply vectorization with language features to attribute representatives. Depending on the vectorization, the feature vector size differs. For one-hot vectors, the vocabulary size determines the feature vector length, while the embedding-size determines the length when applying FastText.

4.4   Creating Training Data

Applying ALR to catalog integration, we need to provide annotated training data. There are two ways of gathering training data. The first option is to assemble and annotate input product catalogs manually. Assuming the input catalog is a CSV file, an employee needs to find corresponding target labels for each attribute representative and eventually include metadata. This process closely relates to the catalog integration process itself. Hence, an automated approach based on analyzing logs from manual interactions in the data pipeline or using input product catalogs and the finally integrated web-shop data is more desirable.

For an automated approach, we need to collect files at two stages of a data pipeline. First, we gather product catalog data after format unification with each file containing the manufacturer's original attribute names and contents. Second, we assemble the related output file after the last human interaction before transferring the product data into a database. In the second stage, the product data has the target schema.

After collecting data, we identify corresponding attribute representatives by their string similarity. If a file from the second stage includes a representative that was not changed by the data pipeline, we can consider a 1:1 relation between input and output attribute names for that representative. However, the data pipeline might have transformed other attribute representatives from the same column during the integration process: For example, application of regular expressions, to extract information from strings into one or multiple target columns, standardization of measurement units, or resolving regular expressions. Consequently, this approach can only identify relations if the same attribute representative is present in both tables since we have no information about the processes inside the data pipeline.

To handle unknown relations, where the data pipeline performed any string manipulation, we can use specialized tokenizers (e.g., a tokenizer for biomedical data [15]). We can then use the cosine similarity of tokens between an attribute representative from the manufacturers' file and all representatives of the related product in the integrated file [21].

For example, assuming we gathered the two files from Fig. 1, the representative *Mouse* matches exactly (similarity equal to 1.0) between input and output. Labels for representatives with perfect similarity are primary labels for a column. Considering the representative from *Product_Name*, we have an uncertain match to the label *Clone* since only *SL-12.1* is present in the sample output. Hence, the similarity score is smaller than 1.0, in contrast to perfect matches. Leveraging these uncertain similarity scores, we can use these labels for a multi-label classification approach by defining a minimum similarity score. We can generate multi-label targets for ALR through the ceiling (if greater or equal than min. similarity) or flooring (if smaller).

With this annotation strategy, we collected 19 files from integration jobs, including a total of ca. 420.000 antibody products (c.f. Table 1).[2] The number of products held in a single file ranges from 3 up to ca. 230.000 products. The files originate from 12 manufacturers and handle different product types (e.g., ELISA Kits, Primary Antibodies, etc.). Depending on the product type and manufacturer, the number of attribute names

---

[2] https://github.com/oschmi/antibody-catalog-integration-dataset.

per catalog ranges from 14 to 65. These catalogs were integrated into a target schema with 94 labels [21].

Table 1. Properties of the catalog integration dataset [21].

Total files	19
Total products	ca. 420.000
Products per file	3 – ca. 230.000
Manufacturers	12
Input attribute range	14–65

4.5 Data Augmentation

Although the annotation strategy is straightforward, it might not be feasible for production environments. Due to the limited amount of gathered data, a model might perform well in test evaluations but not in production. Thus, we employ a data augmentation strategy for production systems to cover wording used by manufacturers not present in the training dataset.

The data augmentation relies on synonym and abbreviation lists, most likely present in or efficiently creatable from every data integration pipeline, since synonym and abbreviation resolution is a typical data preparation stage. With synonyms and abbreviations gathered, we can apply a simple strategy to obtain more data: Instead of using only original columns, we can modify them by replacing attribute names with known synonyms and finally add the modified columns to the training dataset. Consequently, we gain a broad representation of attribute names used by manufacturers not present in the original training dataset. Another strategy could aim to replace representatives from a column with their synonyms. However, this approach only works for BOW columns. We evaluate only the practical impact of data augmentation with the attribute name approach due to this limitation.

5 Evaluation

ALR aims to simplify manual interactions in a data pipeline by recommending possible schema matches and possibly missing extractions. This section evaluates the performance of Attribute Label Ranking (ALR) and extends the original paper by comparing simple and complex neural network architectures and the effect of different preprocessing steps. Our evaluation considers the aspect of theoretical correctness and performance but also includes production evaluations.

5.1 Experimental Scenario

We use a similar experiment to validate the theoretical performance of ALR as Schmidts et al. [21]: The training dataset for the first stage of ALR includes ca. 50.000 products from 7 manufacturers, while the testing dataset contains ca. 50.000 products from 5 manufacturers, distinct from the training dataset. Both datasets contain different product types, such as ELISA Kits, Primary Antibodies, etc. The datasets were annotated as described in Sect. 4.4. In this evaluation, we used a minimum similarity score of 0.5 to find target labels. Depending on the manufacturer, ALR needs to integrate a tabular input file with individual attribute names ranging from 14 to 65 attributes into the target schema.

For this purpose, we train ALR on the training dataset and simulate the integration of product catalogs from the testing dataset. In extension to studying the model performance on two different language features while retaining character features and label similarity features, we evaluate simple language features (one-hot word and subword vectorization) and FastText embeddings with different model architectures (CNN and simple NN). We created all language features on the train set, including any one-hot vocabulary or the FastText embedding specialised for attribute representatives. Furthermore, we evaluate the influence of Unicode normalization and data augmentation.

Since we use a minimum similarity score of 0.5 in this evaluation, all models were trained on data with uncertain matches between input and target schema instead of training and evaluating models on (almost) exact matches as in the original paper due to models trained on uncertain matches outperformed any others [21]. Hence, we train and test all models with target labels reaching a minimum similarity of 0.5 by transforming the raw annotated label score into a one-hot ground truth vector. The target vector for any representative may contain more than one target label.

Evaluating the performance of ALR, we distinguish between two scenarios. In the first scenario, we evaluate predicting the primary label of columns, ignoring unpredictable labels. An unpredictable label occurs when the target label vector equals zero or when the target vector has no primary label (for example, this might happen when two values were greater than 0.5 before transformation to a one-hot target vector). This scenario is the multi-class classification scenario, where we only consider 1:1 relations. In the second scenario, we evaluate models with good performance in the first scenario concerning recommendation and multi-label classification performance. Using a minimum similarity of 0.5 results in a ground truth cardinality [24] of 5. Hence, ALR needs to predict five labels on average for every column in the multi-label classification scenario.

5.2 Classification Results

To compare ALR to other column labeling approaches, we evaluate ALR as a multi-class classification approach instead of a multi-label classification before evaluating the muli-label ranking performance. We only consider 1:1 relations and columns with a primary label for classification. Consequently, we ignore columns without a primary label or columns containing irrelevant data not integrated into the web-shop in the ground truth. The classification result of ALR is the column label with the highest rank. In case ALR cannot predict anything for a column, it returns 0. If there is a label in the ground truth, we count this result as a false negative. Hence, these results lower recall and f_1-score but not precision. We use this definition due to practical relevance: If ALR

Table 2. Overall multi-class classification result of ALR with different model and vectorization setups. Bold font indicates the best performance. All scores represent weighted avg. scores to handle class imbalance.

Model	Precision	Recall	f_1
$NN_{\text{word aug clean}}$	0.8073	0.3197	0.2780
NN_{ngram}	0.8197	0.4832	0.4556
$NN_{\text{ngram aug}}$	0.8196	0.5687	0.5425
$NN_{\text{ngram clean}}$	0.8191	0.4795	0.4595
$NN_{\text{ngram aug clean}}$	0.8239	**0.5687**	**0.5495**
$NN_{\text{ft aug clean}}$	**0.8416**	0.3940	0.3625
$CNN_{\text{ft aug clean}}$	0.5500	0.1636	0.1521

recommends anything, it should be correct. No prediction is better than a wrong prediction considering automated data pipelines.

Table 2 shows the overall weighted avg. classification performance of ALR depending on the model. The model's name indicates the underlying neural network, features, and pre-processing steps. For example, the models NN_{word}, NN_{ngram} and NN_{ft} represent a simple neural network [21] using the corresponding language vectorization: one-hot words, one-hot bi- and tri-grams or FastText embeddings trained on the training dataset. Other features as character and label similarities remain unchanged. The results for the model $NN_{\text{ngram aug}}$ include data augmentation with the strategy discussed in Sect. 4.5. $NN_{\text{ngram clean}}$ includes Unicode normalization.

Analyzing the results in Table 2, we can see that all models with simple NNs achieve a precision score of around 0.82, with $NN_{\text{ft aug clean}}$ reaching the highest score (0.8416) and $NN_{\text{word aug clean}}$ the lowest (0.8073). Comparing the results of $NN_{\text{ngram aug}}$ with $NN_{\text{ngram aug clean}}$ we can see the influence of Unicode normalization for data augmentation improving the result by ca. 0.015. Interestingly, Unicode normalization for raw NN_{ngram} does not improve the result. We provide only detailed n-gram configuration evaluations since the results are entirely transferable to the other models, for which we only report the configuration with the best result.

Considering recall and f_1-score, augmentation based models significantly outperform other approaches with $NN_{\text{ngram aug clean}}$ achieving the best overall recall and f_1-sore (0.5687, 0.5495). Data augmentation leads to an improvement of ca. 0.09. Unicode normalization improves the results again if used combined with data augmentation but not as a standalone preprocessing step. However, language features significantly impact results of recall and f_1-score. While all NN-based models reach comparable precision scores, recall and f_1 depend on the language model used. N-grams reach the best results as in [21]. FastText language features perform better than word one-hot vectors but are still inferior to n-grams regarding recall and f_1-score.

Regarding CNN based ALR, we tried different combinations and network architectures. However, the best CNN we found is inferior to every other simple NN. This result might have different reasons. CNNs might not exploit the data structure to solve

Table 3. Multi-class classification results of ALR depending on column types with different model and vectorization setups. Bold font indicates the best performance. All scores represent weighted avg. scores to handle class imbalance.

Model	BOW			Text		
	Precision	Recall	f_1	Precision	Recall	f_1
$NN_{\text{word aug clean}}$	0.8637	0.2876	0.1827	0.8340	0.3316	0.3107
NN_{ngram}	**0.8941**	0.6301	0.5823	0.8101	0.4285	0.4148
$NN_{\text{ngram aug}}$	0.8829	**0.6575**	**0.6064**	0.8312	**0.5357**	0.5343
$NN_{\text{ngram clean}}$	**0.8941**	0.6301	0.5823	0.8338	0.4234	0.4340
$NN_{\text{ngram aug clean}}$	0.8829	**0.6575**	**0.6064**	**0.8413**	**0.5357**	**0.5460**
$NN_{\text{ft aug clean}}$	0.8683	0.4520	0.4016	0.8386	0.3724	0.3470
$CNN_{\text{ft aug clean}}$	0.8422	0.2238	0.1769	0.5000	0.1786	0.1526

the catalog integration multi-label classification, or data might contain too much noise to receive good results.

Table 3 shows the results differentiated by column class. In general, the overall results apply here again, with n-grams performing best, data augmentation increasing recall and f_1-score, and Unicode normalization improving results. All approaches perform better on BOW than on text. Unicode normalization significantly improves results only for text-based columns, which means that textual columns contain more encoding issues than BOW. Surprisingly, simple word one-hot vectors perform almost on even to FastText embeddings regarding precision in both classes. However, one-hot word vectors have lower recall and f_1-score. Again, CNN performs worst for all classes.

Chen et al. report a micro f_1-score of 0.23 or 0.20 for strings depending on the features used [7]. ALR outperforms their approaches with every configuration despite CNNs, showing the effectiveness of language features in general and using sub-word bi- and trigrams instead of character unigrams for strings since all n-gram based approaches improve the result by at least 0.2 and up to 0.45 for $NN_{\text{ngram aug clean}}$ (micro f_1-score of 0.6575).

5.3   Multi-label and Recommendation Results

To assess whether ALR could be used as a recommendation engine to assist employees in integrating data, we analyze the Label Ranking Average Precision (LRAP), which evaluates the average fraction of labels ranked above a particular label (in our case the primary label) [24] and the $f_{0.5}$-score, which weights precision over recall. We provide these metrics since precision is more important than recall for the recommendation engine. A wrong recommendation could either lead to mistrust in the system or wrongly integrated data in the web-shop.

We calculate the LRAP by using primary labels in the ground truth and then finding the label in the ALR ranking of the corresponding prediction. Contrary to the classification scenario, we include columns with a ground truth of zero and without a primary label. If ALR does not predict a label, and there is no label in the ground truth

Table 4. Label Ranking Average Precision (LRAP) scores of ALR. *Only pred.* shows the LRAP score if ALR made a prediction greater than 0.0. *All* represents every prediction made, even if there is no ground truth available.

Model	LRAP					
	Overall		BOW		Text	
	Only pred.	All	Only pred.	All	Only pred.	All
NN_{ngram}	**0.8567**	0.6009	**0.9725**	0.8046	**0.8077**	0.4215
$NN_{ngram\ aug}$	0.8307	**0.6733**	0.9492	**0.8149**	0.7929	**0.5485**
$NN_{ngram\ clean}$	0.8388	0.6057	**0.9725**	0.8046	0.7853	0.4305
$NN_{ngram\ aug\ clean}$	0.8348	0.6728	0.9492	**0.8149**	0.7979	0.5477
$NN_{ft\ aug\ clean}$	0.8262	0.5382	0.9012	0.7402	0.7991	0.3603

Table 5. Weighted avg. $f_{0.5}$ of ALR with different n-gram configurations. Bold font indicates the best performance.

Model	Overall $f_{0.5}$		
	All	BoW	Text
NN_{ngram}	0.5705	0.7906	0.4636
$NN_{ngram\ aug}$	0.6409	**0.7988**	0.5767
$NN_{ngram\ clean}$	0.5734	0.7906	0.4866
$NN_{ngram\ aug\ clean}$	**0.6473**	**0.7988**	**0.5940**
$NN_{ft\ aug\ clean}$	0.4867	0.6867	0.4005

(ca. 33%), we define the result as correct. In this case, the rank equals one. The latter case, where a primary label is not available, has a minor influence on the score. Table 4 refers to this scenario as *all*. Furthermore, we evaluate how accurate the label ranking is if ALR makes a prediction, ignoring columns where ALR cannot predict any label. This scenario is important for practitioners to gain trust in recommendations (if there is one, it should be right). Again, we only consider the NN-based approaches due to their superior performance.

Table 4 shows the LRAP of predictions of ALR considering the different model configurations and column classes. NN_{ngram} achieves the highest scores (0.8567, 0.9725, 0.8077) if we ignore columns which it cannot predict. If we also take columns without prediction into account, the best performing model is $NN_{ngram\ aug}$ (0.6733, 0.8149, 0.5485). Applying Unicode normalization lowers the result in almost all cases (excepting $NN_{ngram\ clean}$ for textual columns). In general, all model configurations achieve better results on BOW than on text. Surprisingly, FastText could again not achieve better results than n-grams.

Table 5 provides the results for the $f_{0.5}$-score with the same setup as calculating the LRAP. The models $NN_{ngram\ aug}$ and $NN_{ngram\ aug\ clean}$ achieve the best results for BOW columns (0.7988) which corresponds with the highest LRAP in the *all* scenario. The model with Unicode normalization outperforms the raw n-gram based model.

$NN_{ngram\ clean\ aug}$ reaches the highest scores overall (0.6473) and for textual columns (0.5940), closely followed by augmentation without cleaning. The results corresponding to the FastText based model cannot hold the performance of n-gram-based models.

5.4 Limitations and Highlighting Possible Errors

Relying entirely on single columns is the major limitation of ALR. The approach does not include co-occurrences of attribute names in feature vectors. Furthermore, ALR does not utilize the product context to handle ambiguous predictions. Low-quality data from the integration dataset might influence our evaluation due to imbalanced target labels, columns containing duplicated attribute representatives, or different manufactures using a more closely related vocabulary than in other datasets or reality. Especially for BOW-columns, attribute representatives frequently repeat due to the nature of product catalogs.

Another limitation is the usage of a single composed network. Even if ALR handles attribute names and representatives differently, it does not use column structures to handle BOW and unstructured text differently. We need further investigations to figure out if handling BOW and text with specialized networks improves the results since we can differentiate those classes by counting word tokens before applying a neural network.

ALR requires a fixed target schema, and all products need the same context or domain. As a result, changes in the target schema cause retraining of the models behind ALR. However, changes in the target schema of SMEs are rare. If we can apply ALR because we have a fixed target schema and all products originate from the same domain, ALR provides a practical yet straightforward approach to collect and annotate training datasets for SMEs and then assisting manual interactions as a recommendation engine. Because of the annotation strategy, some errors might occur in our evaluation. For example, if the input sample contains the abbreviation *Hu* and the output sample only contains *Human* (c.f. Fig. 1), the simple cos-similarity approach does not find this match. A better annotation strategy could solve those issues. Consequently, ALR sometimes predicts correct results, which are considered as false in our evaluation.

ALR aims to handle noisy and low-quality data from real-world product catalog integration scenarios to meet the requirements of SMEs. In our evaluation dataset, the data quality varies from clean data, ready for integration to attribute representatives with missing whitespaces (e.g., *96test* instead of *96 test*), representatives with misspellings or worse, representatives containing encoding errors and arbitrary strings or numbers (e.g., *™* instead of ^{TM}, *ug* instead of μg). We handled and evaluated the influence of encoding errors, which are measurable in the evaluation. However, other quality issues that we cannot identify automatically may negatively affect the presented results. For example, these issues might result in wrong ground truth data or out of vocabulary errors in the prediction stage.

5.5 Evaluation in Production

We deployed two research prototypes into our partner's productive environment as a recommendation engine to improve their manual integration process in multiple test iterations. According to interviews with the management and reviews of the use case, a single wrong, fully automatic prediction would lead to mistrusting and additional work to correct the integrated data. Moreover, unnoticed incorrect product data in the web-shop might cause a loss of customers. Consequently, we follow this approach.

In the first iteration, we deployed ALR with NN_{ngram} due to its performance compared with NN_{word} in our evaluation. Despite not predicting labels perfectly, a correct prediction reduced the manual matching effort from minutes to seconds if the primary label occurred in the top 3 predictions on 1:1 relations. In 86% of cases where ALR made a prediction, the correct primary label occurred in the top 3. Depending on the manufacturer, 20%–40% of supplied product attributes were irrelevant to integrate into the web-shop.

In the second iteration, we deployed $NN_{ngram\ clean\ aug}$ to improve ALR ability predicting labels for unknown manufacturers. Data augmentation and Unicode normalization lead to an increase of ca. 33% predictions while maintaining the top 3 rate of 86%. These results validate the economic benefit of ALR for practitioners.

6 Conclusion

With Attribute Label Ranking (ALR) we propose a simple yet efficient approach for SME to streamline manual interactions during catalog integration. By applying ALR for column labeling, we extend Chen et al.'s approach [7] with additional features for attribute names and language features for representatives. Additionally, we change column labeling from multi-class classification to multi-label classification. ALR outperforms Chen et al. with every simple neural network, while CNNs seem not applicable for ALR. In addition to Chen et al., ALR can handle textual columns, despite almost every configuration of ALR performs better on BOW columns than on text. The only exception to that result is the recommendation performance of the FastText based simple NN.

Although catalog integration discourages recent advances in exploiting distributions of attribute representatives [18], we were able to produce results on low-quality data that impact and simplify practitioners' daily business. Considering heterogeneous, volatile, and noisy data, we found that simple language features (one-hot vectors) achieved the best results. Using sophisticated embeddings instead of one-hot vectors did not improve the results as expected despite specializing them on antibody product data. Allweyer et al. [1] also reflect these findings on predicting product categories by product names. Word embeddings seem not feasible in a noisy product context, containing many domain-specific abbreviations. However, we could show that already simple data cleaning and augmentation strategies significantly impact real-world applications of ALR.

Due to imbalanced labels and attribute instances in the used product catalogs, further research needs to investigate the performance on datasets from other domains or evaluate ALR over a more extended period in production systems applying the ATTESTATION pattern [23]. Creating datasets from other domains is uncomplicated: A suitable dataset needs at least attribute representatives with corresponding target labels of a fixed schema. Log files of data pipelines may provide these data.

Future research should address the limitations and uninvestigated configurations of ALR. For example, finding a more reasonable annotation strategy for automatic dataset creation could significantly improve existing configurations results. Since ALR ignores column and product context ignoring co-occurrences of labels, future research could extend ALR to handle ambiguous labels by taking these into account and further extending the use case of ALR.

References

1. Allweyer, O., Schorr, C., Krieger, R., Mohr, A.: Classification of products in retail using partially abbreviated product names only. In: Proceedings of the 9th International Conference on Data Science, Technology and Applications - Volume 1: DATA, pp. 67–77. INSTICC. SciTePress (2020). https://doi.org/10.5220/0009821400670077
2. Aumueller, D., Do, H.H., Massmann, S., Rahm, E.: Schema and ontology matching with COMA++. In: Proceedings of the 2005 ACM SIGMOD International Conference on Management of Data, pp. 906–908. ACM (2005)
3. Bernstein, P.A., Madhavan, J., Rahm, E.: Generic schema matching, ten years later. Proc. VLDB Endow. **4**(11), 695–701 (2011)
4. Bizer, C., Primpeli, A., Peeters, R.: Using the semantic web as a source of training data. Datenbank-Spektrum **19**(2), 127–135 (2019). https://doi.org/10.1007/s13222-019-00313-y
5. Bojanowski, P., Grave, E., Joulin, A., Mikolov, T.: Enriching word vectors with subword information. arXiv preprint arXiv:1607.04606 (2016)
6. de Carvalho, M.G., Laender, A.H., Gonçalves, M.A., da Silva, A.S.: An evolutionary approach to complex schema matching. Inf. Syst. **38**(3), 302–316 (2013). https://doi.org/10.1016/j.is.2012.10.002
7. Chen, Z., Jia, H., Heflin, J., Davison, B.D.: Generating schema labels through dataset content analysis. In: Companion Proceedings of the the Web Conference 2018, WWW 2018, pp. 1515–1522. International World Wide Web Conferences Steering Committee, Republic and Canton of Geneva, Switzerland (2018). https://doi.org/10.1145/3184558.3191601
8. Comito, C., Patarin, S., Talia, D.: A semantic overlay network for P2P schema-based data integration. In: 11th IEEE Symposium on Computers and Communications (ISCC 2006), pp. 88–94, June 2006. https://doi.org/10.1109/ISCC.2006.19. ISSN 1530-1346
9. Dessloch, S., Hernandez, M.A., Wisnesky, R., Radwan, A., Zhou, J.: Orchid: integrating schema mapping and ETL. In: 2008 IEEE 24th International Conference on Data Engineering, pp. 1307–1316, April 2008. https://doi.org/10.1109/ICDE.2008.4497540
10. Devlin, J., Chang, M.W., Lee, K., Toutanova, K.: BERT: pre-training of deep bidirectional transformers for language understanding (2019)
11. Foley, J., Bendersky, M., Josifovski, V.: Learning to extract local events from the web. In: Proceedings of the 38th International ACM SIGIR Conference on Research and Development in Information Retrieval, SIGIR 2015, Santiago, Chile, pp. 423–432. ACM, New York (2015). https://doi.org/10.1145/2766462.2767739
12. Gu, B., et al.: The interaction between schema matching and record matching in data integration. IEEE Trans. Knowl. Data Eng. **29**(1), 186–199 (2017). https://doi.org/10.1109/TKDE.2016.2611577
13. Kirsten, T., Thor, A., Rahm, E.: Instance-based matching of large life science ontologies. In: Cohen-Boulakia, S., Tannen, V. (eds.) DILS 2007. LNCS, vol. 4544, pp. 172–187. Springer, Heidelberg (2007). https://doi.org/10.1007/978-3-540-73255-6_15
14. Madhavan, J., Bernstein, P.A., Rahm, E.: Generic schema matching with cupid. In: VLDB, vol. 1, pp. 49–58 (2001)

15. Neumann, M., King, D., Beltagy, I., Ammar, W.: ScispaCy: fast and robust models for biomedical natural language processing. In: BioNLP@ACL (2019). https://doi.org/10.18653/v1/W19-5034
16. Peters, M.E., et al.: Deep contextualized word representations (2018)
17. Pham, M., Alse, S., Knoblock, C.A., Szekely, P.: Semantic labeling: a domain-independent approach. In: Groth, P., et al. (eds.) ISWC 2016. LNCS, vol. 9981, pp. 446–462. Springer, Cham (2016). https://doi.org/10.1007/978-3-319-46523-4_27
18. Pomp, A., Poth, L., Kraus, V., Meisen, T.: Enhancing knowledge graphs with data representatives. In: Proceedings of the 21st International Conference on Enterprise Information Systems, pp. 49–60. SCITEPRESS - Science and Technology Publications, Heraklion (2019). https://doi.org/10.5220/0007677400490060
19. Ristoski, P., Petrovski, P., Mika, P., Paulheim, H.: A machine learning approach for product matching and categorization. Semantic Web **9**(5), 707–728 (2018). https://doi.org/10.3233/SW-180300
20. Schmidts, O., Kraft, B., Siebigteroth, I., Zündorf, A.: Schema matching with frequent changes on semi-structured input files: a machine learning approach on biological product data. In: Proceedings of the 21st International Conference on Enterprise Information Systems, pp. 208–215. SCITEPRESS - Science and Technology Publications, Heraklion (2019). https://doi.org/10.5220/0007723602080215
21. Schmidts, O., Kraft., B., Winkens., M., Zündorf., A.: Catalog integration of low-quality product data by attribute label ranking. In: Proceedings of the 9th International Conference on Data Science, Technology and Applications - Volume 1: DATA, pp. 90–101. INSTICC. SciTePress (2020). https://doi.org/10.5220/0009831000900101
22. Shvaiko, P., Euzenat, J.: A survey of schema-based matching approaches. In: Spaccapietra, S. (ed.) Journal on Data Semantics IV. LNCS, vol. 3730, pp. 146–171. Springer, Heidelberg (2005). https://doi.org/10.1007/11603412_5
23. Sildatke, M., Karwanni, H., Kraft, B., Schmidts, O., Zündorf, A.: Automated software quality monitoring in research collaboration projects. In: Proceedings of the IEEE/ACM 42nd International Conference on Software Engineering Workshops, ICSEW 2020, pp. 603–610. Association for Computing Machinery, New York (2020). https://doi.org/10.1145/3387940.3391478
24. Tsoumakas, G., Katakis, I., Vlahavas, I.: Mining multi-label data. In: Maimon, O., Rokach, L. (eds.) Data Mining and Knowledge Discovery Handbook, pp. 667–685. Springer, Boston (2010). https://doi.org/10.1007/978-0-387-09823-4_34

Designing an Efficient Gradient Descent Based Heuristic for Clusterwise Linear Regression for Large Datasets

Enis Kayış[✉]

Industrial Engineering Department, Ozyegin University, Istanbul, Turkey
enis.kayis@ozyegin.edu.tr

Abstract. Multiple linear regression is the method of quantifying the effects of a set of independent variables on a dependent variable. In clusterwise linear regression problems, the data points with similar regression estimates are grouped into the same cluster either due to a business need or to increase the statistical significance of the resulting regression estimates. In this paper, we consider an extension of this problem where data points belonging to the same category should belong to the same partition. For large datasets, finding the exact solution is not possible and many heuristics requires an exponentially increasing amount of time in the number of categories. We propose variants of gradient descent based heuristic to provide high-quality solutions within a reasonable time. The performances of our heuristics are evaluated across 1014 simulated datasets. We find that the comparative performance of the base gradient descent based heuristic is quite good with an average percentage gap of 0.17% when the number of categories is less than 60. However, starting with a fixed initial partition and restricting cluster assignment changes to be one-directional speed up heuristic dramatically with a moderate decrease in solution quality, especially for datasets with a multiple number of predictors and a large number of datasets. For example, one could generate solutions with an average percentage gap of 2.81% in one-tenth of the time for datasets with 400 categories.

Keywords: Clusterwise linear regression · Heuristics · Gradient descent

1 Introduction

Multiple linear regression (MLR) is a commonly employed method in predictive analytics to identify and quantify the relationship between a set of independent variables and a particular response variable. In many practical settings, however, fitting the same regression hyperplane for all the data points would be suboptimal. The alternative is to fit a separate regression hyperplane for each predefined category of the dataset. However, MLR requires sufficient data to estimate the coefficients of the regression hyperplane that are statistically significant, if they

© Springer Nature Switzerland AG 2021
S. Hammoudi et al. (Eds.): DATA 2020, CCIS 1446, pp. 154–171, 2021.
https://doi.org/10.1007/978-3-030-83014-4_8

exist. This is especially true if the number of categories is very high and thus the number of data points within each category is small. For example, estimating demand function for each stock keeping unit (SKU) could prove to be fruitless, as typical US supermarket carries somewhere between 16000 to 60000 SKUs on average and due to rapidly changing product portfolio and customer preferences, relevant historical demand data for each SKU is quite small.

One solution to the problem stated above is to create clusters of categories with similar regression hyperplanes, and fit cluster-specific regression hyperplanes to make predictions for any of the categories in the particular cluster. A related problem, known as the clusterwise linear regression (CLR), is to cluster data points independent of the category memberships. CLR is known to be a challenging problem to solve exactly, and many heuristics have been proposed in the literature. Our problem is a generalized CLR problem as data points from the same predefined category are constrained to be in the same cluster after the CLR procedure. In line with previous studies, we aim to minimize the total sum of squares errors (SSE) after separate ordinary least squares regressions are applied to each cluster.

Finding exact solutions for the generalized CLR problem is computationally challenging due to the very large number of possible partitions. We are particularly interested in datasets where the number of categories (e.g., SKUs in a demand prediction setting) is very large, which increases the complexity even more. In this paper, we focus on binary clusters. One could extend our methodology to create multi-way partitions in a straightforward fashion. For example, using a greedy approach similar to the classification and regression trees (CART) method to generate decision trees, one can apply the methods presented in this paper consecutively to the resulting partitions to form new two sub-clusters until a termination condition is met. The result would be a multi-way partitioning of the whole dataset.

To create the best binary partitioning, one could cycle through all the variables defining the categories at each iteration and calculate the change in the objective function for all possible binary splits. The type of the category-defining variable determines the complexity of the solution method: If it is an ordered or continuous variable, the number of possible binary splits is equal to one less the number of unique categories. Hence we have an algorithm whose complexity increases linearly with the number of categories.

Splitting on an unordered categorical variable is quite challenging, especially when there are many categories. For a categorical variable with L levels, the number of possible nonempty partitions is equal to $2^{L-1}-1$. When $L > 20$ levels, the number of feasible partitions is more than one million. In this paper, we focus on the case of unordered categorical variable case, as this case is more realistic (e.g., SKU variables are unordered) and it is combinatorially more challenging. Moreover, we are specifically interested in settings where L is very large. Since it is not possible to search through all these solutions, we aim to design an efficient heuristic that can generate high-quality solutions quite fast. We borrow ideas from the gradient descent algorithm which is used to find local optima of a differentiable function.

Kayış (2020) develops some gradient descent based heuristics to solve the generalized CLR problem. In this paper, we focus on solving the problem for large datasets. Thus the speed of the proposed solution is especially critical. Toward this objective, we propose two new variants of the gradient descent based heuristics. Moreover, we evaluate the performance of our heuristics using larger datasets and include a separate section for datasets where multiple predictor variables are present.

The rest of the paper is organized as follows. We review the related literature in Sect. 2. Section 3 presents the formulation of the problem and notation used throughout the paper. We provide a list of heuristics to solve the particular problem in Sect. 4 and compare the performance of these heuristics via simulated datasets in Sect. 5. Section 6 concludes the paper with a discussion on future work that addresses the limitations of the current method and generated datasets and potential avenues for future research.

2   Literature Review

In this section, we provide a brief review of the works on clusterwise linear regression (CLR). CLR is a method that forms clusters of observations with similar regression lines (i.e., hyperplanes). It has been introduced into the literature by Charles (1977) as "régression typologique." Given the wide range of applications for regression models, CLR has also been applied to a wide range of problems in practice. Wedel and Kistemaker (1989) applies CLR to create groups of customers based on preferences while selecting products. Brusco et al. (2003) utilize this method to segment B2B customers of a telecommunications firm based on satisfaction from current products and churn likelihood. Across the weather prediction field, Bagirov et al. (2017) proposes CLR to predict rainfall using five input meteorological variables. Five wine clusters are identified in Costanigro et al. (2009) to fit cluster-specific hedonic price functions using the CLR method. To predict future pavement performance, Luo and Yin (2008) uses the CLR method which is found to have a higher prediction accuracy than a Markov probabilistic model. Olson et al. (2020) leverages CLR to find clusters of neighborhoods. Finally, McClelland and Kronmal (2002) employs the CLR method to analyze the relationship between stroke vulnerability and features derived from MRI scans. Even this shortlist of applications shows that RC could be used in many diverse settings. Since RC enables the researcher to form clusters and analyze the relationship between independent variables and a dependent variable in each cluster, in settings with parsimonious data, this method proposes an advantage to mitigate this data scarcity problem. Next, we summarize the methodological contributions to solve the RC problem.

The early works that provide methods to solve CLR problem include Späth (1979). An exchange algorithm is provided to find hard cluster memberships of each data point to minimize the total sum of squares error (SSE) of all clusters. Indeed the majority of the works in this area, including ours, proposes solutions to the CLR assuming hard clustering. An alternative assumption is that each data point belongs to a particular cluster with a certain probability (i.e. soft clustering). For example, Desarbo and Cron (1988) devises an expectation-maximization algorithm to solve the CLR problem under the soft clustering assumption. Notice, however, that the objective function in this second stream of literature is substantially different: to maximize an appropriately defined likelihood function, which requires additional distributional assumptions on residuals not required under the first stream. In this section, we focus mainly on papers that study the CLR problem under hard clustering and refer readers interested in the soft clustering approaches to Wedel and DeSarbo (1994) and Hennig (1999) for reviews.

Two main questions have to be addressed for a complete CLR application: (1) What is the optimal number of clusters? (2) What are the optimal cluster memberships? There are papers in the literature that proposes methods to address the first question (e.g., Shao and Wu 2005; Khadka and Paz 2017). In this chapter, we focus on addressing the second question assuming the number of clusters is known a priori.

Finding the optimal cluster memberships is a combinatorial problem, thus it is computationally challenging. A limited number of papers presents methods to find exact solutions to CLR. Instead of a traditional big-M formulation, a mixed logical-quadratic programming formulation is suggested in Carbonneaou et al. (2011). The proposed formulation is found to be numerically stable and generate exact global optimal solutions in the experimental datasets. This work is extended in Carbonneaou et al. (2012) with an application of repetitive branch and bound algorithm to solve the mixed-integer nature of the problem.

Since generating exact solutions is computationally costly and feasible only for small datasets, two main approaches are proposed in the literature to generate close-to-optimal solutions: Using simple heuristics and/or mathematical programming based heuristics. A nonlinear mixed-integer programming model is presented in Lau et al. (1999) to solve for the optimal soft clustering of the data points into two clusters. A compact mixed-integer linear formulation is provided in Bertsimas and Shioda (2007) to solve a slight variation of the original CLR problem with an L_1 accuracy measure. Bagirov et al. (2013) proposes an incremental algorithm that constructs initial solutions at each iteration using results obtained at the previous iteration. They find that the proposed algorithm is very efficient even in large datasets that are dense and do not contain outliers based on tests on multiple regression datasets. Joki et al. (2020) provides a support vector machine-based formulation to approximate the clusterwise regression problem with an L_1 accuracy measure that is naturally more robust to outliers. Finally, Wang and Paschalidis (2019) presents a mixed-integer programming formulation for the CLR problem subject to regularization constraints for variable selection.

In this paper, we study a modified version of the original CLR problem. In our problem, observations belonging to the same predefined subgroups are constrained to be in the same cluster. This version is studied only in a handful of papers. Park et al. (2017) defines this problem as generalized clusterwise linear regression, introduces a mixed-integer quadratic programming formulation to solve this version of the CLR problem, and designs and compares the performance of several metaheuristics (e.g., genetic algorithm, column generation, two-stage approach) with synthetic data and real-world retail sales data. Kayış (2020) presents a gradient descent-based heuristic to solve this problem for small datasets. Angün and Altınoy (2019) studies an extension of this problem where the dependent variable is multidimensional and the objective is to minimize the maximum of the sum of regression errors.

We provide two main contributions to the understudied generalized CLR problem. First, we design a fast gradient descent-based heuristic and its variants. Moreover, we present the computational results of the proposed heuristic on large datasets. Combined, we hope to shed light on the applicability of our solution methodology for big data applications.

3   Problem Formulation

We study the problem of splitting a node based on a single categorical variable $s \in \mathbb{R}$ with L unique values which are defined as levels. Let $y \in \mathbb{R}$ be the dependent variable and $\mathbf{x} \in \mathbb{R}^p$ denote the vector of independent variables. The regression hyperplane that represents the relationship between y and $\mathbf{x}$ depends on the value of s. For simplicity, we assume there is a single variable that defines the category of a data point. However, our algorithm can be extended to cases with multidimensional category variables by either forming factors through the concatenation of original variables or searching for the optimal partition variable-wise.

Let $(\mathbf{x}_i', y_i, s_i)$ denote the measurements on subject i, where $i = 1, \cdots, n$ and $s_i \in \{1, 2, \cdots, L\}$ denotes a categorical variable with L levels. The partitioned multiple linear regression model can be stated as:

$$y_i = \sum_{m=1}^{M} \mathbf{x}_i' \beta_m w_m(s_i) + \epsilon_i, \tag{1}$$

where $w_m(s_i) \in \{0, 1\}$ denotes whether the i-th observation belongs to the m-th cluster or not. We require that $\sum_{m=1}^{M} w_m(s) = 1$ for any $s \in \{1, 2, \cdots, L\}$ meaning that each level should be assigned to exactly one cluster. The task at hand is to determine this assignment function $w_m(s)$.

In this paper, we focus on binary partitions, namely $M = 2$, but multi-way partitions can be extended in a straightforward fashion. For example, using a greedy approach similar to the classification and regression trees (CART) method to generate decision trees, one can apply the methods presented in this paper consecutively to the resulting partitions to form new two clusters until a termination condition is met. The result would be a multiple partitioning of the whole dataset. To simplify our notation in binary partitioning, let $w_i := w_1(s_i) \in \{0, 1\}$, which is a mapping from $\{1, 2 \cdots, L\}$ to $\{0, 1\}$. Further, define atomic weights for each level as $\{\tau_1, \cdots, \tau_L\} \in \{0, 1\}^L$, where $\tau_l = 1$ indicates the l-th level is in the left cluster, otherwise it is in the right. Now, one can write the observation-level weights as $w_i = \sum_{l=1}^{L} \tau_l I_{(s_i=l)}$. Thus the number of decision variables reduces from the number of data points n to the number of levels L.

Let the level assignment vector $\boldsymbol{\tau} = (\tau_1, \cdots, \tau_L)'$, $W = \mathrm{diag}\{w_i\}$ and $I - W = \mathrm{diag}\{1 - w_i\}$, the vector of the dependent variable $\mathbf{y} = (y_1, \cdots, y_n)'$, and the design matrix $X = (\mathbf{x}_1, \mathbf{x}_2, \cdots, \mathbf{x}_n)'$. The ordinary least squares regression theory would then imply that, the total sum of squared errors (SSE) of the two clusters can be stated as follows:

$$
\begin{aligned}
Q(\boldsymbol{\tau}) &:= SSE_1 + SSE_2 \\
&:= \|\mathbf{y} - X(X'WX)^{-1}X'W\mathbf{y}\|^2 \qquad\qquad\qquad (2) \\
&\quad + \|\mathbf{y} - X\{X'(I-W)X\}^{-1}X'(I-W)\mathbf{y}\|^2 \\
&:= Q_L(\boldsymbol{\tau}) + Q_R(\boldsymbol{\tau}), \qquad\qquad\qquad\qquad\qquad (3)
\end{aligned}
$$

where the vector of atomic weights $\boldsymbol{\tau}$ is defined on the integer space $\{0,1\}^L$. The objective is to find the vector $\boldsymbol{\tau}$ that minimizes $Q(\boldsymbol{\tau})$. Notice that due to symmetry, one can assume that $\tau_1 = 1$ without loss of generality.

As explained before, the combinatorial optimization problem defined above is a special case of the CLR problem. In the original problem, each data point can belong to any particular partition. However, our formulation requires each data point with the same level to belong to the same partition. Since finding exact solutions to the original CLR problem is computationally prohibitive, our generalized CLR problem, too, is quite challenging to solve for the optimal solution. The mixed-integer programming formulation one could develop for this problem would have a nonlinear objective function as well as the nonlinearity in the constraints. When the number of data points, n, is realistically large, it is computationally prohibitive to solve this optimization problem.

4   Design of Gradient Descent-Based Heuristics

In this section, our aim is to design a heuristic to generate efficient solutions to the generalized CLR problem, since finding the exact solution is computationally costly. The simplest heuristic one could consider is an exhaustive search considering all possible partitions of the levels into two disjoint sets. One could even find the exact solution with this approach, but there is a catch. Assuming a categorical variable with L levels, there are $2^{L-1} - 1$ possible splits an exhaustive search has to go through. Trivially, one could execute this heuristic within a reasonable time when the number of levels is small. However, for a moderate or large number of levels, this option becomes computationally prohibitive, which is the case in most real-life applications. For example, a dataset with 21 different levels requires a search of $1,048,575$ possible splits.

Our aim is to design a gradient descent-based algorithm to generate high-quality solutions for our problem under a reasonable time limit. We borrow ideas from the gradient descent algorithm to find local optima in integer space. This algorithm starts with a random partition of the levels into two nonempty and non-overlapping groups. Then cluster membership of each level are flipped sequentially and the resulting total SSE $Q(\tau)$ as defined in (3)of the resulting clusters are computed for each flip. Next, the flip with the lowest $Q(\tau)$ is selected as the current partitioning and the algorithm iterates in this fashion until convergence. The formal procedure is as follows:

Step 1: Set $i = 1$. Start with a random initial partition of all the levels into two clusters. Let τ^1 denote this partition.

Step 2: Calculate $Q(\tau^i)$. For $l \in \{1, 2, ..., L\}$, do the following: Let $\tilde{\tau}_l^l = 1 - \tau_l^i$ and $\tilde{\tau}_k^l = \tau_l^i$ for $\forall k \neq l$ and compute $Q(\tilde{\tau}^l)$.

Step 3: Let $l^* = argmin_l \, Q(\tilde{\tau}^l)$. If $Q(\tilde{\tau}^l) < Q(\tau^i)$ stop. Otherwise let $i = i + 1$, $\tau^i = \tau^{l^*}$ and repeat Step 2.

This algorithm moves through adjacent partitioning solutions, where two partitions are considered adjacent if only one level has a different cluster. Thus, our heuristic moves through adjacent solutions and is guaranteed to converge to a local optimum. In an effort to achieve global optimum, one could start from multiple random starting partitions and report the best solution. Our algorithm has polynomial complexity in the number of levels assuming that $Q(\tau)$ is locally convex near the initial partition.

In this paper, our aim is to design and compare different variants of this base algorithm. In particular, we develop four variants in an attempt to gradually increase the speed of the base algorithm as follows:

- GD_B: This variant is exactly as defined formally above. Since it starts with a random initial solution, we propose to run it multiple times and report the best solution out of these runs. Multiple runs would clearly increase solution quality at the expense of additional computational time.
- GD_{FI}: In this variant, we start with a fixed initial (FI) partition, in particular we let all the levels to be assigned to the left partition (i.e., $\tau_l^1 = 1$, $\forall l \in \{1, 2, ..., L\}$). Since there is no randomness in this version, a single run is sufficient that would save computational time. However, if there is a local optimum near the initial solution that is not a global one, the solution quality may be poor.
- GD_{FIF}: In an attempt to speed up the algorithm a bit more, we modify GD_{FI} variant by changing the assignments of levels to partitions in only one direction. In particular, we change Step 2 of our base algorithm as follows:
  Step 2': Calculate $Q(\tau^i)$. For $l \in \{l | \tau_l^1 = 1\}$, do the following: Let $\tilde{\tau}_l^l = 0$ and $\tilde{\tau}_k^l = \tau_l^i$ for $\forall k \neq l$ and compute $Q(\tilde{\tau}^l)$.
- GD_{FIS}: This variant is intended to increase the speed of GD_{FIF} by eliminating the need to fit OLS regressions for each level at Step 2. Instead a crude approximation of the potential improvement in SSE reduction will be calculated using the OLS fits for the left and right clusters evaluated at the start of Step 2. Let $q_L(l)$ $(q_R(l))$ be the SSE resulting from using the OLS fit for the left (right) cluster on the data points for which $I_{(s_i=l)} = 1$. Using this notation, one could use $q_R(l) - q_L(l)$ as an approximation of the SSE improvement as a result of moving the l category from the left to the right cluster. Now, we can modify Step 2 and 3 of our base algorithm as follows:

Step 2": Calculate $Q(\boldsymbol{\tau}^i)$. For $l \in \{l | \tau_l^1 = 1\}$, do the following: Let $\tilde{\tau}_l^l = 0$ and $\tilde{\tau}_k^l = \tau_l^i$ for $\forall k \neq l$ and compute $q(l) := q_R(l) - q_L(l)$.
Step 3": Let $l^* = argmin_l\, q(l)$. If $q(l) \leq 0$ stop. Otherwise let $i = i+1$, $\boldsymbol{\tau}^i = \boldsymbol{\tau}^{l^*}$ and repeat Step 2".

The four variants are listed above in the order of decreased computational time, at the expense of decreased solution quality. The selection of the best variant for an application depends on the desired compromise between speed and solution quality. To understand and quantify the rate of decrease in the solution time and quality, we conduct an extensive numerical study.

5 Numerical Study

In this section, we present the findings from a numerical study to understand the quality of the solutions generated by the four variants of our gradient descent heuristic. Simulated datasets are generated to perform the numerical study. We are particularly interested in how fast the solution time and quality decrease as one goes down the list of variants. Moreover, we are also interested in the sensitivity of our results with respect to the number of levels, number of data points, the magnitude of the residuals, and the number and type of underlying clusters. For some cases in our simulated datasets where the optimal partitioning is not known, a random search is used as a benchmark. The random search method simply generates random partitions and returns the one with the smallest total SSE as defined in 3.

In our implementation, we run the base gradient search algorithm, GD_B, 5 times, each time with a different randomly generated initial partitioning, and report the best solution out of 5 replications. The remaining 3 variants are implemented as explained in detail in the previous section. Finally, the random method ($RAND$) evaluates the total SSE of max $4000, 2^{L-1} - 1$ unique random partitions and replicates this procedure 5 times. The best solution out of these 5 replications is reported here as the performance of the random search method. The random search method finds the optimal partitioning when the number of levels is small (i.e., $L \leq 12$). However, the performance of this method deteriorates rapidly as the number of levels increases, as the search space is increasing exponentially fast with the number of levels. Finally, to eliminate problematic OLS fits with a small number of data points, we eliminate solutions with partitions having less than 15 data points from the search space. All computations are carried out on a machine with Intel® Core^{TM} i7-8565U CPU @ 1.80 GHz processor and 16 GB RAM.

5.1 Dataset Generation

We generate three groups of simulated datasets. The first group has a small to moderate number of levels and a single independent variable. The second group is similar to the first but with multiple independent variables. The analysis of the datasets in this group helps us assess the performance of our heuristics as the number of predictors increase. The last group contains our largest datasets with a large number of levels and multiple independent variables. This group sheds light on the performance of our heuristics when used for large datasets. Next, we provide details of the datasets for each group.

The simulated datasets in the first group have the following characteristics. We assume that there is a single independent variable, x, and consider three different regression equation settings. In the first two settings, we consider the cases in which the optimal partition is binary. In the first partition, the underlying regression equations are assumed to have the form $y_i = 10000 - 8 * x_i + \epsilon_i$ for the first partition and $y_i = 5000 - x_i + \epsilon_i$ for the second one. In the first setting, the even-numbered levels are assumed to belong to the first partition and the old numbered partitions are assumed to belong to the second partition. In the second setting, only two levels are assumed to be in the first partition and the rest are assumed to be in the second partition. Variations between the results of these two settings help us analyze the performance with respect to the unequal number of elements in each of the optimal partition. We use the third setting to analyze cases in the optimal partitioning is not binary. In particular, we study 8 partitions and in each partition the underlying regression equation is assumed to have the form $y_i = 10000 - (s_i \bmod 8) - ((s_i \bmod 8) + 1) * x_i + \epsilon_i$. In this last setting, the optimal number of partitions is trivially 8. However, the optimal binary partitioning is not known, unless the exact solution to the generalized CLR problem is known. In all settings, we randomly generated the values for the independent variable x_i uniformly from the interval $[500, 1000]$ and the values for the regression errors ϵ_i from a normal distribution with mean zero and variance σ^2.

For the first group, we generated 672 datasets in total. In each dataset, we change one of the following parameters: The number of levels varied from 8 to 60 in increments of 4. For each number of level L, we consider four variations with respect to the number of data points: $15L, 30L, 60L, 90L$. We let σ to vary from 100 to 400 in increments of 100. Thus we have a full factorial design with $14 * 4 * 4 * 3 = 672$ different datasets.

The dataset in the second group is similar to the first group, but we now have multiple independent variables x_k where $k = 2, 3, ..., K$. Similar to the first group, we consider three different regression equation settings. In the first two settings, the underlying regression equation is assumed to have the form $y_i = 20 + \sum_{p=1}^{K}(2p-1) * x_{pi} + \epsilon_i$ for the first partition and $y_i = 20 + \sum_{p=1}^{K}(2p) * x_{pi} + \epsilon_i$ for the second one. In the third setting, the underlying regression equation is assumed to have the form $y_i = 20 + (s_i \bmod 8) + \sum_{p=1}^{K}((s_i \bmod 8) + 1) * x_{pi} + \epsilon_i$. Regarding the rest of the parameters, we set $\sigma = 10$, varied the number of levels from 40 to 60 in increments of 4 and the number of independent variables K from 2 through 5, and used number of data points from the set $\in \{15L, 30L, 60L, 90L\}$. In total we have $6 * 4 * 4 * 3 = 288$ datasets in the second group.

Finally, the datasets in the third group are generated in the same fashion as those in the second group. However, we have made a few changes due to the significantly increased time requirement for these datasets. The only differences are that the number of levels is either 300 or 400, the number of data points is used from the set $\in \{15L, 30L, 60L\}$ and the number of independent variables K varies from 3 through 5. Hence we have $2 * 3 * 3 * 3 = 54$ datasets in the last group.

5.2   Results Using Datasets with a Single Predictor

We first present results of comparing the five methods using datasets with a single independent variable. Our main performance measure of a method is the percentage gap between the SSE improvement generated by the method at hand and that of the best solution out of the five methods employed. Let SSE_Red_i be the difference between the total SSE assuming all the levels are within a single cluster and the total SSE of the resulting partition obtained by method i. Formally, the percentage gap of method i is calculated as:

$$Gap_i = \frac{\max_i SSE\_Red_i - SSE\_Red_i}{\max_i SSE\_Red_i}.$$

Notice that this performance measure does not give an absolute quality of the method, but rather a comparative performance with respect to the other four methods.

Table 1 presents the summary statistics of the percentage gaps of the five methods across all the generated datasets with a single predictor. Not surprisingly, the GD_B method achieves the best outcome with an average of 0.17% percentage gap. However, the percentage gap could be as large as 38.34%. This result highlights the fact that the descent search method could get stuck in a local minimum which could result in a significant performance loss. The comparative performance of the second variant of our algorithm, GD_{FI}, is expectedly worse off with an average percentage gap of 4.66%. The third variant, GD_{FIF}, provides slightly lower performance with an average percentage gap of 5.91%. The last variant of the gradient descent-based algorithm, GD_{FIS}, uses a crude approximation of SSE reduction instead of a new OLS fit. Based on the results, this approach gives the lowest performance of the variants with an average percentage gap of 6.88%. This ranking of the variants does not change when one considers other summary statistics as well. Finally, the performance of the random search method is expectedly the worst by far in all the summary statistics. It is possible to achieve 0% percentage gap with this method when $L \leq 12$ in which case the random search method becomes an exhaustive search. However, this method could result in significantly low performances when the number of levels is larger.

Table 1. Summary statistics about the percentage gaps of the five methods across 672 datasets in the first group.

	GD_B	GD_{FIF}	GD_{FI}	GD_{FIS}	$RAND$
Average	0.17%	5.91%	4.66%	6.88%	17.98%
Min	0.00%	0.00%	0.00%	0.00%	0.00%
5th Perc.	0.00%	0.00%	0.00%	0.00%	0.00%
25th Perc.	0.00%	0.00%	0.00%	0.00%	0.00%
Median	0.00%	0.00%	0.00%	0.00%	10.72%
75th Perc.	0.00%	7.72%	6.36%	8.79%	30.48%
95th Perc.	0.00%	34.74%	24.56%	34.74%	62.33%
Max	38.34%	65.38%	65.38%	89.95%	74.17%

Figure 1 shows the percentage gaps of five methods as the number of levels increases. First, notice that the performance of the random search method decays quite fast as the number of levels increases beyond 12. As discussed before, when $L \leq 12$, the random search can check each feasible solution, thus could find the optimal partitioning. Moreover, the ranking of the solution qualities generated by four variants of the gradient descent algorithm remains the same at each value of the number of levels parameter. The GD_B variant produces the highest quality solutions when $L \leq 44$. When the number of levels is higher, other variants produce higher quality solutions in only 8 datasets. It is worth mentioning that the initial solution has a significant effect on the performance especially if the number of levels is small: In these cases, the search space is smaller, thus using different initial solutions is effective in overcoming the stacking to a local minimum problem. Moreover, the comparative performance is also worse for the variants that use the fixed initial solution when $L \bmod 8 = 0$ due to our design of the computational experiments: In these cases, there is an equal number of levels in each partition which increases the comparative performance of GD_B method to increase.

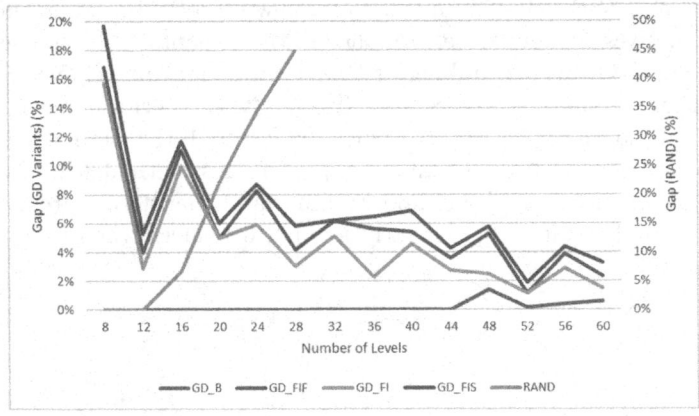

Fig. 1. The average percentage gaps of the five methods.

The first two settings of our numerical study assume that there are two underlying regression equations. For these settings, the optimal binary partition could be found easily by the value of the categorical variable. For datasets generated under these two settings, we compute the number of misclassified levels in each method. Table 2 presents the maximum number of misclassified levels for each method across varying numbers of levels. In line with our findings in Fig. 1, the partitions calculated using the GD_B method has the lowest number of misclassifications. However, the other three variants of the gradient descent algorithm could generate a much higher number of misclassifications, which tend to increase with the number of levels. For one dataset with $L = 20$, the solutions calculated by the other three variants resulted in a very high number of misclassifications and more than 65% percentage gap. This shows that using a fixed initial partition could lead to a local minimum with poor performance. With the random search method, the number of misclassifications increases rapidly with the number of levels. Notice that the fraction of levels that is misclassified is also increasing, which explains the underlying reason for the poor performance of the $RAND$ method.

Table 2. The maximum number of misclassified levels for the five methods.

L	GD_B	GD_{FIF}	GD_{FI}	GD_{FIS}	$RAND$
8	0	1	1	1	0
12	0	1	1	1	0
16	0	1	1	1	1
20	0	9	9	7	3
24	0	1	1	3	4
28	0	1	1	1	6
32	1	1	1	1	
36	0	1	1	1	
40	0	2	1	3	
44	0	1	1	1	
48	1	5	1	9	
52	1	1	1	1	
56	0	1	1	27	
60	1	1	1	1	

How does the distribution of the number of levels within the partitions and the existence of multiple underlying partitions change the performance of each heuristic? Table 3 presents the average percentage gaps of each heuristic across three underlying regression settings defined in Sect. 5.1. The performance of the GD_B method is the best under all three settings, albeit the comparative performance decreases under the second setting due to the higher performance of the other three methods under this setting. The three variants with a fixed initial partition have the best performance in the second setting, which represents the case with an uneven number of levels in each partition (i.e., 2 vs. $L - 2$). For these datasets, most of the levels belong to the same partition. Thus starting with the initial solution of assigning all the levels into a single partition is very close to the optimal partitioning. We also find that the computational times of the $GD_{FI}, GD_{FIF}, GD_{FIS}$ methods for datasets generated under the second setting are significantly smaller, which further corroborates our claim. Finally, the difference between the $RAND$ method and the gradient descent based heuristics is the smallest when there are 8 underlying partitions. This observation could imply that the performance of all the gradient descent based heuristics decreases for datasets with multiple partitions, as the performance of the $RAND$ method is not supposed to differ significantly for these datasets.

Table 3. The average percentage gaps of the five methods across different regression settings.

Regression setting	GD_B	GD_{FIF}	GD_{FI}	GD_{FIS}	$RAND$
1	0.11%	6.15%	6.15%	6.28%	16.86%
2	0.29%	4.31%	0.55%	4.21%	27.64%
3	0.12%	7.26%	7.26%	10.14%	9.44%

The effect of the number of data points (n) on the performance of the heuristics is quite small as shown in Table 4. There is a slight increase in the performance of the GD_B heuristic as n increases. The slight decrease in the comparative performance of $GD_{FI}, GD_{FIF}, GD_{FIS}$ could be attributed to the increased performance of the GD_B method.

Table 4. The average percentage gaps of the five methods across different number of data points.

Number of data points	GD_B	GD_{FIF}	GD_{FI}	GD_{FIS}	$RAND$
$15 * L$	0.39%	9.93%	4.93%	10.38%	17.23%
$30 * L$	0.15%	4.83%	4.83%	6.01%	17.51%
$60 * L$	0.10%	4.14%	4.14%	5.34%	18.00%
$90 * L$	0.06%	4.73%	4.73%	5.79%	19.18%

Table 5 shows the average percentage gaps of each heuristic as the standard deviation of the residuals (σ) varies. We find that, within the range of our numerical study, the variability of the residuals does not have a significant effect on the performance of our heuristics. We should, however, indicate the slightly lower performances of the one-directional variants of the gradient descent-based heuristics.

Table 5. The average percentage gaps of the five methods across varying residual error standard deviation.

σ	GD_B	GD_{FIF}	GD_{FI}	GD_{FIS}	$RAND$
100	0.09%	5.31%	4.69%	6.50%	17.19%
200	0.44%	5.18%	3.80%	6.22%	17.88%
300	0.12%	5.98%	4.49%	6.60%	18.55%
400	0.06%	7.16%	5.65%	8.21%	18.31%

Given the analysis of solution quality, the next question is the required computational times for all heuristics. Table 6 presents the average computation times (in seconds) across a varying number of levels of all five methods. The ranking of the gradient descent based heuristics with respect to average percentage gaps is reversed when one considers the computation times. The GD_B method takes more than five times more computation time as compared to the other 3 variants, which more than offsets the fact that the GD_B method requires 5 replications. We also observe that the difference increases with the number of levels which suggests that the convergence rate with random initial points decreases with the number of levels. Moreover, the $RAND$ method requires quite large computation times. When $L \leq 12$, with a single replication of the $RAND$ method one can search the whole feasible region hence the computational times are comparatively small. However, the random search method stays flat after $L > 12$, as the number of partitions to evaluate reaches the predefined limit of 4000.

5.3   Results Using Datasets with Multiple Predictors

Next, we present results using datasets with multiple independent variables. These results for these datasets shed light on the performance of our methods under multiple predictors and a large number of levels. We have not included $RAND$ and GD_{FIS} in our comparisons for these datasets: The $RAND$ method would be too computationally intensive to evaluate, as the number of levels is too large. The performance of the GD_{FIS} method is very similar to that of GD_{FIF}.

Table 7 shows the average percentage gaps of the three variants of the gradient descent-based heuristics. Comparing to the results in Fig. 1, we find that the performance of GD_B decreases and the performances of the other two variants increase. Since the percentage gap measures comparative performance, one could conclude that the difference between the GD_B method and the other two variants decreases when there are multiple predictors. When the number of levels is also very large, this difference tends to decrease even further. For datasets with 300 levels, the GD_{FI} and GD_{FIF} methods even has a lower average percentage gap than the base heuristic.

Table 6. The average computational times (seconds) of the five methods.

L	GD_B	GD_{FIF}	GD_{FI}	GD_{FIS}	$RAND$
8	0.17	0.02	0.03	0.01	0.14
12	0.52	0.08	0.09	0.02	3.19
16	0.93	0.12	0.15	0.04	29.61
20	1.55	0.19	0.24	0.05	31.83
24	2.35	0.28	0.35	0.07	32.85
28	2.93	0.35	0.46	0.09	30.58
32	3.46	0.41	0.53	0.10	
36	4.72	0.56	0.72	0.15	
40	5.85	0.68	0.87	0.17	
44	7.24	0.82	1.07	0.21	
48	8.72	1.01	1.34	0.28	
52	10.46	1.17	1.54	0.32	
56	12.19	1.34	1.77	0.37	
60	14.54	1.59	2.08	0.43	
All	**5.40**	**0.62**	**0.80**	**0.17**	**9.16**

Table 7. The average percentage gaps of the gradient descent-based heuristics as the number of levels varies.

L	GD_B	GD_{FIF}	GD_{FI}
40	0.99%	3.67%	3.02%
44	0.17%	2.93%	2.93%
48	1.59%	2.72%	2.07%
52	0.11%	1.68%	1.68%
56	0.65%	3.57%	1.50%
60	1.68%	1.79%	1.79%
300	7.20%	2.81%	2.81%
400	4.19%	6.77%	6.77%

We present the average optimality gaps of the three methods as the number of independent variables increases in Table 8. There is not a clear pattern in the results, thus we believe that our results are robust to the number of predictors. It is important to remind that this result is valid for the range of the number of predictors explored in this study.

Table 8. The average percentage gaps of the gradient descent-based heuristics as the number of predictors increases.

K	GD_B	GD_{FIF}	GD_{FI}
2	1.21%	2.29%	1.69%
3	0.11%	2.97%	2.54%
4	0.93%	2.57%	1.94%
5	1.22%	3.07%	2.50%
All	**0.86%**	**2.73%**	**2.17%**

Finally, we report the average computational times (in seconds) of the three methods in Table 9. A comparison with Table 5 shows that there is some increase in the computational time of all the methods for datasets having multiple predictors. Notice that when the number of levels is large, i.e., $L = 400$, the computational time of the GD_B method is about half hour. The other two variants can still solve the problem within almost 3 min. Considering that the performances of GD_{FI} and GD_{FIF} is even better for some cases with large L, the practical use of these variants are more plausible when dealing with large datasets.

Table 9. The average computational time (seconds) of the gradient descent-based heuristics as the number of levels varies.

L	GD_B	GD_{FIF}	GD_{FI}
40	7.21	0.85	1.09
44	9.03	1.00	1.35
48	10.64	1.18	1.51
52	12.68	1.41	1.85
56	15.32	1.75	2.25
60	18.39	1.92	2.53
300	902.80	93.12	120.87
400	2065.26	206.03	271.64

6   Conclusions

We study an extension of the clusterwise linear regression problem. Our aim is to partition the data points such that the resulting sum of square errors from all partitions is minimized. Thus the output would be a set of regression fits that define each cluster. In our problem, observations that belong to the same predefined category should be in the same cluster. This is a challenging problem to solve due to its combinatorial nature. Since exact solutions require a large amount of time, we provide four variants of a gradient descent based heuristic which iterates through solutions in order to find the best binary partition to minimize the total SSE. In our numerical study with 1014 simulated datasets, we find that the comparative performance of our heuristics is very good as compared to the random search method. The performance of the base algorithm is best when each of the true underlying partitions has a similar number of levels and the number of levels is small to moderate.

In many real-life implementations of clusterwise linear regression, the number of levels could be quite large. In an attempt to generate good solutions for these datasets under a reasonable time limit, we design three variants of the base heuristic, which start from the same initial solution and restrict the assignment changes to only one of the partitions. We find that the difference between the base method and these variants decreases with the number of levels when there are multiple independent variables. Given the significantly less time requirement for these variants, there is a practical use case for these methods

There are a number of avenues for future research to further investigate this research problem. First, we need to assess the quality of the generated solutions using a more robust approach. One alternative is to use exact solutions: First, an integer programming formulation should be provided to solve the problem and decomposition techniques, such as Bender's decomposition, should be developed to find the exact solution to our problem. Other meta-heuristics should be tested for large datasets to further understand the practical use of these methods. Two assumptions of our problem, known number of partitions and previously selected independent variables, could be studied to further reap the benefits of clusterwise linear regression. Finally, an evaluation of our methods using real-life datasets would increase our understanding of the problem and our solution methodology.

References

Angün, E., Altınoy, A.: A new mixed-integer linear programming formulation for multiple responses regression clustering. In: 2019 6th International Conference on Control, Decision and Information Technologies (CoDIT), pp. 1634–1639. IEEE (2019)

Bagirov, A.M., Mahmood, A., Barton, A.: Prediction of monthly rainfall in victoria, australia: clusterwise linear regression approach. Atmosp. Res. **188**, 20–29 (2017)

Bagirov, A.M., Ugon, J., Mirzayeva, H.: Nonsmooth nonconvex optimization approach to clusterwise linear regression problems. Eur. J. Oper. Res. **229**(1), 132–142 (2013)

Bertsimas, D., Shioda, R.: Classification and regression via integer optimization. Oper. Res. **55**(2), 252–271 (2007)

Brusco, M.J., Cradit, J.D., Tashchian, A.: Multicriterion clusterwise regression for joint segmentation settings: an application to customer value. J. Mark. Res. **40**(2), 225–234 (2003)

Carbonneau, R.A., Caporossi, G., Hansen, P.: Globally optimal clusterwise regression by mixed logical-quadratic programming. Eur. J. Oper. Res. **212**(1), 213–222 (2011)

Carbonneau, R.A., Caporossi, G., Hansen, P.: Extensions to the repetitive branch and bound algorithm for globally optimal clusterwise regression. Comput. Oper. Res. **39**(11), 2748–2762 (2012)

Charles, C.: Régression typologique et reconnaissance des formes. Ph.D. thesis (1977)

Costanigro, M., Mittelhammer, R.C., McCluskey, J.J.: Estimating class-specific para-
metric models under class uncertainty: local polynomial regression clustering in an
hedonic analysis of wine markets. J. Appl. Econ. **24**(7), 1117–1135 (2009)

DeSarbo, W.S., Cron, W.L.: A maximum likelihood methodology for clusterwise linear
regression. J. Classif. **5**(2), 249–282 (1988)

Hennig, C.: Models and methods for clusterwise linear regression. Models and Methods for Clusterwise Linear Regression. In: Gaul, W., Locarek-Junge, H. (eds.) Classification in the Information Age. Studies in Classification, Data Analysis, and
Knowledge Organization. Springer, Berlin (1999). https://doi.org/10.1007/978-3-
642-60187-3_17

Joki, K., Bagirov, A.M., Karmitsa, N., Mäkelä, M.M., Taheri, S.: Clusterwise support
vector linear regression. Eur. J. Oper. Res. **287**(1), 19–35 (2020)

Kayış, E.: A gradient descent based heuristic for solving regression clustering problems.
In: Proceedings of the 9th International Conference on Data Science, Technology and
Applications (DATA 2020), pp. 102–108. INSTICC, SciTePress (2020)

Khadka, M., Paz, A.: Comprehensive clusterwise linear regression for pavement management systems. J. Transp. Eng. B Pavement **143**(4), 04017014 (2017)

Lau, K.-N., Leung, P.-L., Tse, K.-K.: A mathematical programming approach to clusterwise regression model and its extensions. Eur. J. Oper. Res. **116**(3), 640–652
(1999)

Luo, Z., Yin, H.: Probabilistic analysis of pavement distress ratings with the clusterwise
regression method. Transp. Res. Record J. Transp. Res. Board 2084, 38–46 (2008)

McClelland, R.L., Kronmal, R.: Regression-based variable clustering for data reduction.
Stat. Med. **21**(6), 921–941 (2002)

Olson, A.W., et al.: Classification and regression via integer optimization for neighborhood change. Geograph. Anal. **53**(2), 192–212 (2020)

Park, Y.W., Jiang, Y., Klabjan, D., Williams, L.: Algorithms for generalized clusterwise
linear regression. INFORMS J. Comput. **29**(2), 301–317 (2017)

Shao, Q., Wu, Y.: A consistent procedure for determining the number of clusters in
regression clustering. J. Stat. Plan. Infer. **135**(2), 461–476 (2005)

Späth, H.: Algorithm 39 clusterwise linear regression. Computing **22**(4), 367–373 (1979)

Wang, T., Paschalidis, I.C.: Convergence of parameter estimates for regularized mixed
linear regression models. In: 2019 IEEE 58th Conference on Decision and Control
(CDC), pp. 3664–3669. IEEE(2019)

Wedel, M., DeSarbo, W.S.: A review of recent developments in latent class regression
models. In: Bagozzi, R. (ed.) Advanced Methods of Marketing Research, pp. 352–388.
Blackwell (1994)

Wedel, M., Kistemaker, C.: Consumer benefit segmentation using clusterwise linear
regression. Int. J. Res. Mark. **6**(1), 45–59 (1989)

A Policy-Agnostic Programming Language for the International Data Spaces

Fabian Bruckner[1]([⊠]), Julia Pampus[1], and Falk Howar[2][iD]

[1] Fraunhofer ISST, Emil-Figge-Straße 91, 44227 Dortmund, Germany
{fabian.bruckner,julia.pampus}@isst.fraunhofer.de
[2] TU Dortmund, Otto-Hahn-Straße 14, 44227 Dortmund, Germany
falk.howar@tu-dortmund.de
https://www.isst.fraunhofer.de
https://ls14-www.cs.tu-dortmund.de

Abstract. It is of utmost importance to maintain digital sovereignty in the context of Industry 4.0 and data-driven business models. As data itself becomes a valuable asset, this is a challenge that many companies have to face. This is particularly true as data sharing with third parties is a mandatory component of many modern business models. For its participants, the International Data Spaces (IDS) provide an ecosystem that supports the establishment and protection of their digital sovereignty. In this extended paper, we present the requirements in the area of usage control that have emerged from the IDS. We recapitulate the current state of the domain-specific language D°, which has usage control mechanisms as a core functionality. We then introduce extensions to the policy system of D° and the language itself to meet these requirements. We demonstrate how the policy system can be extended by label-based mechanisms in order to increase the expressiveness of the policy system. These mechanisms can be used to attach metadata to data as well as other language components of D° and therefore allow easy tracing of data and sharing of information between language components such as policies. We introduce a mechanism to D° that allows to dynamically map external identifiers (like the ones used in the IDS) to those used in D°. This allows D° to be combined with other usage control solutions as it facilitates the use of global identities that exceed D°.

Keywords: Usage control · Model-driven software development · Policy-agnostic programming

1 Introduction

Nowadays, the handling and processing of data is the core of many business models [26]. Well-known examples for companies that rely on such data-driven business models are Facebook, Google, and Uber. As a result, data is increasingly developing into an independent, valuable asset on its own. However, not only internet companies are affected by this transition. Due to the transition to Industry 4.0, many manufacturing companies are beginning to produce potentially valuable data. In this context, the integration of information technology in machinery used for industrial production is the

S. Hammoudi et al. (Eds.): DATA 2020, CCIS 1446, pp. 172–194, 2021.
https://doi.org/10.1007/978-3-030-83014-4_9

relevant part of Industry 4.0. This results in enormous amounts of collected data and extended control mechanisms. Prominent examples of business models emerging from Industry 4.0 are predictive maintenance and smart supply chain management.

To compete successfully in the age of Industry 4.0, it is necessary to protect this valuable data. Furthermore, it is absolutely necessary to make self-determined decisions about the use of the data. This is especially true if the data has to be shared with third parties. This ability is known as data or digital sovereignty [7] and includes, for example, the ability to limit the number of times data can be used or to limit the period of time for which it can be used.

It appears that one of the major requirements is reliable mechanisms for protecting the data and regulating its use (by third parties). Usage control can provide a technical solution to these requirements. Usage control is "a fundamental enhancement of the access matrix" [20] and many different approaches have been developed on its basis. The existing solutions have different fields of application. While some of these solutions allow integrating usage control mechanisms into newly developed applications, others are used to add usage control mechanisms to existing software. The label-based approach LUCON is one example of such solutions and allows to track and restrict the usage of data within distributed systems [21].

Since many different companies in various domains are facing similar problems regarding digital sovereignty and usage control, the International Data Spaces (IDS) have been developed [14]. The primary goal of the IDS is to provide its participants with a common ecosystem. The ecosystem allows each participant to define rules that determine how others can use parts of their own data. While the IDS form a basis to provide a common understanding, various verticalizations are developed to meet the specific requirements of domains. Examples for such verticalizations are the Medical Data Space and the Logistics Data Space. It is of utmost importance for the IDS to offer its participants a secure and trustworthy data exchange.

While the IDS do not enforce the usage of specific solutions for usage control, two approaches are being developed in their context. The aforementioned LUCON allows tracking and limiting the usage of data across multiple services and systems [6,21]. The other solution is called MyData and allows to add usage control to existing software [6, 9]. Although these two solutions cover many different use cases, there is no solution that allows considering usage control when developing new services to be used within the IDS.

For this reason, we developed a domain-specific programming language called $D°$ (spoken di'grē). $D°$, which aims at the development of data processing applications. The most important aspect of $D°$ is that it allows considering usage control from the beginning of the development. Usage control is a fundamental component of the language's core, and usage control constructs are integrated directly into $D°$-executables. Furthermore, an important motivation for the development of $D°$ is that we want to simplify the correct use of usage control. This is important because the proper application of usage control and the definition of realistic policies is often challenging [19,25].

This paper is an extended version of the paper "A Framework for Creating Policy-agnostic Programming Languages" presented at DATA 2020, in which we introduced the policy system of $D°$ and demonstrated various concepts of the language [5]. In this paper, we introduce extensions of the policy system of $D°$ that did not fit the aforementioned paper, or were not available at that time. These extensions are motivated by definitions and agreements reached in the IDS. By implementing these extensions, it is possible to define and enforce further policies. In addition, these extensions simplify the application of the policy system. We show how the policy can be extended by a tagging mechanism for various language constructs. This mechanism allows easy data transfer between different policies. In addition, this type of metadata added to language constructs and processed data allows the enforcement of policies that could not be used in the original system. We introduce an extension to the policy system that allows to dynamically map any external identifiers to D°-identifiers. In this way, it is possible to uniquely identify and trace data that uses its own identifier (e.g. IDS-identifiers).

1.1 Related Work

The basis for many different usage control solutions are the $UCON_{ABC}$ models [15,20]. These models are necessary because access control is not capable of fulfilling the data security requirements of modern applications [12,16,20]. These models extend traditional access control, which is based on using attributes of subjects and objects during the authorization process to make usage decisions. Beside various changes to traditional access control (e.g. making subject and object attributes mutable), the major innovation of the $UCON_{ABC}$ models is the addition of obligations and conditions. While obligations "are requirements that a subject must perform before (pre) or during (ongoing) access", conditions are requirements that must be met and are based on the executing system or the environment in general. These extensions and changes allow defining and enforcing many policies that could not be used with traditional access control. Therefore, usage control is a good solution for the requirements of modern applications regarding access control.

There are various approaches in the field of domain-specific languages that implement usage control mechanisms. For example, JFlow extends the Java language with information flow annotations [13]. This allows using statically checked information flows within applications and covers many language features. An additional byte code checker allows these information flow checks to be performed on both source code and bytecode [4]. Since JFlow extends the Java programming language, a certain overhead is required when using JFlow. On top of that, JFlow users are responsible for the correct use of the usage control mechanisms.

Since usage control is a cross-cutting issue and its correct usage and verification can quickly become a challenge [19], this also applies to access control, which features a lower complexity [8]. D° aims to facilitate the correct application of usage control mechanisms.

In order to reduce the complexity of the correct application of usage control mechanisms built into special programming languages, the policy-agnostic programming paradigm has been developed [23,24]. The policy-agnostic programming paradigm is based on the separation of application logic and usage control mechanisms in the development of applications. The two elements must be combined at a later stage of development to form an inseparable unit. This approach makes it possible for the different aspects of applications, namely application logic and usage control, to be developed by experts in each aspect. By automating the combination of usage control and application logic, the correct application of usage control mechanisms can be simplified. Because of the potential for facilitating the correct use of usage control, $D°$ implements the policy-agnostic programming paradigm.

The policy-agnostic programming paradigm has been used in several domain-specific languages. One example is the policy-agnostic language Jeeves [23]. It is possible to use Jeeves standalone or in combination with a host language. In addition, Jeeves has been extended by faceted values to increase its expressiveness [3]. In case Jeeves detects a data flow that violates the defined policies, the data flow is not automatically rejected. Jeeves allows to modify the data if this allows the data flow to comply with the policies. $D°$ does not feature such data manipulating functionalities as these may lead to undesired behavior in scenarios where the integrity of the data is important.

Another domain-specific language that implements the policy-agnostic programming paradigm and focuses on the development of data-centric applications is LIFTY [18]. LIFTY uses program synthesis to insert usage control code into the application logic. According to the policy-agnostic programming paradigm, the actual application logic is developed without considering policies. The main focus of LIFTY is on information flow and the detection of (unintentional) information leaks. These issues are detected and prevented at compile time. $D°$ uses techniques from the field of model-driven software engineering (e.g. code generation) to create a customized policy system for each application. This policy system is capable of enforcing the policies defined for the application and added to the code. The injected policy system operates at runtime and therefore provides a greater expressiveness, as it can evaluate policies based on the application's input data and the system environment.

1.2 Outline

The remainder of this paper is structured as follows. Section 2 presents the policy system, before the modifications are introduced in this paper. The requirements from the IDS that motivate the modifications to the policy system are introduced in Sect. 3. The extensions and modifications applied to the $D°$ policy system are presented in Sect. 4. Section 5 discusses limitations of the policy system and the proposed modifications. In addition, some possible solutions to these limitations are outlined. The results of this paper are discussed in Sect. 6. Furthermore, an outlook on possible future work is given.

2 The $D°$ Language and its Policy System

Before we introduce the extensions to the policy system of $D°$ and the requirements of the IDS that motivated them, this section will give an overview of the policy system and language features of $D°$.

2.1 Language Features

There are various aspects and components of $D°$ that are important for the language but are not covered in detail in this paper. Since some of these components are necessary or at least helpful for the understanding of this paper, they are outlined here.

Type System. D° uses a special type system called Nukleus to define abstract and domain-specific types. The type system is string based and chooses specificity via direct hardware support for data types. For this reason, the representation of data types in Nukleus is not space efficient. The types are organized as a directed acyclic graph. This allows to express complex relationships between different types. New Nukleus types are added to the type system by using one of the supported textual definitions (JSON or yaml). In addition, Nukleus allows the automated testing of data types with provided (positive and negative) values, generation of documentation (based on the type definition), and the generation of fully usable classes in the selected host language.

Host Language. There are various different implementation approaches for domain-specific languages [11,22]. In the following, these approaches are discussed with regard to their suitability for being used in D°.

The pre-processing approach and the embedding approach are very similar in the way developers use the created language. These approaches are based on extending a host language with additional domain-specific features and concepts. The developer writes code in the (general-purpose) host language and can use both the added functionality and all the constructs and features of the host language. This means that the developer is responsible for the (correct) usage of the added elements. The developer can (accidentally or intentionally) only use the host language and ignore the DSL features. Since D° aims to add usage control to all applications while simplifying the correct use of usage control, these approaches are not well suited for D°.

The next approach is interpreting. The domain-specific language has its own syntax and semantic. Code written in the language is passed to an interpreter that executes the code. Since there is no host language that can be used to bypass language features, this approach is better suited for adding usage control to a programming language. The disadvantage of this approach is that in general, interpreted code runs slower than compiled code. Therefore, this approach was not chosen to implement D° as well.

An alternative to interpreted domain-specific languages is provided by the compiling approach. A compiled domain-specific language has its own syntax and semantic, just like the interpreted ones. Instead of interpreting the language's code directly, the code is processed by a compiler. There are two possibilities for compilation. The first possibility is to compile the language code directly into machine executable code. The second possibility is to use a host language. The code of the domain-specific language is first cross-compiled into the used host language. The generated host language code is then interpreted or compiled into an executable format. To take advantage of existing execution environments, D° is implemented as a compiled language with a host language. Our prototypical implementation uses Java as host language.

Extensibility. The main focus of D° is the development of data processing applications. This topic affects almost every domain. Since D° is supposed to be applicable in all different domains, there are many different requirements regarding data types and other language concepts. In general-purpose programming languages, these would often be solved by using libraries. Therefore, it is not possible to provide all functionalities and features (e.g. type definitions) together with D°. In order not to limit the possible fields of application of D°, the language provides an extension system. This system allows the addition of all necessary elements (e.g. policies and type definitions), which are required for a specific domain or use case, to D°. There are well-defined interfaces and rules that must be implemented and followed to add additional elements to D°.

Furthermore, a problem that can be observed is that well-known and accepted methods like e.g. the access matrix do not meet the requirements of modern systems and applications. For this reason, changes and enhancements are required to achieve this [10, 15, 17, 20]. The fact that these methods often support only a limited number of different policies and cannot easily be adapted to new usage scenarios is one of the reasons for this problem. In order to allow users of D° to easily extend the language for new requirements (at least to some extend), extensibility was taken into account from the beginning of the development.

Application Types. Since the data processing scope of D° is very wide, it is not possible to determine in advance what types of applications the users of D° will need. For example, a multi-user service that performs data analysis and needs to be accessed from remote machines may be best implemented as a REST-service. In contrast, a data transformation application that is part of a workflow on a single machine is better implemented as a command line tool.

To make D° usable for all these different scenarios, the D°-compiler is capable of generating various kinds of applications in the host language. The different types are organized in a tree structure to avoid partial duplications. Each new application type is the child of another one and inherits all its elements while adding its own. In addition, each application type has its own execution behavior. For example, some applications require periodic execution, while others are executed only once.

Figure 1 shows a simplified representation of this tree structure. Green nodes are used for application types that can be created by the compiler. Blue nodes are abstract and cannot be created by the compiler. They are used to bundle common configuration items and components. The red node contains the different execution behaviors for applications. When the compiler generates an application, one of the available execution behaviors must be selected.

2.2 Separation of Concerns

This section demonstrates how the policy-agnostic programming paradigm is implemented in D°. As mentioned in Sect. 1.1, the core of the paradigm is the separation of application logic and usage control during application development. The two components have to be combined at a later stage (runtime or compile time).

D° consists of two groups of components. The first group is the language core, which contains the grammar, compiler, runtime environment, component APIs, and more. The second group contains all kinds of language extensions. These extensions are used to provide the actual language constructs at D° and contain all elements that can be used in applications. These include data types, policies, and activities. Activities are the atomic elements of application logic within D°. They can provide an arbitrary amount of logic in the used host language.

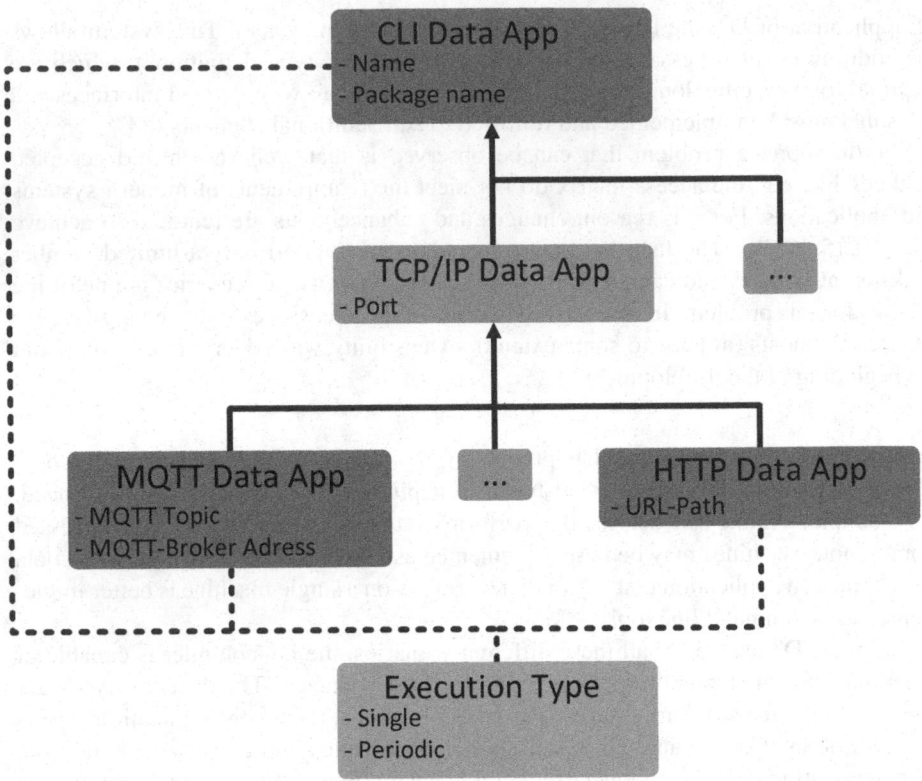

Fig. 1. Schematic illustration of the relationship between data app types. (Color figure online)

While the language core is the same for all applications, the loaded extensions are potentially different for each application. In order to implement the policy-agnostic programming paradigm, D° distinguishes between definitions and instances for activities and policies. The definitions of activities and policies describe the required input parameters of the element and are used to create a link to the implementation. Activity instances are used to combine the activity definition with policies. Policy instances allow the binding of parameters to static values. The definitions build the meta model of all available language elements, while the instances comprise the model of language elements that can be used in applications. This can simplify the usage for static policies (e.g. allow max n uses).

The definition of activities and policies cannot be used directly in D°. In order to create an activity instance that can be used inside an application, the following steps must be performed:

1. Define (if not already existing) necessary data types.
2. Create (if not already existing) the definition and implementation of the activity.
3. Create (if not already existing) the definition and implementation of all policies that should be attached to the activity.

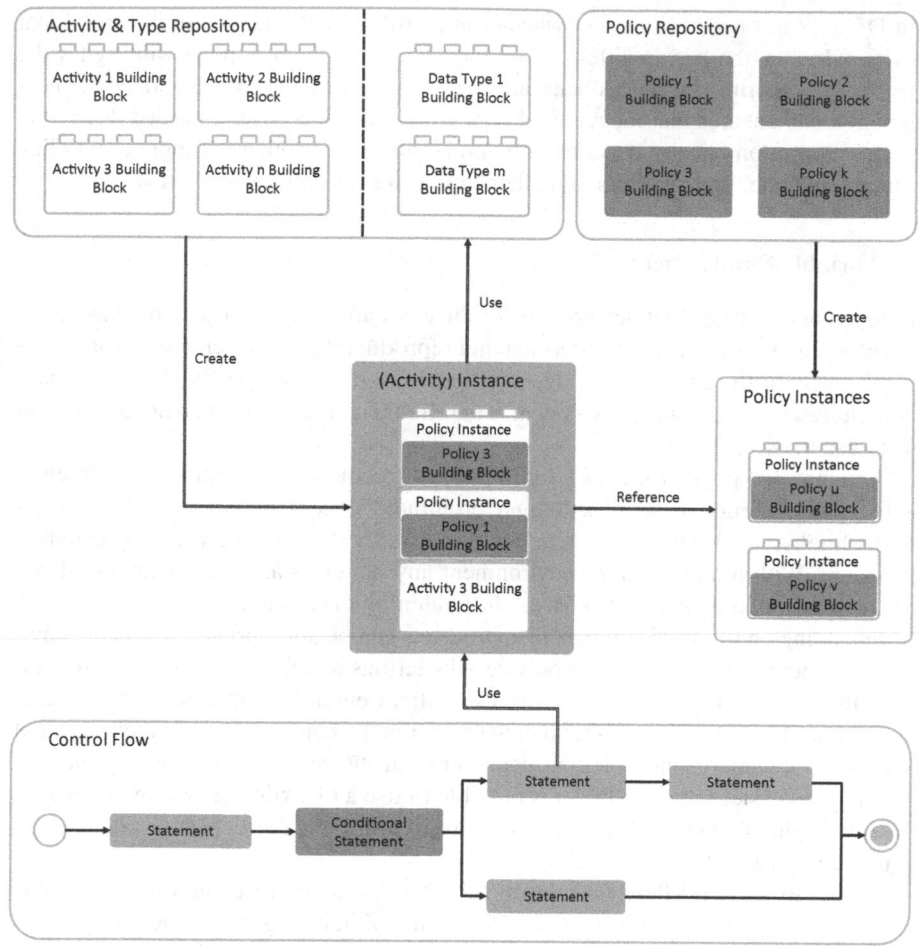

Fig. 2. Diagram showing how building blocks in D° are combined with each other. Reprinted from "a framework for creating policy-agnostic programming languages" [5].

4. Instantiate the policy and bind static values to parameters, if necessary.
5. Instantiate the activity and attach the policy instances to it.

Figure 2 shows a block diagram illustrating the different steps. The repositories contain all available definitions of the different language constructs. These definitions are composed in order to create instances that can be used in applications.

By separating definitions and instances, the policy-agnostic programming paradigm is implemented in D°. Normal developers can implement activities and applications, while policies can be defined and implemented by people with in-depth knowledge of usage control and the D° policy system. The developer who develops applications with D° does not need to consider whether any policies are attached to the individual activities. In fact, there is no difference for the developer. There is no possibility for the developer to determine if any policies are in use. The compiler that generates the host language code ensures that the required policy code is added where needed. Since the D° compiler automatically performs the combination of application logic and policy enforcement code, human errors in implementing usage control are avoided.

2.3 Variable Enforcement

It is necessary to have a defined process for the evaluation of policies. Otherwise, policies enforcement is not clear for users and not reproducible. However, the reproducibility and clarity of the enforcement logic are very important for a policy system. If these two attributes are not granted, the system is unreliable and developers do not understand how to use it.

There are two popular methods for policy enforcement: blacklisting and whitelisting. In a whitelisting system, all actions are prohibited, except those permitted by the so-called whitelist. A blacklisting system works in exactly the opposite way to a whitelisting system. Within a blacklisting environment any action is allowed by default. Only those actions that are on the blacklist are forbidden by the system.

Depending on the application, both approaches can be appropriate. In a secure environment, where it is important that only certain actions are allowed, a whitelisting system is the best choice. However, in an less critical environment, where only certain actions should be forbidden, a blacklisting system is the better choice. Whitelisting and blacklisting are interchangeable, but depending on the requirements, one of the two approaches is easier to use. While it is possible to use a blacklisting system in a highly secure and critical environment, the process of defining the correct set of policies can be quite complex and error-prone.

In order to make D° flexible and well suited for all these different usage scenarios, we defined a process that allows to mix black- and whitelisting. We named the process greylisting. By default, any action in the D° policy system is allowed. It behaves like a blacklisting system. The user can define blacklisting policies that forbid certain actions. In addition, the user can define whitelisting policies that overrule the blacklisting ones.

For example, there is a (blacklisting) policy that prohibits writing files to disk at all. If this policy is combined with a (whitelisting) policy that allows the application to write to its home directory, the application can write files to its home directory, but nowhere else.

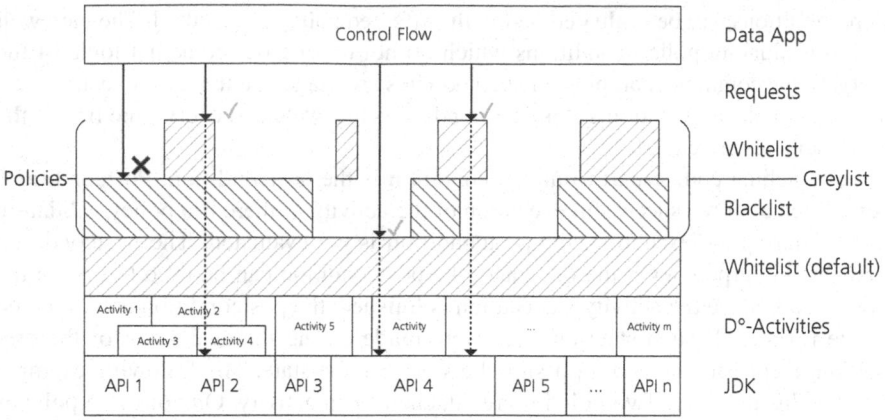

Fig. 3. Schematic representation of greylist enforcement. Reprinted from "a framework for creating policy-agnostic programming languages" [5].

There are special policies that prohibit any action. That way, it is possible to convert the system into a normal blacklisting system.

Figure 3 shows a schematic representation of the described process. The control flow attempts to perform the various activities of an application. These activities use APIs of the host language. However, before an activity triggered by the control flow is executed, the policy system evaluates all relevant policies to determine whether to grant execution. In terms of the figure, the first policy that affects the action to be executed will make the final decision on whether to grant execution. In this way, a well-defined process for evaluating mixed black- and whitelisting policies is defined and used in the D° policy system. This is important in order to predict and reproduce the results of the policy system.

2.4 Policy API and Enforcement

Since D° implements the policy-agnostic programming paradigm, it is not obvious to the developer at what points in time policies are enforced and what kind of tests policies can perform. This becomes clear when inspecting the policy API and the part of the code generator that generates the usage control code. For this reason, this section shows these two components of D°.

The API of D° policies consists of three different endpoints that can be implemented by developers to check policy conditions. Each endpoint is enforced in defined situations. That way, it is possible to define diverse policies in D°. Developers can define any subset of the available policy endpoints for their individual policies. The three endpoints are precondition, postcondition, and the security manager intervention.

Next, the different endpoints are described. The descriptions always assume that an activity is affected by a policy. The reason for this is that the current version of D° only supports adding policies to applications in this way. Policies can only be attached to activity instances. The policies are evaluated each time the activity is invoked.

Preconditions will be evaluated before the affected policy is executed. They are well suited to evaluating policy conditions which do not depend on the actual logic of the activity. Some common examples for such policies are usage counters, time restrictions, and checks on the application's state. Preconditions are evaluated every time before the affected policies are called.

The matching counterpart to the precondition is the postcondition. Postconditions are evaluated after the successful execution of the activity. If there is a policy validation before or during the execution, the postcondition is not evaluated. The postcondition has two main purposes. On the one hand, the postcondition can be used to update the policy's state. Since the activity's execution is finished, the postcondition is best suited for state updates. If such state changes were made during the evaluation of the pre-condition, incorrect data could possibly be stored in the state. The following example illustrates this problem. Two policies are attached to an activity. One of these policies implements a usage counter and performs counter updates during the precondition. If the precondition of the counter policy is evaluated before the other policy, and valida-tion of the second precondition fails, the counter is incremented even though the activity is not performed. On the other hand, postconditions can be used to evaluate policies that depend on the return value of the activity. For example, data validation that exceeds the validation of the data type itself can be performed during the postcondition.

These two endpoints allow the definition of policies that depend on activity inputs and outputs as well as global and/or local state information. Nevertheless, these end-points cannot cover policies that depend on the actual logic of an activity.

For this kind of policies, the intended solution is to use the security manager inter-vention endpoint. When an activity is called, an arbitrary amount of host language code is executed. This host language code uses APIs of the host language. These APIs can be instrumented in order to emit events that trigger the $D°$ security manager. The $D°$ security manager evaluates the security manager intervention on all policies attached to the activity currently being executed. Based on the event type, each policy can decide whether it is affected by the emitted event. The Java language already includes this func-tionality. Various APIs of the JDK (Java Development Kit) are instrumented and ask the Java security manager for permission before execution. Our prototypical implementa-tion uses Java as host language and provides a custom security manager that evaluates $D°$ policies. Examples of APIs used in common policies are those for network commu-nication, file in- and output, and shell command execution.

The security manager intervention allows the implementation of various policies in $D°$, which are otherwise not or not reliably usable. This will be demonstrated below using an example. The functionality of any $D°$ application includes writing files to the disk. In order to prevent excessive disk usage, it is necessary to limit the amount of data that can be used by the application. A policy that tracks and limits the used disk space can be used for this purpose. Without the security manager intervention, the policy must check and track the used disk space in the precondition and postcondition endpoints. The precondition is used to check wheather a requested activity execution exceeds the granted quota. The postcondition is used to update the used disk space. There are problems with this solution:

- The policy needs to transform the input data into the serialization format used by the activity to estimate the correctly used disk space.
- If the activity makes any kind of data modification before writing it to the disk, the policy must make the same modifications. Otherwise, the used disk space is not correct.

Both problems can be solved by adapting the policy to the specific activity. This is problematic because it results in massive code duplications between policies and activities. It also breaks the separation between application logic and policies because the policy developer needs to have knowledge of the activities that will use the policy. In addition, the application developer has to determine which policies are the correct ones for the activities that the application requires. Otherwise, incorrect policies may be assigned to the activities, resulting in a non-functional policy system. This would violate the central aspect of the policy-agnostic programming paradigm.

These issues can be avoided by using the security manager intervention. The policy used in the disk space example would implement the security manager intervention to react to FILE_WRITE events. This way, each time the host language code used to provide the implementation of the activity attempts to execute a file writing operation, the security manager intervention is executed before the file is actually written. In addition, the security manager intervention endpoint can access the data used for the file write operation. Therefore, no code duplication or adaption is necessary. A single policy that

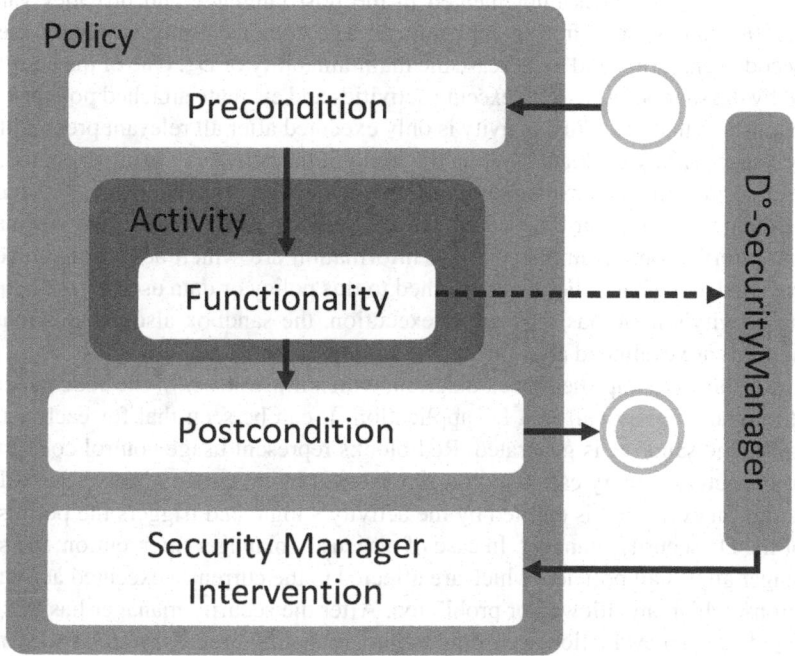

Fig. 4. Schematic representation of the D° policy API data flow. Reprinted from "a framework for creating policy-agnostic programming languages" [5].

limits the used disk space can be added to all activities. In addition, the security manager intervention endpoint promotes the implementation of the policy-agnostic programming paradigm. Complex activities with multiple execution paths can be implemented without any policy consideration. For example, if it is necessary to ensure that a network connection is only established once and there are policies that may or may not attempt to establish that connection, the policy system will not have a problem. This is because the security manager intervention endpoint is only evaluated if the host language's APIs that perform the relevant actions are used.

Figure 4 shows a schematic representation of the policy API and the data flow that takes place during the policy evaluation. The policy is attached to an activity. In addition to the policy API, the D° security manager and the control flow that is executed when the activity is called is displayed. It becomes apparent that the pre- and postcondition of the policy are evaluated each time the activity is called. The security manager intervention endpoint is called by the D° security manager every time the functionality of the activity attempts to access a protected API. This can happen any number of times.

Next, a short demonstration of the code generator is given. The code generator of D° is a critical component as it is responsible of combining application logic and usage control enforcement. It ensures that the control flow shown in Fig. 4 is correctly implemented in every D° application.

In addition to branching operations, a D° application consists of a sequence of activities that are executed sequentially in their order of appearance. To encapsulate the host language code generated for each activity call, D° provides a so-called sandbox. The sandbox is an object that is implemented in the host language and provides various functionalities that are required in applications. The code generator is widely used to simplify code generation and to increase the maintainability of D°. One of the endpoints provided by the sandbox is used to execute activities and evaluate attached policies. This endpoint ensures that the actual activity is only executed after all relevant preconditions have been successfully evaluated. While the logic of the activity is being executed, any number of security manager interventions can occur. When this happens, the sandbox provides endpoints that can be used by the D° security manager in order to retrieve necessary information. Examples of such information are which activity is currently being executed and what policies are attached to this policy or data used by the activity. After the activity's logic has finished its execution, the sandbox also ensures that the postconditions are evaluated after the activity has been executed.

Figure 5 shows a simplified block diagram, which illustrates how the code generator is processing an activity call in a D° application. It can be seen that for each activity call a call to the sandbox is generated. Red blocks represent usage control code that is added to the actual activity call, which is represented by the green nodes. The API call protection is an event that is emitted by the activity's logic and triggers the permission check of the D° security manager. In case of a security manager intervention, the security manager allows all policies, which are affected to the currently executed activity, to state actions, which are allowed or prohibited. After the security manager has this data from all policies, an evaluation according to the greylisting process, which is described in Sect. 2.3, is performed.

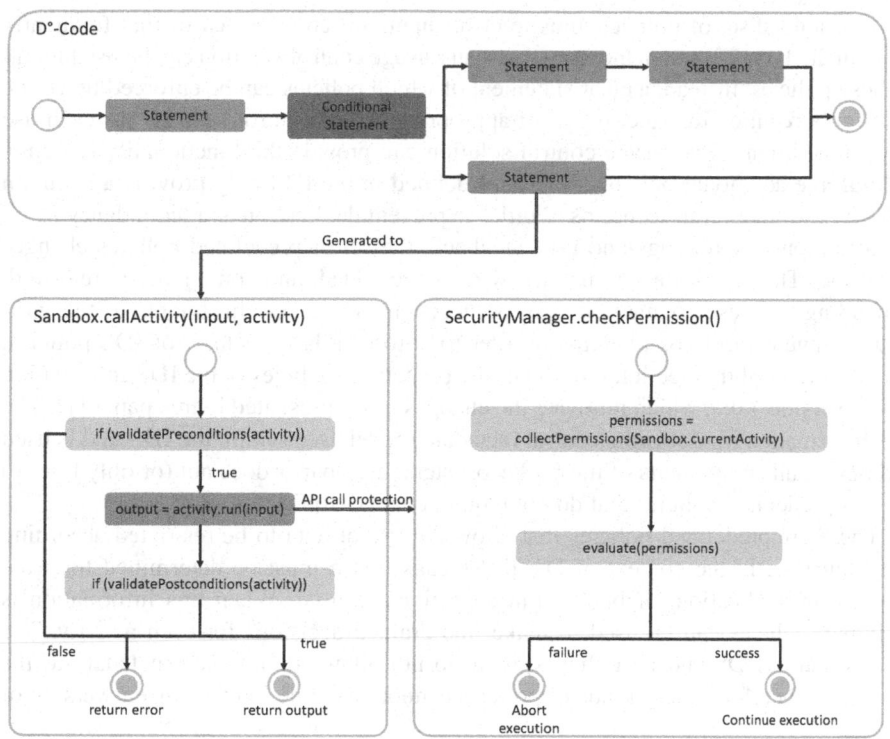

Fig. 5. Simplified representation of the D° code generator aspect that combines application logic and usage control. Reprinted from "a framework for creating policy-agnostic programming languages" [5]. (Color figure online)

3 D° in the Context of the IDS

The aim of IDS is to provide all participants with a common ecosystem that allows and supports the establishment and maintenance of each participant's digital sovereignty. Usage control is an important aspect of this capability. Since the IDS are technology independent, the IDS do not enforce the usage of specific usage control approaches. Nevertheless, there are solutions that have emerged from the IDS [6], one of them is D°.

Instead of prescribing the use of specific usage control solutions, the IDS have defined a set of policies and a common policy specification language (PSL) that is used within the IDS. A common PSL, used by all participants in the IDS, is required to provide a common basis used to define and exchange policies. The PSL used within the IDS is inspired by the Open Digital Rights Language (ODRL) and needs to be converted from the individual usage control solutions to the PSL they are using.

The defined set of policies aims to cover many different use cases that frequently occur in the IDS. It is not mandatory that every usage control solution can be used for all of these policies. Instead, a clear statement of which policies can be enforced by which solution is required to select the most appropriate usage control solution for each use case. In addition, every usage control solution can provide the functionality to define and enforce additional policies. The ones defined in the IDS only provide a common basis for most common scenarios in order to prevent duplication and redundancy.

Based on new findings and user feedback, the set of predefined policies changes over time. The policies are refined, new ones are added, and some may be removed. Depending on these changes, it may be necessary to make adjustments to the individual usage control components in order to enforce a larger subset of IDS policies. The remainder of this section introduces the predefined policies of the IDS Information Model version 4.0.0, which motivate the changes to D° presented in this paper [1]. The IDS Information Model is the central metadata model used within the IDS and is used to describe all components of the IDS ecosystem. This paper does not (or only briefly) address predefined policies that do not require changes to D°.

There are predefined policies that allow the use of data to be restricted according to its purpose. In the context of D°, this means that it must be determined for what purpose an application, or better still, an activity is used. When this information is available, policies can be used to make fine-grained decisions for each activity. The current state of D° and its policy system do not allow adding such metadata to the activities. Therefore, these kinds of policies cannot be defined in the current version of D°.

Other predefined policies lead to similar requirements at the data level. For example, one of the pre-defined policies allows the distribution of data only if it has been encrypted. This requires metadata to describe the current state of the data or what actions have been performed on the data. This is not possible with the current version of D°.

It becomes clear that in many cases policies that require additional metadata cannot be used in the current version of D°. A possible workaround is to perform manual audits on each individual application. However, this is an exhaustive task and also contradicts the policy-agnostic programming paradigm, since the policy audit has to be performed on the application's code.

Not affected by these limitations are policies that require the possibility to store additional data inside the policy. This functionality is already part of D°. Therefore, this type of policy can be implemented in D° without any problems. An example of such a policy is a counter that limits the number of times data or an activity can be used.

As mentioned before, the IDS do not force the use of specific usage control solutions. Therefore, it is common for a single workflow distributed across different applications and systems to use different usage control solutions in different locations. However, it is mandatory that the data processed by the workflow is uniquely identified. The IDS solve this problem by assigning unique identifiers to each data set. The different usage control components must be able to work with these identifiers to retrieve and provide metadata that exceeds the scope of any individual usage control solution.

The current version of D° is not capable of handling such external identifiers. D° uses its own set of identifiers to identify the various elements of applications such as data, policies, and activities. In order to better work together with different usage control solutions within the IDS, functionality that allows to use this IDS identifiers is required.

4   Modifications and Extenstions to D°

This section presents the changes to D° and its policy system, motivated either by the requirements of the IDS or by experience gained during the usage of the current version of D°. These requirements are described in Sect. 3.

4.1   Label-Based Metadata

The predefined policies used within the IDS showed that D° is missing a functionality that allows to add additional metadata to language elements and processed data. In order to make policies requiring such metadata usable within D°, different additions were made to the language and its policy system.

As mentioned before, it is necessary to add additional metadata to instances of data types in order to make policies based on the current state of data usable within D°. The D° type system uses unique identifiers for each instance of data types to manage the instances. By adding the possibility to map these identifiers to any number of labels, the aforementioned polices can be used within D°. The only necessary change is to provide developers with an API to create, read, update, and delete these labels on instances. This API will only be used by developers implementing new activities and policies. There is no difference in the usage of D° for developers who develop D° applications because they do not get in touch with this new functionality. Nevertheless, this addition to D° increases the expressiveness of the policy system. With this addition, it is possible to define policies that require information about actions performed on the data or the state of the data.

Adding metadata to individual data type instances is not sufficient to use all policies mentioned in Sect. 3. While this allows to make decisions based on the state of data, it does not allow to use of all policies that include the behavioral activities that process the data. For example, it is possible for the policy system to determine whether an activity establishes network connections or writes files to disk. However, it is not possible to distinguish whether an activity is used for risk management or for marketing purposes. For these policies, it is necessary to add additional metadata to the activity, because such properties cannot be determined by looking at the activity's code.

In a first step, we have extended the definitions and instances of activities to allow the addition of labels to activities. This enables the addition of labels to activities that describe the activity. Theses labels can contain information about the actions the activity performs (e.g. encrypt and aggregate) and a date describing the usage context (e.g. risk management). The possibility to add labels to both activity definitions and activity instances enhances the flexibility of D°.

The intended way of adding labels to activities is as follows: Labels used to describe functionalities of the activity (e.g. distribute and encrypt) should be added to the definition, as they are the same regardless of the context in which the activity is used in applications. Labels used to add information to activities that are valid for only a single/few applications should be added to the instance. Data about the purpose an activity is used for is one example of good instance labels. This way, the activity definition can be used for all applications by creating matching instances. However, this separation is not enforced by $D°$.

This extension allows to use policies that require general data about activities. Nevertheless, it is not well suited for fine-grained policies. For example, there is an activity that uses more than one input parameter. We know that this activity will distribute the data of one input parameter, because the activity definition is marked with the 'distribute'-label. Now, the applications that uses this activity is processing data whose distribution is prohibited by a policy. Based on the available information, it is not possible to use this data as input for the activity at all, although the data may not be distributed by the activity.

For that reason, we have refined the labeling of activities. In the final version of the labeling extension, it is also possible to add labels to individual input parameters of activities. In the scenario above, the activity input parameter, which would be distributed by the activity, would be labeled accordingly. This would allow for much more fine-grained policy decision making, as the data could be used for any input parameter except the one that would be distributed.

It has to be noted that all mentioned labeling features for adding metadata rely on the correct usage of the developers implementing the activities and policies. For example, a policy that requires input data to be encrypted can only work properly if the activity used to encrypt the data applies the appropriate label to the data. In order to maintain the flexibility and extensibility of $D°$, any valid $D°$-identifier can be used as label. A $D°$ identifier is a sequence of words separated by a single dot. Each word can consist of characters, digits, and the underscore ($_$). Commonly used labels are listed in the $D°$ documentation to simplify choosing the correct labels.

Figure 6 shows a schematic representation of the data flow for policies in $D°$ with the aforementioned labeling mechanisms. It clearly shows the differences from the original data flow, which can be seen in Fig. 4. Three similar but independent extensions have been made in order to make policies based on additional metadata usable within $D°$. The most obvious change is that each instance of a data type can carry metadata in the form of tags. The terms tags and labels are used interchangeable. The other two changes affect the structure of the activities. First, activities themselves have been extended by tags. These affects both the definitions and the instances. These two changes already allow to use many new policies in $D°$. Next, the input parameters of activities were modified to allow the usage of tags as well. This allows more fine-grained policies that could not be used in $D°$, or only under certain circumstances.

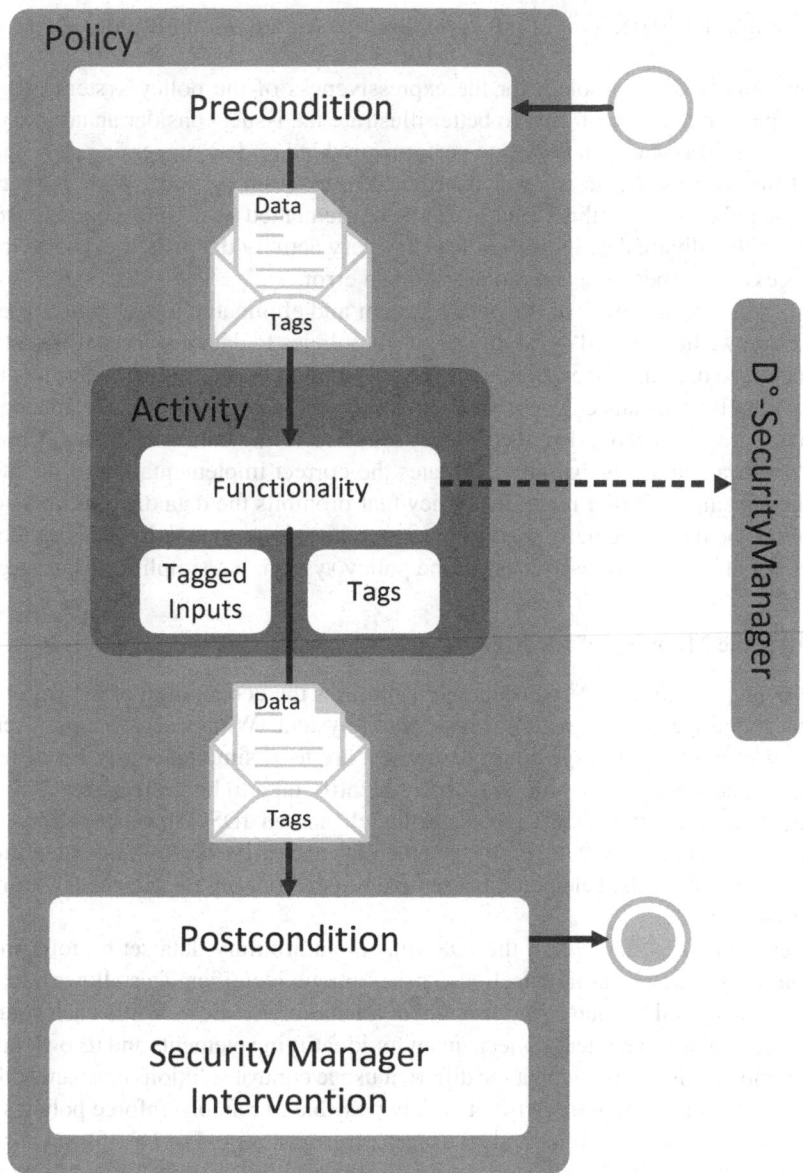

Fig. 6. Schematic representation of the data flow for policies with added labeling in D°.

4.2 Add Policies to Data Instances

In the current version of D°, policies must be attached to activities. Since the individual policy system for each D° application is generated during cross-compilation into the used host language, this has no impact on the expressiveness of the policy system. If the policy system allowed to add, adjust, or remove policies at runtime, this could be a more significant issue, as it is not possible to pass data to applications along with policies.

While this is not a problem for the expressiveness of the policy system, it has a strong impact on the ease of use. To better illustrate the issue, consider an arbitrary $D°$ application. This application is used to perform any kind of data processing. It is important that the processed data is never distributed to external systems. With the current state of the policy system, this scenario can be implemented by adding a corresponding policy to each individual activity, or at least to every activity that uses the data as input. This process is cumbersome and prone to human error.

To increase the usability of the policy system and eliminate the potential source of human error, we have added the ability to attach policies to data instances. Like attaching metadata to data instances, this functionality is based on the unique identifiers used for each data type instance. Every time an activity is called, the policies attached to the activity are evaluated. Also, the policies attached to the data used as input for the activity are evaluated. This greatly facilitates the correct implementation of the aforementioned example. Furthermore, the policy that prohibits the data distribution is only evaluated if the data is actually used as input parameters of an activity. This change to $D°$ does not affect the expressiveness of the policy system, but simplifies its usage.

4.3 Dynamic Mapping of Identifiers

The following addition to $D°$ considerably simplifies the cooperation of $D°$ with other solutions for usage control within a distributed system. Within ecosystems, such as the IDS, where different usage control solutions are used simultaneously for different aspects, it is necessary to be able to globally identify data to be protected by policies. For example, within the IDS, a metadata model, named IDS Information Model, is used to describe and identify all entities, resources, and artifacts. A unique identifier is assigned to each described element in order to uniquely identify the elements within the whole ecosystem.

For example, a policy within the IDS aims at an arbitrary data set by referring to its unique identifier. The policy itself also has a unique identifier. This allows data and policy to be assigned to each other throughout an entire workflow. While each solution for usage control uses an internal mechanism for identifying elements and its own policy representations, it is important that the different usage control solutions can handle these global identifiers as well. Otherwise, it is only possible to reliably enforce policies that only affect the scope of each individual usage control solution. For $D°$, this means that only policies that do not need to obtain data from external systems or supply data to external systems can be used. This is a serious restriction for ecosystems such as the IDS, where digital sovereignty should be established and preserved.

The way in which global identifiers are made available in $D°$, is based on the previous introduced extension: Attaching policies to data instances. The first step is to transfer the global policy into a representation that can be used by $D°$. During this transformation, the global identifier of the target data set is preserved in the $D°$ representation. If required, the global identifier of the policy itself is also preserved. Next, the $D°$ representations are attached to the corresponding input parameters of the application. Every time the logic of the compiled application is executed, the identifiers from the policies attached to the input parameters are collected and corresponding mappings are created.

This allows to use identifiers that are not created and managed by D° to be used in D° applications. The approach is very generic and not limited to the IDS. It can be used within every system where it is necessary to use global identifiers. This is necessary when a global policy has a state, e.g. a limiting usage counter. D° can use the global identifiers to either query the state of a policy from any type of service or send state updates to that service. When all state information is embedded in the policy, the identifiers can be used to identify the correct policies whose states need to be updated after the application's execution.

5 Discussion

This section shows limitations of D°, its policy system, and the introduced modifications. Furthermore, possible solutions for these limitations are outlined.

Since D°, as well as its policy system, is in an early stage of development, there is room for various usability improvements and optimizations. While separating definitions and instances of policies and activities allows for versatile reuse of defined elements and reduces duplicates, it can create overhead for the language's users. Not every activity used as part of an application requires additional policies. However, it is necessary to create an instance that uses the definition. This activity instance does not provide any added value. For an example of an activity instance that does not require policies and is used to log data to the console, see Listing 1.1. Lines 1 and 2 state that the next lines will define an activity instance. Lines 3 to 4 show the name used to call this activity in applications. Lines 5 and 6 contain the reference to the definition of the activity. A more detailed introduction to the semantics and syntax of definitions and instances of language elements can be found in the paper "A Framework for Creating Policy-agnostic Programming Languages" [5].

```
1  PrintToConsole:
2  degree.ActivityInstance:
3  name:
4  Identifier: "PrintToConsole"
5  definition:
6  degree.ActivityReference: "degree.Activity@PrintToConsole"
```
Listing 1.1. Definition of the Log Activity Instance.

It is a very cumbersome process to define these activity instances without attached policies. It leads to a lot of time-consuming overhead costs. This could be avoided completely. Therefore, it is necessary to create one instance for each activity instance on the fly. This workaround is necessary because D° does not allow the direct use of activity definitions in applications.

There is a limitation in the labeling-mechanism introduced in this paper that only affects labels attached to data. The management of these labels is a feature of the type system of D°. Internally, the labels are not part of the data type instances. Instead, they are managed similarly to the external identifiers for data. The information about which labels are attached to a data instance is lost during deserialization. This means, that based on the current state of D°, it is not possible to automatically share labels attached to data.

There are two possible solutions for this issue:

1. Adding the possibility to serialize and deserialize labels that are attached to data instances along with the data instance itself.
2. Providing a common service that can be operated in parallel for any number of applications and provides a key-value store.

While adding data labels to the serialization, the second alternative can provide more functionality to D°. For example, the service could be used to store and exchange the state of used policies between different D° applications. The role of this service would be similar to the one of the Policy Information Point (PIP), which is known from the XACML architecture [2] and MyData [9]. In addition, this service could also be used by other usage control solutions. This way, the service would also promote the collaboration of D° with other usage control solutions.

6   Conclusion

In this extended paper, we have demonstrated that the initially introduced policy system of D°, as well as D° itself, is flexible enough to allow extensions to meet new requirements. We have shown that by adding a comprehensive labeling-mechanism to D°, the expressiveness of the policy system can be improved. By adding the possibility to attach policies directly to data type instances, we have improved the usability of the policy system. In addition, the labeling-mechanism has a positive impact on the usability of the D° policy system. This is because the use of labels provides the possibility to define some policies that can already be used in D° in a different way that can be less complex. We have demonstrated that the usage of external identifiers for policies and data can be added to D° without big modifications to the language. Finally, we have pointed out limitations of the policy system and the proposed additions and possible solutions to them.

Acknowledgments. This work was developed in Fraunhofer-Cluster of Excellence "Cognitive Internet Technologies".

This research was supported by the Excellence Center for Logistics and IT funded by the Fraunhofer-Gesellschaft and the Ministry of Culture and Science of the German State of North Rhine-Westphalia.

References

1. Akyürek, H., et al.: IDS information model v4.0.0 (2020). https://github.com/International-Data-Spaces-Association/InformationModel/releases/tag/v4.0.0
2. Anderson, A., et al.: Extensible access control markup language (XACML) version 1.0. OASIS (2003)

3. Austin, T.H., Yang, J., Flanagan, C., Solar-Lezama, A.: Faceted execution of policy-agnostic programs. In: Proceedings of the Eighth ACM SIGPLAN Workshop on Programming Languages and Analysis for Security, pp. 15–26 (2013)
4. Barthe, G., Naumann, D.A., Rezk, T.: Deriving an information flow checker and certifying compiler for Java. In: 2006 IEEE Symposium on Security and Privacy (S&P 2006), pp. 229–242 (2006)
5. Bruckner, F., Pampus, J., Howar, F.: A framework for creating policy-agnostic programming languages. In: Hammoudi, S., Quix, C., Bernardino, J. (eds.) Proceedings of the 9th International Conference on Data Science, Technology and Applications, DATA 2020, Lieusaint, Paris, France, 7–9 July 2020, pp. 31–42. SciTePress (2020). https://doi.org/10.5220/0009782200310042
6. Eitel, A., et al.: Usage Control in International Data Spaces: Version 2.0 (2019). https://www.internationaldataspaces.org/wp-content/uploads/2019/11/Usage-Control-in-IDS-V2.0_final.pdf
7. Jarke, M., Otto, B., Ram, S.: Data sovereignty and data space ecosystems. Bus. Inf. Syst. Eng. **61**(5), 549–550 (2019). https://doi.org/10.1007/s12599-019-00614-2
8. Jeager, T.: Managing access control complexity using metrices. In: Proceedings of the Sixth ACM Symposium on Access Control Models and Technologies, SACMAT 2001, pp. 131–139. Association for Computing Machinery, New York (2001). https://doi.org/10.1145/373256.373283
9. Jung, C., Eitel, A., Schwarz, R.: Enhancing cloud security with context-aware usage control policies. In: GI-Jahrestagung, pp. 211–222 (2014)
10. Katt, B., Zhang, X., Breu, R.: A general obligation model and continuity: enhanced policy enforcement engine for usage control. In: Proceedings of the 13th ACM Symposium on Access Control Models and Technologies, pp. 123–132 (2008)
11. Kosar, T., Martı, P.E., Barrientos, P.A., Mernik, M., et al.: A preliminary study on various implementation approaches of domain-specific language. Inf. Softw. Technol. **50**(5), 390–405 (2008)
12. Lazouski, A., Martinelli, F., Mori, P.: Usage control in computer security: a survey. Comput. Sci. Rev. **4**(2), 81–99 (2010). https://doi.org/10.1016/j.cosrev.2010.02.002
13. Myers, A.C.: JFlow: practical mostly-static information flow control. In: Proceedings of the 26th ACM SIGPLAN-SIGACT Symposium on Principles of Programming Languages, pp. 228–241 (1999)
14. Otto, B., Jarke, M.: Designing a multi-sided data platform: findings from the International Data Spaces case. Electr. Mark. **29**(4), 561–580 (2019)
15. Park, J.: Usage control: a unified framework for next generation access control. Dissertation, George Mason University, Virginia (2003)
16. Park, J., Sandhu, R.S.: The UCON ABC usage control model. ACM Trans. Inf. Syst. Secur. (TISSEC) **7**(1), 128–174 (2004)
17. Park, J., Zhang, X., Sandhu, R.S.: Attribute mutability in usage control. In: Research Directions in Data and Applications Security, vol. XVIII, pp. 15–29 (2004)
18. Polikarpova, N., Yang, J., Itzhaky, S., Hance, T., Solar-Lezama, A.: Enforcing information flow policies with type-targeted program synthesis. In: Proceedings of the ACM on Programming Languages, vol. 1 (2018)
19. Rajkumar, P.V., Ghosh, S.K., Dasgupta, P.: Application specific usage control implementation verification. Int. J. Netw. Secur. Appl. **1**(3), 116–128 (2009)
20. Sandhu, R.S., Park, J.: Usage control: a vision for next generation access control. In: International Workshop on Mathematical Methods, Models, and Architectures for Computer Network Security, pp. 17–31 (2003)

21. Schuette, J., Brost, G.S.: LUCON: data flow control for message-based IoT systems. In: 2018 17th IEEE International Conference on Trust, Security and Privacy in Computing and Communications/12th IEEE International Conference on Big Data Science and Engineering (TrustCom/BigDataSE), pp. 289–299 (2018)
22. Visser, E.: WebDSL: a case study in domain-specific language engineering. In: Lämmel, R., Visser, J., Saraiva, J. (eds.) GTTSE 2007. LNCS, vol. 5235, pp. 291–373. Springer, Heidelberg (2008). https://doi.org/10.1007/978-3-540-88643-3_7
23. Yang, J.: Preventing information leaks with policy-agnostic programming. Dissertation, Massachusetts Institute of Technology, Massachusett (2015)
24. Yang, J., Yessenov, K., Solar-Lezama, A.: A language for automatically enforcing privacy policies. ACM SIGPLAN Not. 47(1), 85–96 (2012)
25. Zdancewic, S.: Challenges for information-flow security. In: Proceedings of the 1st International Workshop on the Programming Language Interference and Dependence (PLID 2004), pp. 6–11 (2004)
26. Zolnowski, A., Christiansen, T., Gudat, J.: Business model transformation patterns of data-driven innovations (2016)

Coreset-Based Data Compression for Logistic Regression

Nery Riquelme-Granada[1]([✉]), Khuong An Nguyen[2], and Zhiyuan Luo[1]

[1] Royal Holloway University of London, Surrey TW20 0EX, UK
{Nery.RiquelmeGranada,Zhiyuan.Luo}@rhul.ac.uk
[2] University of Brighton, East Sussex BN2 4AT, UK
K.A.Nguyen@brighton.ac.uk

Abstract. The coreset paradigm is a fundamental tool for analysing complex and large datasets. Although coresets are used as an acceleration technique for many learning problems, the algorithms used for constructing them may become computationally exhaustive in some settings. We show that this can easily happen when computing coresets for learning a logistic regression classifier. We overcome this issue with two methods: **A**ccelerating **C**lustering **v**ia **S**ampling (ACvS) and **R**egressed **D**ata **S**ummarisation **F**ramework (RDSF); the former is an acceleration procedure based on a simple theoretical observation on using Uniform Random Sampling for clustering problems, the latter is a coreset-based data-summarising framework that builds on ACvS and extends it by using a regression algorithm as part of the construction. We tested both procedures on five public datasets, and observed that computing the coreset and learning from it, is 11 times faster than learning directly from the full input data in the worst case, and 34 times faster in the best case. We further observed that the best regression algorithm for creating summaries of data using the RDSF framework is the Ordinary Least Squares (OLS).

Keywords: Coresets · Data compression · Logistic regression

1 Introduction

Data-compression techniques are a valuable set of tools for allowing learning algorithms to scale with large datasets. These techniques deviate from the classic algorithmic approach where one needs to write new algorithms in order to improve the running time of the old ones. One then expects these newer versions to converge faster. On the other hand, compression techniques allow the use of the existing, potentially inefficient algorithms, on reduced versions of their input data.

In a nutshell, given some input data $\mathscr{D}$ and a learning algorithm $\mathscr{A}$, a typical compression algorithm would attempt to reduce $\mathscr{D}$ to a much smaller, more manageable, dataset $\mathscr{S}$; once this compressed dataset has been obtained, the original one can be discarded and $\mathscr{A}$ can be run on $\mathscr{S}$ as many times as necessary. Since $\mathscr{S}$ is much smaller than $\mathscr{D}$, the learning process is accelerated and hence the computational burden associated with $\mathscr{A}$ can be better controlled.

© Springer Nature Switzerland AG 2021
S. Hammoudi et al. (Eds.): DATA 2020, CCIS 1446, pp. 195–222, 2021.
https://doi.org/10.1007/978-3-030-83014-4_10

Coresets (or core-sets) [10] are a representative framework of the data-compression family of algorithms, a powerful data-compression paradigm that *provably correctly* approximates the input data $\mathscr{D}$ by constructing a small coreset $\mathscr{C}$, with $|\mathscr{C}| \ll |\mathscr{D}|$. Although there are other interesting compression techniques such as Sketches [15] and Uniform Random Sampling (URS) [4], coresets are very attractive since (i) as opposed to URS, they keep the learning loss bounded, and (ii) as opposed to Sketches, coresets reside in input space *i.e.* the same space where the input data lives. Furthermore, there are well-established approaches for converting, with little effort, any batch algorithm to construct coresets into an online one (See [6], Sect. 7).

This paper expands the line of work started in [17], where the algorithm for constructing coresets for the problem of Logistic Regression (LR) was shown to produce a bottleneck, which in turn caused undesirable extra computational effort in the process of computing the coreset. Hence, some procedures were necessary in order to guarantee the fast compression of the input data. Specifically, in this work we look in-depth at the *Accelerating Clustering via Sampling* (ACvS) and *Regressed Data Summarisation Framework* (RDSF) ideas proposed in [17]. The former is a straight-forward procedure that accelerates the computation of coresets for the problem of Logistic Regression without sacrificing any performance; the latter is a coreset-based framework that uses machine learning to predict what the most *important* portion of the training set is, and constructs a data compression using its predictions. Our contributions are summarised as follows:

- We present and explain the ACvS procedure, proposed in [17], as a simple and effective acceleration technique for reducing the computational overheads that constructing coresets may cause for the problem of Logistic Regression.
- Following the work of [17], we re-visit the RDSF method as a coreset-based compression technique that benefits from a regression algorithm to learn how important the input points are with respect to the LR problem. We also show how RDSF enjoys, following the same acceleration principles involved in ACvS, a fast running time.
- We expand the empirical study presented in [17] in two major ways: (i) we consider two new datasets, ijcnn1 and w8a, and show that ACvS and RDSF efficiently produce good summaries of data; (ii) we present a new set of experiments where different regressors are used as part of the RDSF method. Specifically, we consider the *Ordinary Least Squares* (OLS), *Ridge*, *Lasso* and *Elastic Net* regressors.

The rest of the paper is organised as follows. Section 2 provides the fundamental definitions and discussions on coresets. Section 3 presents an exposition of the ideas originally proposed in [17]: ACvS and RDSF. Section 4 shows our empirical evaluations and the results obtained by using both ideas. Finally, Sect. 5 offers our conclusions and future work.

2   Coresets and Learning

In this section, we consider the problem of efficiently learning a binary LR classifier over a small data summary obtained from the input data. To approach this, we first introduce coresets and their construction. Then, we discuss the well-known Logistic

Regression classifier and the state-of-the-art coreset approach for this particular learning problem called "Coreset Algorithm for Bayesian Logistic Regression" (CABLR) [13]. Finally, we review the computational bottleneck that seems inevitable when using the coreset construction algorithm CABLR for LR.

2.1 Coresets and Their Construction

The framework of coresets is a well-established approach to reduce the size of large and complex datasets. A coreset is a small set of points that approximates a much bigger set of points with respect to a specific function. Formally, let function f be the objective function of some learning problem and let $\mathscr{D}$ be the input data. The set $\mathscr{C}$ is said to be an ε-coreset for $\mathscr{D}$ with respect to f if the following condition holds [10]:

$$|f(\mathscr{D}) - f(\mathscr{C})| \leq \varepsilon f(\mathscr{D}) \tag{1}$$

where $\varepsilon \in (0,1)$ accounts for the error incurred for evaluating f over $\mathscr{C}^1$. This expression establishes the main error bound offered by coresets. Hence, we can potentially suffer some loss when using the coreset; but this loss is bounded and controlled via the ε error parameter. Notice that it is expected that $|\mathscr{C}| \ll |\mathscr{D}|$ holds.

The natural question to ask at this point is how to construct such a set $\mathscr{C}$ for our input data so that we can enjoy the kind of guarantee in formula (1). There are well-known techniques for constructing coresets and they can be summarised as follows:

- **Geometric Decomposition** [2]: this is a fundamental approach for constructing coresets, because the first coreset constructions followed this line of thinking; it relies on discretising the input space of points into cells or grids, and then *snapping* representative points from each grid. This approach has been extensively used in the analysis of *shape fitting* problems such as the *Minimum Enclosing Ball* (MEB) [5].
- **Random Sampling** [9]: this is a more recent result and currently is one of the most successful approaches for constructing coresets. The idea is to compute a probability distribution that, in a well-defined sense, reflects the importance of each input point with respect to function f. Then, one samples the points following the importance distribution and assigns *weights* to each sampled point. Thus, the coreset in this case is a *weighted subset* of the original input data.
- **Gradient Descent** [16]: this line of work uses results from convex optimisation to reduce the coreset construction process to an special case of the popular gradient descent optimiser. Hence, the coreset is constructed iteratively and often implicitly as part of the optimisation of function f.
- **Projection-based Methods** [15]: the most notable projection-based method is that of *sketches*: the idea is to perform projections to sub-spaces of the input space in order to have lower-dimensional points. Hence, coresets constructed following this approach may have the same number of points as the original input data, but because the coreset resides in a much lower dimension *i.e.* the number of dimensions in the coreset is strictly less than the number of dimensions in the original input data, learning-related computations are faster. This set of techniques is largely inspired

---

[1] Instead of using the full input data $\mathscr{D}$.

by the Johnson-Lindenstrauss lemma [7], a result that states that the input data can be embedded in a much lower-dimensional space such that the distances among the points are approximately preserved.

No matter what approach we choose to construct the coreset $\mathscr{C}$, we need a precise definition of f. In machine learning, f is defined as the objective function for the learning problem we are trying to solve. In our case, we want to compute a coreset that allows us to learn a logistic regression classifier with small loss. In the next section we formally define this fundamental learning problem; then, we present a powerful method that falls into the random-sampling family of algorithms to compute coresets.

2.2   Logistic Regression and Sensitivity Framework

Logistic Regression is a well-known statistical method for binary classification problems. Given an input data $\mathscr{D} := \{(x_n, y_n)\}_{n=1}^{N}$, where x_n is d-dimensional feature vector and $y_n \in \{-1, 1\}$ is its corresponding label, the likelihood of observing $y_n = 1$ for x_n can be defined as:

$$p_{logistic}(y_n = 1 | x_n; \theta) := 1/(1 + \exp(-x_n' \cdot \theta)) \tag{2}$$

where $\theta \in \mathbb{R}^{d+1}$ is a *learning parameter* and $x_n' \in \mathbb{R}^{d+1}$ is the feature vector x_n extended with an additional column of ones. The latter is done to account for the bias term.

Similarly, we have

$$p_{logistic}(y_n = -1 | x_n; \theta) := 1 - \frac{1}{(1 + \exp(-x_n' \cdot \theta))}$$
$$= \frac{\exp(-x_n' \cdot \theta)}{(1 + \exp(-x_n' \cdot \theta))} = \frac{1}{(1 + \exp(x_n' \cdot \theta))}. \tag{3}$$

Therefore, the likelihood of observing any y_n can be captured by the expression $p_{logistic}(y_n | x_n; \theta) := 1/(1 + \exp(-y_n x_n' \cdot \theta))$. That is, if $y_n = 1$ the expression will become equivalent to Eq. (2), otherwise it will become equivalent to Eq. (3).

Because the input data $\mathscr{D}$ is assumed to be independent and identically distributed, the log-likelihood function $LL_N(\theta | \mathscr{D})$ can be defined as in [20]:

$$LL_N(\theta | \mathscr{D}) := \sum_{n=1}^{N} \ln p_{logistic}(y_n | x_n; \theta) = - \sum_{n=1}^{N} \ln(1 + \exp(-y_n x_n' \cdot \theta)) \tag{4}$$

which is the objective function for the LR problem. The optimal parameter $\hat{\theta}$ can be obtained using maximum likelihood estimation. Maximising $LL_N(\theta | \mathscr{D})$ is equivalent to minimising $\mathscr{L}_N(\theta | \mathscr{D}) := \sum_{n=1}^{N} \ln(1 + \exp(-y_n x_n' \cdot \theta))$ over all $\theta \in \mathbb{R}^{d+1}$. Finally, the optimisation problem can be defined as:

$$\hat{\theta} := \underset{\theta \in \mathbb{R}^{d+1}}{\arg\min} \mathscr{L}_N(\theta | \mathscr{D}), \tag{5}$$

where $\hat{\theta}$ is the best solution found. Once we have solved Eq. (5), we use the estimated $\hat{\theta}$ to make prediction for any unseen data point.

A Bayesian approach to Logistic Regression allows us to specify a prior distribution for the unknown parameter θ, $p(\theta)$ based on our real-life domain knowledge and derive the posterior distribution $p(\theta|\mathscr{D})$ for a given data $\mathscr{D}$ by applying Bayes' theorem:

$$p(\theta|\mathscr{D}) = \frac{p(\mathscr{D}|\theta)p(\theta)}{p(\mathscr{D})} = \frac{p(\mathscr{D}|\theta)p(\theta)}{\int p(\mathscr{D}|\theta)p(\theta)d\theta}.$$

Exact Bayesian inference for Logistic Regression is intractable. Therefore, no closed-form maximum likelihood solution can be found for determining θ and approximation methods are typically used to find the solution.

The state-of-the-art coreset construction for LR problem, namely *Coreset Algorithm for Bayesian Logistic Regression* (CABLR) was proposed by Huggins *et al.* [13]. Designed for the Bayesian setting, this algorithm uses random sampling for constructing coresets that approximate the log-likelihood function on the input data $\mathscr{D}$.

Huggins *et al.* followed a well-established framework known as the *sensitivity framework* [9] for constructing coresets for different instances of clustering problems such as K-means and K-median. The main idea is to formulate coreset construction as the problem of finding an ε-approximation [14], which can be computed using non-uniform sampling based on the importance of each data point, in some well-defined sense[2]. Hence, each point in the input data is assigned an importance score, *a.k.a.* the sensitivity of the point. An approximation to the optimal clustering of the input data is required in order to calculate such importance scores. For each point, the sensitivity score is computed by taking into account the distance between the point and its nearest (sub-optimal) cluster centre obtained from the approximation. The next step is to sample M points from the distribution defined by the sensitivity scores, where M is the size of the coreset. Finally, each of the M points in the coreset is assigned a positive real-valued *weight* which is the inverse of the point's sensitivity score. The sensitivity framework returns a coreset consisting of M weighted points. The theoretical proofs and details can be found in [9].

However, careless use of this algorithm in the optimisation setting, as we shall see in the next section, may be devastating as computing the clustering of the input data, even with the minimum number of iterations, can become too expensive. The description of CABLR is shown in Algorithm 1 where k number of cluster centres $\mathscr{Q}$, from the input data are used to compute the sensitivities (lines 2–4); then, sensitivities are normalised and points get sampled (lines 5–9); finally, the weights which are inverse proportional to the sensitivities, are computed for each of the sampled points (lines 10–12). Thus, even though the obtained coreset is for LR, CABLR still needs a clustering of the input data as it is common for any coreset algorithms designed using the sensitivity framework.

Remark 1. In the description of Algorithm 1, we hide the coreset dependence on the error parameter ε, defined in Sect. 2.1. There is a good reason for doing this. When theoretically designing a coreset algorithm, there are two error parameters involved:

---

[2] For our discussion, it is enough to state that the sensitivity score is a real value in the half-open interval $[0, \infty)$.

$\varepsilon \in [0,1]$, the "loss" incurred by coresets, and $\delta \in (0,1)$, the probability that the algorithm will fail to construct a coreset. Then, it is necessary to define the minimum coreset size M in terms of these error parameters. The norm is to prove there exists a function $t : [0,1] \times (0,1) \rightarrow \mathscr{Z}^+$, with $\mathscr{Z}^+$ being the set of all positive integers, that gives the corresponding coreset size for all possible error values $i.e.$ $t(\varepsilon_1, \delta_1) := M_1$ implies that M_1 is the minimum number of points needed in the coreset for achieving, with probability $1 - \delta$, the error ε_1. However, in practice, one does not worry about explicitly giving the error parameters as inputs; since each coreset algorithm comes with its own definition of t, one only needs to give the desired coreset size M and the error parameters can be computed using t. Finally, t defines a fundamental trade-off for coresets: the smaller the error parameters, the bigger the resulting coreset size $i.e.$ smaller coresets may potentially lose more information than bigger coresets.[3]

Input: $\mathscr{D}$: input data, $Q_{\mathscr{D}}$: k-clustering of $\mathscr{D}$ with $|Q_{\mathscr{D}}| := k$, M: coreset size
Output: ε-coreset $\mathscr{C}$ with $|\mathscr{C}| = M$
1 initialise;
2 **for** $n = 1, 2, ..., N$ **do**
3 | $m_n \leftarrow$ Sensitivity$(N, Q_{\mathscr{D}})$;   // Compute the sensitivity of each point
4 **end**
5 $\bar{m}_N \leftarrow \frac{1}{N} \sum_{n=1}^{N} m_n$;
6 **for** $n = 1, 2, ..., N$ **do**
7 | $p_n = \frac{m_n}{N \bar{m}_N}$;   // compute importance weight for each point
8 **end**
9 $(K_1, K_2, ..., K_N) \sim$ Multi$(M, (p_n)_{n=1}^{N})$;   // sample coreset points
10 **for** $n = 1, 2, ..., N$ **do**
11 | $w_n \leftarrow \frac{K_n}{p_n M}$;   // calculate the weight for each coreset point
12 **end**
13 $\mathscr{C} \leftarrow \{(w_n, x_n, y_n) | w_n > 0\}$;
14 **return** $\mathscr{C}$

Algorithm 1. CABLR ([13]): an algorithm to construct coresets for Logistic Regression.

2.3 Challenges and Problems

Clustering on large input data is computationally hard [3]. This is why approximation and data reduction techniques are popular choices for accelerating existing clustering algorithms. In fact, the paradigm of coresets has seen great success in the task of approximating solutions for clustering problems (see [1,4,10,12,22]). The sensitivity framework, originally proposed for constructing coresets for clustering problems, requires a sub-optimal clustering of the input data $\mathscr{D}$ in order to compute the sensitivity for each point in $\mathscr{D}$. This requirement transfers to CABLR, described in the previous

---

[3] For CABLR, Huggins $et\ al.$ proved that $t(\varepsilon, \delta) := \lceil \frac{c \bar{m}_N}{\varepsilon^2} [(D+1) log\, \bar{m}_N + log(\frac{1}{\delta})] \rceil$, where D is the number of features in the input data, $\bar{m}_N$ is the average sensitivity of the input data and c is a constant. The mentioned trade-off can be appreciated in the definition of t.

section. If we assume a Bayesian setting as in [13], the time necessary for clustering $\mathscr{D}$ is dominated by the cost of the posterior inference algorithms (see [13]). However, if we remove the burden of posterior inference and consider the optimisation setting, then the situation is very different.

Figure 1 sheds some light on the time spent on finding a clustering compared to all the other steps taken by CABLR to construct a coreset, namely: *sensitivity computation* and *sampling*. The time spent on *learning* from the coreset is included as well.

Evidently, applying a clustering algorithm, even to get a sub-optimal solution as done here, can be dangerously impractical for LR in the optimisation setting, as it severely increases the overall coreset-construction time. Even worse, constructing the coreset is slower than learning directly from $\mathscr{D}$, defeating the purpose of using the coreset as an acceleration technique.

Another interesting issue can be seen at display here: the algorithm used for computing coresets must give us summaries of data that are both quickly-computable and quality-preserving. Disregarding one of these objectives makes our task much easier; that is, we can simply take an uniform random sampling from our input data; no compression algorithm will finish faster, but we will suffer a quality loss that is out of our control. Similarly, we can just avoid performing any data compression/reduction at all, and we will for sure be able to obtain a very high-quality solution; but we should be ready to deal with lots of computational stress, storage overflows and even loss of random access[4].

With coresets for LR, we propose the following research question: *'Can we still benefit from good coreset acceleration in the optimisation setting?'*

We give an affirmative answer to this question through two approaches described in the next section. The key ingredient for both methods is the use of *Uniform Random Sampling* alongside coresets.

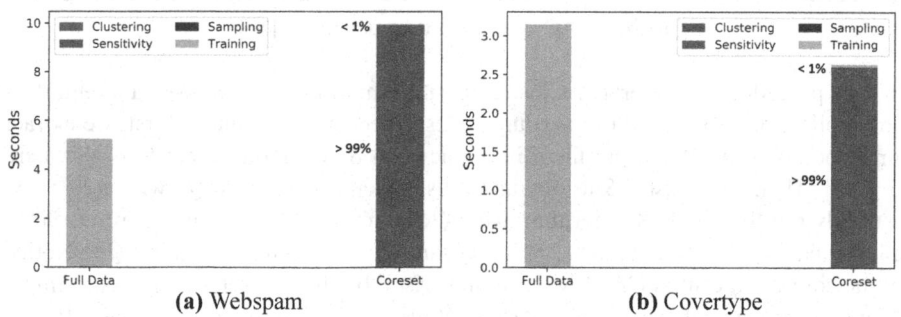

Fig. 1. The bottleneck induced by the clustering process when constructing coresets, as presented in [17].

---

[4] We loose random access when the input data is so large that accessing some parts of the data is more expensive, computationally speaking, than accessing other parts.

3   Two Accelerating Procedures

In this section, we propose two different procedures for efficiently computing coresets for LR in the optimisation setting. Both approaches are similar in the following sense: they both make use of Uniform Random Sampling (URS) for speeding up the coresets computation. URS is the most straightforward and simple way to reduce the size of input dataset by picking as many points as permissible uniformly at random. This is not the first time that the concept of URS comes up alongside coresets; in fact, URS can be seen as a naive approach for computing coresets and it is the main motivation for deriving a more sophisticated sampling approach [4]. In our procedures, however, we see URS as a complement to coresets, not as an alternative to them, which is usually the case in coresets works.

3.1   Accelerating Clustering via Sampling

Input: CABLR: coreset algorithm, $\mathscr{D}$: input data, A: a clustering algortithm, k: number of
        cluster centres, $b \ll |\mathscr{D}|$: uniform random sample size
Output: $\mathscr{C}$: coreset
1 $S \leftarrow \emptyset$;
2 $B \leftarrow |S|$;
3 **while** $B < b$ **do**
4      $s \leftarrow \texttt{SamplePoint}(\mathscr{D})$ // Sample without replacement
5      $S \leftarrow S \cup \{s\}$ // Put s in S
6 **end**
7 $Q_S \leftarrow A(S,k)$ // Run Clustering algorithm on S
8 $\mathscr{C} \leftarrow \text{CABLR}_M(\mathscr{D}, Q_S)$ // Run Coreset Algorithm
9 **return** $\mathscr{C}$

Algorithm 2. ACvS procedure, as defined in [17].

Our first procedure, **A**ccelerated **C**lustering **v**ia **S**ampling (ACvS), uses a straightforward application of URS. The procedure is described in Algorithm 2. First, we extract b input points from $\mathscr{D}$ and put them into a new set S. We require that $b \ll N$, where $N := |\mathscr{D}|$. Then, we cluster S to obtain k cluster centres, namely Q_S with $|Q_S| := k$. We finally run the CABLR algorithm using Q_S as input and compute a coreset. Since we have that $|S| \ll |\mathscr{D}|$, obtaining Q_S is substantially faster than obtaining $Q_{\mathscr{D}}$. Notice that the coreset algorithm CABLR is parameterised by the coreset size M. As a simple example, suppose we have a large dataset that we would like to classify using LR, and to do it quite efficiently, we decide to compress the input data into a coreset. The standard coreset algorithm for LR dictates that we have to find a clustering of our dataset as the very first step. Then we use the clustering to compute the sensitivity of each point. The next step is to sample points according to their sensitivity and to put them in the coreset. Finally, we compute the weight for each point in the coreset. What ACvS proposes is: instead of computing the clustering of our dataset, compute the clustering of a very small set of uniform random samples of it, then proceed as the standard coreset algorithm dictates.

We design this procedure based on the following observation: uniform random sampling can provide unbiased estimation for many cost functions that are additively decomposable into non-negative functions. We prove this fact below.

Let $\mathscr{D}$ be a set of points and let $n := |\mathscr{D}|$; also, let Q be a *query* whose cost value we are interested in computing. We can define a cost function which is decomposable into non-negative functions as $cost(\mathscr{D}, Q) := \frac{1}{n} \sum_{x \in \mathscr{D}} f_Q(x)$.

Most machine learning algorithms can be cast to this form. Here, we are mainly concerned about K-means clustering, where Q is a set of k points and $f_Q(x) := min_{q \in Q} \|x - q\|_2^2$. Let us now take a random uniform sample $S \subset \mathscr{D}$ with $m := |S|$, and define the cost of query Q with respect to S as $cost(S, Q) := \frac{1}{m} \sum_{x \in S} f_Q(x)$. To show that $cost(S, Q)$ is an unbiased estimator of $cost(\mathscr{D}, Q)$ we need to prove that $\mathbb{E}[cost(S, Q)] = cost(\mathscr{D}, Q)$.

Claim. $\mathbb{E}[cost(S, Q)] = cost(\mathscr{D}, Q)$.

Proof. By definition, we have that $cost(S, Q) := \frac{1}{m} \sum_{x \in S} f_Q(x)$. Expanding this, we get

$$\mathbb{E}[cost(S, Q)] = \mathbb{E}[\frac{1}{m} \sum_{x \in S} f_Q(x)] \tag{6}$$

The crucial step now is to compute the above expectation. To do this, it is useful to construct the set $\mathbb{S}$ that contains all the possible subsets S in $\mathscr{D}$. The number of such subsets has to be $\binom{n}{m}$, which implies $|\mathbb{S}| := \binom{n}{m}$. Then, computing the expectation over $\mathscr{S}$ and re-arranging some terms we get

$$\frac{1}{\binom{n}{m}} \frac{1}{m} \sum_{S \in \mathbb{S}} \sum_{x \in S} f_Q(x) \tag{7}$$

Next, we get rid of the double summation as follows: we count the number of times that $f_Q(x)$ is computed. By disregarding overlapping computation of $f_Q(x)$ due to the fact that a point x may belong to multiple subsets $S \in \mathbb{S}$, we quickly obtain that the count has to be $\binom{(n-1)}{(m-1)}$. Then, we write (7) as

$$\frac{1}{\binom{n}{m}} \frac{1}{m} \binom{(n-1)}{(m-1)} \sum_{x \in \mathscr{D}} f_Q(x) \tag{8}$$

Notice that now we have a summation that goes over our original set $\mathscr{D}$. Finally, by simplifying the factors on the left of the summation we have

$$\frac{1}{n} \sum_{x \in \mathscr{D}} f_Q(x) = cost(\mathscr{D}, Q) \tag{9}$$

which concludes the proof.

The imminent research question here is: how does using the ACvS procedure affect the performance of the resulting coreset? We shall show in Sect. 4 that the answer is more benign than we originally thought.

3.2 Regressed Data Summarisation Framework

Our second method builds on the previous one and it gives us at least two important benefits on top of the acceleration benefits given by ACvS:

- *Sensitivity Interpretability:* it unveils an existing (not-obvious) linear relationship between input points and their sensitivity scores.
- *Instant Sensitivity-assignment Capability:* apart from giving us a coreset, it gives as a trained regressor capable of assigning sensitivity scores *instantly* to new unseen points.

Before presenting the method, however, it is useful to remember the following: the CABLR algorithm (Algorithm 1) implements the sensitivity framework, explained in Sect. 2.2, and hence it relies on computing the sensitivity (importance) of each of the input points.

We call our second procedure *Regressed Data Summarisation Framework* (RDSF). We can use this framework to (i) accelerate a sensitivity-based coreset algorithm; (ii) unveil information on how data points relate to their sensitivity scores; (iii) obtain a regression model that can potentially assign sensitivity scores to new data points.

The full procedure is shown in Algorithm 3: RDSF starts by using ACvS to accelerate the clustering phase. The next step is to separate the input data $\mathcal{D}$ in two sets: S, the small URS picked during ACvS, and R, all the points in $\mathcal{D}$ that are not in S. The main step in RDSF starts at line 12: using the clustering obtained in the ACvS phase, Q_S, we compute the sensitivity scores *only* for the points in S and place them in a predefined set Y. A linear regression problem is then solved using the points in S as feature vectors and their corresponding sensitivity scores in Y as targets. This is how RDSF sees the problem of summarising data as the problem of 'learning' the sensitivity of the input points. The result of such learning process is a trained regressor ϕ and RDSF uses it to predict the sensitivities of all the points in R. Hence, RDSF uses S as training set and R as test set.

We finally see that after merging the computed and predicted sensitivities of S and R (line 17 in Algorithm 3), respectively, RDSF executes the same steps as CABLR *i.e.* compute the mean sensitivity (line 18), sample the points that will be in the summary (line 22) and compute the weights (line 23–25).

4 Evaluations

In this section, we show our evaluation results. Similar to [17–19], we rigorously test coresets and coresets-based methods by applying a set of metrics which are standard in machine learning. This work hence puts considerable emphasis on investigating coresets from an empirical standpoint, a perspective that still remains largely unexplored in the coreset community.

Input: $\mathcal{D}$: input data, A: clustering algortithm, k: number of cluster centres, $b \ll |\mathcal{D}|$:
uniform random sample size, M: coreset size
Output: $\tilde{\mathcal{C}}$: Summarised Version of $\mathcal{D}$, ϕ: Trained Regressor
1 initialise;
2 $S \leftarrow \emptyset$;
3 $B \leftarrow |S|$;
4 $N \leftarrow |\mathcal{D}|$;
5 **while** $B < b$ **do**
6 | $s \leftarrow$ SamplePoint$(\mathcal{D})$ // Sample without replacement
7 | $S \leftarrow S \cup \{s\}$ // Put s in S
8 **end**
9 $Q_S \leftarrow A(S,k)$ // Run Clustering algorithm on S
10 $R \leftarrow \mathcal{D} \setminus S$;
11 $Y \leftarrow \emptyset$;
12 **for** $n = 1,2,...,b$ **do**
13 | $m_n \leftarrow$ Sensitivity(b,Q_S) // Compute the sensitivity of each point
         $s \in S$
14 | $Y \leftarrow Y \cup \{m_n\}$;
15 **end**
16 $\hat{Y}, \phi \leftarrow$ PredictSen(S,Y,R) // Train regressor on S and Y, predict
     sensitivity for each $r \in R$
17 $Y \leftarrow Y \cup \hat{Y}$;
18 $\bar{m}_N \leftarrow \frac{1}{N}\sum_{y \in Y} y$;
19 **for** $n = 1,2,...,N$ **do**
20 | $p_n = \frac{m_n}{N\bar{m}_N}$;   // compute importance weight for each point
21 **end**
22 $(K_1,K_2,...,K_N) \sim$ Multi$(M,(p_n)_{n=1}^N)$;   // sample coreset points
23 **for** $n = 1,2,...,N$ **do**
24 | $w_n \leftarrow \frac{K_n}{p_n M}$;   // calculate the weight for each coreset point
25 **end**
26 $\tilde{\mathcal{C}} \leftarrow \{(w_n,x_n,y_n)|w_n > 0\}$;
27 **return** $\tilde{\mathcal{C}}, \phi$

Algorithm 3. The Regressed Data Summarisation Framework ([17]) uses a coreset construction to produce coreset-based summaries of data.

4.1 Strategy

We tested our procedures on 5 datasets, shown in Table 1, which are publicly available[5] and are well-known in the coreset community.

All of our experiments are based on the following five procedures:

- **Full:** no coreset or summarisation technique is used. That is, we simply train a LR model on the entire training set, then predict the labels for the instances in the test set.

---

[5] https://www.csie.ntu.edu.tw/~cjlin/libsvmtools/datasets/ - last accessed in 4/2021.

Table 1. Overview of the datasets considered for evaluation of our procedures.

Dataset	Examples	Features
ijcnn1	141,691	22
Webspam	350,000	254
Covertype	581,012	54
Higgs	11,000,000	28
w8a	64,700	300

- **CABLR:** we obtain a clustering of the input data and run CABLR (Algorithm 1) to obtain a coreset. We then train a LR model on the coreset to predict the labels for the test instances.
- **ACvS:** we use the procedure 'Accelerated Clustering via Sampling', described in Algorithm 2, to accelerate the coreset computation. Once we have obtained the coreset in accelerated fashion, we proceed to learn a LR classifier over it.
- **RDSF:** summaries of data are generated via the 'Regressed Data Summarisation Framework', described in Algorithm 3. Hence, we compute the sensitivity scores only for a handful of instances in the training set. Then, we train a regressor to predict the sensitivity scores for the remaining of the training instances. We sample points according to the sensitivities, compute their weights, and return the data summary. We then proceed as in the previous coreset-based procedures.
- **URS:** for the sake of completeness, we include 'Uniform Random Sampling' as a baseline for reducing the volume of input data; we simply pick the required input points uniformly at random and then train a LR classifier over them.

Our evaluation pipeline can be described as follows: for each of the above approaches, and for each dataset in Table 1, we take the below steps:

a) **Data Shuffling:** we randomly mix up all the available data.
b) **Data Splitting:** we select 50% of the data as training set and leave the rest for testing purposes. The training set is referred as the input data $\mathscr{D}$.
c) **Data Compressing:** we proceed to compress the input data. As previously mentioned, the *CABLR* approach computes a coreset without any acceleration, *ACvS* computes a coreset by using CABLR with an accelerated clustering phase, *RDSF* compresses the input data into a small data summary in an accelerated fashion, and *URS* performs a naive compression by taking uniform random samples of the input data. *Full Data* is the only approach that does not perform any compression on the input data.
d) **Data Training:** we train a Logistic Regression classifier on the data obtained in the previous step. *CABLR, ACvS, RDSF* and *URS* produce a reduced version of the input data while *Full Data* trains the classifier on the full input data $\mathscr{D}$.
e) **Data Assessing:** we finally use the trained Logistic Regression classifiers to predict the labels in the test set and apply our performance metrics, detailed in Sect. 4.2.

We applied the above steps 10 times for each of the five different approaches. Hence, the results we present in the next sections are averaged ones. Regarding the hardware, our experiments were performed on a single desktop PC running the Ubuntu-Linux operating system, equipped with an Intel(R) Xeon(R) CPU E3-1225 v5 @ 3.30 GHz processor and 32 Gb of RAM.

For the coreset implementation, we adapted to our needs the CABLR algorithm as shared by its authors[6]. All of our programs were written in Python. The method used for clustering the input data is the well-known K-means algorithm; and for RDSF, we used linear regression to learn the sensitivities of input points.

4.2   Metrics

As previously mentioned, the empirical performance of coresets has mainly remained a grey area in the past years. We apply the following performance metrics in order to shed some light on, first, the performance of coresets in general, second, the performance of our proposed methods. We consider the following five performance metrics:

1. **Computing time (in seconds):** we measure acceleration in seconds. To make a more meaningful analysis, we further break down time into 5 different stages:
   a) **Clustering:** the time needed to obtain the k-centres for coreset-based approaches.
   b) **Sensitivity:** the time required to compute the sensitivity score for each input point.
   c) **Regression:** the time needed for training a regressor in order to predict the sensitivity scores for input points. The prediction time is also taken into account.
   d) **Sampling:** the time required to sample input points.
   e) **Training:** the time required for leaning an LR classifier.
   Notice that the *Training phase* is the only one present in all of our approaches. Hence, for example, the *coreset* approach does not learn any regressor and thus it is assigned 0 s for that phase. The *URS* approach does not perform any clustering or sensitivity computation, hence those phases get 0 s for this method, etc.
2. **Classification Accuracy:** this measure is given by the percentage of correctly classified test examples. It is commonly used as the baseline metric for measuring performance in a supervised-learning setting.
3. **Area Under the Precision & Recall Curve (PREC/REC):** Precision is defined as $\frac{TP}{TP+FP}$ and Recall can be computed as $\frac{TP}{TP+FN}$ [8], where TP, FP and FN stand for the *True Positives*, *False Positives* and *False Negatives* achieved by a binary classifier, respectively. The curve is obtained by putting the Recall on the x-axis and the Precision on the y-axis. Once the curve has been generated, the area under the curve can be calculated in the interval between 0 and 1. The greater the area, the better the performance.
4. **F1 Score:** is the harmonic average of precision and recall [11] and hence can be computed as $F_1 := 2\frac{PR}{R+P}$, where P is Precision and R is recall [11]. The greater the value, the better the classifier's performance.
5. **Area Under the ROC Curve (AUROC):** provides an aggregate measure of performance across all possible classification thresholds. The curve can be computed

---

[6] https://bitbucket.org/jhhuggins/lrcoresets/src/master - last accessed in 2/2020.

by placing the *False Positives Rate* (FPR) on the *x*-axis and the *True Positives Rate* (TPR) on the *y*-axis, with FPR $:= \frac{FP}{FP+TN}$ and TPR $:= \frac{TP}{TP+FN}$; here, once more, TP, FP and FN stand for the *True Positives*, *False Positives* and *False Negatives* achieved by any binary classifier, respectively. Similar to the area under the precision and recall curve, AUROC is obtained from the curve.

4.3   Acceleration via ACvS and RDSF

We categorise our results according to the five different metrics we just described. Notice that their values are shown as functions of the size of the summaries used for training the LR classifier. Thus, if we look at Figs. 3, 5, 4 and 6, we can see that summary sizes on the x-axes correspond to very small percentages of the training set. Specifically, for the Higgs dataset, which is the largest one, the summary sizes are 0.005%, 0.03%, 0.06% and 0.1% of the input data. For Webspam and Covertype, which are smaller than Higgs, we show results with summary sizes of 0.05%, 0.1%, 0.3%, 0.6% and 1% of the total input data. Finally, for w8a and ijcnn1, which are the smaller datasets, the sizes shown are 1%, 3%, 6%, and 10%. The reason why there are different summary sizes for some of our datasets has to do with the difference in size across datasets. For example, computing a summary of 0.005% of the w8a or the ijcnn1 datasets is unfeasible since these datasets are not very large and hence it is very likely to end up with a extremely small summary of data that only contains points of one class. In other words: the larger the dataset, the more we can compress it.

Computing Time.   Figure 2 summarises our results in terms of computing time. We show in the stacked-bars plots the time spent for each *phase* of the different approaches.

We can clearly see that the *CABLR* approach, which clusters the full input data in order to constructs coresets, is not suitable for the optimisation setting we are considering. Specifically, with respect to the Full method, we notice that for the Covertype dataset, the coreset approach gives a modest acceleration of approximately 1.2 times. The situation becomes more severe for the Webspam, ijcnn1, w8a and Higgs datasets, where using the traditional coreset approach incurs in a learning process which is about 1.9, 2.6, 1.8 and 1.3 times slower than not using coreset at all, respectively.

Hence, by removing the bottleneck produced by the clustering phase, our two proposed methods show that we can still benefit from coreset acceleration to solve our particular problem; that is, our methods take substantially shorter computing time when compared to the *CABLR* approach. In particular, and with respect to Full Data approach, our approach *ACvS* achieves a minimum acceleration of 3.5 times (w8a) and a maximum acceleration of 34 times (Higgs) across our datasets. Regarding *RDSF*, the minimum acceleration obtained was 1.15 times (w8a) and the maximum was 27 times (Covertype).

Notice that our accelerated methods are only beaten by the naive URS method, which should most certainly be the fastest approach.

Finally, notice that the *RDSF* approach is slightly more expensive than *ACvS*. This is the computing price we pay for obtaining more information *i.e.* *RDSF* outputs a trained regressor that can immediately assign sensitivities to new unseen data points; this can

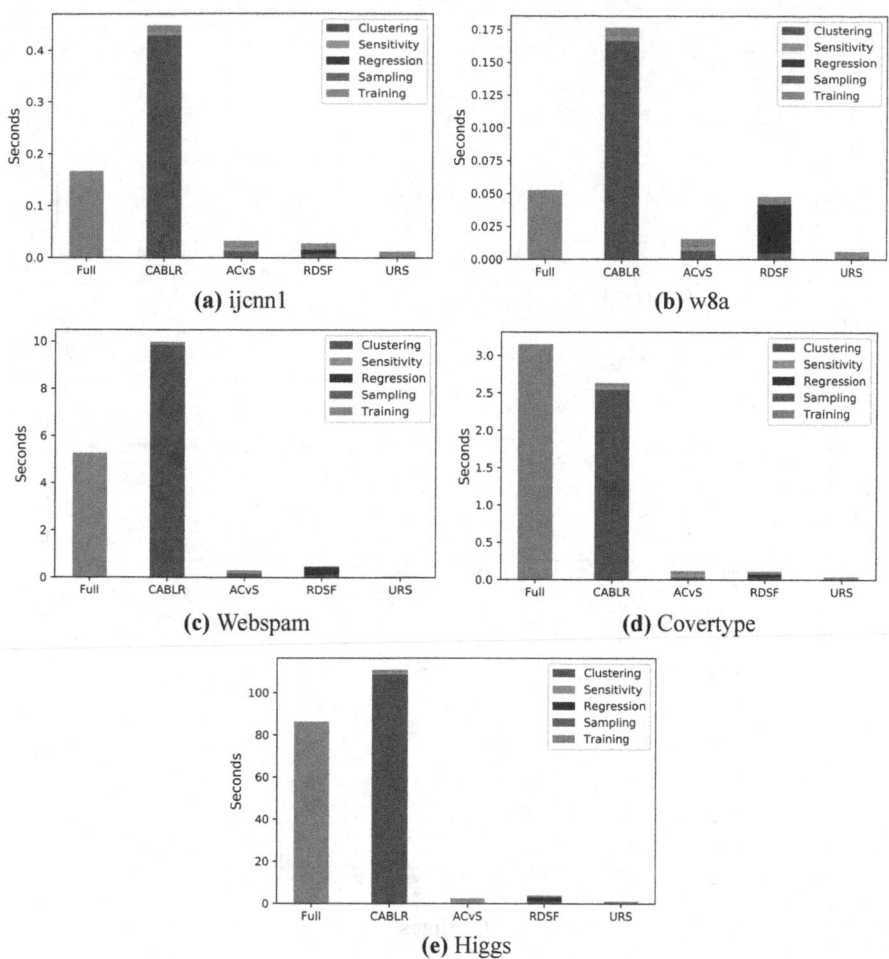

Fig. 2. Comparison of the computing time required by the different procedures.

prove extremely useful in settings when learning should be done *on the fly*. According to our evaluations, RDSF's time can be improved by reducing the number of points used for training the underlying regression algorithm. In general, using 1% of the training set for training the regressor worked well; however, depending on the data, this could be reduced (or increased) in order to achieve better computing time (learning quality).

The natural follow-up question is whether our methods' resulting classifiers perform well. We address this question in great detail in the following sections.

Accuracy. We first look into the baseline metric for measuring the success of a classifier: the accuracy. Figure 3 shows how the accuracy of the methods changes as the sample sizes increase on different datasets. To recall, each of the different methods considered relies on reducing the input data via a coreset-based compression or a random

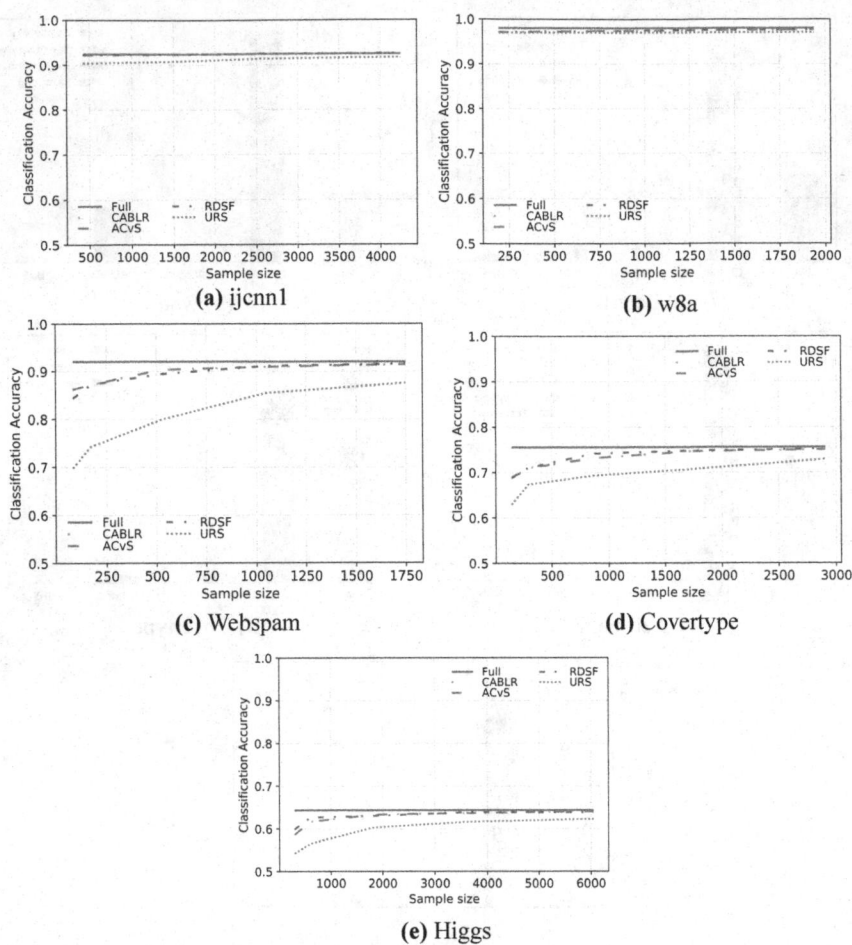

Fig. 3. Comparison of the prediction accuracy achieved by the considered methods.

uniform sample, as described in Sect. 4.1. Hence, we here report the different accuracy scores obtained by training our LR classifier on different samples sizes. As reference, we also include the accuracy of the *Full Data* method as a straight line.

The first observation is that all the methods perform better as the sample sizes increase. Quite surprisingly, we see that in all cases, without exceptions, the ACvS approach achieves the exact same accuracy that the CABLR approach achieves, for all sample sizes. Hence, for coresets, clustering over a sub-sample of the input data does not seem to deteriorate the rate of correct predictions of the resulting classifiers, and greatly accelerates the overall coreset computation, as we could appreciate in the previous section.

We also see that the RDSF approach performs as good as the rest of the coreset-based approaches, with accuracy never lower than the baseline approach (URS). It is generally expected that coresets outperform the URS approach in most situations; and RDSF summaries, even without being strictly a coreset[7], show this behaviour.

Finally, we see that, as sample sizes increase, the gap between coreset performance and URS performance reduces *i.e.* they both get closer and closer to the Full Data approach. A particularly interesting case is that of w8a, which shows a very similar performance for all the methods. This could be an indicator that points in the dataset contribute *almost* equally to the learning problem considered: LR, in this case.

F1 Score. We now present the results of applying the F1 score metric to our LR classifiers for different sample sizes, see Fig. 4.

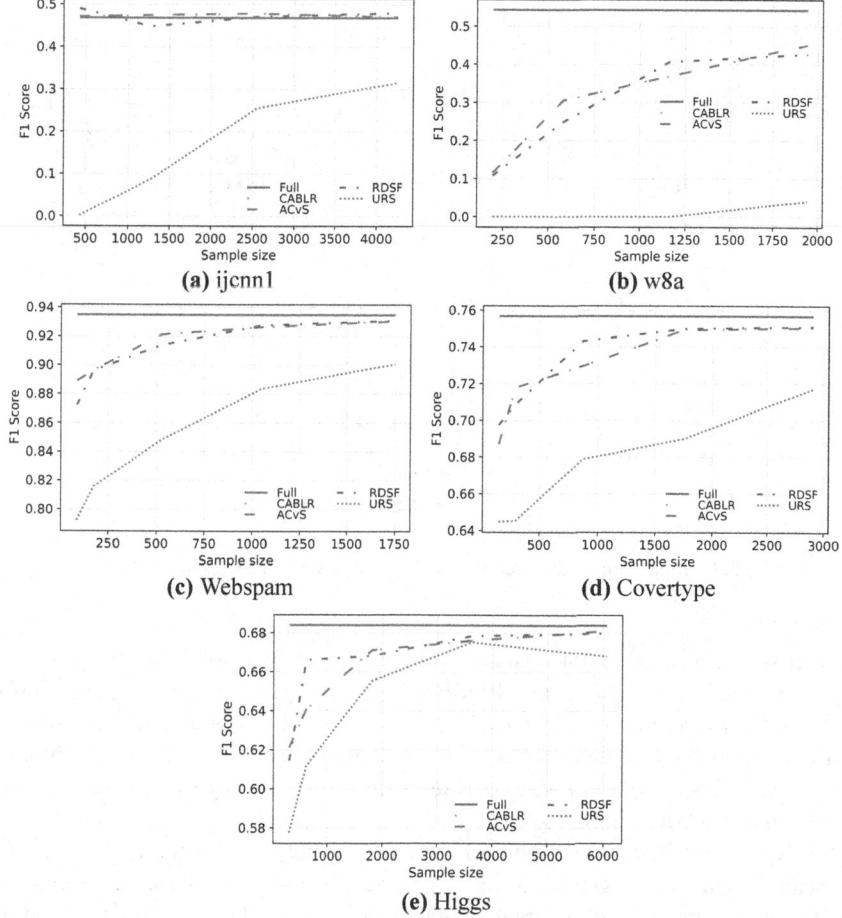

Fig. 4. F1 scores obtained by each of the methods.

---

[7] We carefully distinguish between a coreset and a coreset-based summary. The former requires a theoretical proof on the quality loss.

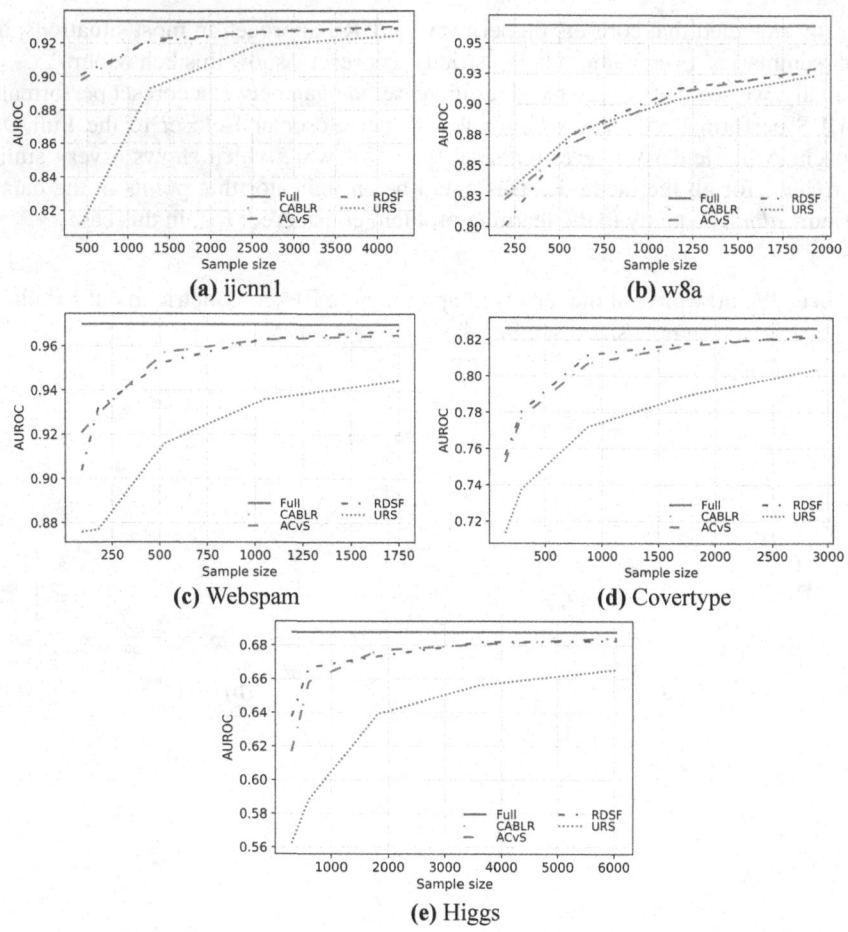

Fig. 5. Comparison of the area under the ROC curve of different methods.

The first observation we make is that, similar to accuracy results, ACvS and CABLR obtain exactly the same scores, and RDSF remains competitive against them. Furthermore, it is fair to say that for the Covertype and Higgs datasets, RDSF has preferable performance compared to the other compression approaches. Hence, we once more see that the advantages of coresets are available in our setting as long as we carefully accelerate the underlying algorithm.

Our experiments reveal that the performance gap between URS and the rest of the approaches becomes even greater for the F1 Score; showing that classifiers trained over coresets are more useful and informative than the ones trained over uniformly randomly selected samples. Furthermore, if we look at the F1 score for ijcnn1 (see Fig. 4a) we can have a glimpse of an interesting phenomenon: we actually obtain better results using coresets than using the full dataset. The fact that we can obtain better results using *less data* is left as an open problem for future exploration.

AUROC. We now present the AUROC score for each of our 5 approaches. Figure 5 shows comparison of the AUROC scores for all methods. The picture is similar to that of F1-score and Accuracy: coreset-based approaches consistently outperform URS. We see indeed that ACvS and RDSF perform competitively traditional coreset approach, achieving their performance in substantially less computing time than coresets (see Sect. 4.3). An intriguing case is that of w8a, which shows that URS is actually slightly better than coreset approaches for small sample sizes. As we previously mentioned, it is highly probably that this is an indication that the input points in the dataset are not very different in terms of their contribution to the LR objective function; or, it could also be the case that the sensitivity distribution, as computed by the coreset-based methods, does not fully account for the structure of the data.

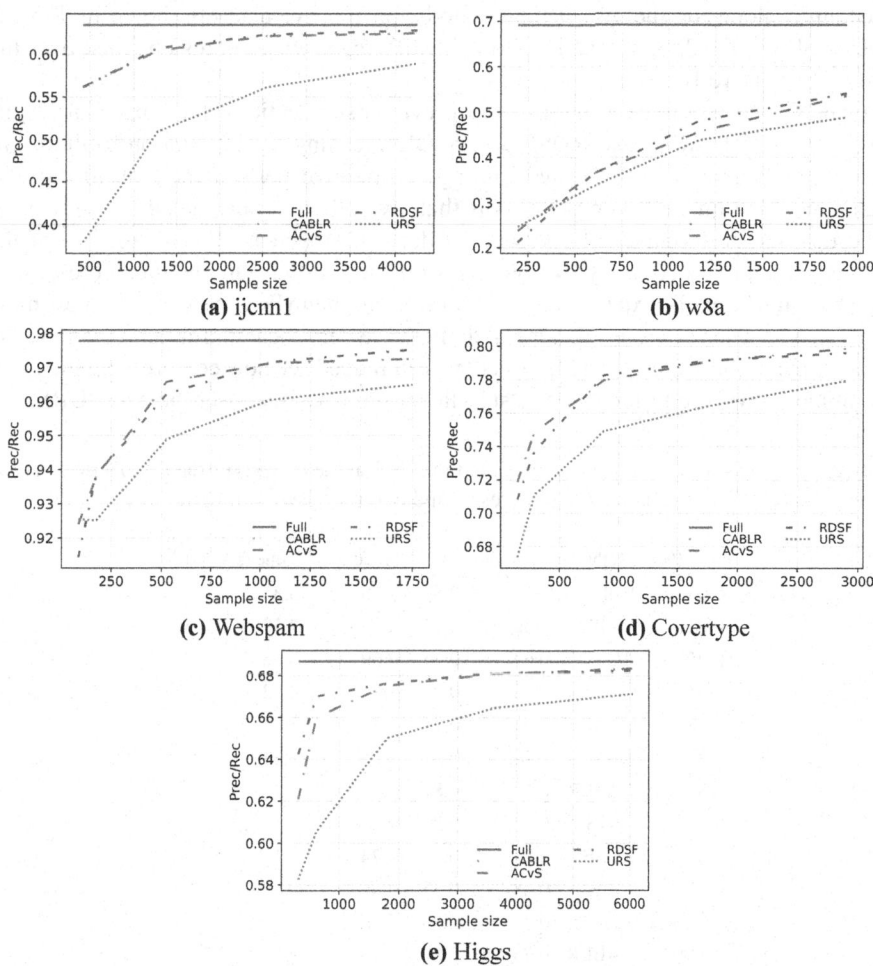

Fig. 6. Comparison of the area under the precision/recall curve of different methods.

Area Under the Precision & Recall Curve. Finally, we present the results concerning the precision and recall score. The behaviour here is similar to that of AUROC. The performance of w8a seems to be different from the rest of the data once more: we see that, for very small sample sizes, URS is even slightly better that the coreset and coreset-based approaches. As the sample sizes increase, the latter outperform the former, although not by much. As we previously mentioned, this could mean that input points in w8a are more or similar for LR and hence we cannot strictly distinguish between redundant and important points. We also see that ACvS gets exactly the same scores when compared to its non-accelerated version; which shows that clustering over the whole input data is not necessary *i.e.* clustering over a small uniform random sample is sufficient.

Summary of Results. This section provides detailed performance information of our procedures, alongside the rest of the methods, on the five datasets shown in Table 1. Specifically, Tables 2, 3, 4, 5 and 6 show the different metric scores obtained over the these 5 datasets, respectively.

Overall, and as shown in the plots in previous sub-sections, the empirical results demonstrated that ACvS and RDSF do provide meaningful acceleration to the traditional Coreset approach, while maintaining competitive performance, in all datasets considered. One important observation is that, even though our procedures give good speed-ups, the performance of coresets are dataset dependent. If the structure of the data can be captured correctly by doing an uniform random sample, then coreset performance should not be expected to be very different than URS. We can see an example of this in w8a, where coresets in general do not give very meaningful improvement. On the other hand, for the rest of the datasets, we can indeed see how compressing the input data in more involved fashion gives a significant improvement over the naive URS.

Table 2. Performance comparison, as presented in [17], on the Covertype dataset. Here, "size" is the percentage of training data used for coresets and coreset-based summaries.

Size (%)	Method	F1 score	ROC	Accuracy	Time (seconds)
0.05	Full	0.76	0.83	0.76	3.35
0.05	CABLR	0.69	0.75	0.69	2.78
0.05	ACvS	0.69	0.75	0.69	0.12
0.05	RDSF	0.70	0.76	0.69	0.12
0.05	URS	0.65	0.71	0.63	0.04
0.3	Full	0.76	0.83	0.76	3.31
0.3	CABLR	0.73	0.81	0.73	2.78
0.3	ACvS	0.73	0.81	0.73	0.13
0.3	RDSF	0.74	0.81	0.74	0.13
0.3	URS	0.68	0.77	0.69	0.05
1	Full	0.76	0.83	0.76	3.71
1	CABLR	0.75	0.82	0.75	3.38
1	ACvS	0.75	0.82	0.75	0.18
1	RDSF	0.75	0.82	0.75	0.18
1	URS	0.72	0.80	0.73	0.07

4.4   The RDSF Technique with Different Regressors

To finish our experiments exposition, we report the results obtained when using RDSF with different regressors in a plug-in/plug-out fashion. More concretely, we consider four different regression approaches: Ordinary Least Squares (OLS), Ridge Regression (RR), Lasso Regression (LSR) and Elastic Net (EN). To remind the reader, RR consists in fitting an OLS regressor with a L_2 regulariser; on the other hand, LSR trains an OLS regressor using a L_1 regulariser. Finally, EN finds an OLS regressor by using a convex combination of both L_1 and L_2 as its the regularisation term.

Depending of what regression algorithm was used to predict the sensitivities of input points, we can have one the following four RDSF instances:

– **RDFS-OLS:** an RDSF instance in which the input points' sensitivity scores were predicted using the ordinary-least-squares regression method. It is worth mentioning that this is the RDSF instance used in [17] and in Sect. 4.3.
– **RDFS-RR:** an instance of RDSF where the sensitivity for input points was predicted using the ridge regression method.
– **RDFS-LSR:** an RDSF instance that uses the lasso method for regression for predicting sensitivity scores.
– **RDFS-EN:** an instance of RDSF in which the sensitivity scores for input points are predicted via the elastic net regression method.

Table 3. Performance comparison, as presented in [17], on the Webspam dataset. Here, "size" is the percentage of training data used for coresets and coreset-based summaries.

Size (%)	Method	F1 score	ROC	Accuracy	Time (seconds)
0.05	Full	0.92	0.94	0.97	5.39
0.05	CABLR	0.86	0.89	0.92	10.15
0.05	ACvS	0.86	0.89	0.92	0.31
0.05	RDSF	0.84	0.87	0.90	0.49
0.05	URS	0.70	0.79	0.88	0.05
0.3	Full	0.92	0.94	0.97	6.54
0.3	CABLR	0.90	0.92	0.96	13.40
0.3	ACvS	0.90	0.92	0.96	0.41
0.3	RDSF	0.89	0.91	0.95	0.64
0.3	URS	0.80	0.85	0.92	0.06
1	Full	0.92	0.94	0.97	6.35
1	CABLR	0.92	0.93	0.97	13.44
1	ACvS	0.92	0.93	0.97	0.45
1	RDSF	0.92	0.93	0.97	0.68
1	URS	0.88	0.90	0.95	0.08

It is important to mention that for this study we only consider three metrics: Area Under the Precision & Recall curve, AUROC and F1 Score. The reason for this decision already sheds the first lights on using different regressors for RDSF: different regressors give summaries of data that, when used to solve the LR problem, give classifiers that do not meaningfully differ in their accuracy score. However, we will see that when more involved performance metrics are considered, the difference in performance becomes more meaningful.

We also highlight that the point of this set of experiments is not to find out which of the RDSF instances considered is faster as the OLS method is by definition the fastest regression algorithm of all, and ridge regression is known to be faster than lasso. Instead, the aim of these experiments is to see whether more involved regression algorithms can help us obtain RDSF summaries that obtain better learning performance.

Figures 7, 8 and 9 show the performance obtained when compressing the input data using different instances of the RDSF framework, specifically in terms of the area under the precision & recall curve, AUROC and F1 score, respectively. Notice that these plots, as the ones found in the previous subsection, have the different sample sizes of the (RDSF) summaries on the x axis and the corresponding performance value on the y axis.

Quite surprisingly, RDSF trained with the simple OLS method seems to be the preferable approach for computing RDSF summaries in general: it is not always the best. But more often than not it gets really close to the best performing method.

Table 4. Performance comparison on the Higgs dataset. Here, "size" is the percentage of training data used for coresets and coreset-based summaries.

Size (%)	Method	F1 score	ROC	Accuracy	Time (seconds)
0.005	Full	0.68	0.69	0.64	89.22
0.005	CABLR	0.62	0.62	0.59	112.44
0.005	ACvS	0.62	0.62	0.59	2.61
0.005	RDSF	0.62	0.64	0.60	4.16
0.005	URS	0.58	0.56	0.54	1.12
0.03	Full	0.68	0.69	0.64	92.22
0.03	CABLR	0.67	0.68	0.633	121.25
0.03	ACvS	0.67	0.68	0.63	2.70
0.03	RDSF	0.67	0.67	0.63	4.46
0.03	URS	0.66	0.64	0.60	1.20
0.1	Full	0.68	0.69	0.64	90.18
0.1	CABLR	0.68	0.68	0.64	123.97
0.1	ACvS	0.68	0.68	0.64	2.61
0.1	RDSF	0.68	0.68	0.64	4.50
0.1	URS	0.69	0.67	0.62	1.29

Table 5. Performance comparison on the w8a dataset. Here, "size" is the percentage of training data used for coresets and coreset-based summaries.

Size (%)	Method	F1 score	ROC	Accuracy	Time (seconds)
1	Full	0.543	0.96	0.98	0.06
1	Coreset	0.11	0.82	0.97	0.18
1	ACvS	0.116	0.82	0.97	0.02
1	RDSF	0.108	0.80	0.97	0.05
1	URS	0	0.82	0.97	0.007
3	Full	0.54	0.96	0.98	0.06
3	Coreset	0.30	0.86	0.97	0.19
3	ACvS	0.30	0.86	0.97	0.02
3	RDSF	0.24	0.87	0.97	0.06
3	URS	0	0.87	0.97	0.01
6	Full	0.54	0.96	0.98	0.05
6	Coreset	0.37	0.91	0.97	0.19
6	ACvS	0.37	0.91	0.97	0.02
6	RDSF	0.407	0.913	0.97	0.05
6	URS	0.0003	0.90	0.97	0.01

Table 6. Performance comparison, as presented in [17], on the ijcnn1 dataset. Here, "size" is the percentage of training data used for coresets and coreset-based summaries.

Size (%)	Method	F1 score	ROC	Accuracy	Time (seconds)
1	Full	0.46	0.93	0.92	0.18
1	Coreset	0.47	0.89	0.92	0.49
1	ACvS	0.47	0.89	0.92	0.03
1	RCP	0.49	0.90	0.92	0.03
1	URS	0.001	0.81	0.90	0.01
3	Full	0.46	0.93	0.92	0.19
3	Coreset	0.47	0.92	0.92	0.45
3	ACvS	0.47	0.92	0.92	0.04
3	RCP	0.44	0.92	0.92	0.03
3	URS	0.08	0.89	0.90	0.02
6	Full	0.46	0.93	0.92	0.19
6	Coreset	0.47	0.92	0.92	0.46
6	ACvS	0.47	0.92	0.92	0.04
6	RCP	0.47	0.92	0.92	0.04
6	URS	0.25	0.91	0.91	0.02

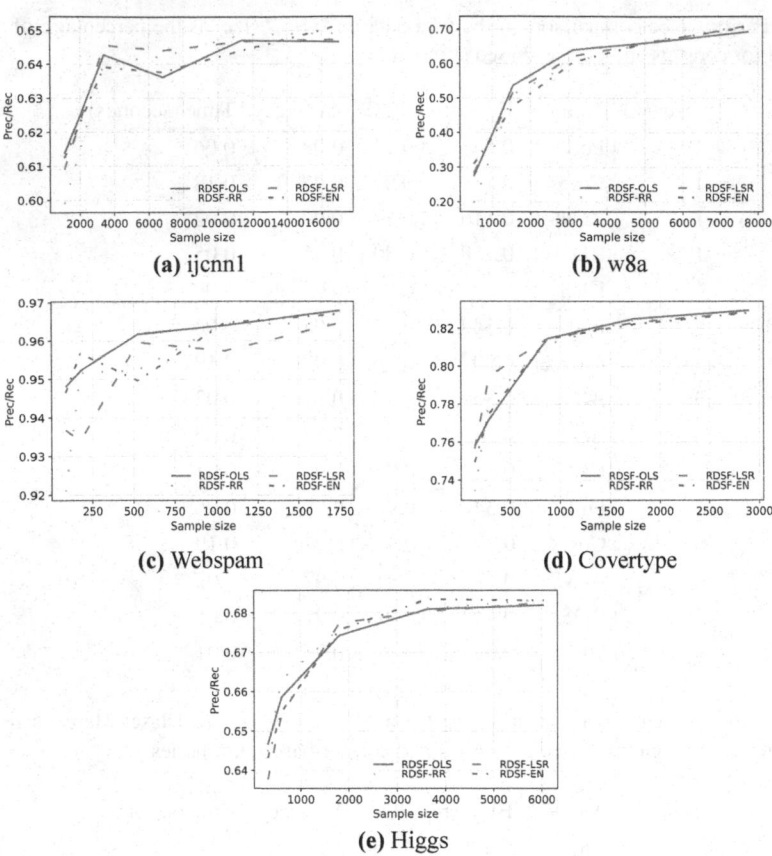

Fig. 7. Comparison of the areas under the precision & recall curve obtained from LR classifiers learned over RDSF summaries. The summaries were computed using different underlying regressors.

This is an enlightening result as OLS is the simplest method of the ones considered, and is seems to provide a very good explanation of the relationship between the input points and their sensitivities. Furthermore, we can make the conclusion that regularisation does not help us much with the task of predicting sensitivities. If we also add up the fact that OLS has a closed-form solution and hence it is computationally very efficient, it becomes really hard to justify the use of any of the other regression algorithms to compress input data via the RDSF framework.

Finally, it is useful to mention that we also considered different sample sizes for the regression problem of sensitivity prediction *i.e.* different values for the parameter b in Algorithm 3; specifically, we tested setting b to 0.01%, 0.05%, 1%, 5%, 10% and 15% of the input data size; however, the behaviour observed is very similar to the results presented here.

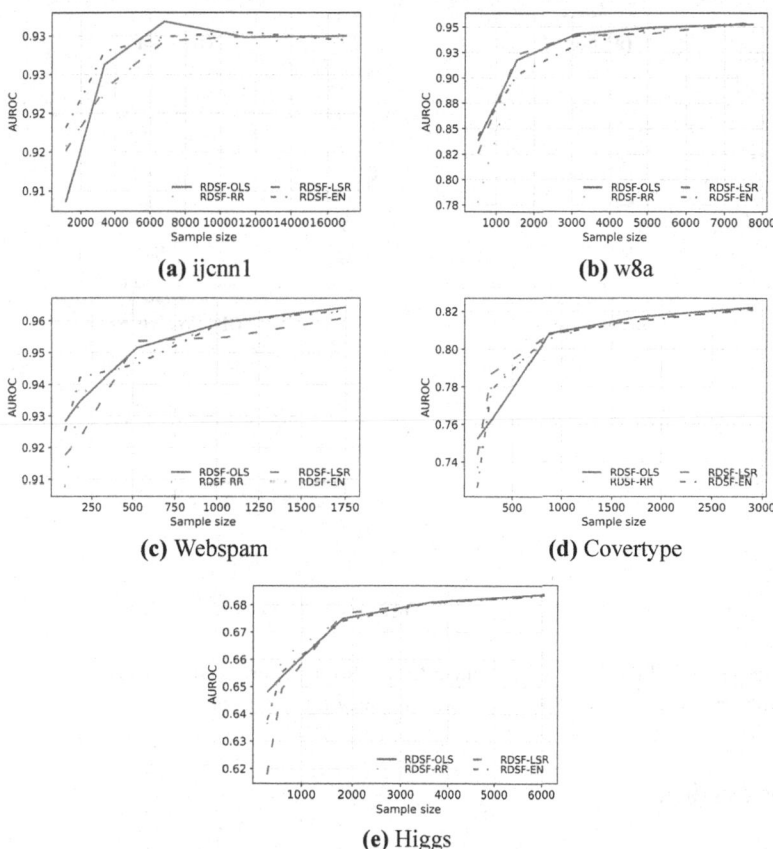

(a) ijcnn1

(b) w8a

(c) Webspam

(d) Covertype

(e) Higgs

Fig. 8. Comparison of the AUROC obtained from LR classifiers learned over RDSF summaries. The summaries were computed using different underlying regressors.

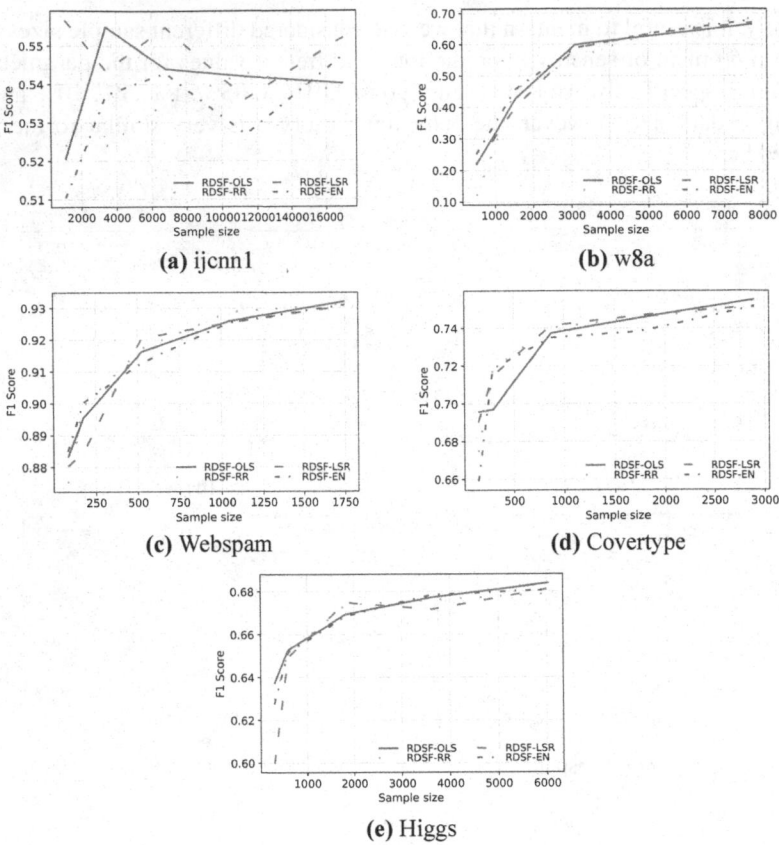

Fig. 9. Comparison of the F1 scores obtained from LR classifiers learned over RDSF summaries. The summaries were computed using different underlying regressors.

5   Conclusion

As modern ever-growing sets of data overshadow our computing resources, scaling up machine learning algorithm is not a trivial task. The most direct algorithmic approach is to write new learning algorithms that overcome the inefficiencies of their old counterparts. A less direct approach consists of using the well-known algorithms we currently possess over a reduced version of their input data. We have presented the paradigm of coresets: a framework that correctly compresses the input data with respect to an specific learning problem. We have shown that for the optimisation setting, the algorithm for constructing coresets for the problem of Logistic Regression relies on a clustering phase that, more often than not, creates a bottleneck in the compression process.

To circumvent this, we proposed two methods that ease this computational bottleneck: Accelerating Clustering via Sampling (ACvS) and Regressed Data Summarisation Framework (RDSF). Both methods achieved substantial overall learning acceleration while maintaining the performance accuracy of coresets. This implies that coresets can still be efficiently used to learn a logistic regression classifier in the optimisation setting.

Interestingly, we observed that, even though CABLR involves input data clustering, this can be relaxed in the practical sense. Furthermore, our calculations indicate that CABLR must be used with the clustering done over a small subset of the input data in the optimisation setting (*i.e.* the ACvS approach). Our empirical evaluations confirm that, by doing so, one will not be sacrificing learning performance.

With respect to RDSF, we believe this will open a new research branch for coresets: we could pose the computation of data compression via coresets as solving a small-scale learning problem in order to solve a large-scale one. It is interesting to see that the sensitivities of input points can be explained by a simple linear regressor. Most importantly, we believe that this method could be of powerful use in the *online learning setting* [21]. This is because RDSF allows us to obtain a fully trained regressor capable of assigning sensitivity scores to new incoming data points. We leave the use of these methods in different machine learning tasks as future work.

Acknowledgements. This research is supported by AstraZeneca and the Paraguayan Government.

References

1. Ackermann, M.R., Märtens, M., Raupach, C., Swierkot, K., Lammersen, C., Sohler, C.: StreamKM++: a clustering algorithm for data streams. J. Exp. Alg. (JEA) **17**, 2–4 (2012)
2. Agarwal, P.K., Har-Peled, S., Varadarajan, K.R.: Geometric approximation via coresets. Comb. Comput. Geom. **52**, 1–30 (2005)
3. Arthur, D., Vassilvitskii, S.: K-Means++: the advantages of careful seeding. In: Proceedings of the Eighteenth Annual ACM-SIAM Symposium on Discrete Algorithms, pp. 1027–1035. Society for Industrial and Applied Mathematics (2007)
4. Bachem, O., Lucic, M., Krause, A.: Practical coreset constructions for machine learning. arXiv preprint arXiv:1703.06476 (2017)
5. Bădoiu, M., Clarkson, K.L.: Optimal core-sets for balls. Comput. Geom. **40**(1), 14–22 (2008)
6. Braverman, V., Feldman, D., Lang, H.: New frameworks for offline and streaming coreset constructions. CoRR abs/1612.00889 (2016). http://arxiv.org/abs/1612.00889
7. Dasgupta, S., Gupta, A.: An elementary proof of the Johnson-Lindenstrauss lemma. International Computer Science Institute, Technical report **22**(1), 1–5 (1999)
8. Davis, J., Goadrich, M.: The relationship between precision-recall and ROC curves. In: Proceedings of the 23rd International Conference on Machine Learning, pp. 233–240 (2006)
9. Feldman, D., Langberg, M.: A unified framework for approximating and clustering data. In: Proceedings of the Forty-Third Annual ACM Symposium on Theory of Computing, pp. 569–578. ACM (2011)
10. Feldman, D., Schmidt, M., Sohler, C.: Turning big data into tiny data: constant-size coresets for K-means, PCA and projective clustering. In: Proceedings of the Twenty-Fourth Annual ACM-SIAM Symposium on Discrete Algorithms, pp. 1434–1453. SIAM (2013)
11. Goutte, C., Gaussier, E.: A probabilistic interpretation of precision, recall and *F*-score, with implication for evaluation. In: Losada, D.E., Fernández-Luna, J.M. (eds.) ECIR 2005. LNCS, vol. 3408, pp. 345–359. Springer, Heidelberg (2005). https://doi.org/10.1007/978-3-540-31865-1_25

12. Har-Peled, S., Mazumdar, S.: On coresets for k-Means and k-Median clustering. In: Proceedings of the Thirty-Sixth Annual ACM Symposium on Theory of Computing, pp. 291–300. ACM (2004)
13. Huggins, J., Campbell, T., Broderick, T.: Coresets for scalable Bayesian logistic regression. In: Advances in Neural Information Processing Systems, pp. 4080–4088 (2016)
14. Mustafa, N.H., Varadarajan, K.R.: Epsilon-approximations and epsilon-nets. arXiv preprint arXiv:1702.03676 (2017)
15. Phillips, J.M.: Coresets and sketches. arXiv preprint arXiv:1601.00617 (2016)
16. Reddi, S.J., Póczos, B., Smola, A.J.: Communication efficient coresets for empirical loss minimization. In: UAI, pp. 752–761 (2015)
17. Riquelme-Granada, N., Nguyen., K.A., Luo., Z.: On generating efficient data summaries for logistic regression: a coreset-based approach. In: Proceedings of the 9th International Conference on Data Science, Technology and Applications - Volume 1: DATA, pp. 78–89. INSTICC. SciTePress (2020). https://doi.org/10.5220/0009823200780089
18. Riquelme-Granada, N., Nguyen, K., Luo, Z.: Coreset-based conformal prediction for large-scale learning. In: Conformal and Probabilistic Prediction and Applications, pp. 142–162 (2019)
19. Riquelme-Granada, N., Nguyen, K.A., Luo, Z.: Fast probabilistic prediction for kernel SVM via enclosing balls. In: Conformal and Probabilistic Prediction and Applications, pp. 189–208. PMLR (2020)
20. Shalev-Shwartz, S., Ben-David, S.: Understanding Machine Learning: From Theory to Algorithms. Cambridge University Press, New York (2014)
21. Shalev-Shwartz, S., et al.: Online learning and online convex optimization. Found. Trends Machine Learn. 4(2), 107–194 (2012)
22. Zhang, Y., Tangwongsan, K., Tirthapura, S.: Streaming k-means clustering with fast queries. In: 2017 IEEE 33rd International Conference on Data Engineering (ICDE), pp. 449–460. IEEE (2017)

Product Classification Using Partially Abbreviated Product Names, Brands and Dimensions

Oliver Allweyer[1], Christian Schorr[2(✉)], Andreas Mohr[1], and Rolf Krieger[2]

[1] retailsolutions GmbH, Campus, Saarbrücken, Germany
{oliver.allweyer,andreas.mohr}@retailsolutions.de
[2] Institute for Software Systems, Trier University of Applied Sciences,
Environmental Campus Birkenfeld, Birkenfeld, Germany
{c.schorr,r.krieger}@umwelt-campus.de

Abstract. Retail companies are looking for ways to support or automate the data entry process for product master data which is currently often a time-consuming and cost-intensive manual process. The basis which many attributes and business processes in master data management depend on is the classification of articles to a certain product category. In this paper we propose a machine learning approach to classify articles according to the Global Product Classification schema by their product name, brand name and other attributes such as the product weight and dimensions. One of the challenges in our data set is posed by the product names containing a significant amount of abbreviations, for which we implement several preprocessing strategies. Additionally, the data set suffers from class imbalance and missing values that must be considered. Different classification algorithms, data imputation methods and feature combination strategies are evaluated. We show that automatic classification can be performed successfully based on the partly abbreviated product names despite the challenges mentioned. A simple Support Vector Machine model shows to outperform more sophisticated models and the brand names. The product dimensions and other additional attributes did not increase prediction quality.

Keywords: Machine learning · Product data · Automated product classification

1 Introduction

Product data form the basis for many different business processes in retail companies. Incomplete or defective master data are one of the most common reasons for poor data quality. This not only prevents effective data-driven innovation, but also adversely affects reporting and logistics. Product data records in enterprise resource planning systems (ERP) consist of a great variety of descriptive and process-controlling attributes. Some retailers' product data amount to millions of records, with more than a thousand new

---

This paper is an extension of the paper "Classification of products in retail using partially abbreviated product names only" by Allweyer et al. [2].

© Springer Nature Switzerland AG 2021
S. Hammoudi et al. (Eds.): DATA 2020, CCIS 1446, pp. 223–244, 2021.
https://doi.org/10.1007/978-3-030-83014-4_11

data records created each day. Because managing product data involves considerable effort and high costs, many companies are looking for ways to automate data entry and maintenance.

Since many attributes depend on the nature of a product, it is essential to know the product's affiliation to a certain category right at the start of the data generation process. Typical retail product ranges can for example contain food, office supplies, clothing or electronics. Therefore, an essential step in data entry is the classification of a product which assigns it a category. This decision depends on various criteria such as the structure of the classification system used and the characteristics of the product. Often the search for similar products with existing categorizations is a reasonable approach. The product might already be categorized in a different classification system such as the Global Product Classification (GPC) standard described in [1]. In most cases, mapping categories between different classification systems is not a trivial task.

Little information may be available at the time of data entry. The very first step is usually the entering of a product name, which is often constrained by system limitations such as character encoding and length, as well as company-specific conventions such as including brand names, the color, or the packaging size. This often very short product name provides a possibility for an automated classification of products, but poses some unique challenges compared to traditional text classification.

This paper extends the work reported in [2], where we presented a machine learning model that classifies retail food products by GPC codes based on the partially abbreviated product name (see Sect. 2). Using the same data set, we now examine how additional categorical and numerical attributes such as the brand name, the product weight and the product dimensions can be employed to increase the prediction quality. We explore different methods of feature engineering and data pre-processing to leverage the additional attributes and assess the pre-processing of the product name in greater detail. In addition, model architectures for feature concatenation and the influence of oversampling were analyzed in more detail.

This paper is structured as follows. First, we present a literature overview of the use of machine learning to classify product data and short texts (Sect. 2) and summarize the findings of [2]. In Sect. 3 we first describe and analyze the underlying product data set, which will be used in the subsequent sections to train and evaluate classification models. In Sect. 3.2 the evaluation process for the considered machine learning algorithms is explained. Next, we describe the approaches for data preprocessing and feature engineering and the experimental setup, in which we compare the impact of each different approach on classification performance (Sect. 3.3–3.6). The results of these experiments are presented and discussed in Sect. 4. Section 5 concludes with a summary of our results and suggests possibilities for further research.

2   Related Work

In this section, approaches from recent literature for the classification of products and the classification of short texts are described. Many of the previous works use the product name and, if available, the product description for product classification. In some cases, additional textual, categorical and numerical attributes are included. The results of the different approaches and model architectures are usually not directly comparable, since the work is based on different data sets, the amount of data varies considerably, different attributes are used as features, and different classification systems and different metrics are used for evaluation.

A comprehensive comparison of classification algorithms can be found in [3]. They evaluate the performance of Naïve Bayes, logistic regression, neural networks and Support Vector Machines (SVM) with 10-fold cross-validation on three data sets with product names and categories of a total of 46,000 items from three different online stores. After cleansing of numbers, punctuation and stop words, the texts are lowercased and tokenized. Bag-of-words representations with uni- to 4-grams are used as features. The optimal hyper parameters are determined by grid search. On two of the data sets, the Naïve Bayes classifier achieves the highest AUROC measure and statistical significance for all data sets. In [4], the classification of product names is differentiated from the classification of texts. Typical text classification techniques such as stemming, tokenization and feature representation are examined for a training data set of 10 million product records from an online store, which are distributed relatively evenly across 29 classes except for one class, and a test data set with 7 million products. A Support Vector Machine is used for classification. The experiment shows that the general modeling approach can be transferred from text to product classification. However, the following differences emerge from the experiment: Stemming and the removal of stop words have a negative influence on the classification for the product names under consideration and should not be applied. Binary and TF-IDF representation of the tokens achieve similar results. The use of bigrams and feature transformation with a polynomial kernel apparently works better than usual for text classification because of the brevity of the product names. A similar problem is considered in [5]. Two data sets from different vendors with 21 and 24 categories are classified using Naïve Bayes and a bag-of-words model. The investigation of different preprocessing steps shows that the removal of stop words (stemming), lowercasing, and the removal of numbers have little to no impact. A Decision Trees model achieves a slightly higher accuracy than Naïve Bayes.

Cevahir et al. investigate several classification techniques on a set of product descriptions categorized according to a UNSPSC scheme [6]. Naïve Bayes scores best compared to k-Nearest-Neighbors and a naive approach based on cosine similarity, reaching an accuracy of 86% at the lowest hierarchy level. About 40% of the data set belonging to categories with sparse coverage have been excluded. Contrary to intuitive expectations, the hierarchical classification shows a significantly worse result: Naïve Bayes achieves an accuracy of only 38%–42%. The authors explain this with a high number of wrong decisions that are made at a higher hierarchical level and thus prevent a correct classification at the lower levels. In [7] a classification model is presented that assigns products to one of 28,338 possible categories from a five-level taxonomy based on Japanese and English product names and descriptions. The model combines Deep Belief Nets, Deep Autoencoders and k-Nearest Neighbors and is trained on approximately 150 million product records. Challenges of the data set are identified in the unbalanced and sparse distribution across the categories, differences in the lengths of names and descriptions, and the unverifiable validity of the categories assigned by retailers. First, classification is performed at the highest level, which has only 35 categories, and then at the leaf categories. The probability distribution scores of the different classifiers are averaged to determine the category with the highest overall confidence. The authors of [8] also consider deep learning with a hierarchical taxonomy. They use Fasttext to represent product names with 100-dimensional word embeddings based on bigrams. Their data set comprises 1 million product names of which 72% are used for model training. Any preprocessing of the names such as stemming has a negative effect. The leaf categories are best classified with an attention-based LSTM, which outperforms convolutional and recurrent neural networks with a precision and recall of 83%. The best result is achieved by a combination of single label and multi label models.

Despite some differences [8], the classification of short texts can be considered a generalization of product title classification. In [9] an overview of the classification of short texts is given. They highlight sparseness as a particular challenge: "a short text only contains several to a dozen words with a few features, it does not provide enough words co-occurrence or shared context for a good similarity measure" [9]. Short texts are difficult to standardize – they contain spelling errors and noise. Due to these characteristics, the bag-of-words model is deemed poorly suited for capturing similarities in short texts.

Two short texts on a similar topic often do not share common words or use them ambiguously. Many sources therefore enrich short texts with additional texts from external sources such as search engines or knowledge databases. The authors of [9] propose a method for semi-supervised learning with unlabeled text corpora as "background knowledge" to support text representation and classification. However, their definition of short texts includes news headlines, chat and mobile short messages, which is not applicable to our problem, since these types of texts have a more pronounced grammatical and syntactical structure.

In [10] it is shown how classification for a large number of products can be managed in a real-world scenario by implementing a hybrid system called Chimera that combines machine learning with manual rules and crowdsourcing. In their use case, several millions of products from the Walmart group have to be classified into more than 5,000 categories. First, a product is preprocessed in a "gatekeeper" module and classified directly, if the product name is already known to the system. The preprocessing of the product names includes stemming, lowercasing and stop word removal. A classification based on expert rules defined by analysts is then combined with the prediction of a machine learning model based on the product name. Out of several algorithms studied, Naïve Bayes, k-Nearest-Neighbors and Perceptron work best for the latter. By means of weighted voting, a list of categories with the highest confidence is compiled. A subset of the classified items is evaluated by crowdsourcing for continuous quality assurance. Items that could not be classified as well as predictions that were marked as incorrect by the crowd workers are passed on to analysts for review, who adjust the rules and algorithms accordingly. Over a six-month period, Chimera classified 93% of 14 million Walmart items with 93% accuracy. Over 20,000 rules were defined.

Most of the presented approaches share the assumption that both product names and product descriptions are available in natural language. In our application, the classification must be performed based on very short and partly abbreviated product names without further detailed product descriptions. Consequently, we expect that models based on harnessing the natural language syntax and structure, like most deep learning approaches, are not suitable for our task. In many cases, relatively good results can already be achieved with simple models like Naïve Bayes or Support Vector Machines. Deep learning approaches are successfully employed for larger data sets in the order of one million records and outperformed by simpler algorithms for smaller data sets. Methods that are proven useful for text classification do not necessarily work for short product names. Depending on the available data, the preprocessing of texts such as stemming, lowercasing and the removal of stop words has different effects on the classification.

Multi-level taxonomies can be used to build a hierarchical model architecture with interdependent classifiers at the individual levels. However, this method sometimes performs worse than a single classifier for all categories at the lowest level. When dealing with unbalanced data, the summary or exclusion of the smallest categories a strategy that is applied by several authors.

In [2], we focused on the impact of text preprocessing strategies and different machine learning algorithms. The data set we tested the algorithms on consists of 144,000 product names classified according to the hierarchical GPC standard. It is described in more detail in Sect. 3.1. Analysis of the data shows a significant class imbalance. Therefore, we put special consideration on choosing significant evaluation metrics where good performance in a large category does not skew the results and decided on a weighted combination of micro- and macro-averaged metrics. We found that on our data set, lowercasing and the removal of all special characters from the product names has a slightly beneficial influence on classification performance. A simple learning algorithm, the Support Vector Machine, outperformed Decision Trees, Random Forests and simple neural networks. The Word2Vec embedding model had a detrimental impact compared to the less complex bag-of-words and TF-IDF text representation. Our model reached a weighted F_1 score of 93.8% on GPC family level, 91.2% on class level and 86.0% on the lowest level. A hierarchically descending classification did not increase the F_1 score on the lower levels. The biggest opportunity for classification improvement has been identified in gathering more training data. However, our data set contains additional attributes that have not been utilized in [Data-Paper] yet. In Sects. 3 and 4, we investigate if these attributes can increase classification performance compared to our preceding contribution.

3   Feature Engineering and Model Development

3.1   Test Data

The product data set we conducted our experiments on corresponds to those in [2]. It was provided by a large retail company in Germany with over 1000 stores and is described and analyzed below. It contains over 144,000 retail products of the segment "Food/Beverages/Tobacco" with text attributes like the product name and numerical attributes like weight and dimensions. The data is classified according to the Global Product Classification Scheme (GPC), a global classification standard used by over 1.5 million companies [1]. It consists of a four-level hierarchy with the levels segment, family, class and brick, each of which are identified by a unique code. The scheme groups products by their physical characteristics. Every product can be assigned to exactly one brick code. Company-specific categorical attributes present in the data set are *product category* with the variants "single material" and "display", and *product type* with the values "commodity", "fresh food" and "full goods".

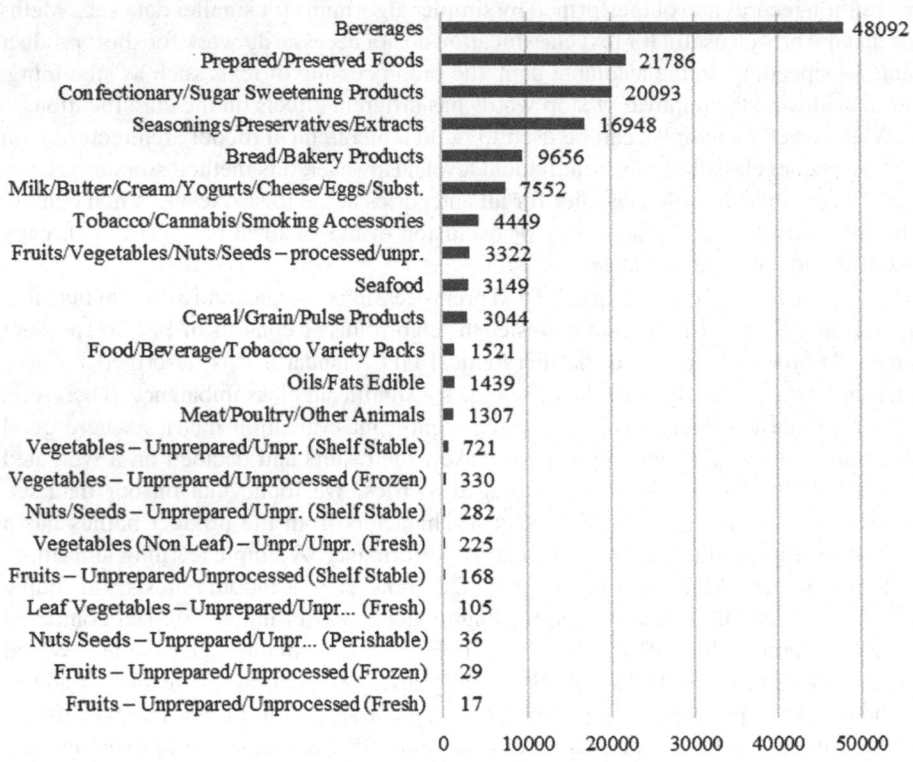

Fig. 1. Number of products per GPC family [2].

As Fig. 1 shows, the data set exhibits a highly unequal distribution across, as well as within the GPC families. The most numerous of the 22 families contained in the data set is "Beverages" with more than a quarter of all items. 60% of the beverages are in the class "Alcoholic Beverages", followed by "Non Alcoholic Beverages – Ready to Drink" and "Coffee/Tea/Substitutes". The classes "Non Alcoholic Beverages – Not Ready to Drink" and "Beverages Variety Packs" contain only a few products. The second and third most common families after beverages are "Prepared/Preserved Foods" with 12% and "Confectionery/Sugar Sweetening Products" 11% of the products. The families "Fruits – Unprepared/Unprocessed (Fresh)" and "Fruits – Unprepared/Unprocessed (Frozen)" are the smallest GPC families with 17 and 29 entries respectively. The arithmetic mean is 15,390 products per family, the median is 7,111 with a standard deviation of 24,151. The classification by product category also shows a strong imbalance: 91.7% of the products are "single material"; likewise, 83.4% of the products have the product type "commodity".

All products feature a German product name. For 21.3% of the products a product description is available and for 9.8% a brand name. As outlined in [2] the product name is normally between 4 and 61 characters long, with an accumulation of 20 to 36 characters. Splitting the product name with spaces as separators into individual tokens, we see that most product names consist of 2 to 7 tokens. Often the product name contains a brand name ("Milka Oreo Riegel"). Some products also contain numerical information such as quantities or percentages (e.g. for foods containing fat or alcohol), places and regions (e.g. for wine bottles) or descriptive characteristics such as "coarse", "fine", "vegan" or "organic". Sometimes terms are difficult to classify and understand, for example, strongly abbreviated terms or products designated with unknown proper names, but which are not trademarks. There are some quantity indications ("2-pack", "1/2", "3ST"), weight, volume and price indications in the product name. Most product names do not contain numbers, 28.9% contain one token with a number, 11.1% two or more such tokens. By counting the points contained in a product name as signifiers, the number of abbreviations is heuristically determined: 21.1% of product names contain one abbreviation, 10.1% contain two and 9.8% contain three or more abbreviations. The (unabbreviated) brand names are contained as the first token in the product name for 37% of the items. There is a total of 1,900 different brand names.

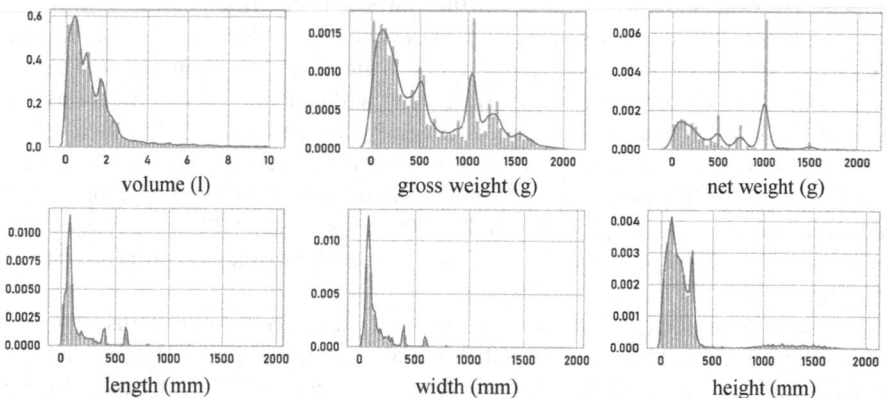

Fig. 2. Distribution of numerical values.

The physical properties of the products are furthermore described by the numerical attributes gross weight, net weight, volume, length, height and width. Dimensions, volume and gross weight are each defined for 83–84% of the data set, while net weight is defined for only 28.4%. The distribution of the attribute values excluding missing values is shown in Fig. 2. For the volume, a high standard deviation and an unplausible high maximum is noticeable. Since the volume of more than half of the products ranges within an interval of 1.79 L, this high maximum indicates faulty outliers. Similar conclusions can be drawn for gross and net weight, although the values are more distributed and the outliers are not quite as distinct. For example, a pack of waffles has the highest net weight of 15,000 kg at dimensions of 40 × 60 × 137 cm, which is clearly erroneous. There is a striking peak in net weight: 25,075 products have a net weight of 1 kg. At the gross weight, this tip is slightly shifted to the right. Comparing net and gross weight, it is noticeable that the net weight is equal to the gross weight for 16.9% of the products. With 32 products, it is even higher than the gross weight. For 76% of the products, the net weight is at least half as high as, but not equal to the gross weight. The dimensions have conspicuously small minima – products that are common in retail will rarely be 0.1 mm wide or high. The same applies to the minima of net and gross weight with 0.01 g and 0.02 g respectively. Clusters of the same length, width and height indicate dummy values: 5,787 items have the same length, width and height of 1 mm each. The volume calculated from the dimensions differs from the maintained volume in 36.8% of cases.

As a result, the analysis of the numerical attributes shows that our data set contains numerous errors. Due to the outliers, median and quartiles are more meaningful measures than the arithmetic mean. Outliers and dummy values should be cleaned before using the data for model training.

3.2 Evaluation Process and Classification Algorithms

Different classification algorithms and the approaches to feature engineering presented in Sects. 3.3–3.6 are evaluated with respect to their influence on the classification of products. The evaluation process used for this purpose is described below.

Categories with extremely small group sizes are excluded from the data set for each GPC level, respectively. This is done by setting a threshold for the minimum size of a category based on the largest category, based on the data exploration. Categories with less than 0.1% of the entries of the largest category are excluded. At family level, for example, three out of 22 families are excluded. However, these excluded families contain only 82 of over 144,000 items. The size of the training record is shown in Table 1. With small variations, there are approximately 144,000 items at each GPC level. We set aside a manually selected subset (around 7% of the data set) for evaluation purposes and use the remaining data for training and testing.

The selection of the classification algorithms is based on the algorithms frequently used in literature. The considered classification algorithms are Naïve Bayes (NB) [11], Single-Layer Perceptron (SLP) [12], Multi-Layer Perceptron (MLP), Logistic Regression with stochastic gradient descent [13], Support Vector Machine (SVM) [14], Decision Trees and Random Forests [15]. As a baseline, we use only the product name without any preprocessing, represented as bag-of-words based on unigrams with a Naïve Bayes classifier. Classification performance is measured on family level to decide which feature combinations and transformations to select. Parameter optimization is done via grid search. Performance is measured with five-fold cross-validation (stratified cross-validation with prior shuffling, see [16]). Results did not improve significantly with finer partitioning. For the algorithms' implementation, the Python framework Scikit-Learn [17] is chosen. Using Scikit-Learn pipelines, it is possible to implement advanced combinations of data transformers and estimators that can be evaluated on training and test data in an automated manner.

The metrics used for evaluating the classification performance are precision, recall and F_1 score with weighted averaging as defined in [2] to account for class imbalance. The weighted F_1 score is used as the main decision criterion. Depending on the application, it may be sufficient to output several plausible GPC codes if the result is uncertain. The selected set would then be limited to a handful of codes for manual classification. To measure the accuracy for this use case, the success metric "correct class among the n most probable" A_{topn} is defined for the final evaluation [see also 3, 5, 6]. For prediction, instead of a single label with the highest probability, a list of all learned labels with prediction probabilities is computed and sorted by descending probability. A_{topn} for a set of data is then the quotient of the size of the subset for which the correct label is among the n most probable predicted labels and the size of the entire set. A_{top1} is the normal accuracy. The metric is measured for $n \in \{2, 3\}$. With a hierarchical classification scheme, it is also of interest how precise a classifier works on a higher level than the one it has been trained on. For a misclassified brick code, the brick code may still belong to the correct class or family. To measure this accuracy, the labels of the parent levels are assigned to the predicted labels and their accuracy is measured for each classification at brick or class level. These metrics are called A_{class} and A_{family}.

Table 1. Data set size after excluding categories with a small number of products [2].

GPC level	Categories	Evaluation data	Training data
Family	19	9,930	134,256
Class	72	10,008	134,067
Brick	245	9,829	133,728

3.3 Normalization and Representation of Text Attributes

The textual attributes such as product name, product description and brand name exhibit high informational content. Often it is possible to assign a category to a product intuitively by manual consideration of the short product name and the brand. This information is to be used for the automatic classification. The most essential attribute is the product name which is present in all our data records (see Sect. 3.1). The influence of the brand name, which is contained only sparsely, is to be examined. The longer product description is not used as a training feature because it does not fit our use case of classifying with little information available but is employed in enriching the preprocessing as described below.

The data exploration showed that there are several steps of preprocessing that could be applied such as lowercasing, cleaning of special characters, numbers, and umlauts. An overview about common preprocessing techniques is given in [18]. Stemming and lemmatization are not used since the names contain almost no inflected verbs or adjectives. Using all preprocessing steps, the product name "LAVAZZA ARMONICO WHOLE BEAN COFF.BL. MED.ROAST 12OZ" is transformed to "lavazza armonico whole bean coff bl med roast oz". This example highlights that the product names contain a high amount of abbreviations.

In order to resolve the abbreviations, a normalization dictionary is created with the usage of the brand names and product descriptions as introduced in [2]. A simple approach would consist of finding the full counterpart for each abbreviated token in the brand or the product description and adding this tuple to the dictionary. However, for most abbreviations there is much ambiguity because they correspond to more than one full word. For instance, the abbreviation "gem." could stand for "gemahlen" ("ground"), "gemischt", "gemixt" (both "mixed"), "Gemenge" ("mixture") or "Gemüse" ("vegetable"). To distinguish between these cases based on the surrounding context, a normalization method based on 3-grams is proposed. For each abbreviated token whose full word is known from the brand or product description, an entry consisting of the preceding token, the succeeding token, the token itself and the non-abbreviated correspondence is added to the dictionary, each token preprocessed with the steps described above. The result contains 24.807 entries with 6.666 normalizations. To substitute an abbreviated token t_i in the training and test set with the surrounding tokens t_{i-1} and t_{i+1}, all normalization entries for t_i with preceding and succeeding tokens $norm_{pre}$ and $norm_{succ}$ are ranked by a similarity score based on the Levenshtein distance d:

$$\text{sim}\big((t_{i-1}, t_{i+1}), (norm_{pre}, norm_{succ})\big) = \frac{1}{d\big(t_{i-1}, norm_{pre}\big) + d\big(t_{i+1}, norm_{succ}\big) + 1}$$

(1)

The normalization entry with the highest similarity score is used to replace the abbreviated token. The quality of this normalization method is evaluated by manual review and presents a mixed picture. For the review, the subset of products with normalized product name and both missing product description and brand name are considered, because these products have not been included to build the normalization dictionary. This set contains 14,544 food product names.

For some product names, the substitution of abbreviations works well, for example for "KR.APFELTEE" ("kraeuter apfeltee"/"herbal apple tea") and "UBENA PFEFFER WEISS GESCHR." ("ubena pfeffer weiss geschrotet"/"ubena pepper white crushed"). Oftentimes, the substitution is not completely correct, but close to the correct normalization: the term "ORA.MANG." in "FRUIT2GO ORA.MANG.EW0,75" is transformed into "orange mango-karotte-hafer" ("orange mango carrot oat") instead of "orange mango". Diverging inflections occur, such as in "oppmann schloss wuerzburger rotsiegel" which should read "… wuerzburg rotsiegel", a sparkling wine brand. In some cases, not every abbreviation is replaced ("MAGGI WIRTSH. NUDELN I.RAHM-SAUCE" – "maggi wirtshaus nudeln i rahm sauce"). For product names with a high amount of abbreviations, the similarity score is low for any possible normalization entry, and the normalization produces incorrect results: "A.GEW.F.GR.CURRY 77G" is normalized to "a gewuerztraminer&riesling f grauburgunder curry g". A threshold for a minimum similarity score could be used to mitigate this problem. For brand names, the method gravitates towards the most frequently occurring brands. Brand name tokens containing a dot ("Dr. Oetker") are incorrectly regarded as abbreviations. The impact of normalizing the product names using the proposed method on classification is analyzed.

As described in [2] different methods of textual representation are compared. The baseline representation of product names as bag-of-words is contrasted with the TF-IDF representation and the word2vec model, and the respective impact on classification is measured. For bag-of-words and TF-IDF, combinations of n-gram intervals from [1, 1] to [4, 4] are used, with 4-grams being a reasonable upper limit for the mostly shorter texts.

We compare word2vec with 100, 200 and 300 dimensions. We chose 300 dimensions as an appropriate upper limit based on the results by [19], who found the difference between 300 and 600 dimensions to be negligible, even on a far greater data set. All textual representation methods are trained on the names in the training set, the respective test set is excluded. In a subsequent experiment, the performance gain by adding the brand name is analyzed.

3.4 Preprocessing and Transformation of Numerical Attributes

Analysis of the data set showed that the numerical attributes contain a lot of errors and missing values. From the analysis results described in Sect. 3.1, an approach for cleaning these attribute values is derived. We define a lower limit for dimensions and weights and discard implausibly low values as well as dummy values and discrepancies in gross weight and net weight. Upwards outliers are cleaned using the Z-score [see 20] with a threshold of 3. After this cleaning process, 94–98% of values are still present for each attribute. Dimensions and weights have a higher correlation than before cleaning.

Due to the drastic amount of missing values for some of the numerical attributes, excluding these records from the training set would not be reasonable. Instead, these values should be imputed with plausible approximations. To this end, we compare a simple imputation with the column's median to an interpolation technique based on k-Nearest-Neighbors regression [see 21].

Besides using the preprocessed numerical attributes for classification without further transformation, standardization and discretization techniques are also examined. The considered techniques are normalization to the interval [0, 1] and binned to 5, 25 and 100 bins. The discrete attributes are represented as one-hot vectors.

We evaluate how well the classification based only on numerical attributes as well as on both numerical and categorical attributes performs. The categorical attributes product category and product type are encoded as one-hot vectors. The impact of the preprocessing and transformation approaches described above is measured in combination with the algorithms Naïve Bayes, Linear Perceptron, Decision Trees and Random Forests. As a baseline we use the normalized attributes without preprocessing, imputed with the median and classified using Naïve Bayes. For the best performing model, we then evaluate the improvements by the kNN-based imputation technique introduced above. The optimal combination of k and the sample size s is determined for $k \in \{1, 2, 3, 5, 15\}$ and $s \in \{10,000, 50,000\}$.

3.5 Feature Combination

The possibilities to concatenate features can be summarized in three model pipeline architectures. The original features can be concatenated in the first step, before a transformation is applied (see Fig. 3a). For text attributes, string concatenation with a blank space is employed. If the features must be transformed differently from each other, the concatenation can be applied to the transformed feature vectors instead (see Fig. 3b). Finally, multiple machine learning models that have been trained on different features can be linked to a *meta learner* by concatenating their predictions as training features for a subsequent model (see Fig. 3c).

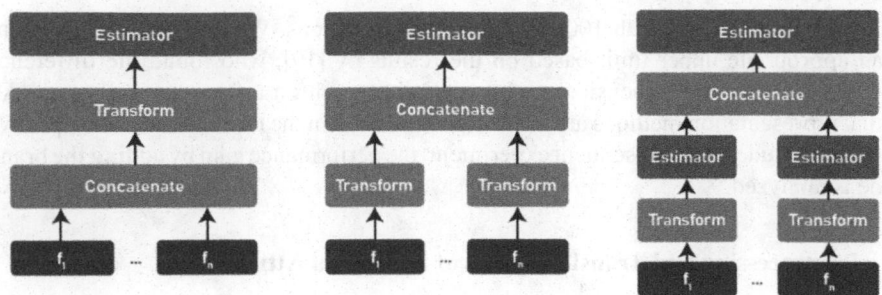

Fig. 3. Different model architectures for feature concatenation: a. concatenation of features before transformation, b. concatenation of transformed features, c. model stacking.

The best performing models for text-based and numerical attribute-based classification are combined per feature concatenation as well as per model stacking, and the performance gain is evaluated.

3.6 Oversampling

We evaluate whether the classification of the balanced test set is improved by using SMOTE (Synthetic Minority Over-sampling Technique, see [22]). As a naïve oversampling method to compare this technique to, we evaluate random oversampling by duplication of data records in underrepresented classes.

4 Results and Discussion

4.1 Baseline and the Impact of Text Pre-processing

As a baseline, we train a Naïve Bayes model using only the product name as feature, without any pre-processing. The product name is encoded using bag-of-words with unigrams. The baseline model reaches a weighted F_1 score (see Sect. 3.2) of 0.918, a precision of 0.918 and a recall of 0.920.

The pre-processing methods for text presented in Sect. 3.3 are compared to the baseline model, again using bag-of-words and Naïve Bayes. The results of the pre-processing step analysis with Naïve Bayes are assumed to be valid for other classifiers as well. The results are listed in Table 2, with the best values for each individual metric highlighted in bold.

As outlined in [2] converting the product names into lowercase strings (lowercasing) seems to have the greatest positive effect on classification. The precision of lowercase text ranks among the three highest precision values. When comparing the F_1 values, the result can be increased by 0.1% with the removal of special characters or umlauts. The removal of numbers has surprisingly negative effects: the weighted F_1 is 0.3% lower than the baseline F_1 score.

The classification after normalization of abbreviations works even 0.1% worse than the baseline. The reason for this could be a high number of wrong substitutions of

Table 2. Classification results for different pre-processing strategies according to [2] (feature: product name, label: family code, 5-fold cross-validated).

Pre-processing method	Pr_{wg}	Pr_{ma}	Re_{wg}	Re_{ma}	F_{1wg}	F_{1ma}
No pre-processing (baseline)	0.918	0.766	0.920	0.627	0.918	0.656
Lowercase	**0.921**	0.770	**0.923**	0.631	0.920	0.659
Remove special characters	0.919	0.768	0.920	0.629	0.918	0.659
Remove umlauts	0.919	0.766	0.920	0.629	0.918	0.658
Remove numbers	0.916	0.761	0.918	0.629	0.915	0.658
Lowercase, remove special characters	**0.921**	**0.771**	**0.923**	**0.634**	**0.921**	**0.661**
Lowercase, remove special characters and umlauts	**0.921**	0.768	**0.923**	**0.634**	**0.921**	**0.661**
Lowercase, remove special characters, umlauts and numbers	0.919	0.767	0.921	0.633	0.919	**0.661**
Lowercase, remove special characters; substitute abbreviations	0.918	0.764	0.919	0.632	0.917	0.659

Table 3. Classification algorithms and optimized hyperparameter settings.

Algorithm	Parameter 1	Parameter 2	Parameter 3
Naïve Bayes	alpha = 0.1	-	-
Single-Layer Perceptron	alpha = 0.001	max_iter = 500	-
Multi-Layer Perceptron	alpha = 0.001	max_iter = 500	layer_size = 25
Logistic Regression	alpha = 0.001	max_iter = 500	-
Support Vector Machine	C = 1.0	max_iter = 500	-
Decision Trees	max_depth = 1000	max_leaf_nodes = 1000	-
Random Forests	max_depth = 1000	max_leaf_nodes = 1000	n_estimators = 100

abbreviations that falsify the classification. On the other hand, during normalization, numbers are removed in the same step, which is likely to have a negative impact. At this point, more detailed investigations would be necessary to quantify the result of the normalization and to measure the influence of the normalization independently from the removal of numbers. Besides introducing a similarity score threshold for normalizations with low probability (see Sect. 3.3), manually adding popular abbreviations and brand names could be considered to improve the quality of normalization.

Overall, the differences between the pre-processing methods are minor. On family level, weighted F_1 has been increased by a maximum of 0.3% compared to the baseline. The combination of lowercasing and removing special characters and umlauts is selected as the most appropriate text pre-processing strategy.

4.2 Impact of Classification Algorithms and Text Representation

The bag-of-words approach is compared to TF-IDF representation and word2vec embedding with different machine learning algorithms (see Sect. 4.2), optimizing different hyperparameters for each model via grid search. The feature vector consists of the lowercased product name with special characters and umlauts removed. Table 3 shows the resulting parameter combinations. The cross-validated weighted F_1 scores of some representative combinations are plotted in Fig. 4 (for a comparison of weighted and macro precision and recall scores, see [2]).

Bag-of-words and TF-IDF hardly differ from each other in their results. Bag-of-words works better for some algorithms (Naïve Bayes and Support Vector Machine, among others) TF-IDF for others (Perceptron). Only in logistic regression does TF-IDF perform about 50% worse than bag-of-words. The influence of n-gram intervals also appears similar for most algorithms. For the intervals [1, 2], [1, 3], and [1, 4], all classifiers except logistic regression achieve the best results for both bag-of-words and TF-IDF. Especially when omitting unigrams, the performance decreases noticeably. For example, Naïve Bayes achieves on bag-of-words with unigrams and bigrams (interval [1, 2]) an F_1 score of 0.926, with only bigrams 0.792, with only trigrams 0.519, and with only 4-grams merely 0.304. TF-IDF and the other classifiers show the same tendency.

Generally, Word2Vec embedding is less successful than bag-of-words and TF-IDF. For the linear models, the best Word2Vec model performs on average 20% worse than the best bag-of-words or TF-IDF model. The only exception is again the logistic regression: Here Word2Vec achieves in the best case a 4.8% higher value than the best bag-of-words model. Word2Vec achieves a comparatively better result in Decision Trees and Random Forests. The first algorithm achieves a maximum F_1 of 0.794 on the bag-of-words model and a maximum F_1 of 0.709 on Word2Vec, and 0.823 and 0.766 for Random Forests. Word2Vec benefits from high dimensionality: In all cases considered, the 300-dimensional embedding achieves a significantly higher F_1 than the 100- and 200-dimensional embedding. This applies to the newly trained model as well as to the pre-trained model. The latter performs about 25% worse than the newly trained embedding, which suggests that many of the proper names and special terms in the data set are not included in the vocabulary of the pre-trained Word2Vec model.

The model that best classifies products by their product name is the Support Vector Machine using the bag-of-words model with uni- and bigrams achieving an F_1 score of 0.938. In summary, the linear models perform better on the simpler text representations, while the tree-based models seem to make better use of the more complex structure of word vectors in Word2Vec.

4.3 Impact of the Brand Name

The Support Vector Machine model that has been selected as the best performing classifier on the product name is trained on an extended feature vector which consists of the product name and the brand name. The brand name is only maintained for 9.8% of the product records considered. Since the brand name is not present in the majority of the data set, it is questionable if there is any improvement to be expected. Nonetheless, we investigate whether the concatenation position in the pipeline – before or after the

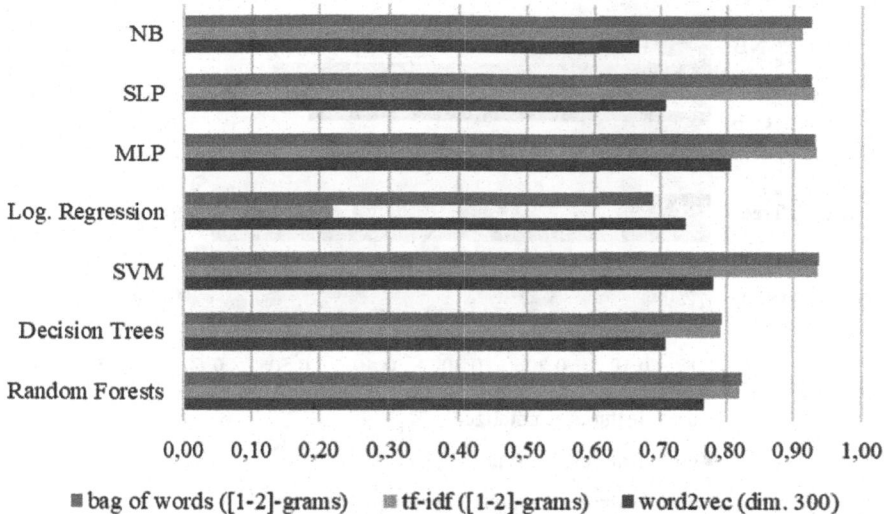

NB

SLP

MLP

Log. Regression

SVM

Decision Trees

Random Forests

0,00   0,10   0,20   0,30   0,40   0,50   0,60   0,70   0,80   0,90   1,00

■ bag of words ([1-2]-grams)   ▦ tf-idf ([1-2]-grams)   ■ word2vec (dim. 300)

Fig. 4. Weighted F_1 scores of combinations of classification algorithms and text representations of feature "product name" (pre-processed), measured on family level (5-fold cross-validated).

bag-of-words encoding – plays a crucial role. With regard to the bag-of-words model, in the first case the brand name is treated as part of the text and is incorporated into the vocabulary in a single model. In the second case, a separate bag-of-words model is trained, whose vocabulary contains only the brand names.

It is observed that the addition of the brand name increases the precision and the F_1 score by a maximum of 0.1% with minimal differences between the concatenation approaches. For the cross-validated metrics, the best result is achieved with feature combination, i.e. concatenation after separate bag-of-words transformations (see Sect. 3.5) with a weighted F_1 score of 0.939 on family level (for classification scores on all GPC levels, see Table 5). We conclude that for products with the brand name present, adding it improves classification performance slightly. The most successful model for classification on the text features is therefore a Support Vector Machine with product names and brand names as bag-of-words features.

4.4 Baseline for Categorical and Numerical Features and Impact of Preprocessing

The classification using only numerical features (dimensions, weights and volume, see Sect. 3.4) reaches at most a weighted F_1 score of 0.697 on family level (see Fig. 5). The algorithms Random Forests and Decision Trees perform best and second best. The considered linear algorithms perform significantly worse, with Naïve Bayes reaching a maximum F_1 of 0.519 at family level (see Fig. 5). The recall is significantly lower than the precision in all cases.

The cleaning of the numerical attributes according to the procedure described in Sect. 3.4 as well as the inclusion of the categorical attributes product category and product type have different effects at different levels, with small deviations of up to 0.5% for F_1. At family level, the uncleaned numerical attributes without categorical attributes

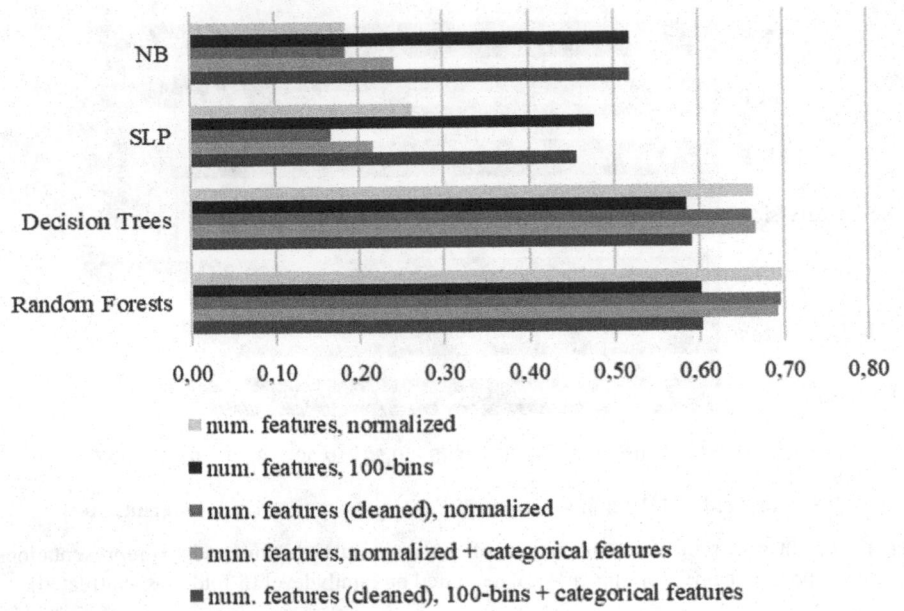

num. features, normalized

num. features, 100-bins

num. features (cleaned), normalized

num. features, normalized + categorical features

num. features (cleaned), 100-bins + categorical features

Fig. 5. Weighted F_1 scores of combinations of numerical features (median-based imputation), categorical features, and classification algorithms, measured on family level (5-fold CV).

are most successful, at class level the cleansed numerical attributes without categorical attributes perform best and at brick level the combination of uncleaned numerical and categorical attributes achieves the highest results.

When comparing the standardization procedures normalization and binning, normalization works best for Random Forests and Decision Trees. Binning achieves the maximum F_1 of 0.631 at family level with 25 bins for Random Forests. The opposite can be observed for the linear models: For Naïve Bayes and Single Layer Perceptron, the F_1 increases with increasing bin number, for normalization F_1 is the lowest. In comparison with the best text-based classifier (see Sect. 4.2), the F_1 of the best attribute-based model is 24–38% lower.

The kNN-based imputation of missing values was tested using a Random Forests pipeline using numerical attributes without prior preprocessing. For the imputation parameters k and s (see Sect. 3.4), the optimal values found were $k = 2$ and $s = 50,000$ at family level, with a maximum difference in F_1 of 0.5% between the worst and best performing combinations. Regarding our dataset it turns out that the more sophisticated kNN-based imputation does not outperform the simpler median-based imputation: The F_1 of the best performing pipeline with kNN-based imputation (0.692 at family level) is still about 0.5% lower than the best performing pipeline with median-based imputation (0.697 at family level, see above).

4.5 Impact of Categorical and Numerical Features

It is investigated whether textual, numerical and categorical features combined by feature concatenation after transformation or model stacking increase prediction quality (see Sect. 3.5).

In the comparison between feature combination and model stacking, the models of the second category clearly win (see Table 4). The best weighted F_1 achieved at family level with concatenation is 12.7% below the best of the stacked models. For concatenation, Random Forests and SVM were compared, with SVM scoring less than half as well as the Random Forest models. In model stacking, Random Forests and Decision Trees were the strongest, whereas Naïve Bayes, Single Layer Perceptron and SVM did not give a useful result.

The combination of textual and numerical or categorical attributes did not improve the model performance. The strongest combined pipelines performed slightly worse than the best text-based model with a weighted F_1 score of 0.937. Consequently, it can be assumed that the meta-learners, who perform a classification using the classes predicted by the text-based and attribute-based model, almost always trust the prediction of the text-based model and discard the prediction of the attribute-based model.

Table 4. Classification results for different combinations of text features and numerical/categorical features (label: family code, 5-fold cross-validated).

Model pipeline	Pr_{wg}	Pr_{ma}	Re_{wg}	Re_{ma}	F_{1wg}	F_{1ma}
Feature Combination + SVM	0.721	0.427	0.399	0.176	0.371	0.157
Feature Combination + Random Forests	0.834	0.656	0.823	0.403	0.810	0.456
Stacked Models + NB	0.179	0.125	0.366	0.169	0.230	0.129
Stacked Models + SLP	0.133	0.026	0.359	0.059	0.192	0.034
Stacked Models + SVM	0.025	0.010	0.147	0.056	0.042	0.017
Stacked Models + Decision Trees	**0.936**	0.795	**0.938**	**0.701**	**0.937**	0.735
Stacked Models + Random Forests	**0.936**	**0.797**	**0.938**	**0.701**	**0.937**	**0.736**

4.6 Impact of Oversampling

The SMOTE procedure for oversampling underrepresented classes, tested on the best product name-based classification model (see Sect. 4.2), does not improve the classification result: at family level, a weighted F_1 score of 0.913 is achieved, which is about 2.5% below the normal value. Also, precision and recall are lower with 0.920 and 0.908. As a reference method, random oversampling by duplication of products is also measured. Here, F_1 is 0.1% below the normal value, i.e. significantly higher than SMOTE, but achieving no improvement over the unbalanced data set.

Based on the assumption that SMOTE is less suitable for the bag-of-words model, the same experiment is performed for an SVM model with TF-IDF-encoded attributes – but with similar results. Since the classification of short product names with SMOTE works slightly worse, but still relatively well, it is concluded that the procedure for encoded texts itself does work, but that the class imbalance in the test set does not have as strong a negative effect on classification that it would have to be corrected with oversampling.

4.7 Evaluation on Different Hierarchy Levels

The model with the highest score on family level (see Sect. 4.3) is now evaluated on the lower GPC hierarchy levels class code and brick code. For this purpose, the metrics Precision, Recall and F1, as well as A_{top2}, A_{top3}, A_{class} and A_{family} (see Sect. 3.2) are considered, each measured on the three hierarchy levels with fivefold cross-validation. The results are depicted in Table 5. As expected, prediction quality decreases with increasing number of labels. The weighted F_1 score drops by 2.4% from family to class code, with possible labels increasing from 19 to 72 (see Table 1), and by 5.1% from class to brick code (245 different categories). Precision and recall also decrease accordingly.

The probability that the correct brick code of a product lies among the top 2 predicted brick codes with the highest confidence is 93.1% (see A_{top2}) and for the top 3 up to 95.1%.

As the metrics A_{class} and A_{family} (see Sect. 3.2) show, classification on the lowest GPC level (brick code) achieves just as good a result for higher GPC levels as the classification on those levels, meaning even if products are assigned to the wrong brick code, the brick still belongs to the correct GPC class for 91,6% of products. Therefore, a hierarchical descending classification approach is not considered necessary.

Compared to the final model from [2] (SVM classifying only the product name, see Sect. 4.2), weighted F_1 has been increased by 0.1% on family level, 0.3% on class level and 0.4% on brick level.

Table 5. Classification results of best text-based model on different GPC levels.

Label	Pr_{wg}	Re_{wg}	F_{1wg}	A_{top2}	A_{top3}	A_{class}	A_{family}
Family code	0.939	0.941	0.939	0.976	0.986	-	0.941
Class code	0.914	0.916	0.915	0.958	0.970	0.916	0.941
Brick code	0.865	0.869	0.864	0.931	0.951	0.916	0.942

4.8 Evaluation on Balanced Evaluation Set

Finally, the influence of class imbalance on classification performance is discussed. For this purpose, the best model from Sect. 4.3 is evaluated on the evaluation set (see Sect. 3.2) at family level. For a better visual comparison of the wrong assignments in relation to the size of the family, a balanced data set is generated from the evaluation set by random oversampling. Figure 6 shows the confusion matrix for this experiment. The families are sorted by their first occurrence in the test set. In each field (x, y) the absolute number of items with predicted label x and actual label y is entered. The products in the diagonal from (x_{min}, y_{max}) to (x_{max}, y_{min}) are correctly classified.

The dominance of the family "Beverages" (5020), which is the biggest product family in the data set (see Fig. 1), is striking. In general, some items are incorrectly assigned to the families in the first four columns (5010, 5020, 5019, 5017) (false positives). About half the families are slightly to strongly underrepresented (5029 to 5031). Nevertheless, they are assigned reasonably well. A family with a particularly high number of false negatives is "Food/Beverage/Tobacco Variety Packs" (5023) whose products are often misclassified as "Beverages" (5020), "Prepared/Preserved Foods" (5019) or "Seasonings/Preservatives/Extracts" (5017). In the case of these mixed products, classification based on the brand name and the short description alone is often difficult, even if they are reviewed manually: Among the false negatives which were wrongly classified as beverages are products such as "Tee Fee Cocoa Tea" and "Lehner Premium Pils", among the seasonings products such as "Collitali Black Pepper" and "Salmar Fleur de Sel".

The measured precision for the balanced evaluation set is 0.823, accuracy and F_1 only 0.725 and 0.719 respectively. This discrepancy between precision and F_1 indicates an unequal distribution. The impression is reinforced when looking at the misclassified items that are accumulated in the lower half of the diagram. Compared to the lower left quarter, the upper left quarter performs better. The bright diagonal line in the diagram is a visual indicator of an overall satisfactory result. As expected, the classification performs worse for products in underrepresented families, but the general result can be considered successful. The benefit of using diverse groups like mixed packs without additional attributes for a more precise differentiation might be critically questioned.

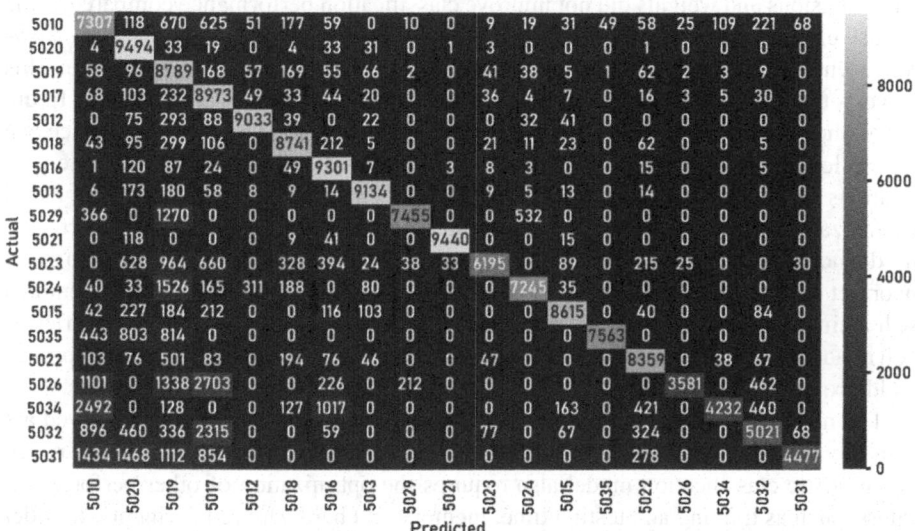

Fig. 6. Confusion matrix for classification at family level on a balanced evaluation set with random oversampling.

5 Outlook

In summary, our results have demonstrated that the automated classification of food products during the first stages of product data entry can be performed solely based on the product name. The results of [2] have been confirmed. Standard algorithms like Support Vector Machines are able to achieve satisfactory results without the need for hyper-specialized models that are expensive to train and harder to optimize. Our method could be applied to other product data sets with similar challenges such as very short product names with a lot of abbreviated tokens and underrepresented classes.

In order to improve the prediction quality, the greatest potential is expected to be found in increasing the size of the training data set. Our training set of about 144,000 products is rather small compared to many other data sets from the machine learning literature, and the structure of the text attributes is relatively homogeneous in terms of word order and absence of verbs, connectives and filler words. Special attention should be paid to the enlargement of underrepresented categories. Text from other sources could increase the robustness against differently structured product names. By adding more and varied data sets, the model which has been trained only on products in the food segment can be extended to other GPC segments. It has to be examined if the same model is able to differentiate between different segments with sufficient accuracy or whether a narrow-down approach is necessary, e.g. by a higher-level model in the GPC hierarchy or by manual rules. Class imbalance is another factor that should be inspected with high priority in subsequent experiments. The SMOTE approach did not improve prediction quality for underrepresented categories.

The combination of text-based classification and numerical attributes such as product dimensions and weights did not improve classification performance compared to the exclusively text-based models. Insufficient data quality might be an explanation, however even with sophisticated cleaning and imputation the observation holds true. This suggests that the most relevant information is to be found in the text attributes and future efforts should concentrate on those, besides gathering a larger data set. For instance, we tried to leverage longer product descriptions, where available, to find appropriate substitutions for abbreviated tokens in the short product names by creating a context-based normalization dictionary. Although some abbreviations could be normalized correctly, this did not positively influence prediction quality. Therefore, it is suspected that too many incorrect normalizations occurred. The normalization entries that have been assembled with a simple heuristic might be improved by a manual review of incorrect entries as well as adding well-known domain-specific abbreviations. A machine learning approach could provide higher robustness when replacing these abbreviations.

The methods investigated here as well as the research approaches we reviewed are primarily aimed at achieving the best possible classification quality. The practical use of an automatic classification model also requires the optimization of other performance criteria such as training and testing time, memory and hardware requirements. In order for the category suggestions to be verified by users and for detected errors and exceptions to be included to improve future predictions in a transparent way, the maintainability and interpretability of the model must be ensured. One way to achieve these criteria could be the integration of the model into a system that could contain for example a reference database with audited products, an expert rule module for known exceptions, a platform for quality monitoring and a module for the continuous model improvement through online training. Finally, it can be assumed that machine learning will be increasingly used for automatic product classification in the future. We hope that the results of our work will accelerate the development and implementation of suitable models in practice.

Acknowledgements. This work was funded by the German Ministry of Education and Research under grant FKZ 01IS18018.

References

1. GS1 Germany Homepage: Global Product Classification (GPC). https://www.gs1-germany.de/gs1-standards/klassifikation/produktklassifikation-gpc. Accessed 30 Oct 2020
2. Allweyer, O., Schorr, C., Krieger, R., Mohr, A.: Classification of products in retail using partially abbreviated product names only. In: Proceedings of the 9th International Conference on Data Science, Technology and Applications, pp. 67–77 (2020)
3. Chavaltada, C., Pasupa, K., Hardoon, D.R.: A comparative study of machine learning techniques for automatic product categorisation. In: Cong, F., Leung, A., Wei, Q. (eds.) ISNN 2017. LNCS, vol. 10261, pp. 10–17. Springer, Cham (2017). https://doi.org/10.1007/978-3-319-59072-1_2
4. Yu, H., Ho, C., Arunachalam, P., Somaiya, M., Lin, C.: Product title classification versus text classification. In: Online (2012)
5. Shankar, S., Lin, I.: Applying machine learning to product categorization. http://cs229.stanford.edu/proj2011/LinShankar-Applying%20Machine%20Learning%20to%20Product%20Categorization.pdf. Accessed 30 Oct 2020
6. Ding, Y., et al.: GoldenBullet: automated classification of product data in E-commerce. In: Proceedings of BIS 2002, Poznań, Poland (2002)
7. Cevahir, A., Murakami, K.: Large-scale multi-class and hierarchical product categorization for an E-commerce giant. In: Proceedings of COLING 2016, pp. 525–535. The COLING 2016 Organizing Committee, Osaka, Japan (2016)
8. Yu, W., Sun, Z., Liu, H., Li, Z., Zheng, Z.: Multi-level deep learning based ecommerce product categorization. In: The 2018 SIGIR Workshop On eCommerce. Ann Arbor (2018)
9. Song, G., Ye, Y., Du, X., Huang, X., Bie, S.: Short text classification: a survey. J. Multimedia **9**(5) (2014)
10. Sun, C., Rampalli, N., Yang, F., Doan, A.: Chimera: large-scale classification using machine learning, rules, and crowdsourcing. In: Proceedings of the VLDB Endowment, vol. 7 (2014)
11. Maron, M.: Automatic indexing: an experimental inquiry. J. ACM **8**(3) (1961)
12. Rosenblatt, F.: The perceptron: a probabilistic model for information storage and organization in the brain. Psychol. Rev. **65**(6), 386–408 (1958)
13. Taddy, M.: Stochastic gradient descent. In: Business Data Science: Combining Machine Learning and Economics to Optimize, Automate, and Accelerate Business Decisions, pp. 303–307. McGraw-Hill, New York City (2019)
14. Cortes, C., Vapnik, V.: Support-vector networks. Mach. Learn. **20**(3), 273–297 (1995)
15. Ho, T.: Random decision forests. In: Proceedings of the 3rd International Conference on Document Analysis and Recognition, pp. 278–282. IEEE, New York City (1995)
16. Kohavi, R.: A study of cross-validation and bootstrap for accuracy estimation and model selection. In: Proceedings of the 14th International Joint Conference on Artificial Intelligence vol. 2, no. 12, pp. 1137–1143. Morgan Kaufmann Publishers Inc., San Francisco (1995)
17. Scikit-Learn Homepage. https://scikit-learn.org. Accessed 30 Oct 2020
18. Uysal, A., Gunal, S.: The impact of preprocessing on text classification. Inf. Process. Manage. **50**(1), 104–112 (2014)

19. Mikolov, T., Chen, K., Corrado, G., Dean, J.: Efficient estimation of word representations in vector space. arXiv:1301.3781 (2013)
20. Garcia, F.: Tests to Identify Outliers in Data Series. Pontifical Catholic University of Rio de Janeiro, Industrial Engineering Department, Rio de Janeiro, Brazil (2012)
21. Jonsson, P., Wohlin, C.: An evaluation of k-nearest neighbour imputation using Likert data. In: Proceedings of the 10th International Symposium on Software Metrics, pp. 108–118 (2004)
22. Chawla, N., Bowyer, K., Hall, L., Kegelmeyer, W.: SMOTE: synthetic minority over-sampling technique. J. Artif. Intell. Res. **16**, 321–357 (2002)

Algebraic Expressions with State Constraints for Causal Relations and Data Semantics

Susumu Yamasaki$^{1(\boxtimes)}$ (iD) and Mariko Sasakura$^{2(\boxtimes)}$ (iD)

^{1} School of Science and Technology, Okayama University, Okayama, Japan
^{2} Department of Computer Science, Okayama University, Okayama, Japan
sasakura@cs.okayama-u.ac.jp

Abstract. This paper deals with algebraic expressions constrained by states for causal relations. Abstracted from procedural and reference data relations, Heyting algebra expressions of some form may be adopted as theoretical basis of a language system with state constrains for data representations. Query operations for such algebraic expressions are presented by 3-valued model theory of algebraic expressions, where the unknown value is available and negatives are used in two ways. Model theory of algebraic expressions is given by both prefixpoint of associated nonmonotonic mappings and predicates of corresponding queries, such that semantics is denotational. As regards state traverses and transitions accompanied by queries at states, algebraic structure is presented in a semiring structure, where alternation for selections of state transitions, and concatenation of state transitions are involved in. Models of algebraic expressions denote queries such that they are organized into sequences on a semiring structure. In terms of model construction and semiring structure, this paper presents data semantics abstracted for state constraint expressions of causal relations.

Keywords: Causal relation · Algebraic approach · State constraint

1 Introduction

Based on the discussion of reference data and causal relation [27], this paper makes a fully abstract description of algebraic expressions for data and operations in state constraint systems where algebraic expressions are causal relations, constrained by states and models of expressions as queries are retrieval operations with state transitions.

State constraint expressions for procedure construction can be associated with logical procedures and problem solving in answer set programming [7], as well as a language system theory [26].

Reference data in distributed systems may be viewed from inductive structure among reference names at computing environments, such that state constraint expressions may be abstracted into causal relations.

Motivated by state constraint systems regarding procedural and data constructions by induction, this paper treats semantics for state constraint expressions of causal relations as inductive constructions of informations, and for full abstraction from data and operations in distributed environments.

S. Hammoudi et al. (Eds.): DATA 2020, CCIS 1446, pp. 245–266, 2021.
https://doi.org/10.1007/978-3-030-83014-4_12

The significance of aims at data semantics for state constraint expressions comes from logical database abstraction of representation and manipulation. To formulate semantics, concretized query and representation of negative information must be theoretically described well. As relevant topics and methodologies, we must see the backgrounds as follows.

(a) On the one hand, procedural semantics is expressed and systemized by denotational approach in the book [17], although the procedural method is really based on operational implementation for programs to be executed. On the other hand, the procedures may be abstracted into functions, in terms of functional programs [2]. Compared with those established views, procedural interpretation of predicates and construction may be regarded as close up to data representation with states as computing environments.
(b) Logics with knowledge [19] are so suggestive that causal relations and query predicates may be designed even from algebraic approach closely related to logic. From model theoretic views with treatments of negatives, the argumentation is formulated by means of 3-valued logic into the semantics for defeasible reasonings [10]. Compared with default or defeasible logic in AI programming, defeasibility is beforehand assumed in the given rules, but the causal relation consisting of rules by algebraic expressions is simpler without treating ambiguity of rules containing default negation.
(c) As regards state transitions, abstract state machine is formulated in the book [5] and paper [20] on weighted automata theory. Regarding structure of streams possibly caused by abstract state transitions, there is the note [21]. These ideas inspire the method for representation on the state traverse of this paper.

With respect to such backgrounds of algebraic and logical perspectives, this paper is based on algebraic approach to the representations of reference data, with causal relations and query predicates, as well as state transitions constraining algebraic expressions. As a whole, model theory of algebraic expressions and algebraic structure regarding state transitions may be built into data semantics for a state constraint system.

Concerning procedural construction and reference data constrained by states, algebraic expressions are abstracted and captured as causal relations, whose model theories are developed in Heyting algebra whose expressions may be possibly infinite for covering universal first-order logic to computing, and for constructive concepts with correspondence to intuitionistic logic. As regards traverses through states, semiring is characterized for state constraint systems. The theoretical aspect of Heyting algebra expressions and model theories are primarily developed, as well as algebraic structure for state transitions caused by models denoting queries on algebraic expressions. These aims are theoretical frameworks for data semantics regarding inductive structures of reference data, from the steps as follows.

(i) Reference data in state constraint systems are examined, such that simple inductive structure of distributed reference links is abstracted into causal relations of Heyting algebra expressions.
(ii) Heyting algebra expressions are analyzed to abstractly represent inductive structures of causal relations. The model theory of algebraic expressions is hard,

because the mapping associated with expressions is nonmonotonic such that classical fixed point theory cannot be always adopted. Some prefixpoint may be inductively constructed as a model. This paper gives the constructions of models of algebraic expressions, in terms of predicates for queries on causal relations. Although the model theory is not so easy, it is well discussed in non-classical framework over a 3-valued domain. In addition to non-classical discussions, we have an adjusting tool to get approximations of predicates by the classical idea on negation by failure. Queries for algebraic expressions are approximately realized, by negation as failure rule, such that it is sound with respect to models.

(iii) Default negation popular in AI is now taken by regarding it as a mapping in the algebra, so that we have algebraic expressions with both strong negation (caused by Heyting implication to the least element) and default negation. This paper contains detailed model theory of expressions with double negation. An approximation tool may be constructed to be sound with respect to the models by predicates for queries.

(iv) State transitions are abstracted into semiring structure, caused by models of algebraic expressions. In accordance with finite state automata, star semiring has been given, on the one hand [25]. From the view on nondeterministic alternation of traverses, more complex semiring may be defined in this paper, on the other hand.

The paper is organized as follows. Section 2 is concerned with descriptions of structures for causal relations in procedural interpretation and reference data of state constraint systems. In Sect. 3, we have Heyting algebra expressions for causal relations, whose model theories may be solved for predicates on queries to be defined. Theoretical aspects are in more details provided than the paper on language system based on algebra [26]. Adjusting derivations as approximating queries are introduced for implementation tool regarded as data retrieval. In Sect. 4, model theories of algebraic expressions with double negation are originally developed, covering model theories of Sect. 3. Section 5 presents an algebraic structure in terms of semiring, by constructing the models of algebraic expressions for concatenation and alternation regarding state transitions. Concluding remarks and related works are summarized in Sect. 6.

2   State Constraint Expressions

Some state constraint systems are viewed as containing causal relations in distributed systems, where procedural construction and reference data are in inductive structures which algebraic expressions of causal relation may represent.

2.1   State Constraint Systems

At the state to reflect computing and communication environments, procedures, and data expressions may be constructed. We here have an abstraction of state constraint systems from the viewpoint of data representations and semantics in distributed environments.

Procedural Structures. As in problem solving by answer set programming [12] with respect to its Herbrand base, a procedure structure may be defined in terms of a first-order logic predicate pr (as a procedure name), followed by the conjunction of

$$pr_1, \ldots, pr_m \text{(as a procedural body)}$$

for predicates $pr_1, \ldots, pr_m$ ($m \geq 0$). This view may be extended by regarding the predicate possibly containing negations, as well as constrained by states. The procedure may be thus constructive under the state to be abstracted from programming and data environments. That is, for some (abstract) state s, the form

$$s : pr^1 \text{ followed by } pr^1_1, \ldots, pr^1_{m_1},$$
$$\ldots,$$
$$\ldots,$$
$$pr^n \text{ followed by } pr^n_1, \ldots, pr^n_{m_n} \triangleright s'$$

is supposedly constructed to denote the whole procedure, where a state transition to another state s' with some implementation regarding the whole procedure (data of procedural names) and procedure evocations.

In place of the predicate logic, more abstract expressions based on Heyting algebra can be taken for a language system [26], whose intuitive meaning is given in tabular form of Table 1, with procedures $expression_1, \ldots, expression_n$. It may denote causal relations of intuitionistic propositional logic formulas to implement data operations as well as state transitions.

Table 1. A language system is constructive with algebraic expression.

State	Algebraic expressions	(to)	States
s	$expression_1$	$\triangleright$	s_1
	$expression_2$	$\triangleright$	s_2
	...	.	.
	...	.	.
	$expression_n$	$\triangleright$	s_n

Reference Data. A more general representation of reference data is here examined, from the simple one of the paper [27]. A distributed system is to supposedly consist of sites, where:

(i) the site (state) contains pages, and
(ii) the page denotes references which are inductively linked to other references from other pages, where the pages may be from other sites.

Example 1. We can think of distributed reference data, represented by algebraic elements, with algebraic expressions assigned to states. As an illustration of producer and consumer representation states, we may write references, with possible transfer of data from a state s_1 (for producer data) to another s_2 (for consumer data):

> at state s_1,
> $\{required[s_2], productive[s_1], over[s_1]\}$
> linked from $transferred[s_1]$,
> $\{productive[s_1], not\ over[s_1]\}$ linked from $stored[s_1]$, and
> at state s_2,
> $\{not\ stored[s_2]\}$ linked from $required[s_2]$,
> $\{(stored[s_2]\}$ linked from $not\ required[s_2]$,

where (i) *not* means a negative of reference, and (ii) each element (with state name attached) is a variable over an algebraic domain.

For example, the reference $transferred[s_1]$ is assigned to the state s_1, and is linked with the references $required[s_2]$, $productive[s_1]$ and $over[s_1]$. The reference $transferred[s_1]$ would be evaluated as 1 (active) at state s_1 if we have evaluated references of:

(i) $required[s_2]$ (at state s_2) as 1 (active),
(ii) $productive[s_1]$ (at state s_1) as 1 (active), and
(iii) $over[s_1]$ (at state s_1) as 1 (active),

where the state s_1 is supposedly transited to the state s_2.

The other relations among references may be analyzed in the similar views with respect to their activities involving inactivity (denoted 0) as well as the unknown (denoted 1/2) in 3-valued domain for evaluation:

(a) At state s_1, the reference $stored[s_1]$ contains the references $productivity[s_1]$ and $not\ over[s_1]$. The reference inactivity $not\ over[s_2]$ is shown at state s_1 in case that the reference $over[s_2]$ is inactive, evaluated as 0.
(b) The reference $required[s_2]$ contains the inactive reference $not\ stored[s_2]$ at state s_2, where the name $required[s_2]$ is referred to if $stored[s_2]$ is inactive. The reference inactivity $not\ required[s_2]$ contains the reference $stored[s_2]$, where $required[s_2]$ should be inactive if $stored[s_2]$ is active.

This construction could be also captured in term of propositional logic formulas with negations. In this paper, it would be represented by Heyting algebra expressions (denoting intuitionistic logic) as a more abstract framework.

As a description abstracted from Example 1, we have a formal representation of reference data of state constrains, not mentioned in the previous paper [27].

At a site s, a page supposedly contains a reference name and the page contents, followed by a reference name 1 (of a page) from a state $s_1, \cdots$, and a reference name n (of a page) from a state s_n. After the page representation, a transit to another state s' is given with right hand direction symbol. It is formally defined in Backus-Naur Form, by induction without description on the page contents.

$$Syst:: = null_{Syst} \mid s : P \triangleright s; Syst$$
$$P:: = null_P \mid p; P$$
$$p:: = r \text{ flb } ref$$
$$ref:: = null_{ref} \mid r; ref$$

where:

(a) The colon ":" is used for a delimiter. The semicolon ";" denotes a concatenation operation. The mnemonic "flb" stands for "followed by" as in the programming language *Lucid*.
(b) $null_{Syst}$, $null_P$ and $null_{ref}$ are the empty sequences, on the domain of systems, pages and references, respectively.
(c) *Syst* is a system variable, and *s* is a state variable.
(d) *p* is a page variable such that *P* denotes a sequence of pages.
(e) *r* is a reference variable such that *ref* denotes a sequence of references, where *r* may be settled with a state variable such that a form of $R[s]$ is taken for a reference name variable *R* and a state variable *s*.

Without the content of each page, the relation among references may be compiled in a page, that is, the page involves a reference followed by a sequence of references.

To a reference (variable) $R[s]$, the 3-valued domain may be taken to make assignments: Reference activities, "active" (linked), "unknown" and "inactive" (not linked), can be evaluated as 1, 1/2 and 0, respectively, in 3-valued domain $\{1, 1/2, 0\}$, with respect to communications between states for data (name) transfers.

2.2   Causal Relation in Terms of Algebraic Expressions

Abstracting procedure constructions and reference data representations, we now adopt Heyting algebra expressions to denote inductive structure of procedure and reference constructions. Regarding state constraints, Sect. 5 is concerned with effects of procedural or data operations, based on algebraic methods, for state transitions. As we make use of in [27], Heyting algebra (HA) is a bounded lattice $(A, \vee, \wedge, \bot, \top)$, equipped with the partial order $\sqsubseteq$, and with an implication $\Rightarrow$:

 (i) The elements $\bot$ and $\top$ are the least and the greatest elements of the set *A*, respectively, with respect to the partial order $\sqsubseteq$.
(ii) The *join* (least upper bound) $\vee$ and the *meet* (greatest lower bound) $\wedge$ are defined for any two elements of *A*.
(iii) As regards the implication $\Rightarrow$, for elements *a*, *b* and *c* in *A*, $a \Rightarrow b$ is defined such that

$$c \sqsubseteq (a \Rightarrow b) \text{ iff } (a \wedge c) \sqsubseteq b.$$

The element $a \Rightarrow \bot$ is denoted as "*not a*" (a negative) for $a \in A$, where *not* $\bot = \top$ and *not* $\top = \bot$. As is well known, we note some algebraic properties on the HA:

$$((a \Rightarrow b) \bigwedge (b \Rightarrow c)) \sqsubseteq (a \Rightarrow c),$$
$$a \sqsubseteq not\ (not\ a),$$
$$(a \bigwedge (a \Rightarrow b)) \Rightarrow b,$$
$$not\ (a \bigvee b) = not\ a \bigwedge not\ b.$$

Therefore the expression $a \Rightarrow b$ may be regarded as representing a causal relation between the cause denoted a and the effect denoted b. The implication $\Rightarrow$ is more abstract than the classical (e.g. propositional) logic implication.

The causal relation is now taken in a form of expressions, for the denotation of reference data, with (a) the meet of n elements (for $n \geq 0$) (which denote data or their negatives) as the cause, (b) Heyting implication and (c) the element, for datum or its negative, as the effect. Then the expression F (over the underlined set A of the algebra) of the following form is regarded as (a meet of) causal relations to abstract inductive structures of reference data:

$$\bigwedge_{j} (l_1^j \bigwedge \cdots \bigwedge l_{n_j}^j \Rightarrow l^j)$$

where l_i^j denotes a or $a \Rightarrow \bot$ (*not a*) for $a \in A$.

With respect to the effect of algebraic expressions for implementation and operation on data, model theory is abstract and theoretical basis. In accordance with intuitionistic logic, model theory in Heyting algebra can be examined in 3-valued domain, where the unknown is admitted as in Example 1, and 3-valued domain models are differently studied from 2-valued domain problem solving [12] and from argumentation [10] in AI. With respect to model theory, the form of algebraic expressions is to be a little restricted for consistency in the following sections.

3   Model Theory of Algebraic Expressions

Regarding algebraic expressions constrained by states, we examine 3-valued domain model theories as basis for state constraint systems. In this section, the model of expressions is interpreted as a set of queries concerning causal relations which algebraic expressions denote. This section comprizes several propositions, because they are essential for model theories of expressions, with proofs exhaustive for theoretical senses of propositions.

As a standard form, we aim at the expression F (over the underlined set A of the algebra) of the form $\bigwedge_j (l_1^j \bigwedge \cdots \bigwedge l_{n_j}^j \Rightarrow l^j)$, written as a set of the rules

$$\cup_j \{l_1^j \bigwedge \cdots \bigwedge l_{n_j}^j \Rightarrow l^j\}.$$

The rule $l_1^j \bigwedge \cdots \bigwedge l_{n_j}^j \Rightarrow l^j$ is abbreviated as $exp^j \Rightarrow l^j$, with $l_1^j \bigwedge \cdots \bigwedge l_{n_j}^j$ (the meet) by exp^j, for convenience of representations in model theories of expressions. We refer to l_i^j by "l_i^j of exp", on the assumption of commutativity for the meet operation. The set of rules is also referred to by the same name F with a condition to avoid inconsistency that for each $a \in A$, if there is a rule of the form $exp \Rightarrow a$ then there is no rule of the form $exp' \Rightarrow not\ a$.

3.1   Evaluation of Expressions

To begin model theories on the set of rules over a 3-valued domain, we have an evaluation $ev : (2^A \times 2^A) \to A \to \{0, 1/2, 1\}$ to an element $a \in A$ with respect to a pair $(I, J) \in 2^A \times 2^A$ $(I \cap J = \emptyset)$.

$$ev_{(I,J)}(a) = \begin{cases} 1 & \text{if } a \in I \\ 0 & \text{if } a \in J \\ 1/2 & \text{otherwise} \end{cases}$$

Following the definition of implication $\Rightarrow$ and meet $\wedge$, we have the evaluations with respect to the pair (I, J) $(I \cap J = \emptyset)$ as follows.

(i) For *not a* $(a \in A)$:

$$ev_{(I,J)}(not\ a) = \begin{cases} 1 & \text{if } ev_{(I,J)}(a) = 0 \\ 0 & \text{otherwise} \end{cases}$$

(ii) For a meet *exp*:

$$ev_{(I,J)}(exp) = \begin{cases} 1 & \text{if } ev_{(I,J)}(l) = 1 \text{ for any } l \text{ of } exp \\ 0 & \text{if } ev_{(I,J)}(l) = 0 \text{ for some } l \text{ of } exp \\ 1/2 & \text{otherwise} \end{cases}$$

(iii) For a rule $exp \Rightarrow l$:

$$ev_{(I,J)}(exp \Rightarrow l) = \begin{cases} 1 & \text{if } ev_{(I,J)}(exp) \text{ is less than or} \\ & \text{equal to } ev_{(I,J)}(l) \\ 0 & \text{if } ev_{(I,J)}(l) = 0 \\ 1/2 & \text{otherwise} \end{cases}$$

(iv) For a set of rules $\cup_j \{exp^j \Rightarrow l^j\}$:

$$ev_{(I,J)}(\cup_j \{exp^j \Rightarrow l^j\}) = \begin{cases} 1 & \text{if } ev_{(I,J)}(exp^j \Rightarrow l^j) = 1 \text{ for any } j \\ 0 & \text{if } ev_{(I,J)}(exp^j \Rightarrow l^j) = 0 \text{ for some } j \\ 1/2 & \text{otherwise} \end{cases}$$

Note that 0 is defined as less than 1/2, and 1/2 is as less than 1, in 3-valued domain, where "*not a*" is just for an element "$a \Rightarrow \perp$" of A, with *not* as strong negation. For an expression F, if $ev_{(I,J)}(F) = 1$ with the pair (I, J) such that $I \cap J = \emptyset$, then the pair (I, J) is said a 3-valued model of F.

With $exp \Rightarrow a$ and $exp' \Rightarrow not\ a$ (where exp and exp' are meets of some elements), some cognitive functions of acknowledgement and neglect may be simply represented.

Example 2. We assume the set

$$A' = \{Ac(a) \mid a \in A\} \cup \{Neg(b) \mid b \in A\}.$$

Then the HA algebra $(A, \vee, \wedge, \perp, \top)$ (with the partial order $\sqsubseteq$, a subset of $A \times A$) may be expanded to the algebra

$$(A \cup A', \vee, \wedge, \perp, \top)$$

with the partial order $\sqsubseteq_0$ (which is a subset of $(A \cup A') \times (A \cup A')$), where:

$$\sqsubseteq_0 = \sqsubseteq \cup \{(Ac(d), Ac(e)) \mid d, e \in A' \text{ such that } (d,e) \in \sqsubseteq\}$$
$$\cup \{(Neg(d), Neg(e)) \mid d, e \in A' \text{ such that } (d,e) \in \sqsubseteq\}.$$

In this expanded algebra, and with some meets exp_1 and exp_2,

$exp_1 \Rightarrow a$ is assumed to the acknowledgement of a by $a \Rightarrow Ac(a)$, and
$exp_2 \Rightarrow (not\ b)$ is assumed to the neglect of b by $not\ b \Rightarrow Neg(b)$.

As cognitive response, $Ac(a)$ or $Neg(b)$ may be expected with some state constraining the expressions from which the element a or b is derived.

We here examine *prefixpoint as model* of the expression F, over the 3-valued domain $\{0, 1/2, 1\}$. With the set A for an expression F, a mapping

$$\Psi_F : 2^A \times 2^A \to 2^A \times 2^A, \ \Psi_F(I_1, J_1) = (I_2, J_2)$$

can be defined: The mapping Ψ_F is associated with a set F of rules as follows.

(1) For some rule $exp \Rightarrow a$,
   (i) if exp is the empty such that it is regarded as $\top$, then a is in I_2.
   (ii) if b is in I_1 for any b of exp and c is in J_1 for any $not\ c$ of exp, then a is in I_2.
(2) (i) In case that there is no rule $exp \Rightarrow a$ and no rule $exp' \Rightarrow not\ a$ for $a \in A$, a is in J_2.
   (ii) For any rule $exp^j \Rightarrow a$, if b is in J_1 for some b of exp^j, or c is not in J_1 for some $not\ c$ of exp^j, then a is in J_2.
   (iii) For some rule $exp' \Rightarrow not\ a$, if b is not in J_1 for any b of exp' and c is in J_1 for any $not\ c$ of exp', then $a \in J_2$.

By the subset inclusion "$\subseteq_c$", we mean the relation that $(I_1, J_1) \subseteq_c (I_2, J_2)$ if $I_1 \subseteq I_2$ and $J_1 = J_2$. If $\Psi_F(I, J) \subseteq_c (I, J)$ and $I \cap J = \emptyset$, then (I, J) can be a model of F, that is, $ev_{(I,J)}(F) = 1$.

Proposition 1. *Assume a pair $(I, J) \in 2^A \times 2^A$ for a given expression F (a set of rules) with the element set A. If $\Psi_F(I, J) \subseteq_c (I, J)$ and $I \cap J = \emptyset$, then the pair (I, J) is a model of F.*

Proof. Let $\Psi_F(I, J) = (I_0, J_0) \subseteq_c (I, J)$. For each $a \in A$ such that $exp \Rightarrow a$ or $exp' \Rightarrow not\ a$, any rule in F should be evaluated as 1 for the following reason.

(i) If $a \in I_0 \subseteq I$, then $ev_{(I,J)}(exp \Rightarrow a) = 1$ for any rule $exp \Rightarrow a$ with $ev_{(I,J)}(a) = 1$.

(ii) If $a \in J_0 = J$, then (a) there is no rule of the form $exp \Rightarrow a$ and of the form $exp' \Rightarrow not\ a$, or (b) $ev_{(I,J)}(a) = 0$ for any rule $exp \Rightarrow a$, or (c) $ev_{(I,J)}(not\ a) = 1$ for any rule $exp' \Rightarrow not\ a$.

   (a) Unless there is a rule of the form $exp \Rightarrow a$ or of the form $exp' \Rightarrow not\ a$, the evaluation of the set F remains to be the same.
   (b) For any rule $exp \Rightarrow a$ (if exists), $ev_{(I,J)}(exp) = 0$ as well as $ev_{(I,J)}(a) = 0$. This is caused by the definition of the mapping Ψ_F where b is in J for some b of exp, that is, $ev_{I,J}(b) = 0$, or c is not in J for some $not\ c$ of exp, that is, $ev_{(I,J)}(not\ c) = 0$. Therefore the rule $exp \Rightarrow a$ must be evaluated as 1 (i.e. $ev_{(I,J)}(exp \Rightarrow a) = 1$).
   (c) For any rule $exp' \Rightarrow not\ a$, $ev_{(I,J)}(not\ a) = 1$ for $a \in J$. Thus we can have $ev_{(I,J)}(exp' \Rightarrow not\ a) = 1$.
(iii) In case that $a \notin I \cup J$:
   (a) For any rule $exp \Rightarrow a$, $ev_{(I,J)}(exp) = 0$ or $1/2$ as well as $ev_{(I,J)}(a) = 1/2$. Thus $ev_{(I,J)}(exp \Rightarrow a) = 1$.
   (b) For any rule $exp' \Rightarrow not\ a$, $ev_{(I,J)}(exp') = 0$ as well as $ev_{(I,J)}(not\ a) = 0$. Thus $ev_{(I,J)}(exp' \Rightarrow not\ a) = 1$.

Therefore all the rules may be evaluated as 1 with respect to the pair (I,J) such that the pair is a model, as long as $I \cap J = \emptyset$.   Q.E.D.

3.2   Query Predicates of Success and Failure

In what follows, we suppose the set A (for HA expressions) and the expression F as a set of rules. We have got a procedure with respect to construction of some model (I,J). This is a query procedure for algebraic expressions applicable to data retrieval.

Definition 1. For query a to be an effect for the expression, the predicates of success $Suc_F(a)$ and failure $Fail_F(a)$ may be inductively defined for $a \in A$ and a given expression (a set of rules) F, with such predicates as "not $Fail_F(a)$".

 (i) If there is a rule $exp \Rightarrow a$ such that $Suc_F(b)$ for any b of exp, and $Fail_F(c)$ for any c with $not\ c$ of exp, then $Suc_F(a)$.
(ii) (a) If there is no rule $exp \Rightarrow a$ and no rule $exp' \Rightarrow not\ a$ for $a \in A$, then $Fail_F(a)$.
    (b) For any rule $exp \Rightarrow a$ with $a \in A$, if $Fail_F(b)$ for some b of exp, or not $Fail_F(c)$ for some $not\ c$ of exp, then $Fail_F(a)$.
    (c) If there is a rule $exp' \Rightarrow not\ a$ for $a \in A$ such that not $Fail_F(d)$ for any d of exp', and $Fail_F(e)$ for any $not\ e$ of exp', then $Fail_F(a)$.

Proposition 2. *For an expression F, let a pair $(I,J) \in 2^A \times 2^A$ be*

$$I = \{a \mid Suc_F(a)\} \text{ and } J = \{b \mid Fail_F(b)\}.$$

Then $\Psi_F(I,J) \subseteq_c (I,J)$, and (I,J) is a model of F if $I \cap J = \emptyset$.

   Proof. (1) Let $\Psi_F(I,J) = (I_0,J_0)$. We prove by induction on the predicate definition that $(I_0,J_0) \subseteq_c (I,J)$.

(i) If $a \in I_0$, for some rule $exp \Rightarrow a$ (exp may be $\top$), then $b \in I$ for any b of exp and $c \in J$ for any *not* c of exp, such that $Suc_F(b)$ for any b of exp and $Fail_F(c)$ for any *not* c of exp. (We have no condition if $exp = \top$ for the rule $exp \Rightarrow a$.) Then $Suc_F(a)$. That is, $a \in I$, by which $I_0 \subseteq I$.

(ii) If $a \in J_0$, then the following examinations are to be made for $a \in J$, which shows $J_0 \subseteq J$.

    (a) If there is no rule of the form $exp \Rightarrow a$ and of the form $exp' \Rightarrow not\ a$, then $Fail_F(a)$. That is, $a \in J$.

    (b) For any rule $exp \Rightarrow a$, $b \in J$ for some b of exp, or $c \notin J$ for some *not* c of exp. Thus $Fail_F(b)$ for some b of exp, or not $Fail_F(c)$ for some *not* c of exp. It follows that $Fail_F(a)$, and thus $a \in J$.

    (c) Let $a \in J_0$ for some rule $exp' \Rightarrow not\ a$. Then $d \notin J$ for any d of exp' and $e \in J$ for any *not* e of exp'. It follows that not $Fail_F(d)$ for any d of exp' and $Fail_F(e)$ for any *not* e of exp'. By the predicate definition, $Fail_F(a)$. Thus $a \in J$.

By similar induction, we can have $J \subseteq J_0$.

(2) By the relation of (1) with Proposition 1, the pair (I,J) is a model of F, if $I \cap J = \emptyset$.

                                                              Q.E.D.

The significance of Proposition 2 is to suggest constructive views on predicates of $Suc_F(a)$ and $Fail_F(a)$ for a model (I,J) of the given expression F, where the pair (I,J) may be regarded as organized by the predicates.

However, the predicate "not $Fail_F(a)$" is not so practical, where it is of use in the inductive definition of the predicate $Fail_F(a)$. It is primarily from nonmonotonicity of the mapping Ψ_F associated with a given expression F as causal relation. That is, it is not always the case for monotonicity of Ψ_F that $\Psi_F(I_1,J_1) \subseteq_c \Psi_F(I_2,J_2)$ if $(I_1,J_1) \subseteq_c (I_2.J_2)$. To make it more practical, we have simple predicates for queries concerning the expression F. The predicates $pos_F(a)$ and $neg_F(a)$ are definable, such that

(i) if $pos_F(a)$ then $Suc_F(a)$ and "not $Fail_F(a)$", and
(ii) if $neg_F(a)$ then $Fail_F(a)$.

Formally, the predicates are defined inductively as follows.

Definition 2. (i) If there is a rule $exp \Rightarrow a$ such that $pos_F(b)$ for any b of exp, and $neg_F(c)$ for any *not* c of exp, then $pos_F(a)$.

(ii) (a) If there is no rule $exp \Rightarrow a$ and no rule $exp' \Rightarrow not\ a$ for $a \in A$, then $neg_F(a)$.

    (b) For any rule $exp \Rightarrow a$ such that $neg_F(b)$ for some b of exp, or $pos_F(c)$ for some *not* c of exp, then $neg_F(a)$.

    (c) If there is a rule $exp' \Rightarrow not\ a$ such that $pos_F(d)$ for any d of exp', and $neg_F(e)$ for any *not* e of exp', then $neg_F(a)$.

These predicates $pos_F(a)$ and $neg_F(b)$ are sound with respect to a model (I,J) constructed by the predicates $Suc_F(a)$ and $Fail_F(b)$.

Proposition 3. *Assume an expression F over the set A of algebraic elements. Let*

$$I = \{a \mid Suc_F(a)\} \ and \ J = \{b \mid Fail_F(b)\}$$

such that $I \cap J = \emptyset$. It follows that

(i) *if $pos_F(a)$ then $a \in I$, and*
(ii) *if $neg_F(a)$ then $a \in J$.*

Proof. By the inductive definitions and assumption such as $I \cap J = \emptyset$,

(a) if $pos_F(a)$ then $Suc_F(a)$,
(b) if $neg_F(a)$ then $Fail_F(a)$, and
(c) $Suc_F(a)$ and $Fail_F(a)$ are exclusive, such that if $pos_F(a)$ then not $Fail_F(a)$.

This may conclude the proposition.   Q.E.D.

3.3   Adjusting Procedure for Queries

A procedure may be constructed, in accordance with the definitions of the predicates $pos_F(a)$ and $neg_F(b)$. The procedure contains the rule of "negation as failure" for derivation: with failure, it is negated.

(1) With a given expression F, *query* of the *sequence* "X?" is assumed, where $X = y_1; \ldots; y_n (n \geq 0)$ with y_i being a or *not a* for $a \in A$ and with the concatenation operation ";" (which is regarded as $\bigwedge$), where in case of "$n = 0$", X is *null* (the empty query). A sequence query may be denoted as $y; X$? (with y being b or *not b* for $b \in A$, and with X a sequence query), or $Y; X$? with Y and X sequence queries.
(2) The notations $\langle X?\ suc \rangle$, and $\langle X?\ fail \rangle$ stand for the cases of the query X? to be a success, and a failure, respectively.
   There are routines of succeeding and failing derivations constructed for queries to be analyzed:
   (i) $\langle null?\ suc \rangle$.
   (ii) $\langle x; X?\ suc \rangle$, if $x = a$ (for $a \in A$) and there is $Y \Rightarrow x$ in F such that $\langle Y; X?\ suc \rangle$.
   (iii) (a) $\langle x; X?\ suc \rangle$, if $\langle a?\ fail \rangle$ for $x = not\ a$, and $\langle X?\ suc \rangle$.
         (b) $\langle x; X?\ suc \rangle$, if $\langle a?\ fail \rangle$ for $x = not\ a$ where there is some $Y' \Rightarrow x$ in F with $\langle Y'?\ suc \rangle$, and $\langle X?\ suc \rangle$.
   (iv) $\langle x; X?\ fail \rangle$, if there is no rule $Y \Rightarrow a$ and no rule $Y' \Rightarrow not\ a$ in F for $x = a \in A$, or $\langle X?\ fail \rangle$.
   (v) $\langle x; X?\ fail \rangle$, if $x = a$ ($a \in A$) such that $\langle Y?\ fail \rangle$ for any Y (where $Y \Rightarrow x$ in F), or $\langle X?\ fail \rangle$.
   (vi) (a) $\langle x; X?\ fail \rangle$, if $x = not\ a$ such that $\langle a?\ suc \rangle$, or $\langle X?\ fail \rangle$.
        (b) $\langle x; X?\ fail \rangle$, if $x = a$ such that $\langle Y'?\ suc \rangle$ for some Y' (where $Y' \Rightarrow not\ a$ in F), or $\langle X?\ fail \rangle$.

By induction on the definitions of predicates $pos_F(a)$ and $neg_F(b)$, and on the derivations $\langle a?\ suc \rangle$ and $\langle b?\ fail \rangle$, we can see:

Proposition 4. *For a given expression F,*

(i) $pos_F(a)$ iff $\langle a?\ suc \rangle$, and
(ii) $neg_F(a)$ iff $\langle a?\ fail \rangle$.

Proof. (1) We prove by induction that (a) if $pos_F(a)$, then $\langle a?\ suc \rangle$, and (b) if $neg_F(a)$, then $\langle a?\ fail \rangle$.

(i) $\langle null?\ suc \rangle$ is assumed without any condition.

(ii) If $pos_F(a)$ by $\top \Rightarrow a$, then $\langle a?\ suc \rangle$, because $\top$ is regarded as *null* such that $\langle \top?\ suc \rangle$.

(iii) If $pos_F(a)$ by $exp \Rightarrow a$, then $pos_F(b)$ for any b of exp and $neg_F(c)$ for any *not* c of exp. By induction hypothesis, $\langle b?\ suc \rangle$ and $\langle c?\ fail \rangle$ (deriving $\langle not\ c?\ suc \rangle$). Because exp contains b and *not* c as sequence elements, by the definition of adjusting, $\langle exp?\ suc \rangle$. It follows that $\langle a?\ suc \rangle$.

(iv) If $neg_F(a)$ without any rule $exp \Rightarrow a$ and any rule $exp' \Rightarrow not\ a$ for $a \in A$, then $\langle a?\ fail \rangle$ by the definition of adjusting.

(v) If $neg_F(a)$ for any rule $exp \Rightarrow a$, then $neg_F(b)$ for some b of exp, or $pos_F(c)$ for some *not* c of exp. By induction hypothesis, $\langle b?\ fail \rangle$, or $\langle c?\ suc \rangle$ (deriving $\langle not\ c?\ fail \rangle$). Because exp contains b or *not* c, $\langle exp?\ fail \rangle$ for any form exp. It follows that $\langle a?\ fail \rangle$.

(vi) If $neg_F(a)$ for some rule $exp' \Rightarrow not\ a$, then $pos_F(d)$ for any d of exp' and $neg_F(e)$ for any *not* e of exp. By induction hypothesis, $\langle d?\ suc \rangle$ and $\langle e?\ fail \rangle$ (deriving $\langle not\ e?\ suc \rangle$). Because exp' contains d and *not* e, $\langle exp?\ suc \rangle$. It follows that $\langle a?\ fail \rangle$ by the definition of adusting for a rule $exp' \Rightarrow not\ a$.

(2) We prove by induction that (a) if $\langle a?\ suc \rangle$, then $pos_F(a)$, and (b) if $\langle a?\ fail \rangle$, then $neg_F(a)$.

(i) (a) If $\langle a?\ suc \rangle$ with a rule $\top \Rightarrow a$ (where $\langle null?\ suc \rangle$ for the sequence *null* in correspondence with $\top$), then $pos_F(a)$ by the predicate definition for the rule $\top \Rightarrow a$. (b) Assume that $\langle a?\ suc \rangle$ with a rule $Y \Rightarrow a$ for $\langle Y?\ suc \rangle$. Because Y is a sequence, containing b such that $\langle b?\ suc \rangle$ and *not* c such that $\langle not\ c?\ suc \rangle$ (derived from $\langle c?\ fail \rangle$), by induction hypothesis, $pos_F(b)$ for any b of Y and $neg_F(c)$ for any *not* c of Y. Then $pos_F(a)$ by the definition of the predicate.

(ii) Assume that $\langle not\ a?\ suc \rangle$ (a) by $\langle a?\ fail \rangle$, or (b) $\langle a?\ fail \rangle$ with a rule of the form $Y' \Rightarrow not\ a$ such that $\langle Y'?\ suc \rangle$. In case of (a), $neg_F(a)$, by induction hypothesis. In case of (b), for the sequence Y', $\langle d?\ suc \rangle$ for any d of Y' and $\langle not\ e?\ suc \rangle$ (derived from $\langle e?\ fail \rangle$) for any *not* e of Y'. By induction hypothesis, $pos_F(d)$ for any d of Y' and $neg_F(e)$ for any *not* e of Y'. It follows that $neg_F(a)$ with the rule $Y' \Rightarrow not\ a$.

(iii) Assume that $\langle a?\ fail \rangle$ with (a) no rule of the form $Y \Rightarrow a$ and of the form $Y' \Rightarrow a$, or (b) any rule of the form $Y \Rightarrow a$ such that $\langle Y?\ fail \rangle$. In case of (a), $neg_F(a)$ by the predicate definition. In case of (b), for a sequence Y, $\langle b?\ fail \rangle$ for some b of Y or $\langle not\ c?\ fail \rangle$ (derived from $\langle c?\ suc \rangle$) for some *not* c of Y. By induction hypothesis, $neg_F(b)$ for some b of Y or $pos_F(c)$ for some *not* c of Y. It follows from any rule $Y \Rightarrow a$ that $neg_F(a)$.

(iv) Assume that (a) $\langle not\ a?\ fail \rangle$ by $\langle a?\ suc \rangle$, or (b) $\langle a?\ fail \rangle$ with a rule $Y' \Rightarrow not\ a$ such that $\langle Y'?\ suc \rangle$. In case of (a), $pos_F(a)$ by induction hypotyhesis. In case of (b), $\langle Y'?\ suc \rangle$. For the sequence Y', $\langle d?\ suc \rangle$ for any d of Y' and $\langle not\ e?\ suc \rangle$ (derived from $\langle e?\ fail \rangle$) for any *not* e of Y'. By induction hypothesis, $pos_F(d)$ for any d of Y', and $neg_F(e)$ for any e of Y', such that $neg_F(a)$.

Q.E.D.

The predicates $Suc_F(a)$ and $Fail_F(b)$ are meaningful for algebraic expressions, with $pos_F(a)$ and $neg_F(b)$ for adjusting as approximations of the predicates.

4 Negatives in Algebraic Expressions

With respect to the predicates $pos_F(a)$ and $neg_F(b)$ approximating $Suc_F(a)$ and $Fail_F(b)$, we here examine another negation. It is known as default negation in AI for data and knowledge representations. Even if algebraic expressions contain double negation in 3-valued domain, the predicates for queries may be constructed. Abstract and theoretical propositions are given with exhaustive proofs, which may be needed for basis of state constraint systems with algebraic expressions, more extended from the language system [26]. The intuitive meanings are captured with the similar representations to those in Sect. 3.

Given a Heyting algebra

$$(A, \bigvee, \bigwedge, \top, \bot)$$

equipped with the partial order $\sqsubseteq$ and implication $\Rightarrow$ (which can define a negation *not* such that $a \Rightarrow \bot$ is *not* a for the least element $\bot$ of A), we have a "mapping"

$$\sim\; : A \to A$$

such that $\sim b \sqsubseteq \sim a$ if $a \sqsubseteq b$ (and thus $\sim\bot = \top$ and $\sim\top = \bot$). We can regard the mapping $\sim$ as *default* negation different from *strong* negation *not*, following the evaluation in 3-valued domain as below. From logical views which algebraic expressions may denote, "$\sim$" is mentioned as default negation.

4.1 Expressions with Double Negation

We extend the evaluation function *ev* of expressions over the 3-valued domain $\{0, 1/2, 1\}$ by taking, with respect to the pair $(I,J) \in 2^A \times 2^A$ $(I \cap J = \emptyset)$:

$$ev_{(I,J)}(\sim a) = \begin{cases} 0 & \text{if } ev_{(I,J)}(a) = 1 \\ 1/2 & \text{if } ev_{(I,J)}(a) = 1/2 \\ 1 & \text{if } ev_{(I,J)}(a) = 0 \end{cases}$$

We now study model theory on the set G of rules each of which takes a more general form $Exp \Rightarrow L$ than the form $exp \Rightarrow l$ in the expression F of Sect. 3, where

(i) L is a, *not* a or $\sim a$ for $a \in A$, and
(ii) Exp is a meet $L_1 \bigwedge \ldots \bigwedge L_n$ ($\top$ if $n = 0$) such that each L_i $(1 \leq i \leq n)$ is b, *not* b or $\sim b$ for $b \in A$, and L_i may be pointed out by "L_i of Exp".

The set G supposedly follows a condition to escape from inconsistency that for each $a \in A$, if there is a rule of the form $Exp \Rightarrow a$, then there is neither a rule of the form $Exp' \Rightarrow$ *not* a nor a rule of the form $Exp'' \Rightarrow \sim a$. The evaluation *ev* is extended in the case of expressions including the default negation $\sim$.

(i) For *not* a $(a \in A)$:

$$ev_{(I,J)}(not\ a) = \begin{cases} 1 & \text{if } ev_{(I,J)}(a) = 0 \\ 0 & \text{otherwise} \end{cases}$$

(ii) For a meet Exp:

$$ev_{(I,J)}(Exp) = \begin{cases} 1 & \text{if } ev_{(I,J)}(L) = 1 \text{ for any } L \text{ of } Exp \\ 0 & \text{if } ev_{(I,J)}(L) = 0 \text{ for some } L \text{ of } Exp \\ 1/2 & \text{otherwise} \end{cases}$$

(iii) For a rule $Exp \Rightarrow L$:

$$ev_{(I,J)}(Exp \Rightarrow L) = \begin{cases} 1 & \text{if } ev_{(I,J)}(Exp) \text{ is less than or} \\ & \text{equal to } ev_{(I,J)}(L) \\ 0 & \text{if } ev_{(I,J)}(L) = 0 \\ 1/2 & \text{otherwise} \end{cases}$$

(iv) For a set of rules $\cup_j \{Exp^j \Rightarrow L^j\}$:

$$ev_{(I,J)}(\cup_j\{Exp^j \Rightarrow L^j\}) = \begin{cases} 1 & \text{if } ev_{(I,J)}(Exp^j \Rightarrow l^j) = 1 \text{ for any } j \\ 0 & \text{if } ev_{(I,J)}(Exp^j \Rightarrow l^j) = 0 \text{ for some } j \\ 1/2 & \text{otherwise} \end{cases}$$

Example 3. At some closed gate, it may be open when the obstacle (which is denoted by *obst*) is negated, but while the obstacle negation is default, an examination is needed. Such a circumstance is represented by algebraic expressions as a set (or sequence) of rules.

$$not\ obst \Rightarrow awareness,$$
$$\sim obst \Rightarrow default,$$
$$closed \wedge awareness \Rightarrow open,$$
$$closed \wedge default \Rightarrow examination,$$

where *obst, awareness, default, closed, open* and *examination* are algebraic elements which may be evaluated over 3-valued domain.

As an extended version of a prefixpoint of the mapping Ψ_F (in Sect. 3), we now have a prefixpoint model of the expression G, over the 3-valued domain $\{0, 1/2, 1\}$, if it exists, although it is not always available. With the set A for an expression G, a mapping

$$\Phi_G : 2^A \times 2^A \rightarrow 2^A \times 2^A, \ \Phi_G(I_1, J_1) = (I_2, J_2)$$

can be defined as a more abstract one than Ψ_F with more exhaustive checks:

(1) For some rule $Exp \Rightarrow a$:
    (i) if Exp is the empty such that it is regarded as $\top$, then a is in I_2.
    (ii) if b is in I_1 for any b of Exp, c is in J_1 for any *not* c of Exp, and d is in J for any $\sim d$ of Exp, then a is in I_2.
(2) (i) In case that there is no rule $Exp \Rightarrow a$, no rule $Exp' \Rightarrow not\ a$ and no rule $Exp'' \Rightarrow \sim a$ for $a \in A$, a is in J_2.
    (ii) For any rule $Exp^j \Rightarrow a$, if b is in J_1 for some b of Exp^j, c is not in J_1 for some *not* c of Exp^j, or d is in I_1 for some $\sim d$ of Exp^j, then a is in J_2.
    (iii) For some rule $Exp' \Rightarrow not\ a$, if b is not in J_1 for any b of Exp', c is in J_1 for any *not* c of Exp', and d is in J_1 for any $\sim d$ of Exp', then $a \in J_2$.

(iv) For some rule $Exp' \Rightarrow \sim a$, if b is in I_1 for any b of Exp', c is in J_1 for any *not* c of Exp', and d is in J_1 for any $\sim d$ of Exp', then $a \in J_2$.

If $\Phi_G(I,J) \subseteq_c (I,J)$ (with the set inclusion $\subseteq_c$) and $I \cap J = \emptyset$, then (I,J) can be a model of G. The proof contains more exhaustive examinations of cases, however, Proposition 5 is of a more abstract sense with the similar account for Proposition 1.

Proposition 5. *Assume a pair* $(I,J) \in 2^A \times 2^A$ *for a given expression G (a set of rules) with the element set A. If* $\Phi_G(I,J) \subseteq_c (I,J)$ *and* $I \cap J = \emptyset$, *then the pair* (I,J) *is a model of G.*

Proof. Let $\Phi_G(I,J) = (I_0,J_0) \subseteq_c (I,J)$. For each $a \in A$ such that $Exp \Rightarrow a$, $Exp' \Rightarrow not\ a$ or $Exp' \Rightarrow \sim a$, any rule in G should be evaluated as 1 with respect to (I,J).

(i) If $a \in I_0 \subseteq I$, then $ev_{(I,J)}(Exp \Rightarrow a) = 1$, for any rule $Exp \Rightarrow a$ with $ev_{(I,J)}(a) = 1$.

(ii) If $a \in J_0 = J$, then (a) there is no rule of the form $Exp \Rightarrow a$, of the form $Exp' \Rightarrow not\ a$ and of the form $Exp'' \Rightarrow \sim a$, or (b) $ev_{(I,J)}(a) = 0$ for any rule $Exp \Rightarrow a$, (c) $ev_{(I,J)}(not\ a) = 1$ for any rule $Exp' \Rightarrow not\ a$, or (d) $ev_{(I,J)}(\sim a) = 1$ for any rule $Exp' \Rightarrow \sim a$.

    (a) Unless there is a rule of the form $Exp \Rightarrow a$, of the form $Exp' \Rightarrow not\ a$ or of the form $Exp'' \Rightarrow \sim a$, the evaluation of the set G remains to be the same.

    (b) For any rule $Exp \Rightarrow a$ (if exists), $ev_{(I,J)}(Exp) = 0$ as well as $ev_{(I,J)}(a) = 0$. This is caused by the definition of the mapping Φ_G where b is in J for some b of Exp (i.e. $ev_{(I,J)}(b) = 0$), c is not in J for some *not* c of Exp (i.e. $ev_{(I,J)}(not\ c) = 0$), or d is in I for some $\sim d$ of Exp (i.e. $ev_{(I,J)}(\sim d) = 0$). Thus $ev_{(I,J)}(Exp) = 0$. Therefore the rule $Exp \Rightarrow a$ must be evaluated as 1.

    (c) For any rule $Exp' \Rightarrow not\ a$, $ev_{(I,J)}(not\ a) = 1$ for $a \in J$. Thus we have $ev_{(I,J)}(Exp' \Rightarrow not\ a) = 1$.

    (d) For any rule $Exp' \Rightarrow \sim a$, $ev_{(I,J)}(Exp' \Rightarrow \sim a) = 1$, because, for $a \in J$, $ev_{(I,J)}(not\ a) = 1$.

(iii) In case that $a \notin I \cup J$:

    (a) For any rule $Exp \Rightarrow a$, $ev_{(I,J)}(Exp) = 0$ or $1/2$ and $ev_{(I,J)}(a) = 1/2$. Thus $ev_{(I,J)}(Exp \Rightarrow a) = 1$.

    (b) For any rule $Exp' \Rightarrow not\ a$, $ev_{(I,J)}(Exp') = 0$ as well as $ev_{(I,J)}(not\ a) = 0$. Thus $ev_{(I,J)}(Exp' \Rightarrow not\ a) = 1$.

    (c) For any rule $Exp' \Rightarrow \sim a$, $ev_{(I,J)}(Exp') = 0$ or $1/2$. Because $ev_{(I,J)}(not\ a) = 1/2$, $ev_{(I,J)}(Exp' \Rightarrow not\ a) = 1$.

Thus all the rule may be evaluated as 1 with respect to the pair (I,J) such that the pair is a model, as long as $I \cap J = \emptyset$.   Q.E.D.

4.2 Predicates for Modeling

With respect to query a to be an effect for the expression, the predicates of success $Suc_G(a)$ and failure $Fail_G(a)$ may be inductively defined for $a \in A$ and a given expression (a set of rules) G as follows. These predicates are similarly organized to the manner for the predicates $Suc_F(a)$ and $Fail_F(a)$ of Sect. 3, however, they are more general with double negation, involving the predicate like "not $Fail_G(a)$" for the organizations, as well.

(1) If there is a rule $Exp \Rightarrow a$ such that $Suc_G(b)$ for any b of Exp, $Fail_G(c)$ for any *not a* of Exp and $Fail_G(d)$ for any $\sim d$ of Exp, then $Suc_F(a)$.

(2) (i) If there is no rule $Exp \Rightarrow a$, no rule $Exp \Rightarrow not\ a$ and no rule $Exp'' \Rightarrow \sim a$ for $a \in A$, then $Fail_G(a)$.

 (ii) If there is a rule $Exp \Rightarrow a$ such that $Fail_G(b)$ for some b of Exp, not $Fail_G(c)$ for some *not c* of Exp, or $Suc_G(d)$ for some $\sim d$ of Exp, then $Fail_G(a)$.

 (iii) If there is a rule $Exp' \Rightarrow not\ a$ such that not $Fail_G(e)$ for any e of Exp', $Fail_G(f)$ for any *not f* of Exp' and $Fail_G(g)$ for any $\sim g$ of Exp', then $Fail_F(a)$.

 (iv) If there is a rule $Exp' \Rightarrow \sim a$ such that $Suc_G(e)$ for any e of Exp', $Fail_G(f)$ for any *not f* of Exp' and $Fail_G(g)$ for any $\sim g$ of Exp', then $Fail_F(a)$.

The predicates $Suc_G(a)$ and $Fail_G(a)$ are of use for the construction of modeling the set G of rules. The following proposition is an extended version of Proposition 2 with the similar account, where its proof contains more exhaustive checks.

Proposition 6. *Assume a pair* $(I, J) \in 2^A \times 2^A$ *for an expression G over the set A. Let*

$$I = \{a \mid Suc_G(a)\} \text{ and } J = \{b \mid Fail_G(b)\}.$$

Then $\Phi_G(I, J) \subseteq_c (I, J)$, *and* (I, J) *is a model of G if* $I \cap J = \emptyset$.

Proof. (1) Let $\Phi_G(I, J) = (I_0, J_0)$. We prove by induction on the predicate definition that $(I_0, J_0) \subseteq_c (I, J)$.

 (i) Assume that $a \in I_0$. Then there is a rule $Exp \Rightarrow a$ such that $b \in I$ for any b of Exp, $c \in J$ for any *not c* of Exp and $d \in J$ for any $\sim d$ of Exp. By the assumed definitions of I and J, $Suc_G(b)$ for any b of Exp, $Fail_G(c)$ for any *not c* of Exp and $Fail_G(d)$ for any $\sim d$ of Exp. It follows that $Suc_G(a)$. That is, $a \in I$ and thus $I_0 \subseteq I$.

 (ii) When $a \in J_0$, there are cases as follows, which are examined for a to be included in J and which show that $J_0 \subseteq J$.

 (a) If there is no rule of the form $Exp \Rightarrow a$, of the form $Exp \Rightarrow not\ a$ and of the form $Exp'' \Rightarrow \sim a$ for $a \in A$, then $Fail_G(a)$. Thus $a \in J$.

 (b) For any rule $Exp \Rightarrow a$, b is not in J for some b of Exp (i.e. not $Fail_G(b)$), c is in J for some *not c* of Exp (i.e. $Fail_G(c)$) or d is in J for some $\sim d$ of Exp (i.e. $Fail_G(d)$). Then $Fail_F(a)$, and thus $a \in J$.

 (c) If there is a rule $Exp' \Rightarrow not\ a$ such that e is not in J for any e of Exp' (i.e. not $Fail_G(e)$), f is in J for any *not f* of Exp' (i.e. $Fail_G(f)$) and g is in J for any $\sim g$ (i.e. $Fail_G(g)$), then $Fail_G(a)$, and $a \in J$.

 (d) If there is a rule $Exp' \Rightarrow \sim a$ such that e is in I for any e of Exp' (i.e. $Suc_G(e)$), f is in J for any *not f* of Exp' (i.e. $Fai_G(f)$) and g is in J for any $\sim g$ of Exp' (i.e. $Fail_G(g)$), then $Fail_G(a)$, and $a \in J$.

 By similar induction, we can have $J \subseteq_c J_0$.

(2) With Proposition 5, (I, J) is a model of G if $I \cap J = \emptyset$.   Q.E.D.

The predicates $Suc_G(a)$ and $Fail_G(a)$ may be approximated, if the predicates $pos_G(a)$ and $neg_G(a)$ are constructed by the extensions of the predicates $pos_F(a)$ and $neg_F(a)$ for the expression F (of Sect. 3).

The predicates $pos_G(a)$ and $neg_G(a)$ are defined inductively in a similar but a more general manner.

(1) If there is a rule $Exp \Rightarrow a$ such that $pos_G(b)$ for any b of Exp, $neg_G(c)$ for any *not c* of Exp and $neg_G(d)$ for any $\sim d$ of Exp, then $pos_G(a)$.

(2) (i) If there is no rule $Exp \Rightarrow a$, no rule $Exp' \Rightarrow not\ a$ and no rule $Exp'' \Rightarrow \sim a$ for $a \in A$, then $neg_G(a)$.

(ii) For any rule $Exp \Rightarrow a$ such that $neg_G(b)$ for some b of Exp, $pos_G(c)$ for some *not c* of Exp or $pos_G(d)$ for some $\sim d$ of Exp, then $neg_G(a)$.

(iii) If there is a rule $Exp' \Rightarrow not\ a$ such that $pos_G(e)$ for any e of Exp', $neg_G(f)$ for any *not f* of Exp' and $neg_G(g)$ for any $\sim g$ of Exp, then $neg_G(a)$.

(iv) If there is a rule $Exp' \Rightarrow \sim a$ such that $pos_G(e)$ for any e of Exp', $neg_G(f)$ for any *not f* of Exp' and $neg_G(g)$ for any $\sim g$ of Exp, then $neg_G(a)$.

These predicates are sound with respect to a model (I, J) constructed by the predicates $Suc_G(a)$ and $Fail_G(b)$, in the same sense of Proposition 3, for the reason: (i) If $pos_G(a)$, then $Suc_G(a)$. (ii) If $neg_G(a)$, then $Fail_G(a)$. (iii) If the predicates $Suc_G(a)$ and $Fail_G(a)$ are exclusive for any $a \in A$, and $pos_G(a)$, then "not $Fail_G(a)$".

Proposition 7. *Assume an expression F over the set A of algebraic elements. Let*

$$I = \{a \mid Suc_G(a)\} \ and \ J = \{b \mid Fail_G(b)\}$$

such that $I \cap J = \emptyset$. With respect to the pair (I, J),

(i) *if $pos_G(a)$ then $a \in I$, and*
(ii) *if $neg_G(a)$ then $a \in J$.*

5   Semiring Structure

This section is concerned with the primary algebraic structure in abstract state machine [27], however, we here take algebraic expressions with double negation for causal relation data in terms of effects of queries. The algebraic expression is called by the name G. For algebraic expressions G, the queries $Suc_G(a)$ and $Fail_G(a)$ are assumed as retrieval tools. Approximating predicates $pos_G(a)$ and $neg_G(a)$ may be admitted, as well, such that queries are available at each state where the expressions are constructed.

At each state constraint as illustrated in Example 1, data operations like queries in (algebraic) expressions cause state transitions. Because the model of the expressions is closely related to queries such as predicates of Sect. 4, models may be captured as causing state transitions in such a state constraint system. When traversing the states (sites), models may be regarded as being concatenated to other models of another state, when reference data is considered.

Given an algebraic expression G over the set A, we may have a pair

$$(I, J) \in 2^A \times 2^A,$$

which is assumed as a 3-valued model of G, and can be regarded as defining state changes (transitions). With the set A, we can have denumerable expressions $G_1, G_2, \ldots,$ causing state changes, which are in accordance with causal relations. Then the 3-valued models of expressions $G_1, G_2, \ldots$ may be assumed as the pairs

$$(I_1, J_1), (I_2, J_2), \ldots.$$

As regards state transitions, concatenation and alternation are needed, to denote the implementation senses.

(1) Concatenation: By means of the set concatenation "." (which gets the set of sequences obtained from taken elements of sets), we might have

$$(I_1, J_1) \bullet \ldots \bullet (I_n, J_n)$$
$$= (I_1 \cdot \ldots \cdot I_n$$
$$-\{w \mid \text{some element of } w \text{ of } I_1 \cdot \ldots \cdot I_n \text{ is in } J_1 \cup \ldots \cup J_n\}, J_1 \cup \ldots \cup J_n),$$

with multiplication "$\bullet$" to express the sequence formation.

(2) Alternation: Different from the case in the star semiring [25], alternations are realized by direct sums. From implementation views, the "sum" means *nondeterministic* selections as alternation.

With alternation aspects, let R_A (R, for short with the assumption of the set A) be the set of "direct sums" of the form

$$\Sigma_l(pSeq_l, nSet_l)$$

with l ranging indexes, where each pair $(pSeq_l, nSet_l)$ consists of a set $pSet_k$ of sequences and a set $nSet_k$, concerned with models (I_l, J_l) of some expression G_k over A.

The operations $+$ (addition–alternation) and $\circ$ (multiplication–concatenation) on R are defined:

(1)
$$\Sigma_i(pSeq_i, nSet_i) + \Sigma_j(pSeq_j, nSet_j) = \Sigma_{k=i,j}(pSeq_k, nSet_k).$$

(2)
$$\Sigma_i(pSeq_i, nSet_i) \circ \Sigma_j (pSeq_j, nSet_j)$$
$$= \Sigma_{i,j}(pSeq_i \cdot pSeq_j$$
$$-\{uv \mid u \in pSeq_i, v \in pSeq_j, u : \text{ inconsistent to } nSet_j\}$$
$$-\{uv \mid u \in pSeq_i, v \in pSeq_j, v : \text{ iconsistent to } nSet_i\}, nSet_i \cup nSet_j),$$

where
  (i) the sequence uv is constructed by concatenation of sequences u and v,
  (ii) by saying that u and v are inconsistent to (the sets) $nSet_j$ and $nSet_i$, respectively, it means that u and v contain some element in $nSet_j$ and $nSet_i$, respectively, and
  (iii) the operation $\cdot$ is the set concatenation, consisting of concatenated sequences.

With the identity 0_Σ for addition $+$, and the identity $(\{\varepsilon\}, \emptyset)$ for multiplication $\circ$, we finally have a semiring R_A regarding sequences caused by models of expressions:

Proposition 8. *The structure* $\langle R_A, +, \circ, 0_\Sigma, (\{\varepsilon\}, \emptyset) \rangle$ *is a semiring.*

Proof. (1) We can have identities with respect to the addition and multiplication in terms of alternation and concatenation, respectively, if we care the direct sum of the "form" $\Sigma_i(pSeq_i, nSet_i)$.

(i) $\Sigma_i(pSeq_i, nSet_i)$ is denoted $\emptyset_\Sigma$, if the direct sum is the empty. It is the identity with respect to $+$.

(ii) The empty sequence in A^* is represented by ε. $(\{\varepsilon\}, \emptyset)$ is the identity with respect to $\circ$.

(2) We can see the conditions of a semiring as follows.

(i) The operation $+$ is defined so that commutative and associative laws may obviously hold. With the identity $\emptyset_\Sigma$, $\langle R, +, \emptyset_\Sigma \rangle$ is a commutative monoid (a commutative semigroup with the identity).

(ii) The operation $\circ$ is associative, so that $\langle R, \circ, (\{\varepsilon\}, \emptyset) \rangle$ is a semigroup with the identity $(\{\varepsilon\}, \emptyset)$, that is, a monoid.

(iii) Left and right multiplications over addition are both distributive:

$$\Sigma_i(pSeq_i, nSet_i) \circ (\Sigma_j(pSeq_j, nSet_j) + \Sigma_k(pSeq_k, nSet_k))$$
$$= (\Sigma_i(pSeq_i, nSet_i) \circ \Sigma_j(pSeq_j, nSet_j))$$
$$+ (\Sigma_i(pSeq_i, nSet_i) \circ \Sigma_k(pSeq_k, nSet_k)).$$
$$(\Sigma_j(pSeq_j, nSet_j) + \Sigma_k(pSeq_k, nSet_k)) \circ \Sigma_i(pSeq_i, nSet_i)$$
$$= (\Sigma_j(pSeq_j, nSet_j) \circ \Sigma_i(pSeq_i, nSet_i))$$
$$+ (\Sigma_k(pSeq_k, nSet_k) \circ \Sigma_i(pSeq_i, nSet_i)).$$

(iv) $\emptyset_\Sigma \circ \Sigma_i(pSeq_i, nSet_i) = \Sigma_i(pSeq_i, nSet_i) \circ \emptyset_\Sigma = \emptyset_\Sigma$.
That is, annihilation holds for $\circ$, with the identity $\emptyset_\Sigma$ regarding $+$.

Q.E.D.

6   Conclusion

Concluding remarks and related works are briefly summarized, with respect to the views in data science and knowledge engineering.

6.1   Primary Contribution

This paper gives model theories of Heyting algebra expressions over 3-valued domain, for data semantics of causal relations constrained by states. The models of algebraic expressions are mentioned from both prefixpoint approach and predicates of queries on algebraic expressions. To approximate queries, adjusting derivations (based on negation as failure rule) are designed such that they may be sound with respect to the models of expressions. As regards denotations of state transitions, a semiring algebra is designed for sequences of queries on algebraic expressions to construct an explicit structure. Compared with our previous works, novel contents are included in the senses:

(i) The form of the expressions is general enough to describe formulas of intuitionistic propositional logic and universal by a form of possibly infinite rule set, apart from the form restriction in representation of reference data in the paper [27]. As a knowledge engineering tool to analyze algebraic expression queries, negation as failure rule is applied to sound procedure.

(ii) The expression of this paper may contain two kinds of negation, strong negation caused by Heyting implication and default negation over 3-valued domain, where model theory is elaborated, on the basis of the model theory of expressions without default negation. This model theory is relevant to those in logic programming with default and strict negations [24], but more general, with the predicates for queries.

(iii) The semiring of this paper is different from the star semiring of the paper [25], with the explicit representation for nondeterministic alternation to constructions of query sequences. The semiring structure is formally constructed with respect to state transitions virtually caused by dynamic traverses through queries, which is related to automata theory [5] rather than context-free language aspects [23].

6.2   Related and Advanced Works

We list up several works which are relevant to this paper in data science and engineering, and contain advanced results in software and knowledge engineering.

(a) The action is formulated as a key role with respect to state transitions. In concretized actions as programs of dynamic logic, acting and sensing failures are discussed as advanced works [22]. Actions are also captured in logical systems from the viewpoints of sequential process, as in the papers [8, 11].

(b) As regards computing environments related to state concepts, mobile ambients [3, 16] have been formulated with environments for communication.

(c) Concerning fixed point theory, the papers [4, 14] are classical enough to formulate the proof systems with fixed points and their approximations.

(d) The paper [1] presents the belief predicate with the credence function of agents, concerning epistemic contradictions. Such predicates must be designed on the algebra, when this paper is applied to modal logic

(e) There is a paper [15] presenting second-order propositional frameworks, with epistemic and intuitionistic logic. With the second-order (quantified) propositions, the paper [9] involves dependence and independence concepts, which may control implementations of programs or queries if data base is designed with such concepts. For an extension of propositional modal logic without quantification, the paper [6] introduces relations and terms with scoping mechanism by lambda abstraction.

(f) "Distributed knowledge" is discussed [18], with quantified variables ranging over the set of agents. Concerning applications of the second-order predicates to knowledge, the paper [13] contains the concept of knowing.

References

1. Beddor, B., Goldstein, S.: Believing epistemic contradictions. Rev. Symb. Log. **11**(1), 87–114 (2018)
2. Bertolissi, C., Cirstea, H., Kirchner, C.: Expressing combinatory reduction systems derivations in the rewriting calculus. Higher Order. Symbolic Comput. **19**(4), 345–376 (2006)
3. Cardelli, L., Gordon, A.: Mobile ambients. Theoret. Comput. Sci. **240**(1), 177–213 (2000)

4. Dam, M., Gurov, D.: Mu-calculus with explicit points and approximations. J. Log. Comput. **12**(1), 119–136 (2002)
5. Droste, M., Kuich, W., Vogler, H. (eds.): Handbook of Weighted Automata. EATCS, Springer, Heidelberg (2009). https://doi.org/10.1007/978-3-642-01492-5
6. Fitting, M.: Modal logics between propositional and first-order. J. Log. Comput. **12**(6), 1017–1026 (2002)
7. Gebser, M., Schaub, T.: Modeling and language extensions. AI Mag. **3**(3), 33–44 (2016)
8. Giordano, L., Martelli, A., Schwind, C.: Ramification and causality in a modal action logic. J. Log. Comput. **10**(5), 625–662 (2000)
9. Goranko, V., Kuusisto, A.: Logics for propositional determinacy and independence. Rev. Symb. Log. **11**(3), 470–506 (2018)
10. Governatori, G., Maher, M., Autoniou, G., Billington, D.: Argumentation semantics for defeasible logic. J. Log. Comput. **14**(5), 675–702 (2004)
11. Hanks, S., McDermott, D.: Nonmonotonic logic and temporal projection. Artif. Intell. **33**(3), 379–412 (1987)
12. Kaufmann, B., Leone, N., Perri, S., Schaub, T.: Grounding and solving in answer set programming. AI Mag. **3**(3), 25–32 (2016)
13. Kooi, B.: The ambiguity of knowability. Rev. Symb. Log. **9**(3), 421–428 (2016)
14. Kozen, D.: Results on the propositional Mu-calculus. Theoret. Comput. Sci. **27**(3), 333–354 (1983)
15. Kremer, P.: Completeness of second-order propositional S4 and H in topological semantics. Rev. Symn. Log. **11**(3), 507–518 (2018)
16. Merro, M., Nardelli, F.: Behavioral theory for mobile ambients. J. ACM **52**(6), 61–1023 (2005)
17. Mosses, P.: Action Semantics. Cambridge University Press, Cambridge (1992)
18. Naumov, P., Tao, J.: Everyone knows that some knows: quantifiers over epistemic agents. Rev. Symb. Log. **12**(2), 255–270 (2019)
19. Reiter, R.: Knowledge in Action. MIT Press, Cambridge (2001)
20. Reps, T., Schwoon, S., Somesh, J.: Weighted pushdown systems and their application to interprocedural data flow analysis. Sci. Comput. Program. **58**(1–2), 206–263 (2005)
21. Rutten, J.: On Streams and Coinduction. CWI, Amsterdam (2001)
22. Spalazzi, L., Traverso, P.: A dynamic logic for acting, sensing and planning. Log. Comput. **10**(6), 787–821 (2000)
23. Winter, J., Marcello, B., Bonsangue, M., Rutten, J.: Coalgebraic characterizations of context-free languages. Formal Methods Comput. Sci. **9**(3), 1–39 (2013)
24. Yamasaki, S.: Logic programming with default, weak and strict negations. Theory Pract. Log. Program. **6**(6), 37–749 (2006)
25. Yamasaki, S.: Semantics and algebra for action logic monitoring state transitions. In: Proceedings of the 2nd International Conference on Complexity, Future Information Systems and Risks, vol. 1, pp. 110–115. SCITEPRESS Digital Library (2017)
26. Yamasaki, S.: Theoretical basis of language system with state constraints. In: Proceedings of the 5th International Conference on Complexity, Future Information Systems and Risks, vol. 1, pp. 80–87. SCITEPRESS Digital Library (2020)
27. Yamasaki, S., Sasakura, M.: Reference data abstraction and causal relation based on algebraic expressions. In: Proceedings of the 9th International Conference on Data Science, Technology and Applications, vol. 1, pp. 207–214. SCITEPRESS Digital Library (2020)

An Environmental Study of French Neighbourhoods

Nelly Barret[1] , Fabien Duchateau[1(✉)] , Franck Favetta[1] , Aurélien Gentil[2],
and Loïc Bonneval[2]

[1] LIRIS UMR5205, Université de Lyon, UCBL, Lyon, France
`nelly.barret@etu.univ-lyon1.fr`,
`{fduchate,ffavetta}@liris.cnrs.fr`
[2] Centre Max Weber, Université de Lyon, Lyon, France
`{aurelien.gentil,loic.bonneval}@univ-lyon2.fr`

Abstract. Neighbourhoods are key places for daily activities and many studies in social sciences, health or biology use this spatial concept as an impact factor. Conversely, the neighbourhood environment is rarely defined (e.g., in terms of landscape or main social class). In this paper, we propose six descriptive variables for this environment, and we provide a dataset of 270 annotated neighbourhoods. Next, we detail two methods (prediction and spatial computation) for describing environment of remaining neighbourhoods, and we show in our set of experiments an acceptable quality.

Keywords: Neighbourhood · Environment · Data integration · Machine learning · Prediction · Spatial computation

1 Introduction

Neighbourhoods are a very common concept in studies from diverse domains such as health, social sciences, or biology. For instance, Japanese researchers investigated the relationships between social factors and health by taking into account not only behavioural risks, but also housing and neighbourhood environments [38]. In a British study, authors describe how living areas have an impact on physical activities, from which they determine a walkability index at the neighbourhood level for improving future urban planning [16]. Smarts cities also consider neighbourhoods as an ideal unit division for measuring urban quality [18]. Lastly, a survey describes the luxury effect, i.e., the impact of wealthy neighbourhoods on the surrounding biodiversity [27]. In addition to the essential role of the neighbourhoods, these examples also show that the definition of neighbourhood is subject to various interpretations [8,20,24], which may depend on the point of view (e.g. administrative, functional, economic). The definition (mainly in terms of borders) and description (features) of a neighbourhood is therefore a complex task.

This paper is an extended version of a short paper published in the DATA 2020 proceedings [3]. This work has been partially funded by LABEX IMU (ANR-10-LABX-0088) from Université de Lyon, in the context of the program "Investissements d'Avenir" (ANR-11-IDEX-0007) from the French Research Agency (ANR), during the HiL project.

© Springer Nature Switzerland AG 2021
S. Hammoudi et al. (Eds.): DATA 2020, CCIS 1446, pp. 267–292, 2021.
https://doi.org/10.1007/978-3-030-83014-4_13

When studying neighbourhoods, one of the challenges is to compare them according to some criteria. Different works have proposed solutions to tackle this issue. It is possible to exploit social networks data to detect similar neighbourhoods between cities [26] or in the same city [13,41]. Accommodation advertisements (rental or buying) are also used for predicting price and neighbourhood characteristics [39]. In a neighbourhood search, researchers assume that they have users, so they can compare their profiles to annotated ones [40] or their original neighbourhood with regards to target ones [4]. However, most of these works have a limited scope (e.g., a few cities) or the multiple comparison criteria make it difficult to understand the differences between two neighbourhoods. In a recent paper, we have proposed to compare environments of neighbourhoods [3]. In this extended version, we provide a complete description of the environment variables, a few improvements for computing this environment as well as a new method (for the *geographical position* variable), and an updated experimental validation including two extra experiments.

In the context of the HiL project[1], we aim at studying the impact of the neighbourhood environment when people moves in another city, i.e., we plan to answer questions such as *"do they choose a similar environment?"* and *"how does their possible salary increase affect their choice of neighbourhood?"*. Indeed, the choice of a neighbourhood may be difficult, especially without any prior knowledge about the future city. One may look for a vibrant neighbourhood with many pubs while other may prefer a quiet residential area close to schools and parks. To reach this goal, it is necessary to characterize environment of neighbourhoods in a simple way (i.e., with a few attributes, such as type of buildings, location of the neighbourhood in the city, main social class, etc.). Such description is useful for comparing neighbourhoods, for instance in social science studies or when searching for accommodations. However, in large countries, there are too many neighbourhoods (e.g., about 50,000 for France) and it is not possible to manually describe environment for each of them. We tackle this problem using an exploratory methodology and machine learning.

This paper includes the following contributions:

- Description of a neighbourhood environment. Based on the literature in social sciences and on a survey of 155 individuals, we propose a list of six variables (each with a limited number of values) to define this neighbourhood;
- Dataset `mongiris`. We describe which and how data have been integrated for about 50,000 French neighbourhoods (e.g., number of bakeries, average income), and we provide 270 neighbourhoods annotated with their environment. The resulting dataset named `mongiris` is publicly available;
- Methods for computing environment. We present one method using machine learning to predict environment, with a focus on the selection of the most interesting features. The `predihood` tool used to configure classifiers and to visualize neighbourhoods on a map is publicly available. Another method enables the computation of the *geographical position* variable;
- Experimental validation. A set of experiments on the French territory demonstrates the benefits of our proposals, as well as possible clues for improvement.

---

[1] HiL project, http://imu.universite-lyon.fr/projet/hil/.

We first introduce related work (Sect. 2). Next, we describe variables representing the environment of a neighbourhood (Sect. 3). Methods for computing environment are detailed in Sect. 4 while Sect. 5 presents and analyses experimental validation. Section 6 concludes and highlights perspectives.

2 Related Work

Most works dealing with modelling (urban) environment falls in the energy and transportation domains [35]. Multiple projects focus on studying neighbourhoods, but they do not aim at defining and describing their environments. As explained in the literature, the concept of neighbourhood is difficult to describe due to various perceptions [34], and each work provides its own definition and borders for neighbourhoods [8,20,24].

A first category of works relies on social networks, which contain a wealth of geolocated information, especially tweets, likes or check-ins. In the Livehoods project, the goal is to discover city's dynamics from its resident's behaviour [13]. Spatial and social proximities are used as input features of a spectral clustering algorithm, and the evaluation compares the machine-learning based algorithm fed with 18 million check-ins against the neighbourhood description from 27 interviews. In the same fashion, Le Falher et al. discover similar neighbourhoods between cities [26]. To reach this goal, they use classification algorithms applied on social networks data, namely *Information Theoretic Metric Learning* and *Large Margin Nearest Neighbour*. These algorithms build a matrix with human activities occurring in places along with surrounding points of interest, and the classes come from Foursquare categories. Next, they use the Earth Mover distance to measure the effort for "transforming" one area into another one. The Hoodsquare approach from Zhang et al. aims at detecting boundaries and similar areas [41]. Each neighbourhood is described as a vector of features (e.g., place types, Foursquare check-ins, temporal information) and similarity metrics such as Cosine similarity compute a similarity score between two neighbourhoods. Location recommendation is another motivation [29]. Authors do not rely on the user point of view, but rather on the location to neighbourhood characteristics. They assume that locations in the same neighbourhood share more similar user preferences, and that locations in the same region may share similar user preferences, thus leading to a two-level matrix factorization solution.

Another category exploits profiles of inhabitants. Researchers in South Korea have proposed to find the most relevant neighbourhood and accommodation based on similar user profiles [40]. They have built a database of residents, which includes information such as household composition, budget, accommodation preferences and distance from home to work. A new profile is compared to existing ones using case-based reasoning, and recommendations are adjusted consequently. A recent project *my neighbourhood, my neighbours*[2] analyses the relationships between residents in their neighbourhood. About 2,500 inhabitants from various areas (city centres, urban and peri-urban) in two cities (Lyon and Paris) have answered a survey about their vision of their neighbourhood, city and profile. Descriptions of residents provide an overall qualification

---

[2] Project *mon quartier, mes voisins*, http://mon-quartier-mes-voisins.site.ined.fr/.

of each considered neighbourhood. Preliminary results show that the neighbour perception strongly varies according to density and to social characteristics (e.g., young people include city centres while older ones constraint it to a few streets). Besides, they question the relevance of neighbourhoods in peri-urban areas. These results about neighbour representation confirm previous studies such as the one from Pan Ké Shon [32].

The last category relies on objective criteria that characterize neighbourhoods. The study from Tang et al. compares Airbnb announcements in San Francisco to determine their price and neighbourhood location [39]. The features include structured information (e.g., type of accommodation, number of rooms), bag of words (most frequent terms in the announcement), word class (among nine predefined classes such as nature, nightlife or culture), text sentiment and visual characteristics. In the VizLIRIS prototype, users may search for and visualize ideal neighbourhoods in the context of job transfers [4]. Hundreds of features are available to describe each area, such as the number of transportation means, the average income or inhabitants classified per socio-professional class. Distance-based algorithms (e.g., KMeans) are used for recommending neighbourhoods similar to selected ones while clustering algorithms enable the detection of similar neighbourhoods in a given area. In addition to scientific literature, many online applications produce neighbourhood recommendations, as described in the following list (centred on France and non exhaustive). The website DataFrance[3] integrates data from diverse French sources, such as indicators provided by the National Institute of Statistics[4] (INSEE), geographical information from the National Geographic Institute[5] (IGN) and surveys from newspapers for prices (L'Express[6]). The search for neighbourhoods which satisfy user criteria is performed manually through the interface. Kelquartier[7] describes the main French cities using quantitative criteria (e.g., average income, density of schools, density of shops). A manual search for neighbourhoods includes tens of criteria about the area (e.g., density of restaurants, schools), about real estate (e.g., building seniority, ratio of landlords) and about inhabitants (e.g., income, age, type of household). Home in Love[8], vivroù[9] and Cityzia[10] are more oriented towards users as they take into account itineraries (e.g., from and to work) or life style. All aim at recommending the most relevant neighbourhood(s). Finally, ville-ideale[11] is a collaborative website for evaluating French cities. Users can give a score (out of 10) for each of the ten categories, from healthcare to security or culture. Although limited to the city or district level, user comments frequently include mentions of neighbourhood, which may be useful for a (manual) assessment of the quality of a neighbourhood. Social science works also highlight the double perception

---

[3] DataFrance, http://datafrance.info/.

[4] INSEE, http://www.insee.fr/en/.

[5] IGN, http://www.ign.fr/.

[6] L'express, http://www.lexpress.fr/.

[7] Kelquartier, http://www.kelquartier.com/.

[8] Home in Love company (in French), http://homeinlove.fr/.

[9] Vivroù, http://www.vivrou.com/.

[10] Cityzia, http://www.cityzia.fr/.

[11] Ville idéale, http://www.ville-ideale.fr/.

of the neighbourhood, either from the inside (residents' perception) or from the outside (objective criteria) [2, 17].

Our contribution differs from existing works on several points. First, some works are limited to a few cities, which is not possible when studying population's trajectories. Indeed, rural migration is still very active, thus requiring a description of all areas. Relying on social data implies prior analysis in order to avoid bias (e.g., over-represented class of people or activities). User profiles are an interesting direction, but it requires a long and costly study to collect all necessary information (which, moreover, people may not be willing to provide). Criteria are not directly available for describing the environment of a neighbourhood, although some of them provide an insight (e.g., the average income is a clue for determining social class, but it is not sufficient and often relative to a local context). Besides, too many criteria makes it difficult both for obtaining a simple representation of the area and for comparing and understanding the choice of a neighbourhood. Finally, there is no work which aim at associating both perceptions of the neighbourhood (inside and outside), and it is a real challenge to automate what qualitative studies are able to do, but at larger scale.

3 Environment of a Neighbourhood

As previously explained, the notion of neighbourhood varies according to the point of view, making it more difficult to define representative criteria. Besides, most studies provide description about quality of life (e.g., security, health), which may include bias and subjectivity. In order to obtain a simple description of neighbourhoods, social science researchers have studied information about residents and their neighbourhoods and they have extracted a list of six descriptive variables for neighbourhoods. Our proposal focuses on France, but could be applied to similar countries.

3.1 Neighbourhood Definition

Neighbourhoods have a different definition according to usage [2, 8, 20]. For instance, geographers mainly rely on natural borders while inhabitants have a less precise vision of the boundaries. Voting and cadastral definitions are typically used by administrative employees. Historical or economical divisions may also impact the definition.

In our context, we have chosen a small division unit of the French territory named IRIS[12] to represent our neighbourhoods. They are produced by the National Institute of Statistics (INSEE) and are considered of good quality due to their frequent updates and wide use by many organizations. An IRIS usually includes between 2,000 up to 5,000 residents, and consequently are rather small in cities while their size increases in the countryside. These units are constrained by geographic and demographic criteria and their borders are easily identifiable and stable in the long term. There exist three types of IRIS: housing (accounting for around 90% of the dataset), activities or business (e.g., industrial area, university campus), and miscellaneous (e.g., parks, forests). The French territory is split into 49,800 IRIS. In the rest of the paper, we use the term

---

[12] IRIS definition, http://www.insee.fr/en/metadonnees/definition/c1523/.

neighbourhood instead of IRIS. Indeed, although they are defined as statistical division units, IRIS are considered as a reliable approximation of the perceived neighbourhood: in outside urban areas, they are usually similar to the town, and in large cities, they enable to estimate the diversity of people (and environment elements) which are met in daily activities [31]. Last, one of the objectives of this paper is to check whether an approach based at the IRIS level is sufficient to simulate the perceived neighbourhood.

3.2   Methodology for Defining Environment

We have analysed data from a company(see Footnote 8) specialized in accompanying the search of an accommodation during job transfers. The dataset is not available for confidentiality reasons. At the time of writing, it includes 155 customers (each representing an household), thus 310 locations (previous accommodation before the job transfer, and the new one). Some customers came from other countries (no neighbourhood information), and several neighbourhoods were redundant (e.g., several people moving to the same village close to a large industrial factory). Our dataset results in a total of 270 distinct neighbourhoods. For each customer, hundreds of information are available in various categories:

- Personal information (names, birthdate, household composition, etc.);
- Work information (label, socio-professional category, salary, etc.) both for the previous job and the new one;
- Tax information, which may explain some situations, for instance when people have other incomes than salaries;
- Address of the previous accommodation, and address of the new accommodation (which was discovered using the company's services). From these data, we deduce the neighbourhoods;
- Expenses (credit, rental, monthly bills, etc.);
- Accommodation (description from real-estate agencies, type of heat-system, presence of amenities such as garden, parking or swimming-pool, shared equipments, etc.);
- Profile (optional and filled in by customers);
- Ideal accommodation (optional and filled in by customers);
- Expectations about the future neighbourhood (optional and filled in by customers);
- A narrative analysis, written by social science researchers, about the life style and story of the household (e.g., marriage, type of neighbourhood), including assumptions about the job transfer (social trajectory) and about accommodation search.

The main idea is to study the environment of these households, mainly in terms of social, material and natural aspects. Our methodology is independent from households' profiles, and it includes the exploitation of household data and data from Google Maps, namely aerial and street views, photographs of buildings, urban furniture, parked cars, type and brand of shops, leisures and park areas. The virtual exploration of a neighbourhood enables a detailed observation of the environmental surroundings of each address, in a variable radius. The closest environment (400 m radius) is always analysed, and if needed, further exploration is performed[13]. A careful attention was taken about seasons

---

[13] The scale differences for analysing the environment make it difficult to automate the process, hence one of the objectives of this paper.

(e.g., less green areas visible in winter) as well as the date of street views (no more than four years). A description of the neighbourhood based on these observations are stored so that objective and fine-grained comparisons between two addresses are possible at very small scale (usually smaller than the neighbourhood). Finally, this exploration provides means of comparison between both accommodations of the same customer for studying residential choices. Note that this manual observation step takes several hours (per address/neighbourhood) when rigorously performed.

From this analysis, neighbourhoods were characterized and classified into six categories, built using an inductive process (popular in social sciences). The various decisions which led to this classification involve (a part of) arbitrary choices and subjectivity. But our methodology consists in classifying using very detailed and meticulous observation and interpretation, rather than relying on more "objective" data produced by different providers. Three additional verifications were performed to comfort our decisions, namely investigation with related social science works, consistency with external data sources about neighbourhoods (DataFrance (see Footnote 3) and KelQuartier (see Footnote 7)) and consistency between departure neighbourhood and arrival neighbourhood of an household (given their situation). For this last point, an initial question deals with the comparison of both neighbourhoods. Indeed, the context of job transfer implies that employees usually search for a similar neighbourhood to the one they come from, mainly for securing the residence change [36]. If two neighbourhoods are not similar, researchers check how information about the household (e.g., salary increase, children) and/or the city (e.g., moving from a costly city to a small town) could explain the differences between both neighbourhoods. Redundant neighbourhoods (where different people originate or arrive) were also exploited as a verification means. This methodology provides a solid background for defining the environment of a neighbourhood, which is presented in the next section.

3.3 Six Variables for Environment Neighbourhood

Social science researchers followed the previously mentioned methodology to define 6 environment variables, whose goal is to facilitate the description and the comparison of neighbourhoods. These variables are summarized in Table 1 along with their list of values. *Building type* refers to the most common buildings in the neighbourhood. *Usage* represents local activities and *landscape* defines the space conceded to green areas. *Social class* stands for the stratification of a population according to position in the social hierarchy. *Morphological position* can be seen as the relationship to centrality. *Geographical position* denotes the direction towards the city centre of the closest city.

Let us now provide more details about each variable:

Building Type. We have distinguished five categories. *Large housing estates* are composed of similar residential towers, such as social housing or winter sports apartments. A neighbourhood classified as *buildings* usually stands for areas with heterogeneous buildings. *Mixed* neighbourhoods are typically found in cities and combine other possible values. Contrary to *housing subdivisions*, individual *houses* (both in cities and rural areas) are heterogeneous in terms of construction period or architecture;

Table 1. Environment variables and their possible values.

Environment variable	Values (comments)
Building type	Large housing estates (homogeneous tower conglomerate)
	Mixed (both buildings and houses)
	Buildings (heterogeneous)
	Housing subdivisions (homogeneous)
	Houses (heterogeneous)
Usage	Residential area (few local shops)
	Shopping (areas with many local shops)
	Other activities (mixed zones with factories, companies and some houses, usually outside cities)
Landscape	Urban (high density of buildings, near absence of green areas)
	Green areas (built area, but with some natural spaces)
	Forest (high density of green areas or forests)
	Countryside (crop fields and natural areas)
Social class	Lower
	Lower middle
	Middle
	Upper middle
	Upper
Morphological position	Central
	Urban (in the main town, but not in the centre)
	Peri-urban (at the periphery of the city)
	Rural (area further than urban and peri-urban areas)
Geographical position (9 different values)	Centre
	North
	North East
	East
	...

Usage. Three main categories enable to classify the studied environments. In a *residential area* neighbourhood, there is almost no shop. They are usually found at the periphery of urban areas or in housing subdivisions. *Shopping* areas, usually in city centres, are marked by a high density of local shops. The last category (*other activities*) corresponds in general to areas located at the borders between urban and peri-urban, with houses surrounded by companies, large commercial zones and factories. This variable could include more categories (e.g., arts, education, nightlife, work), as in the Hoodsquare project [41]. However, in our context of job transfer (with many people searching in peri-urban areas), the main goal is to distinguish the usage in peri-urban areas (and not necessarily those in urban zones). Besides, adding more general categories would not be sufficient as users are interested in specific types of point of interest (e.g., kindergarten or elementary school, bakery, organic shops);

Landscape. Four types of sceneries have been identified according to the density of surrounding green areas and plants as well as their natural state. Neighbourhoods classified as *urban* imply a quasi-absence of plants. *Green areas* offers a significant presence of parks, gardens or tree alleys, but they are delimited and maintained. *Forest* are wooded neighbourhoods where green areas are strongly visible. Finally, the *countryside* value includes agricultural and farming spaces, as well as natural zones with few buildings (mountains, vast forests);

Social Class. This variable is one of the most studied in social sciences [9,23,31]. In our context, we defined 5 groups of social class, ranging from *lower, lower middle* and *middle* up to *upper middle* and *upper*. To perform this classification, we rely on various revealing clues from our observations of the people living in the studied neighbourhoods: architectural aspects of buildings, position in the city, type and brand of local shops, type and brand of parked cars, configuration of outdoor spaces, etc. Social class is certainly the environment variable which involves the most difficult interpretation. The difference between a middle-upper area and an upper one, or at the other end of the social hierarchy, between a lower and a lower-middle neighbourhood, may not be visible from the external view of a neighbourhood, especially in urban and central which includes more social diversity [14]. However, and although the choices between close classes may be tenuous, we note that our observations were clearly sufficient to determine the main trend (i.e., rather lower, rather middle or rather upper), which are critical in peri-urban settings;

Morphological Position. The morphology criterion has been divided into four values: *central, urban, peri-urban* and *rural*, each denoting a placing according to the centrality of a geographic area. Neighbourhoods in each category may share trends or characteristics. This variable also enables sociologists to study phenomena such as rural flight and urban planning.

Geographical Position. This variable indicates the direction towards the city centre of the closest city. This is an essential information for peri-urban neighbourhoods. Indeed, a central morphologic area may not be geographically centred (e.g., the main shopping and service area of the peri-urban town Vénissieux is central, but the city centre of the largest city Lyon is located north). Urban areas were not built at random, and people with a similar lifestyle tend to live in the same neighbourhood. For instance, it is well-known that East districts were poorer due to industrial pollution coming from West winds [37]. Thus, detecting the geographical position can help when analysing population in neighbourhoods. In rural areas, this variable represents the direction of the closest large city. Note that our work does not take into account poly-centralities (i.e., secondary cities, which may be as attractive as the largest city for surrounding peri-urban towns).

3.4   An Example of Environment in Lyon Part Dieu

To illustrate these environment variables, let us describe the neighbourhood *Part Dieu*, in the city centre of Lyon, France. In the INSEE data, this neighbourhood is identified with code *693830301* and is located in Lyon 3rd district. Its activity type is A, which stands for a commercial, services, or industrial area (i.e., which includes more workers than residents). Figure 1 depicts views of this neighbourhood: the left picture shows the border of the neighbourhood while the right one provides an aerial view. We notice that it includes the main railway station of the city, business towers including a large mall,

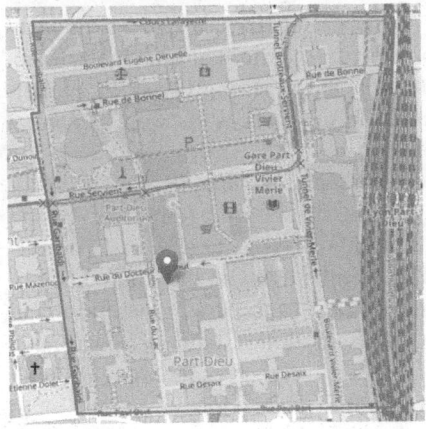
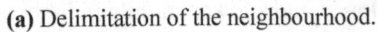

(a) Delimitation of the neighbourhood.   (b) Aerial view.

Fig. 1. The *Part Dieu* neighbourhood, Lyon, France (source Google Maps).

movie theatre, the main library, the auditorium, hotels and some important administrative buildings.

Social science researchers have described the environment of *Part Dieu* neighbourhood as shown in Table 2. The building type is mainly composed of buildings, and its usage is indeed dedicated to shopping as the first floor of most buildings is dedicated to merchant activities. Although we notice some trees in the aerial view, the perception is clearly urban in the neighbourhood. The last variables are easier to check, since this neighbourhood is obviously central (in the city) and in the centre of the closest city. Researchers also provided a short description about the accommodation in its area. For the household living in *Lyon Part Dieu*, the comment is *"Building from the 1930's, along the Jean-Jaurès avenue, close to many shops"*.

Table 2. Environment variables for neighbourhood *Part Dieu*, in Lyon.

Building type	Buildings
Usage	Shopping
Landscape	Urban
Social class	Upper middle
Morphological	Central
Geographical	Centre

3.5 Statistics and Representativeness

To conclude this section, we provide statistics about the classifications of our 270 neighbourhoods and their representativeness with regards to the whole country.

Table 3 depicts the value distribution per variable. We note that households either live in buildings (apartments), houses or mixed areas, and half of them are located in residential areas according to the *usage* variable. The *social class* variable is over-represented by the middle and upper middle classes. The type of *landscape* is typical from cities (urban and green areas), which is consistent not only with the morphological situation focused around the centre and urban areas, but also with the job transfer context. Finally the *geographical position* shows some favoured directions such as Centre, East, North and South.

Table 3. Statistics of neighbourhoods according to environment variables.

Building type	
Large housing estates	11
Mixed	89
Buildings	91
Housing subdivisions	34
Houses	45

Social	
Lower	11
Lower middle	13
Middle	89
Upper middle	124
Upper	33

Usage	
Residential area	145
Shopping	91
Others	34

Geographical	
Centre	58
North	43
North East	17
East	55
South East	18
South	34
South West	8
West	26
North West	11

Landscape	
Urban	102
Green areas	122
Forest	24
Countryside	22

Morphological	
Central	89
Urban	74
Peri-urban	93
Rural	14

Next, we check how representative our dataset of 270 annotated neighbourhoods is with regards to the total number of French neighbourhoods (49,800). It only represents 0.6% of this total, which may not be sufficient for machine learning algorithms used for predicting environment of the remaining neighbourhoods.

Building Type and Usage. Both variables are difficult to verify, as there are few additional information about the composition of neighbourhoods.

Morphological Position. This variable indicates whether a neighbourhood is inside or far from a city. Based on the INSEE methodology for constructing their division unit(see footnote 14), one third of the neighbourhoods (16,100) are found in cities with more than 10,000 inhabitants and most towns with more than 5,000 inhabitants. Remaining locations (33,700) were considered as sparsely populated and a single unit is affected to each one. Assuming these small towns are rural areas, they account for 68% of the whole dataset, while our annotated dataset only includes 5% of rural neighbourhoods. This difference is easily understandable due to our context of job transfers, mainly to the benefit of big cities.

Landscape. This variable is closely related to the morphological position. If we assume that forest and countryside are representative of rural areas, they obtain a representation of 17%, which is disconnected from the 68% expected in France but consistent with the 5% previously mentioned rural neighbourhoods.

Social Class. Classification of the population according to wealth is not an easy task, and many studies have their own definitions and categories. According to Bigot et al. [7], the French population includes 59% of households belong to the middle class (in a broad meaning, thus encompassing lower and upper middles). This middle class is defined with incomes ranging from 70% to 150% of the median income (1,750 euros for 2014), which corresponds to 71% of neighbourhoods in the country. Conversely, our dataset includes 82% of middle class neighbourhoods.

Geographical Position. Although this variable is more balanced, a few directions appear more frequently (e.g., South, East, North). Providing an explanation for these cases requires more research in social sciences. The centre value is the most represented, since it is correlated with the central morphological position. A comparison with the whole dataset is difficult: computing the direction of the closest city for all areas depends on several parameters, as shown in Sect. 4.4.

To summarize, we have identified six environment variables from a dataset of 270 annotated neighbourhoods. Compared to the full set of neighbourhoods, the *morphological* and *landscape* variables are biased, and the *social class* variable includes a small bias too. The dataset is not representative of the whole country as it focuses on moving employees. Besides, we are less interested in urban neighbourhoods, contrary to similar works which mainly study old or sensitive neighbourhoods, thus promoting peri-urban study. Even without a fair representativeness, our dataset is interesting as it provides a diversity of environments. However, identified biases may have an impact for predicting environment of any neighbourhood, as described in the next section.

4   Computing Environment

To compare resident's moves between neighbourhoods, it is important to annotate the environment of all neighbourhoods. Manual annotation is a time-consuming process (see Sect. 3.2), thus an automatic solution is preferable. We propose two approaches for computing the environment of a neighbourhood: prediction (using machine learning algorithms) and spatial computation (only for the *geographical position* variable). Figure 2 depicts the whole process. First, data description aims at gathering and collecting relevant data sources about neighbourhoods. They are integrated into a merged database named *mongiris*. From this point, the top approach predicts the environment by selecting relevant features and applying machine learning training and testing while the alternative approach enables the computation of the *geographical* variable.

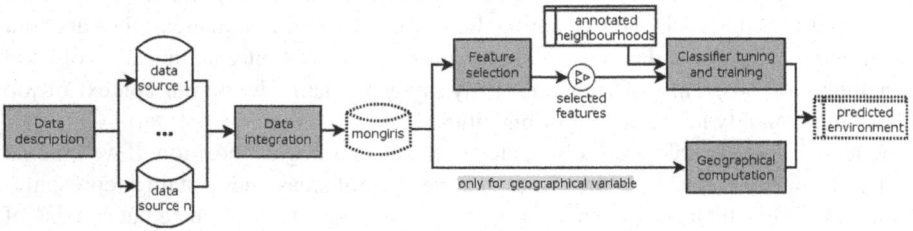

Fig. 2. Process for computing environment of any neighbourhood.

4.1 Data Description

A predictive approach requires features to build a model and classify instances. The adoption of Open Data principles has led to a wealth of information available in different data sources [1]. Following is a description of considered data sources:

- **IRIS Data.** As explained in Sect. 3.1, we selected the unit division IRIS as neighbourhoods, a choice also supported by the fact that they come with many indicators about population, buildings, shops, leisures, education, etc. These data are updated every 4 years, and we use the 2016 version. First, each neighbourhood includes 17 descriptive information (identifier, name, city name, postcode, administrative department, administrative region, type, etc.). These indicators are mostly useful for visualization. The remaining hundreds of indicators are either quantities (e.g., number of bakeries, of elementary schools, of buildings built before 1950, of tennis courts), unit quantities (e.g., average income, average income for the agricultural class), coefficients (e.g., Gini coefficient[14], S80/S20 ratio[15]), percentages (e.g., percentage of unemployed people, percentage of fiscal households) or string values (e.g. notes about incomes);
- **Spatial Data.** Each neighbourhood has a geometry (i.e., list of coordinates delimiting a polygon), which is useful for cartographic visualization. From this geometry, it is possible to compute the surface of the neighbourhood, an important feature either as an indicator[16] or for normalizing other data;
- **Prices.** This information is valuable in the sense that it can leverage several environment variables. For instance, costly accommodations are typically found in richer neighbourhoods, situated in the city centres or close to remarkable locations such as green areas or historic buildings. Prices in large cities are usually higher than in small cities, thus peri-urban neighbourhoods of large cities may have comparable prices to central areas in small cities. Local context is therefore needed to wisely exploit prices. In addition, this kind of sensible or monetizable information is usually incomplete or rarely available for free. It is available as open data at a higher cartographic level (administrative department), which is not sufficiently accurate to be useful. In DataFrance (see Footnote 3), prices are only available for 600 cities, based on a newspaper survey. Real estate agencies own such data, but it may be biased (e.g., towards a specific type of accommodation), incomplete (e.g., specific to a region) and/or confidential. The recent DVF project[17] provides prices of all sold buildings per year, but it requires more work for deduplication (sales are filled in at the parcel level, but not at the accommodation level) and exploitation (issues related to local context, spatial conflicts, management of the annual sales) [12]. Besides there is no database about rents. Currently, we have not included any price information;
- **List of Points of Interest (POI).** IRIS data only provide a number of shops, but not their names. Yet, the presence of a given brand may convey information about the neighbourhood. For instance, an organic shop is usually found in middle or upper

---

[14] Gini coefficient, http://en.wikipedia.org/wiki/Gini_coefficient.
[15] S80/20 ratio, http://www.insee.fr/en/metadonnees/definition/c1666.
[16] Neighbourhoods in cities tend to be small while those in rural areas have a larger size.
[17] Accommodation prices in France, http://app.dvf.etalab.gouv.fr/.

class neighbourhoods. Providers could be private companies (e.g., Bing Maps, Here) or collaborative projects (e.g., Open Street Map), but there may be limitations (e.g., data usage policies, numbers of daily queries, management of obsolete locations and updated ones). Although the GeoAlign tool could be used to gather POI with a high degree of completeness [5], it requires a deeper study to select the most relevant brands.

These data sources provide heterogeneous models, formats and semantics, thus an integration step and a quality check is required.

4.2 Data Integration

Relevant data about neighbourhoods are extracted from identified data sources (using dumps, API, queries), but they need to be merged into a single model. Since we manipulate spatial objects, we have chosen the GeoJSON format[18] to store neighbourhoods and their features.

Data integration is a common task [22]. Spatial data is stored according to the OGC standard Geometry Model [19] while IRIS features are scattered in tens of CSV files (one for population, another one for education, etc.), produced at different periods, by different persons and using various concept representations. Thus, data may contain anomalies, inconsistencies or missing values and need to be cleaned through data cleaning or data wrangling processes [15].

First, we have performed a manual schema matching step [6], i.e. the detection of corresponding attributes between data sources. There is no need to use a dedicated tool since the attributes' overlapping is limited and renaming headers in CSV files solves most label heterogeneity issues. The next step is record linkage or data matching [11], which consists in detecting equivalent information (e.g., tuples, entities, values) between data sources, mainly in order to avoid duplicates in the merged database. Each IRIS has its own identifier, but the following modifications may occur from one data source to another: some IRIS were simply missing (e.g., no information about education in this neighbourhood), several IRIS were merged into a single new one or split into smaller units (e.g., due to diverse federations of towns[19], more than 1,250 in 2020). We developed a Python script to enable the detection of these challenging modifications, based on names (both IRIS and city) comparisons and area juxtaposition.

During the integration of data sources into a single database, we computed the surface of polygons. A few neighbourhoods have incorrect boundaries such as overlapping edges in their geometries and they have been corrected using GIS tools. Moreover, there may be some unknown values (e.g., no information about the number of florists in a small town). These values have been replaced by the median score of the column: zero values are not acceptable (already a specific meaning, i.e., a neighbourhood does not have a given feature) and the average is more sensitive to outliers. Another issue is the difference of units and meaning between indicators (e.g., quantities, percentages, quantiles). Some classification algorithms require comparable information. Social science

---

[18] GeoJSON format, http://geojson.org/.
[19] Federation of towns, http://en.wikipedia.org/wiki/Communes_of_France#Intercommunality.

researchers suggested that population and population density were the most relevant normalization factors. Both the size and the number of residents have an impact on the characteristics of a neighbourhood (e.g., two areas may have 5,000 residents, but one of them is a large rural area around a village while the other is a small city area). Consequently, all indicators have been normalized according to the population density. Lastly, we have created a new attribute labelled *grouped indicators*, which reflects the characteristics of a neighbourhood with a higher level of abstraction. For example, the grouped indicator *health* sums up the number of doctors, pharmacies, hospitals, etc. Local commerces (which exclude large supermarkets) aggregate the number of bakeries, butcheries, open markets, etc. In total, 30 grouped indicators have been defined and added as features for each neighbourhood.

In the end, we obtain a consolidated MongoDB database named `mongiris`[20]. It contains 49,800 French neighbourhoods fully covering the country. Each of them includes an average of 550 raw indicators from data sources and 30 grouped indicators. A Python API is also provided to facilitate the querying of the database (e.g., retrieve a neighbourhood from its code, get a list of all surrounding neighbourhoods of a given one).

4.3 Predicting Environment

Our neighbourhoods include a number of indicators, and they can be used for predicting the environment of any neighbourhood. One of the issue is the high number of indicators (550 in average), which may degrade the performance of machine learning techniques due to over-fitting. Indeed, Lillesand et al. have established that a reasonable number of features f is given by the formula $10f > n > 100f$, with n the size of training data [28]. In our context, we have 270 annotated examples, thus we should use between 3 and 27 indicators as features.

To solve this problem, we reduce the number of features as follows. Descriptive features (17) such as city or neighbourhood names are removed, as well as indicators that are either empty or filled in with the same value[21] (59). INSEE indicators can also be very detailed. For instance, one field counts the number of "tennis courts", a second one stands for the number of "tennis courts with at least one covered", and another one about the number of "tennis courts with at least one lighted". A hierarchy of all indicators has been semi-automatically built, and 213 over-detailed ones have been removed (only "tennis courts" is kept as feature in the previous example). Most neighbourhoods still have many features (362 remaining for those with the maximum of 647). Next, we study the correlation between indicators using the Spearman coefficient [30]. When a pair of indicators obtains 100% correlation, we discard the one which is the most detailed (i.e., at lower levels in our hierarchy).

A last option for reducing the number of indicators is to produce lists of selected features for each variable. Feature importance is a popular method to reach this goal [21], but it may promote the same category of indicators (e.g., population, incomes) to the detriment of category diversity. We therefore propose Algorithm 1, an algorithm

---

[20] Mongiris database, http://gitlab.liris.cnrs.fr/fduchate/mongiris.

[21] Indicators from INSEE may not be filled in (empty or default value), especially for data provided by local communities (small towns may not have the resources to manage this task).

based on existing feature selection techniques. It first generates ranked lists of features (lines 3 and 4) based on the Extra Trees (ET) and Random Forest (RF) techniques. The output of these algorithms are merged, and the resulting table sorted with indicators at the higher level of our hierarchy ranked first (lines 5 and 6). To avoid strong impact of a single category, an indicator is removed if its parent is already in the list (lines 8 to 10), else it is added in the resulting set F' (line 12). Merged indicators are then sorted by score (line 13). In the end, we obtain several list of features noted L_v^k which contain the most k relevant indicators for variable v. We have chosen to retain several lists containing from 10 to 100 indicators due to the complexity of prediction.

Algorithm 1. Selection of relevant features (adapted from [3]).

```
    input  : set of indicators I, set of variables V
    output: lists of features L_v^k
1   for v ∈ V do                              /* for each environment variable */
2   │   L_v, F' ⟵ ∅;
3   │   F_v^ET ⟵ ET.rank_features(I);          /* selected features of Extra Trees */
4   │   F_v^RF ⟵ RF.rank_features(I);    /* selected features of Random Forest */
5   │   F ⟵ F_v^ET ∪ F_v^RF;
6   │   F ⟵ sort(F);/* sort from general to specific w.r.t. hierarchy */
7   │   for f ∈ F do
8   │   │   p_f ⟵ parent(f);
9   │   │   if p_f ∈ F' then
10  │   │   │   └ p_f.score ⟵ p_f.score + f.score;    /* boost parent score in F' */
11  │   │   else
12  │   │   │   └ F' ⟵ F' + {f};                        /* add feature in F' */
13  │   F' ⟵ sort(F');                       /* sort by descending score */
14  │   for k ∈ [10, 20, 30, 40, 50, 75, 100] do  /* generate lists of various size */
15  │   │   └ L_v^k ⟵ top-K(F', k);
```

When features have been selected, the next step is the prediction using machine learning. We are in a classification problem[22] since the objective is to classify a neighbourhood according to the possible values of an environment variable. Thus we generate one instance of a classifier per variable. The main issue is to choose a relevant classifier and to correctly tune its parameters (e.g., thresholds, weights, distance metric), which have a considerable impact on the achieved quality [25]. Due to the complexity of adjusting these parameters, we have developed the predihood[23] tool to ease this task.

This machine learning based method is general (i.e., applicable to all variables), but the geographical variable can be directly computed using cartographic systems, as presented in the next part.

---

[22] Predicting all variables at the same time is a multi-output classification problem, which is more complicated to manage and more adapted to correlated classes.

[23] Predihood tool, http://gitlab.liris.cnrs.fr/fduchate/predihood.

4.4 Computing Geographical Variable

Rather than predicting the direction of the closest city, it is possible to directly compute this value. Let us describe this idea. Starting from a given neighbourhood, we search for a large city by iteratively increasing the search radius. When a large city is found, two representative points for the neighbourhood and the city are calculated, and the direction between these points is then computed.

Several questions arise from this idea. First, how to define a large city? And how to compare the surface of a neighbourhood with the one of a city? How to deal with the centre value, which does not include a clear definition? To enable some flexibility in our approach with regards to these questions, various parameters were introduced:

- MAX_DISTANCE is the maximum radius to search within;
- MIN_CITY is the minimum number of neighbourhoods so that the city can be considered as a large one;
- DISTANCE_CENTRE is the distance below which a neighbourhood is considered in the centre of the found city;
- INCREASE_RADIUS is the distance to be added to the search radius at each iteration;
- REF_POINTS is a method for representing the neighbourhood and the city, either by their centroids or by their nearest points;
- ANGLE_DIRECTIONS is the choice of angles, either *45* (for all directions) or *30–60* (small angles for the four major cardinal points and higher value for corners such as NW, NE, SE and SW, in order to better reflect human estimation).

Algorithm 2 presents our approach for computing the direction of the largest city given an input neighbourhood. Previously mentioned parameters appear in small capital letters. The recursive function *compute_city* (lines 1 to 9) is in charge of returning the largest city by an iterative search. It collects all neighbourhoods in the considered area, and groups them according to city postcode. The city with the highest number of neighbourhoods is extracted from this counting, and its number of neighbourhoods is compared to a threshold value to decide whether it is a sufficiently large city. If not, the function calls itself by incrementing the search radius. The main procedure starts at line 10. It first computes the reference points of both the neighbourhood and its city, so that it checks whether the former is in the city centre (lines 11 to 14). If not, a search for large city τ is performed (line 15), and its reference point is also calculated (line 17). To compute the direction between both reference points, we compute the difference between their coordinates (lines 18 and 19). To use the arctangent function, we first check that both points are not located on the same longitude (lines 20 to 23), and we compute the angle between both points (line 24). As the arctangent function returns values in the range $[-90, +90]$, the function *get_direction_from_angle* performs some adjustments (e.g., adding 180 for dials on the West side), and it returns the cardinal direction according to the choice of angles (line 25).

This algorithm is generic due to various parameters, and we show in the next section how their tuning affects the overall quality.

Algorithm 2. Computation of geographical variable.

---

input : neighbourhood η
output: direction

```
1  function compute_city(point, radius)
2      if radius > MAX_DISTANCE then                              /* no large city found */
3          return ∅;
4      N ⟵ get_neighbours(point, radius);
5      c ⟵ extract_largest_city(N) ;              /* neighbourhoods grouped by city */
6      nb_c ⟵ count_neighbourhoods(c);
7      if nb_c > MIN_CITY then    /* number of neighbourhoods above threshold */
8          return c;
9      return compute_city(point, radius + INCREASE_RADIUS);

10  c_η ⟵ get_city(η) ;                            /* city of the neighbourhood */
11  p_η ⟵ get_ref_point(η, METHOD) ;        /* reference point of neighbourhood */
12  p_{c_η} ⟵ get_ref_point(c_η, METHOD) ;              /* reference point of city */
13  if Δ(p_η, p_{c_η}) < DISTANCE_CENTRE then      /* neighbourhood in city centre */
14      return 'Centre';

15  τ ⟵ compute_city(p_η, 1000) ;               /* large city for the neighbourhood */
16  if τ ≠ ∅ then                                   /* a large city has been found */
17      p_τ ⟵ get_ref_point(τ, METHOD) ;         /* reference point of large city */
18      δ_y ⟵ p_η.y − p_τ.y;
19      δ_x ⟵ p_η.x − p_τ.x;
20      if δ_x = 0 and δ_y > 0 then                 /* dial N, avoids divide by zero */
21          return 'North';
22      if δ_x = 0 and δ_y < 0 then                 /* dial S, avoids divide by zero */
23          return 'South';
24      angle ⟵ 180 × arctan(δ_y/δ_x)/π ;   /* angle in [-90, +90], East at 0 */
25      direction ⟵ get_direction_from_angle(angle, ANGLE_DIRECTIONS);
26      return direction;
```

---

5   Experimental Validation

Three experiments are presented in this section: quality results of the prediction with various classifiers (Sect. 5.1), without rural neighbourhoods (Sect. 5.2), and quality results of the geographical computation (Sect. 5.3).

For experiments based on machine learning, we use the popular scikit-learn library for machine learning [33]. The annotated neighbourhoods are split into 80% training data and 20% evaluation data, as recommended in the literature [10]. We use accuracy as quality metric, i.e. the fraction of correct predictions, which is the average quality obtained by 10 runs.

An open discussion concludes this section.

5.1 Predicting with Different Classifiers

In this first experiment, the main objective is to correctly predict the values for each environment variable of a neighbourhood (Sect. 4.3). We have used 5 scikit-learn algorithms[24]: Logistic Regression (LR), Random Forest (RF), K-Nearest Neighbours (KNN), Support Vector Classification (SVC), and AdaBoost (AB). Many parameters have an impact in machine learning [25], and we tested several configurations (e.g., weights, maximum depth in trees, number of neighbours, distance metric) to retain the best one. We also measure the impact of the proposed lists for selecting indicators (see Sect. 4.3). Tables 4 to 9 provide the accuracy score (percentage) computed for each variable using different algorithms. In these tables, the baseline list I stands for all indicators (i.e., no feature selection) while L^k represents a list of k selected features. The <u>underlined scores</u> indicate the best result for an algorithm (i.e., by column). A **bold score** means that the corresponding list of features achieves a better score than the list I. The highlighted cells correspond to the best score in the whole table.

Table 4 presents the quality results for the *building type* variable. Without feature selection, quality spans from 36% to 57%. Smaller lists enable an improvement over list I (e.g., L^{20}). The best score is achieved by RF with list L^{20}.

Table 5 shows prediction quality for the *usage* variable. The scores without selection range from 51.1% to 64.5%. A few of the smallest lists perform better than the baseline one, but without significant improvement. RF obtains the best results with list L^{50}.

Table 6 provides accuracy scores for the *landscape* variable. Similarly to previous results, small lists are able to improve quality over list I with three algorithms. SVC obtains the same score whatever the list of features.

Table 7 depicts quality results for the *social class* variable. The lists of selected features, either small or large depending on the algorithm, allows a better quality in a few cases. The best score is slightly above 50%, which shows that this variable is difficult to predict. Yet, many features describe incomes (median, per decile) and population characteristics (number of students, employees, farmers, unemployed, etc.).

Table 8 details quality obtained for the *morphological position*. The L^{10} list mainly wins against the baseline list, except with SVC which achieves similar scores (44%) whatever the features.

Table 9 is dedicated to *geographical position*. Scores are far lower than for other variables (33% as best value), which is not surprising given the *a-priori* irrelevant indicators for this prediction. Still, small lists mostly perform better than the baseline. As shown in Sect. 5.3, these results can be improved by computing the value of the geographical variable instead of predicting it.

To conclude this experiment, we note that best scores range from 33% for geographical position and 50% for *social class* to 60–65% for the remaining four variables. Although algorithms obtain different scores with the baseline list, their results mainly improve by a few percent (in average per column) when using other lists of features, which could demonstrate that current indicators are not sufficient or useful. Our algorithm for feature selection has also proven useful, since many lists outperform the baseline (whatever the algorithm or variable). Lists of 20 up to 50 features are particularly

---

[24] Other algorithms such as Stochastic Gradient Descent or Nearest Centroid have been tested, but they mostly follow the same trend or achieve insufficient accuracy.

Table 4. Prediction quality for variable *building type* (from [3]).

	LR	RF	KNN	SVC	AB
I	46.6	57.0	55.2	45.5	36.5
L^{10}	44.3	**59.3**	<u>**57.8**</u>	44.7	**41.7**
L^{20}	**49.2**	**60.0**	56.3	43.6	**43.6**
L^{30}	45.1	**58.9**	**55.9**	43.6	32.1
L^{40}	46.2	**59.3**	54.8	43.2	27.6
L^{50}	46.6	**58.9**	54.8	45.5	32.4
L^{75}	44.3	**58.2**	55.2	<u>**45.9**</u>	32.0
L^{100}	43.6	57.0	55.2	45.5	36.5

Table 5. Prediction quality for variable *usage* (from [3]).

	LR	RF	KNN	SVC	AB
I	52.9	64.5	59.3	<u>51.1</u>	55.6
L^{10}	52.6	61.2	<u>**63.8**</u>	49.6	**59.6**
L^{20}	**55.9**	64.1	**63.0**	49.6	**56.6**
L^{30}	51.1	61.2	**62.3**	49.6	**60.8**
L^{40}	<u>**57.8**</u>	63.0	**60.8**	49.2	**56.3**
L^{50}	**56.3**	<u>**64.9**</u>	62.2	46.6	<u>**61.1**</u>
L^{75}	50.7	63.4	**60.8**	51.1	**58.2**
L^{100}	**53.7**	64.5	59.3	51.1	55.6

Table 6. Prediction quality for variable *landscape* (from [3]).

	LR	RF	KNN	SVC	AB
I	53.7	60.8	59.6	<u>47.7</u>	50.3
L^{10}	48.1	**62.7**	59.6	<u>47.7</u>	**51.8**
L^{20}	51.5	<u>**63.0**</u>	60.4	<u>47.7</u>	**52.6**
L^{30}	50.3	60.8	**61.9**	<u>47.7</u>	**52.5**
L^{40}	49.2	**62.7**	61.5	<u>47.7</u>	49.2
L^{50}	47.7	**61.5**	61.1	<u>47.7</u>	48.1
L^{75}	52.6	**62.3**	59.3	<u>47.7</u>	48.5
L^{100}	<u>**56.3**</u>	60.8	59.6	<u>47.7</u>	50.3

Table 7. Prediction quality for variable *social class* (from [3]).

	LR	RF	KNN	SVC	AB
I	44.4	51.1	42.1	45.5	36.5
L^{10}	43.6	46.6	**43.9**	44.7	**41.7**
L^{20}	39.1	46.6	**45.1**	43.6	**43.6**
L^{30}	41.4	49.6	**45.1**	43.6	32.1
L^{40}	39.1	**51.8**	<u>**46.6**</u>	43.2	27.6
L^{50}	42.1	48.1	**44.3**	45.5	32.4
L^{75}	<u>**45.1**</u>	48.1	**44.0**	<u>**45.9**</u>	32.0
L^{100}	40.7	51.1	42.1	45.5	36.5

Table 8. Prediction quality for variable *morphological* (from [3]).

	LR	RF	KNN	SVC	AB
I	46.6	59.7	58.2	<u>44.7</u>	45.8
L^{10}	<u>**48.5**</u>	60.0	<u>**60.8**</u>	44.0	**49.9**
L^{20}	44.0	**61.2**	58.5	44.4	48.5
L^{30}	39.2	**61.2**	58.2	44.4	48.8
L^{40}	33.5	**61.2**	58.6	44.4	<u>**50.7**</u>
L^{50}	36.1	59.3	57.4	44.4	**46.2**
L^{75}	41.3	60.8	57.1	<u>44.7</u>	49.2
L^{100}	43.2	59.7	58.2	<u>44.7</u>	45.8

Table 9. Prediction quality for variable *geographical* (from [3]).

	LR	RF	KNN	SVC	AB
I	22.0	<u>33.6</u>	27.2	25.0	15.6
L^{10}	**25.3**	29.9	**27.6**	24.6	<u>**21.9**</u>
L^{20}	**26.1**	31.3	<u>**29.5**</u>	25.3	20.1
L^{30}	**26.1**	31.7	**28.3**	<u>**27.2**</u>	17.5
L^{40}	<u>**29.1**</u>	32.8	**28.3**	24.6	17.1
L^{50}	**25.0**	32.1	27.2	23.8	**19.0**
L^{75}	24.6	32.8	27.2	25.0	**17.9**
L^{100}	24.6	<u>33.6</u>	27.2	25.0	15.6

effective. However, the improvement is not significant (a few percent at best compared to baseline). On the contrary, larger lists (top-100) usually provide the same quality as the baseline. Among the ten algorithms and configurations we have tested so far, Random Forest seems to be the most interesting in our context because it achieves all best scores. Some algorithms were not suitable, for instance SVC requires many features (best results with all indicators or with largest lists of features).

5.2 Removing Rural Neighbourhoods

In Sect. 3.5, we have shown that there was a bias in the dataset due to rural neighbourhoods. This experiment aims at measuring their impact. The 14 rural areas (around 5% of annotated neighbourhoods) have been removed from the dataset, and new accuracy scores (percentage) are shown for the Random Forest classifier in Table 10. Note that results are similar with other classifiers. Numbers inside parenthesis represent the gain or loss compared to the whole dataset of 270 neighbourhoods, and **bold values** highlight the gains. Without rural neighbourhoods, one could expect that classifiers now focus on distinguishing urban areas and thus improve accuracy. On the contrary, their absence involves a decrease in terms of overall quality, up to 13% in some cases. A possible explanation is that these neighbourhoods are easy to predict. Indeed, they usually include indicators with missing values or specific values (e.g., low density, less shops and restaurants, high number of farmers). However, the morphological variable acts as an exception with improved results (up to 7.6%). This is mainly due to the thin border between rural and peri-urban neighbourhoods, which disappear in this setup. This experiment finally confirms the benefit of the feature selection process, since most lists of selected features achieve better results than the list I and smaller lists (L^{10} to L^{30}) tend to minimize the loss.

Table 10. Prediction quality without rural neighbourhoods (RF classifier).

	Building	Usage	Landscape	Social	Morphological	Geographical
I	43.4 (-13.6)	54.1 (-10.4)	58.7 (-2.1)	40.6 (-10.5)	58.0 (-1.7)	29.9 (-3.7)
L^{10}	48.4 (-10.9)	56.6 (-4.6)	59.4 (-3.3)	44.1 (-2.5)	61.9 (**+1.9**)	33.5 (**+3.6**)
L^{20}	51.2 (-8.8)	57.6 (-6.5)	59.8 (-3.2)	44.1 (-2.5)	66.2 (**+5.0**)	33.5 (**+2.2**)
L^{30}	50.5 (-8.4)	58.4 (-2.8)	62.3 (**+1.5**)	42.7 (-6.9)	64.7 (**+3.5**)	30.3 (-1.4)
L^{40}	50.5 (-8.8)	56.9 (-6.1)	60.9 (-1.8)	40.2 (-11.6)	64.7 (**+3.5**)	33.1 (**+0.3**)
L^{50}	49.1 (-9.8)	55.1 (-9.8)	60.1 (-1.4)	39.9 (-8.2)	66.9 (**+7.6**)	30.6 (-1.5)
L^{75}	49.8 (-8.4)	57.6 (-5.8)	60.1 (-2.2)	39.5 (-8.6)	62.6 (**+1.8**)	29.6 (-3.2)
L^{100}	47.7 (-9.3)	57.3 (-7.2)	59.1 (-1.7)	38.8 (-12.3)	60.8 (**+1.1**)	29.9 (-3.7)

5.3 Computing Geographical Variable

In Sect. 4.4, we have presented a method for calculating the direction of the closest city (i.e., value of the geographical environment variable). This experiment aims at checking whether the proposed method is efficient in terms of accuracy. Remind that we identified six important parameters to compute the direction of the closest city. Preliminary experiments have shown that three of them could be fixed: the REF_POINTS is either set to *centroid* or *nearest points*, but the latter value has problems in case of close locations. The ANGLE_DIRECTIONS parameter can be tuned to *45* or *30–60*, but the second option

Table 11. Accuracy for variable *geographical* according to parameters maxd (MAX_DISTANCE in kms), minc (MIN_CITY) and dcent (DISTANCE_CENTRE in kms).

maxd	minc	dcent	Acc.	maxd	minc	dcent	Acc.	maxd	minc	dcent	Acc.
30	15	0.5	34.0	40	15	0.5	32.8	50	15	0.5	31.6
30	15	1.0	35.6	40	15	1.0	34.4	50	15	1.0	32.4
30	15	1.5	**38.9**	40	15	1.5	37.3	50	15	1.5	**34.8**
30	15	2.0	37.7	40	15	2.0	36.4	50	15	2.0	**34.0**
30	20	0.5	33.6	40	20	0.5	32.8	50	20	0.5	31.6
30	20	1.0	35.2	40	20	1.0	34.4	50	20	1.0	32.4
30	20	1.5	**38.1**	40	20	1.5	37.3	50	20	1.5	**34.8**
30	20	2.0	**37.3**	40	20	2.0	36.4	50	20	2.0	**34.0**
30	25	0.5	30.8	40	25	0.5	30.8	50	25	0.5	30.0
30	25	1.0	32.4	40	25	1.0	32.4	50	25	1.0	30.8
30	25	1.5	34.8	40	25	1.5	**34.8**	50	25	1.5	**33.2**
30	25	2.0	**34.0**	40	25	2.0	**34.0**	50	25	2.0	**32.4**

outperforms in all tests. In addition, the INCREASE_RADIUS parameter, which does not affect much the results, is set to 2 kilometres. Table 11 provides accuracy results when varying the remaining three parameters. A single run (270 neighbourhoods) takes about five minutes.

We observe that quality decreases as the maximum distance grows. In France, a large city is typically found within 40 kilometres. As for the minimal number of neighbourhoods to be considered as a large city, 15 is the best trade-off because quality slightly decreases with higher numbers. Another comment is that a higher DIS-TANCE_CENTRE value (bold scores) achieves better results than smaller distances. This means that centred neighbourhoods are usually up to 2 kilometres around the city's reference point. The best score is 38.1% (green cell), which is slightly above the best scores of the predictive approach (33%). In addition, detailed results enable a better understanding of the complexity for this variable. First, several issues are related to the **city definition**. Indeed, it is based on a minimum number of neighbourhoods, which is a hard threshold value and thus not adaptative to different situations. We also found cases in which two cities were roughly at the same distance of the considered neighbourhood: our algorithms selects the one with the highest number of neighbourhoods, but experts may have considered other elements such as direct roads, natural obstacles, etc. Last, a frequent case deals with neighbourhoods inside cities: the returned direction depends on the DISTANCE_CENTRE parameter, either *centre* when the neighbourhood is below the threshold value, or one of the eight cardinal points otherwise. In small cities, a high threshold value tends to incorrectly return *centre*. Two other issues are related to the **subjectivity of the expertise**. When manually checking for the direction, experts may not take into account the whole surface of both city and neighbourhoods (thus resulting in predicting the next value of the dial, e.g., South East instead of East). With an algorithm (using centroids and a dial divided in 8 parts), results are consistent between them, but may still be inaccurate due to lack of human perception (e.g., a city which includes a large forest inside its borders). Besides, Google Maps may give focus to small towns (e.g., *La Chaise-Dieu*, a touristic village of 700 inhabitants, appear at the same level of bigger cities with tens of thousand residents). Finally, the last problems concern the **three major French cities** (Paris, Lyon, Marseille), which are divided into boroughs. Inside one borough, values may be different (between *centre* and another direction) which makes the computation more difficult. Next, neighbourhoods in surrounding cities of Paris, Lyon and Marseille are usually sufficiently populated to be elected as large city, and if the choice between the major city and the smaller surrounding cities is quite clear for a human, our algorithm may be wrong because it stops when the closest city satisfies the minimum number of neighbourhoods. All these identified issues show that these results could still be improved.

5.4 Discussion

These results are promising and show that an approach based on statistical division units (IRIS) provides an acceptable quality with regards to neighbourhood perception. Improvements are still possible, especially by addressing the representativeness issues presented in Sect. 3.5 or by programming heuristics to enhance the computation of geographical position (e.g., around major cities). The number of annotated neighbourhoods is also limited due to the time-consuming manual annotation (as explained in Sect. 3.2), which may negatively impact the results.

We finally provide answers to research questions about the trends of people who moves to another city in the context of job transfers. Households from our dataset mostly belong to the middle and upper-middle social classes, and they usually stay in this category, which means that their choice of neighbourhood should not drastically change. Half of them were occupants prior to moving, one fourth owned their accommodation while the remaining fourth was hosted (mostly students about to leave their parent's home). After the move, a large majority ends up as occupants, either because they need time to discover their new city before buying, or because their new job is temporary, or they are first-time workers. Households were more or less fairly divided into the 5 types of buildings (except for under-represented *large housing estates*), but half of them resides in buildings after the move. This can be explained by the weight of first-time workers, who may not afford to live in houses or mixed areas. In a similar fashion, residents tend to leave residential neighbourhoods in favour of shopping zones, an expected situation due to the job transfer context. This trend is confirmed by the morphological position, since rural and peri-urban and even urban become less attractive to the benefit of central areas (which doubles its score). Landscape is partly correlated to morphological position and neighbourhood usage, and urban areas, which accounts for one third of the shares before moving, represent half of the neighbourhoods in the end. This comparison between start and arrival neighbourhoods enables a better understanding of residential choices in this context.

6 Conclusion

In this paper we first present a new set of six variables for describing the environment of neighbourhoods. They were derived from a manual observation of various elements such as customer's information, aerial views and raw indicators about the neighbourhood. Due to the job transfer context, most of the 270 annotated neighbourhoods were located in peri-urban areas, which results in a bias compared to the 49,800 neighbourhoods in France. The main challenge was to check whether this manual observation process could be automated to describe neighbourhood environment of the whole country. We first integrated different data sources into the single database mongiris(see Footnote 20). Next, we proposed two approaches for computing environment variables, based on machine learning techniques and on a spatial computation of the *geographical position* variable. The former approach, implemented in the predihood (see Footnote 23) tool, requires a specific pre-process for selecting a subset of indicators while the latter involves different parameters to take into account open questions such as the definition of a large city. Our experimental validation confirms that it is possible to use statistical unit divisions as neighbourhoods and to predict their environment with an acceptable quality. Yet, this computation is still a difficult task and our results could be improved.

We envision different perspectives to this work. First, we have shown that the number of examples is low (less than 1% of the dataset) and not sufficiently heterogeneous. Increasing and varying the number of examples could therefore help in improving the quality. Designing heuristics for spatial computation or using different classifiers than the ones provided by scikit-learn are also clues for achieving a better quality. Another possibility could be the generation of a bigger synthetic dataset, which share similarities with the 49,800 neighbourhoods. The mongiris database includes hundreds of indicators for each neighbourhood. Other data sources such as the prices of sold accommodations or the type/brand of specific points of interest were presented but not integrated due to the need of enhanced thinking. Using new indicators and applying our feature selection algorithm could reveal whether they are useful for the prediction. Besides, indicators from INSEE are updated every couple of years. Observing the dynamics of a few indicators could reveal trends about the environment of neighbourhoods (e.g., evolution of unemployed people). Other application domains may have different needs about the environment (e.g., pollution degree, stopover possibilities for migratory birds), and a last perspective is to discuss with researchers and practitioners from other fields to adapt the description of the environment.

References

1. Attard, J., Orlandi, F., Scerri, S., Auer, S.: A systematic review of open government data initiatives. Gov. Inf. Q. **32**(4), 399–418 (2015)
2. Jean-Yves, A., Bacque Marie-Hélène, G.P.F.: Le quartier. Enjeux scientifiques, actions politiques et pratiques sociales. La Découverte (2007). https://www.cairn.info/le-quartier-9782707150714.htm
3. Barret, N., Duchateau, F., Favetta, F., Bonneval, L.: Predicting the environment of a neighborhood: a use case for France. In: International Conference on Data Management Technologies and Applications (DATA), pp. 294–301. SciTePress (2020)

4. Barret, N., Duchateau, F., Favetta, F., Miquel, M., Gentil, A., Bonneval, L.: À la recherche du quartier idéal. In: Extraction et Gestion des Connaissances, pp. 429–432 (2019)
5. Barret, N., Duchateau, F., Favetta, F., Moncla, L.: Spatial entity matching with geoalign. In: ACM GIS SIGSPATIAL, p. 580–583. ACM (2019)
6. Bellahsène, Z., Bonifati, A., Rahm, E.: Schema Matching and Mapping. Springer, Heidelberg (2011). https://doi.org/10.1007/978-3-642-16518-4
7. Bigot, R., Croutte, P., Müller, J., Osier, G.: Les classes moyennes en europe. Le CRÉDOC, Cahier de recherche 282 (2011)
8. Bonneval, L., et al.: Étude des quartiers : défis et pistes de recherche. In: Extraction et Gestion des Connaissances (2019). http://dahlia.egc.asso.fr/atelierDAHLIA-EGC2020.html
9. Bourdieu, P.: What makes a social class? On the theoretical and practical existence of groups. Berkeley J. Sociol. **32**, 1–17 (1987)
10. Bruce, P., Bruce, A.: Practical Statistics for Data Scientists: 50 Essential Concepts. O'Reilly (2017). https://books.google.fr/books?hl=fr&lr=&id=ldPTDgAAQBAJ
11. Christen, P.: Data Matching: Concepts and Techniques for Record Linkage, Entity Resolution, and Duplicate Detection. Springer, Heidelberg (2012). https://doi.org/10.1007/978-3-642-31164-2
12. Coulondre, A.: Ouvrir la boîte noire des marchés du logement. Métropolitiques (2018). https://metropolitiques.eu/Ouvrir-la-boite-noire-des-marches-du-logement.html
13. Cranshaw, J., Schwartz, R., Hong, J., Sadeh, N.: The livehoods project: utilizing social media to understand the dynamics of a city. In: ICWSM Conference (2012)
14. Dennis, G.: The American Class Structure. New York Wadsworth Publishing (1998)
15. Donoho, D.: 50 years of data science. J. Comput. Graph. Stat. **26**(4), 745–766 (2017). https://doi.org/10.1080/10618600.2017.1384734
16. Frank, L.D., Sallis, J.F., Saelens, B.E., Leary, L., Cain, K., Conway, T.L., Hess, P.M.: The development of a walkability index: application to the neighborhood quality of life study. Br. J. Sports Med. **44**(13), 924–933 (2010)
17. Galster, G.: On the nature of neighbourhood. Urban Stud. **38**(12), 2111–2124 (2001)
18. Garau, C., Pavan, V.M.: Evaluating urban quality: indicators and assessment tools for smart sustainable cities. Sustainability **10**(3), 575 (2018)
19. GIS, O.: Consortium Inc., OpenGIS simple features specification for SQL (1999). http://www.gismanual.com/relational/99-049_OpenGIS_Simple_Features_Specification_For_SQL_Rev_1.1.pdf
20. Guest, A.M., Lee, B.A.: How urbanites define their neighborhoods. Population Environ. **7**(1), 32–56 (1984). https://doi.org/10.1007/BF01257471
21. Guyon, I., Elisseeff, A.: An introduction to variable and feature selection. J. Mach. Learn. Res. **3**(3), 1157–1182 (2003)
22. Halevy, A., Rajaraman, A., Ordille, J.: Data integration: the teenage years. In: Proceedings of the 32nd International Conference on Very Large Data Bases, pp. 9–16. VLDB Endowment (2006). http://portal.acm.org/citation.cfm?id=1164127.1164130
23. Hoyt, H.: The Structure and Growth of Residential Neighborhoods in American Cities. Scholarly Press (1972)
24. Jenks, M., Dempsey, N.: Defining the neighbourhood: challenges for empirical research. Town Plann. Rev. 153–177 (2007)
25. Jordan, M.I., Mitchell, T.M.: Machine learning: trends, perspectives, and prospects. Science **349**(6245), 255–260 (2015)
26. Le Falher, G., Gionis, A., Mathioudakis, M.: Where Is the Soho of Rome? Measures and algorithms for finding similar neighborhoods in cities. In: ICWSM, vol. 2, 3–2 (2015)
27. Leong, M., Dunn, R.R., Trautwein, M.D.: Biodiversity and socioeconomics in the city: a review of the luxury effect. Biol. Lett. **14**(5), 20180082 (2018)

28. Lillesand, T., Kiefer, R.W., Chipman, J.: Remote Sensing and Image Interpretation. Wiley, Hoboken (2015)
29. Liu, Y., Wei, W., Sun, A., Miao, C.: Exploiting geographical neighborhood characteristics for location recommendation. In: Conference on Information and Knowledge Management, pp. 739–748 (2014). https://doi.org/10.1145/2661829.2662002
30. Mukaka, M.M.: A guide to appropriate use of correlation coefficient in medical research. Malawi Med. J. **24**(3), 69–71 (2012)
31. Oberti, M., Préteceille, E.: La ségrégation urbaine. La Découverte (2016)
32. Pan Ké Shon, J.L.: La représentation des habitants de leur quartier: entre bien-être et repli. Économie et statistique **386**(1), 3–35 (2005)
33. Pedregosa, F., Varoquaux, G., Gramfort, A., Michel, V., Thirion, B., Grisel, O., Blondel, M., Prettenhofer, P., Weiss, R., Dubourg, V., Vanderplas, J., Passos, A., Cournapeau, D., Brucher, M., Perrot, M., Duchesnay, E.: Scikit-learn: machine learning in Python. J. Mach. Learn. Res. **12**, 2825–2830 (2011)
34. Reibel, M.: Classification approaches in neighborhood research: introduction and review. Urban Geogr. **32**(3), 305–316 (2011)
35. Salim, F.D., et al.: Modelling urban-scale occupant behaviour, mobility, and energy in buildings: a survey. Build. Environ. **183**, 106964 (2020)
36. Sigaud, T.: Accompagner les mobilités résidentielles des salariés: l'épreuve de l'entrée en territoire. Espaces et sociétés **162**(3), 129–145 (2015)
37. Tabard, N.: Des quartiers pauvres aux banlieues aisées: une représentation sociale du territoire. Economie et statistique **270**(1), 5–22 (1993)
38. Takada, M., Kondo, N., Hashimoto, H.: Japanese study on stratification, health, income, and neighborhood: study protocol and profiles of participants. J. Epidemiol. **24**(4), 334–344 (2014)
39. Tang, E., Sangani, K.: Neighborhood and price prediction for San Francisco Airbnb listings (2015). cs229.stanford.edu/proj2015/236report.pdf
40. Yuan, X., Lee, J.H., Kim, S.J., Kim, Y.H.: Toward a user-oriented recommendation system for real estate websites. Inf. Syst. **38**(2), 231–243 (2013). https://doi.org/10.1016/j.is.2012.08.004
41. Zhang, A.X., Noulas, A., Scellato, S., Mascolo, C.: Hoodsquare: modeling and recommending neighborhoods in location-based social networks. In: Social Computing, pp. 69–74. IEEE (2013)

Phenomena Explanation from Text: Unsupervised Learning of Interpretable and Statistically Significant Knowledge

Giacomo Frisoni (iD) and Gianluca Moro$^{(\boxtimes)}$ (iD)

Department of Computer Science and Engineering – DISI, University of Bologna,
Cesena Campus, Via dell'Università 50, 47521 Cesena, Italy
{giacomo.frisoni,gianluca.moro}@unibo.it

Abstract. Learning knowledge from text is becoming increasingly important as the amount of unstructured content on the Web rapidly grows. Despite recent breakthroughs in natural language understanding, the explanation of phenomena from textual documents is still a difficult and poorly addressed problem. Additionally, current NLP solutions often require labeled data, are domain-dependent, and based on black box models. In this paper, we introduce POIROT, a new descriptive text mining methodology for phenomena explanation from documents corpora. POIROT is designed to provide accurate and interpretable results in unsupervised settings, quantifying them based on their statistical significance. We evaluated POIROT on a medical case study, with the aim of learning the "voice of patients" from short social posts. Taking Esophageal Achalasia as a reference, we automatically derived scientific correlations with 79% F1-measure score and built useful explanations of the patients' viewpoint on topics such as symptoms, treatments, drugs, and foods. We make the source code and experiment details publicly available (https://github.com/unibodatascience/POIROT).

Keywords: Descriptive text mining · Unsupervised learning · Natural language understanding · Natural language processing · Explainability

1 Introduction

With the continuous growth of the amount of textual data on the Web, it is increasingly difficult for humans to consume information of interest at the same rate as it is produced and accumulated over time. Consequently, natural language understanding (NLU) is becoming a widely felt need. New analytical tools are sought to support the development of answers to priority questions, starting only from unlabeled text documents and avoiding their manual reading.

The problem of explaining phenomena from text belongs to the area of descriptive text mining, and applies to a large number of completely different domains. For example, we may want to investigate the causes of destructive plane crashes from aviation reports, or the reasons behind negative opinions from

© Springer Nature Switzerland AG 2021
S. Hammoudi et al. (Eds.): DATA 2020, CCIS 1446, pp. 293–318, 2021.
https://doi.org/10.1007/978-3-030-83014-4_14

customer reviews. As COVID-19 has recently shown[1], one of the areas that can benefit most from these solutions is Health. Beyond the scientific literature, more and more patients are gathering in large online communities to share experiences and to look for answers to questions in order to safely improve their quality of life (QoL). For instance, "which are the most effective and safe medical treatments from patients' viewpoint?", "what contributes to the failure of a certain medical treatment?", "what are the most difficult daily activities for patients?", or "which foods cause or lighten a certain symptom?".

Discovering the reasons that explain some phenomena expressed within a corpus of textual documents requires bringing out semantic relationships among unbounded combinations of relevant concepts, such as symptoms, treatments, drugs, and foods. The knowledge contained in the text can be seen as a set of correlations accompanied by their statistical significance (e.g., "citrus fruit" ↔ "acid reflux": 87%, "GERD" ↔ "PPIs": 82%), enabling sorting, selection and filtering. Therefore, learning this type of knowledge requires the overcoming of several challenges: (i) we need to deal with semantics; (ii) an automatic learning process is preferred to avoid the necessary guidance of a human analyst, but having the ability to combine human skills during analysis is equally important; (iii) unsupervised approaches are necessary because the data is mostly unlabeled; (iv) domain independent solutions are studied to extend their applicability; (v) the extracted relations must come from the analysis of the whole corpus; (vi) we would like to statistically quantify the results in order to recognize their significance; (vii) the interpretability of the results and of the process by which to obtain them must be possible. These are not simple properties to achieve, and the vast majority of existing techniques only partially solve them.

To meet these requirements, we present a novel descriptive text mining methodology of PhenOmena ExplanatIon fROm Text (POIROT) that discovers statistically significant evidences. The solution consists of modules that can be adapted to the specific problem under consideration. The essential components of the contribution include document preprocessing, document classification, term weighting, and language modeling for the representation of the text in a latent semantic space. The adoption of information retrieval (IR) and statistical hypothesis testing, within the space thus constructed, makes it possible to derive and quantify semantic correlations between terms, documents and classes. The generation of a textual explanation for the phenomenon of interest is carried out incrementally. Moreover working with a latent low rank space, generated with efficient randomized matrix factorization algorithms, reduces the original data dimensions by order of magnitudes and this allows to apply the methodology to very large corpora and vocabularies.

To evaluate the effectiveness of POIROT, we conducted experiments on a medical case study to capture the "voice of patients" (i.e., a set of problems, experiences, and feelings often not reported to doctors) from the social posts

---

[1] NLU Kaggle competition on COVID-19. https://www.kaggle.com/allen-institute-for-ai/CORD-19-research-challenge.

shared by a community of people living with rare diseases (RDs). To this end, the results have been validated with domain experts.

In this paper we describe the full version of the methodology we preliminarily presented in [20]. In particular in this work we introduce new modules to empower the language model component based on LSA with pLSA and LDA, perform new experiments with extended gold standards (>50 new correlations), present the pseudocode of the algorithms that discover explanations and publicly release both the data and source code we have developed. The rest of the paper is organized as follows. Section 2 discusses the related works. In Sect. 3 we introduce the methodology and the mathematical framework behind POIROT and its modules, highlighting the differences between an interactive and fully automatic use. In Sect. 4, we show the application of the contribution on a real medical case study focused on Esophageal Achalasia, presenting the experiments and the results obtained. Finally, Sect. 5 sums up the work with conclusive remarks.

2 Related Work

The explanation of phenomena from textual data constitutes a task related to *descriptive analytics* and *diagnostic analytics*, which have the objective of identifying patterns to summarize historical data ("what happened?") and uncover the reasoning behind certain results ("why did it happen?"). However, text mining and data mining solutions for this purpose do not directly address the above-mentioned questions but treat such analyzes as a set of easier sub-tasks that can provide useful results for manually constructing answers. Phenomena explanation is also completely different from predictive text mining, where instead the goal is to estimate the likelihood of a future outcome based on labeled data [47], such as text classification and sentiment analysis.

In [1], the authors apply data mining techniques for descriptive phrase extraction, using *episode rules* (i.e., a variant of the association rules) and statistically quantifying their significance. Nevertheless, episode rules are not sufficiently expressive and require a different construction form depending on the problem.

Aspect-based Sentiment Analysis gives some details on the reason behind an overall opinion rating by assigning individual scores to each known feature that characterizes a target entity (e.g., cleanliness, food, quietness and kindness for a hotel). On the other hand, it is applied to data that are labeled and restricted to an expected comparison schema, where most of the time the choice of the aspects to be evaluated is carried out manually by an expert user. According to [31], it is interesting to observe that there are four main lines of work for the unsupervised extraction of aspects from the text: (i) frequent nouns and noun phrases identification, (ii) nouns in conjunction with opinion words, (iii) topic modeling, (iv) latent associations between terms used in documents and opinion ratings. POIROT, although independent of sentiment analysis, is linked to the approaches belonging to the fourth group.

Topic Modeling techniques, such as Latent Dirichlet Allocation (LDA) [3], allow us to discover the topics covered within a collection of text documents and to label the latter with topic mixtures. They cannot provide phenomena explanations or fine-grained correlations between concepts, despite being unsupervised and interpretable.

Deep Learning (DL) models [6,36,40] have outperformed human performance on a broad spectrum of NLP tasks, including machine translation and question answering, which are different from phenomena explanation. DL solutions are highly supervised (i.e., require large labeled datasets to achieve satisfactory results), can be easily fooled with adversary inputs [27,39], and are not designed to explain the learned knowledge. In medicine, above all, where wrong decisions by a system can be harmful, the ability to explain models or to make them interpretable is considered essential [35]. This lack of reliability and transparency has recently opened a new research thread called Explainable Artificial Intelligence (XAI) [23,32], also sparking a renewed interest in statistical and symbolic approaches. *Explainability* seeks to give answers on how a black-box model achieves the results it produces (e.g., the features considered by a classification model that distinguishes benign from malignant tumor cells), but not on *why* a phenomenon occurs. Moreover, the explanation of the internal mechanics of a neural network provided by current XAI solutions is almost always local, when instead the explanation of a phenomenon requires a global point of view. For instance, if a typical XAI solution can detect the terms most responsible for the class prediction of a single text document, a phenomena explanation task may require the identification of the most representative terms for the documents belonging to the class on the entire corpus.

Decision Trees [44] can be used to explain knowledge with a symbolic and interpretable model, where the highest nodes are the most important ones. With them, we can discover the most relevant terms for a certain class (e.g., "pain" for negative opinion class), but we cannot detect fine-grained interclass correlations, such as those between drugs, symptoms, and so on.

3   Methodology

In this section, we present the overall framework of POIROT, whose architectural diagram is shown in Fig. 1. The methodology can be used both to extract knowledge *interactively* (i.e., the user is part of the learning process and can explore the data during the analysis) and *automatically* (i.e., without man-in-the-analysis). Section 3.1 illustrates the interactive mode, while Sect. 3.2 shows the transition to a fully automatic one. Section 3.3 formalizes the pseudocode.

3.1   Interactive Knowledge Extraction

POIROT comprises several stages, following a general knowledge discovery process. All the phases are illustrated in detail below, paying attention to the importance of their combination.

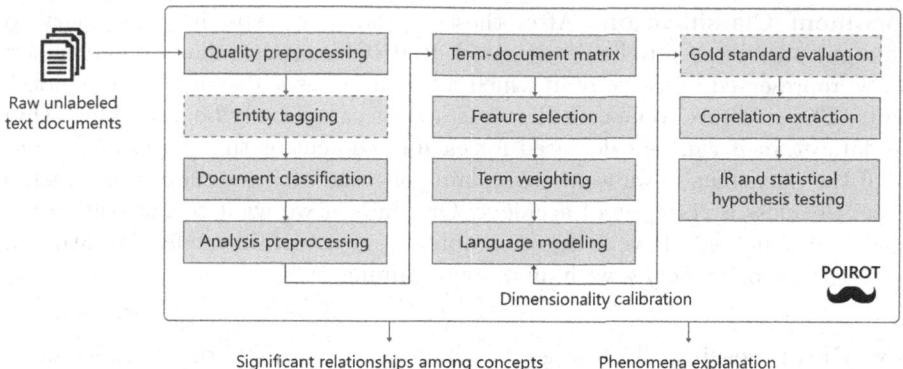

Fig. 1. POIROT architectural diagram. The boxes with dashed outline refer to optional modules.

Quality Improvement. As an initial stage, a text transformation pipeline can be applied to improve the quality of documents within the corpus. In fact, the latter typically have numerous imperfections, such as grammatical and spelling errors, and various types of noise, including slang words, unnecessary information, and inconsistencies in symbol encoding. For example, given a document *"i suffrer from achalasiaaa"*, we want to improve it in *"I suffer from achalasia"*. Cleaning the text promotes the recognition of correlations and simplifies the analysis through dimensionality reduction, also improving the results of all subsequent steps.

Entity Tagging. Optionally, pre-trained named entity recognition (NER) and named entity linking (NEL) systems can be used for the unsupervised classification of terms into predefined categories (e.g., drugs, symptoms, foods, places) and for their alignment with related entries in existing knowledge bases (KBs, e.g., Wikidata, DBpedia, Freebase). Advanced NER systems can detect several hundreds of very fine-grained types organized in hierarchical taxonomies [30, 42]. The results linked to the recognized entities can be reported directly within the documents to increase their information content, carrying out an entity tagging operation. For instance, *"I suffer from achalasia"* can be augmented to *"I suffer from <e>achalasia<t>/medicine/disease</t><wl>Q661015</wl></e>"*. After this stage, we distinguish between entity terms (i.e., labeled) and standard terms (i.e., unlabeled), where the latter refer to verbs, adjectives, or specific domain concepts that do not fall within the adopted taxonomy. Entity tagging normalizes the various ways of referring to entities thanks to their identifier, allows more in-depth analyzes based on entity types, and favors greater interpretability of the phenomenon explanation. By exploiting the links with external KBs, it is also possible to extend the amount of initial data (in a small data perspective).

Document Classification. After these preliminary steps, it is necessary to define the phenomenon to be investigated. POIROT assumes that a phenomenon can be represented by the way in which a certain class is distributed over documents. The attribute to be considered as a class can already be available within the dataset, or it can be calculated for each document at this stage. For example, if the phenomenon we want to explain concerns why destructive air crashes occur, the class is the type of accident. Or again, if we want to investigate the reasons why patients have a negative opinion on a certain medical treatment, the classification coincides with an opinion mining task.

Text Preprocessing. This stage has the objective of preparing data for analysis. It typically includes transformations such as case-folding, replacement of punctuation and numbers with spaces (except for entity tags), and stopword removal. By standardizing the inflected forms of a word, lemmatization increases the similarity between terms and facilitates the identification of latent correlations. N-Gram tokenization, both at the word and character level, is another central aspect. Subword models can be very powerful [4], but they require additional steps to reconstruct the words and return a meaningful explanation. Consequently, the next stages of the methodology refer to a unigram word-level approach for greater clarity.

Term-Document Matrix Construction. A large and sparse term-document matrix is extracted from the corpus, where each row stands for a unique term t, each column stands for a unique document d, and each cell contains the frequency with which t appears in d.

Feature Selection. This stage aims to further prune less relevant terms and to define the model vocabulary. One possible approach is to keep only the terms with a percentage frequency above a certain threshold, such as 1%. From a co-occurrence point of view, each term should appear at least twice. The percentage threshold for standard terms should be distinct from that for entity terms. In fact, depending on the domain and the specific corpus, an entity with a strong interesting type for the analysis (e.g., a drug) might actually be poorly mentioned in the documents. This phase has a strong impact on the model size and on computation times. However, caution must be exercised because the more terms we eliminate, the weaker the latent correlations become.

Term Weighting. Raw counts do not consider the significance a term has in the documents in which it appears. To better represent the importance of each term in each document, term weighting methods are applied to the term-document matrix. A good comparison of the available schemes and their effectiveness is illustrated in [17]. We suggest a variation of the classic tf-idf, making use of a factor inverse to the Shannon entropy of the term in the non-local part of the formula. See Eq. 1.

$$w_{t,d} = log(1 + tf_{t,d}) \times (1 - shannonEntropy(tdm))$$ (1)

This phase determines the norms of the vector representations for the terms in the latent semantic space, and therefore strongly affects the phenomenon explanation that will be constructed.

Language Modeling. This stage involves the application of a language model (LM) to bring out semantic similarities between terms and documents within a latent vector space. Operating at the semantic level would not be possible with a Boolean research model based on lexical matches. POIROT can be used with different LMs: (i) *algebraic*, like Latent Semantic Analysis (LSA) [13,28]; (ii) *probabilistic*, like Probabilistic Latent Semantic Analysis (pLSA) [26] and Latent Dirichlet Allocation (LDA); (iii) *neural*, like BERT [10] and SBERT [41]. In this paper, we focus on LSA, pLSA, and LDA, reinterpreting and extending them in light of recent developments in the NLP field. There are several reasons behind this choice.

– They allow a coherent representation of terms and documents in a common space. Despite recent developments, word and document embeddings are meant to work only on words and documents in a mutually exclusive manner.
– They allow us to perform analyzes on spaces with a small number of dimensions (even just two). On the other hand, word embeddings require a large number of features to work properly. For example, BERT uses 768 hidden units, and this number has been largely surpassed by other SOTA models in recent months.
– Their algebraic/probabilistic nature, together with the limited number of dimensions, makes them more interpretable models than alternatives based on deep neural networks.
– They do not require labeled data and training.

Latent Semantic Analysis. LSA induces global knowledge indirectly from local co-occurrence data. It performs a mapping of a term-document matrix (eventually weighted) into a low-dimensional latent semantic space. The mapping is based on Singular Value Decomposition (SVD), a linear algebra technique that factorizes a matrix C into the product of three separate matrices (Eq. 2).

$$\underset{M \times N}{C} = \underset{M \times M}{U} \underset{M \times N}{\Sigma} \underset{N \times N}{V^T}$$ (2)

U and V are two orthogonal matrices, and Σ is a diagonal matrix containing the singular values of C in descending order. Formally, $\Sigma = diag(\sigma_1, \ldots, \sigma_p)$ where $\sigma_1 \geq \sigma_2 \geq \cdots \geq \sigma_p \geq 0$ and $p = min(M, N)$. The singular values in Σ are the components of the new dimensions, and the first of them capture the greatest variation of the data (i.e., contain more information). SVD reduces dimensionality by selecting only the k largest singular values, and only keeping the first k columns of U, and the first k rows of V^T. So, given a matrix C $M \times N$ and a positive integer k, SVD finds the matrix $C_k = U_k \Sigma_k V_k^t$ of rank at most k (between all matrices with k linearly independent vectors) that minimizes the difference with the original matrix $X = C - C_k$, according to the Frobenius norm (Eq. 3). The positions of all terms and documents in the latent semantic space are obtained from the products of matrices $U_k \times \Sigma_k$ and $V_k \times \Sigma_k$, respectively. The value of the hyperparameter k can be calibrated to delete noise and unnecessary data, as well as better capture the mutual implications of terms and documents. Though some heuristics are available, establishing it optimally is still an empirical issue.

$$\|X\|_F = \sqrt{\sum_{i=1}^{M}\sum_{j=1}^{N} X_{ij}^2} \tag{3}$$

Figure 2 sums up this process. Though its text representation is basic and relatively simple, LSA is a powerful technique for capturing knowledge that closely matches human semantic similarities, proving to have the potential to address Plato's Problem [29]. However, it should be noted that statistical LMs can represent probabilistic knowledge in a more natural way. The computational cost of LSA is the same as SVD: $O(min\{MN^2, M^2N\})$. No-exact solutions for SVD reduce costs by several orders of magnitude [25,45] and sometimes allow for a decrease in execution times from a few hours to a few minutes.

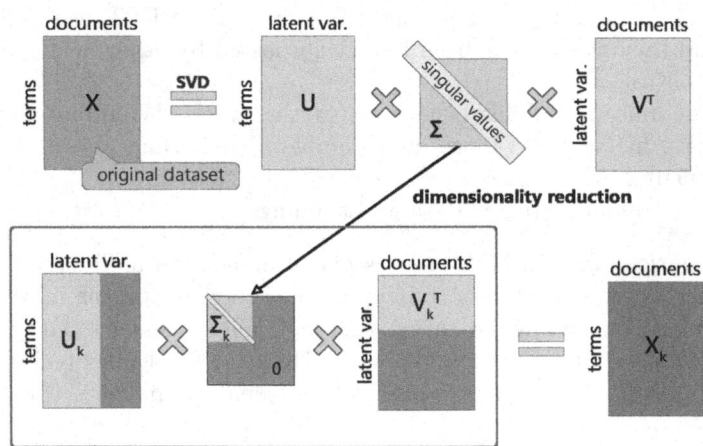

Fig. 2. LSA dimensionality reduction through SVD [20].

Probabilistic Latent Semantic Allocation. While LSA is based on the application of SVD to text processing and IR, pLSA adopts a probabilistic approach to reach the target. It is a statistical language model that, similarly to LSA, can be used to discover hidden structures in a collection of texts (where each latent dimension is seen as a topic t) and to factorize a matrix for unsupervised dimensionality reduction. The goal of pLSA is to maximize the predictive probability $P(w, d)$ of each entry inside the original term-document matrix, by estimating some parameters via likelihood maximization (i.e., a non-convex optimization problem that can be solved with the Expectation-Maximization algorithm). The parameters to be learned depend on the problem formulation, for which there are two variants (Eq. 4). The second one, called "symmetric", underlines the parallelism with LSA, and it is precisely the formulation considered in this paper. Since pLSA is based on probability distributions, the matrices resulting from the factorization have the property of being non-negative and normalized.

$$P(w, d) = P(d) \sum_t P(t|d) P(w|t) = \sum_t P(t) P(d|t) P(w|t) \approx U \Sigma V^T \quad (4)$$

Latent Dirichlet Allocation. LDA is a generative statistical model that constitutes a probabilistic extension of LSA, where documents are interpreted as a soft mixture of topics, and the distribution of topics is assumed to have a sparse Dirichlet prior. This sparse nature is linked to the assumption that documents are covered only by a small set of topics and that topics are characterized only by a small set of frequent words. LDA is a generalization of pLSA (i.e., a Bayesian version), and the two models coincide in the case of uniform Dirichlet prior distribution [22]. The Bayesian approach can avoid data overfitting, which is typical of pLSA with small datasets. A LDA model trains to output $P(t|d)$ and $P(w|t)$, similarly to the asymmetric formulation of pLSA. To make the transition to the symmetrical formulation required by our work it is necessary to calculate $P(t)$ and $P(d|t)$. The first one can be calculated taking into account the significance of each topic in the $P(t|d)$ distribution of each document d (Eq. 5), while the second one can be derived by applying the Bayes rule (Eq. 6). Finally, as in Σ from SVD, the rows and the columns of the resulting matrices can be sorted in descending order with respect to $P(t)$.

$$P(t) = \frac{\sum_d P(t|d)}{|t|} \quad (5)$$

$$P(d|t) = \frac{P(t|d) \times P(d)}{P(c)} \quad (6)$$

The similarity between the vectors modeled by LSA, pLSA, and LDA can be calculated with the cosine similarity metric (Eq. 7).

$$sim(A, B) = cos(\theta) = \frac{A \cdot B}{\|A\| \, \|B\|} = \frac{\sum\limits_{i=1}^{n} A_i B_i}{\sqrt{\sum\limits_{i=1}^{n} A_i^2} \sqrt{\sum\limits_{i=1}^{n} B_i^2}} \quad (7)$$

2D Space Representation. After the construction of the latent semantic space, the visualization of the terms and documents within it allows to:

- identify the correlations between terms and terms, documents and documents, and terms and documents;
- have a graphical feedback on the distribution of documents and their class;
- recognize the presence of any clusters;
- understand the effectiveness of the model and, if necessary, intervene again on the previous phases to apply corrections.

Even if the new latent space is made up of k dimensions, a 2D representation is more suitable for human observation, moreover the first eigenvalues, which are even the highest ones and follow a hyperbolic distribution, give the highest weight and importance to the corresponding first latent dimensions, therefore they well approximate the real position of the data in the full space with all latent dimensions. Under this point of view, t-SNE [34] can be useful for compressing the original dimensions and minimizing divergences, however it is not essential because as mentioned the first latent dimensions are sufficient to approximate the data distribution in the latent space. For example, the choice of the two dimensions to be adopted for visualization purposes can be made directly from the matrix Σ_k. Since singular values represent the decreasing importance of dimensions in the new space, choosing the first two of them without too much mutual difference is a good approximation and avoids a strong crushing of the data along an axis. In any case, generally one does not go beyond the fourth dimension, because the information captured is much lower than the previous ones. As shown in Fig. 3, the *power law curve* is a valid tool to make this decision. To prevent terms and documents from being displayed at different scales, a good practice is to normalize vectors. The cosine similarity allows the visual recognition of semantically related terms and documents. For instance, terms frequently mentioned together in the corpus will probably form a small angle with the origin. However, having compressed an originally high-dimensional space into only two dimensions, close terms in the graph may not necessarily be such. A complete representation of the latent semantic space can be obtained by superimposing the normalized vectors of terms and documents (Fig. 4), also coloring them according to their class for better understanding (i.e., NER type for the terms, if available). In the case of a probabilistic language model such as pLSA or LDA, the visualization is limited to the positive quadrant only.

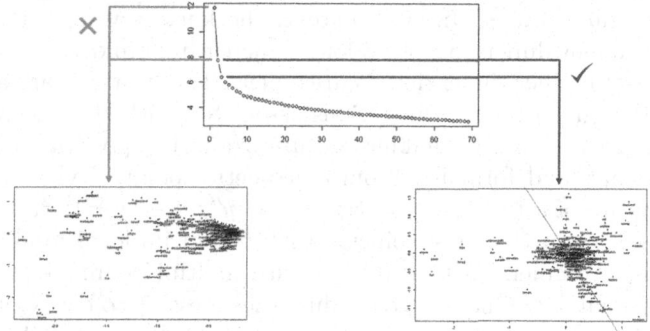

Fig. 3. 2D visualization of the latent semantic space, starting from the power law curve obtained after the SVD decomposition (LSA). In the first case (dimensions 1 and 2), the resulting terms distribution is not satisfactory and takes the form of an ellipsoid. In the second case (dimensions 2 and 3), the distribution is less concentrated and consequently it is better for visual observations [20].

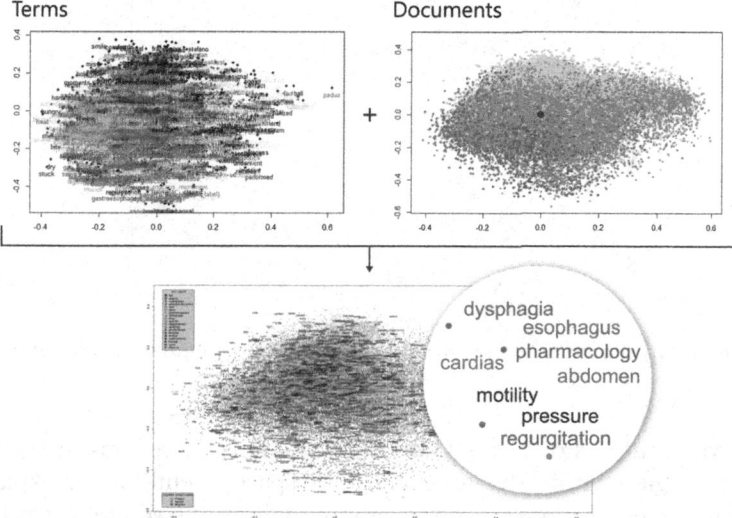

Fig. 4. Graph of the latent semantic space with normalized and overlapping terms and documents.

Dimensionality Choice. The use of only two dimensions is suitable for visualization purposes, but generally not for the continuation of the analysis where this could cause a significant loss of information. The dimensionality k of the latent semantic space can be further reduced to lighten the computational load required by the subsequent phases. The choice of the optimal number of dimensions to work with can be made by searching for a *knee point* in the descending sequence of singular values. In this context, the knee is where the benefit of including subsequent dimensions is no longer increasing rapidly and is no longer worth the cost of further dimensional enrichment. The idea is that the informative contribution given by the dimensions associated with the eigenvalues that follow a knee point is lower, making an approximation possible. This can be done both visually and formally. From a geometric point of view, considering that the curvature of a function $y = f(x)$ is $c = y''/(1 + (y')^2)^{3/2}$, a valid number of dimensions can therefore coincide with one of its local minima (Fig. 5). Typically it is recommended to run tests with multiple minima to choose the potentially optimal one. One way to conduct these tests is to check the semantic consistency with respect to a query of the first N documents similar to it (i.e., query precision).

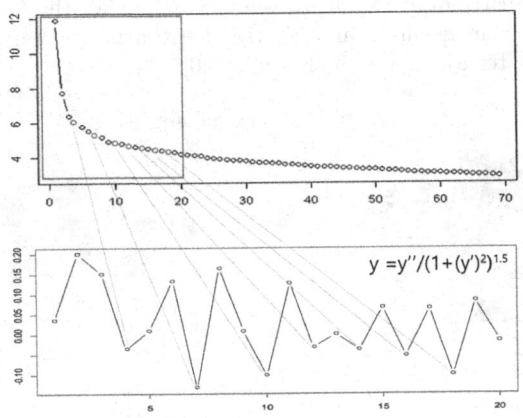

Fig. 5. Knee points in the curvature function for singular values [20].

Qualitative Analysis of Class Distribution. This phase aims to identify the areas to investigate within the latent semantic space, useful for the explanation of the phenomenon of interest. In the case of uniform distribution, within each quadrant with which we can imagine dividing the space, it should be identified a number of documents for class proportional to the original one in the corpus. It follows that the areas to be explored are those with unexpected concentrations of documents belonging to the desired class (Fig. 6). The recognition of these areas can be done directly by observing the approximate bidimensional representation previously constructed.

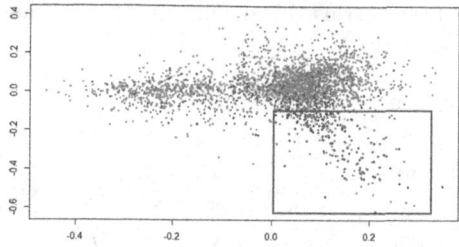

Fig. 6. Example of unusual concentration of documents belonging to a certain class (colored in red), in the 2D representation of the latent semantic space [20]. (Color figure online)

Phenomena Explanation. This is the last phase of the methodology, intending to discover the explanation for the phenomenon of interest. The various elements required to complete the task in question are described below.

Query Fold-in. One of the most interesting features of LSA, pLSA, and LDA is the ability to fold-in[2] new documents, realizing the transposition of queries in the latent semantic space. A query q is equivalent to a set of terms in C, and therefore to an artificial document. It must undergo the same preliminary transformations that the cell entries of C received before model construction (i.e., quality preprocessing, entity tagging, analysis preprocessing, term weighting). Transforming a query vector q in a new document q_k means transforming it into a row of the matrix V_k. Since $V = C^T U \Sigma^{-1}$, it follows that $q_k = q^T U_k \Sigma_k^{-1}$. The position of the query in the latent semantic space is given by $q^T U \Sigma^{-1} \Sigma = q^T U$. A statistical LM requires the prediction of the topic mixture for q.

Semantic Similarities. The next steps require the calculation of semantic similarities between terms, documents, and queries (i.e., concepts). Literature work on LSA, pLSA, or LDA typically focuses on the application of language models and the general use of cosine similarity, but neither describes nor offers solutions to these more comprehensive types of operations. Consequently, we propose an expansion of the foundational algebra necessary for the objective of the research. Within the reconstructed term-document matrix C_k (Eq. 2), the semantic similarities between the pairs of terms or documents are measured with the cosine of the respective scalar products ($C_k C_k^T = U_k \Sigma_k^2 U_k^T = (U_k \Sigma_k)(U_k \Sigma_k)^T$ or $C_k^T C_k = V_k \Sigma_k^2 V_k^T = (V_k \Sigma_k)(V_k \Sigma_k)^T$), and the specific instances of U_k or V_k. Table 1 introduces the equations for calculating all the similarities between the vectors in the transformed space. Note that cosine similarity in an LSA model belongs to the range $[-1, 1]$, while in a pLSA/LDA model it belongs to $[0, 1]$ and can be interpreted as a probability.

First Term Selection. The composition of a probabilistic explanation for the phenomenon we have chosen to analyze is carried out incrementally and is based on

---

[2] Folding is the process of adding new vectors to a space after its construction, without rebuilding it.

Table 1. Similarities between terms (u), documents (v) and queries (q) in the latent semantic space.

v_i and v_j	$cosSim(v_i\Sigma_k, v_j\Sigma_k)$
u_i and u_j	$cosSim(u_i\Sigma_k, u_j\Sigma_k)$
q and v_j	$cosSim(q^T U_k, v_j\Sigma_k)$
u_i and v_j	$cosSim(u_i\Sigma_k^{1/2}, \Sigma_k^{1/2} v_j)$
u_i and q	$cosSim(u_i\Sigma_k^{1/2}, \Sigma_k^{-1/2} U_k^T q)$

the construction step by step of a query. In particular, the resulting explanation will consist of a set of terms that best characterize the phenomenon in the latent semantic space. First, the most representative term must be visually identified in the area highlighted in the previous stage. In doing this, it is necessary to focus on the terms placed in a central position within the area itself and at a greater distance from the origin (with a high 2-norm and so a high relevance). The selected term can be seen as the first one of the explanation query. In order to mathematically demonstrate the correlation between the folded-in query q and the class c representing the phenomenon, the chi-squared (χ^2) test can be used in conjunction with R-precision (Eq. 8). To give the query the possibility of retrieving all the documents to which it refers, R is set equal to the number of instances of class c.

$$\chi^2(\mathbb{D}, q, c) = \sum_{e_q \in \{0,1\}} \sum_{e_c \in \{0,1\}} \frac{(N_{e_q e_c} - E_{e_q e_c})^2}{E_{e_q e_c}} \tag{8}$$

where:

$\mathbb{D}$ = corpus (repository of documents)
q = query
c = class
e_q = p-a in the top-R identified by q
e_c = p-a of the class
$N_{e_q e_c}$ = observed number of documents with e_t and e_c
$E_{e_q e_c}$ = expected number of documents with e_t and e_c.

While the number of documents observed is inherent in the data, the expected frequencies are calculated supposing the term t and the class c are independent, namely $E_{e_q e_c} = |\mathbb{D}| \cdot P(t) \cdot P(c)$. For example, $E_{11} = |\mathbb{D}| \cdot ((N_{11} + N_{10})/|\mathbb{D}|) \cdot ((N_{11} + N_{01})/|\mathbb{D}|)$. The higher χ^2, the lower the probability that the hypothesis of independence between q and c holds. The LM alone is not sufficient to compute the level of statistical significance for the phenomenon explanation. To obtain it, we consider the p-value derivable from the χ^2 distribution table between q and c with a degree of freedom equals to 1 as the contingency chi-square matrix is 2×2. A p-value threshold (e.g., 0.005) must be established to determine whether the null hypothesis is rejected or not. In the case of statistical dependence, let n_c be the number of documents belonging to class c in top-R and $|c|$ the number of instances of class c (used as R-precision), it is possible to say that the query characterizes a number of instances related to the phenomenon being described equal to $n_c/|c| \cdot 100$, with a probability corresponding to the p-value for the calculated χ^2.

Explanation Construction by Iterative Refining. After having formally verified the relevance of the term chosen for the class associated with the unusual concentration, it is possible to proceed with the explanation enrichment. The analysis, therefore, continues with the search for the terms closest to q. Among the terms with greater similarity and 2-norm, we choose the one that, if linked to the explanation so far composed, leads to the creation of the most significant query (i.e., lowest p-value after the re-execution of the chi-squared test). The process is repeated iteratively, as long as the confidence indicated by the p-value does not fall below the specified threshold. By alternating searches for query-term and query-document correlations, the proposed approach progressively make the phenomenon explanation more specific (Fig. 7). If there are more areas to investigate (e.g., because they deal with different topics), it is possible to construct an explanation for each of them. Once the analysis is complete, POIROT returns one or more set of terms that do not have a sentence structure but are often easily interpretable. Taking advantage of the results obtained by NER and NEL systems, as we did in [21], it is also possible to build a knowledge graph (KG) [7,8] to increase the power of expressivity and interrogability.

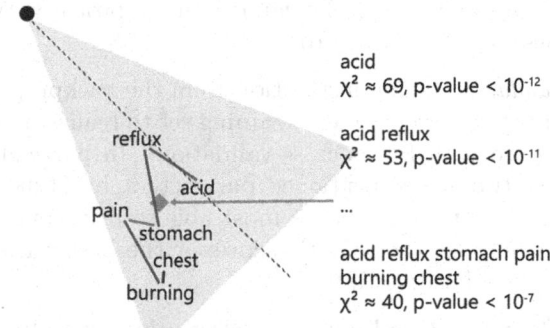

Fig. 7. Example of phenomenon explanation. At each step, the query is enriched with a semantically close term, and the correlation with the class tends to decrease.

Evaluation. There are different ways to evaluate the correctness of the results produced by POIROT in its various parts. The phenomenon explanation can be interpreted and compared to the already existing one from scientific reports or other sources. As regards the correlations between concepts as a whole, they are deductible directly from the clusters of similar vectors in the transformed space. In this work, we suggest a formal approach based on the definition of a set of known gold standards (i.e., positive and negative known correlations expressed by an expert user). Each gold standard represents a correlation between two artificial documents (i.e., sets of terms): $x_1, \ldots, x_n \leftrightarrow y_1, \ldots, y_m$. An example of positive correlation (known in the literature for its truth) is "alcohol" $\leftrightarrow$ "acid reflux". Vice versa, an example of negative correlation (known in the literature for its falsity) is "lung" $\leftrightarrow$ "gastroenterology". The effectiveness of the model can be proven with the same theoretical framework underlying POIROT (i.e., by making fold-in of the two known queries involved by each gold standard, applying the chi-squared test between the vectors, and verifying that the resulting p-value is below a certain threshold for positive examples and above for negative ones). This allows us to create a confusion matrix and to calculate different metrics, such as the F1-measure score.

3.2 Automatic Knowledge Extraction

In this section, we discuss a possible solution to fully automate the execution of POIROT.

Dimensionality Calibration. Concerning the dimensionality, two main parameters can be identified: the number of dimensions of the transformed space produced by the selected LM and the one to be considered for the analysis (not necessarily equal to the first). Not knowing in advance how many topics there are in the corpus, the choice of these values is not simple; it cannot be standardized for all application cases and is typically carried out empirically. We propose two different approaches to address this problem.

Based on Gold Standards. Taking inspiration from the backpropagation mechanism, gold standards can be reused as a training set to realize a semi-supervised calibration phase (also with k-fold cross-validation). In particular, it is possible to iterate on the two above mentioned parameters, build more models, and choose the combination of values that is most able to bring out known correlations (e.g., by searching for the best F1 score, or the best ratio between True Positive Rate and False Positive Rate).

Based on Space Geometry. Good dimensionality values can also be established with an unsupervised approach based on the geometric characteristics of the space. Specifically, we propose to evaluate two main factors: (i) high-norm vectors, (ii) independence between dimensions in terms of covariance around the origin.

Area(s) Identification in the Space. The automated version of POIROT must still be able to manage the choice of the area(s) to investigate within the space. Again, we propose more techniques to achieve this goal.

Starting Query. If we have a concept for which to verify the correlation with the investigated phenomenon, we can indicate a starting query. In this way, a point in space is identified, and—moving from it—the continuation of the analysis can enrich the provided description with other statistically significant terms. In a medical domain, for example, this query can express information that we want to examine, such as symptoms and medical treatments.

First Term Selection. As an alternative to a starting query, we can consider all the terms with a norm greater than a threshold, and apply the chi-squared test on each of them to verify their correlation with the class. The term chosen is the one with minimum p-value and highest norm. This approach is indicated in the case of a single area with non-random concentration and has the risk of selecting a scarcely relevant first term. In this regard, a valid preprocessing is fundamental.

Clustering. In the case of several areas of interest, the most suitable technique for their automatic recognition is clustering. Some hierarchical clustering techniques [46] do not require prior knowledge about the number of clusters or the height at which to cut the dendrogram, but only a minimum confidence threshold (i.e., p-value) for the clusters to return. It is thus possible to construct multiple explanations for the phenomenon, starting from the centroids of the clusters obtained.

Correlation Extraction. Semantically similar sets of terms or documents can be automatically extracted with clustering techniques (as described above) or more efficiently with approximated k-NN algorithms, like LSH [9,33]. The degree of correlation can be quantified in a probabilistic form. While this is natural with statistical LMs, it may alternatively require the mapping of cosine similarity from $[-1,1]$ to $[0,1]$, or the calculation of the chi-squared test between terms. The tags of the NER system allow to extend interrogability, and to search for correlations between entities of specific types (e.g., drug $\leftrightarrow$ symptom) [21].

3.3 Algorithm

This section introduces the pseudocode for the core part of POIROT, summarizing the salient aspects of the previous sections. Algorithm 1 illustrates the main function with the calls to the implementations of the various modules, while Algorithms 2 and 3 are focused on the steps necessary for the construction of the target phenomenon explanation.

4 Case Study and Experiments

In this section, we show the application of POIROT to a medical case study with the aim of capturing the "voice of patients" from their conversational messages on social media communities. We argue that extracting knowledge from the text and easily finding explanations for phenomena of various kinds can be the right step towards a future of inclusion, capable of avoiding the data loss concerning the personal experience (also called "real world") of patients. In addition to the impact that solutions of this type can have also for caregivers and researchers, the problem acquires even more interest considering the challenges it poses in NLP [18]. Posts and comments are unlabeled, short, full of noise, and with a

---

Algorithm 1. Main.

   Input   : $D \leftarrow$ Documents, $GS \leftarrow$ Gold standards, $SQ \leftarrow$ Starting query,
              $C \leftarrow$ Investigated class
   Output: $PExpl$
   $D \leftarrow$ QualityPreprocessing(D);
   $D \leftarrow$ EntityTagging(D);
   $D \leftarrow$ DocumentClassification(D);
   $Corpus \leftarrow$ AnalysisPreprocessing(D);
   $Tdm \leftarrow$ TermDocumentMatrix$(Corpus)$;
   $Tdm \leftarrow$ FeatureSelection(Tdm);
   $Tdmw \leftarrow$ TermWeighting(Tdm);
   $U_K, \Sigma_K, V_K^T \leftarrow \text{LM}_{Min\_K}(Tdmw, GS)$;
   $Tksrs \leftarrow U_K \times \Sigma_K^{1/2}$;
   $Tls \leftarrow U_K \times \Sigma_K$;
   $Dls \leftarrow V_K^T \times \Sigma_K$;
   $PExpl \leftarrow$ PhenomenonExplanation$(\dots)$;

Algorithm 2. Utils.

   MakeQuery $(Text, U_K, \Sigma_K)$
   $\quad$ | $Qv \leftarrow$ FoldIn$(Text)$;
   $\quad$ | $Qwv \leftarrow$ TermWeighting(Qv);
   $\quad$ | $Qls \leftarrow Qwv^T \times U_K$;
   $\quad$ | $Qk \leftarrow Qls \times \Sigma_K^{-1}$;
   $\quad$ | $Dksrs \leftarrow Qk \times \Sigma_K^{1/2}$;
   $\quad$ | **return** $Text, Qls, Qk, Dksrs$;
   QueryClassCorrelation $(Q, U_K, \Sigma_K, Dls, DCs, C, Min)$
   $\quad$ | $Q \leftarrow$ MakeQuery(Q, U_K, Σ_K);
   $\quad$ | $QDSims \leftarrow \forall d \in$ rows(Dls) CosSim$(d_{Min}, Q.Qls_{Min})$
   $\quad$ | $QvsC \leftarrow$ ConfusionMatrix(
   $\quad$ | $\quad$ GetD(TopH$(QDSims, |C \in DCs|))$, $Class = C)$
   $\quad$ | $Pvalue \leftarrow \chi^2(QvsC)$;
   $\quad$ | **return** $Q, Pvalue$;

---

lot of grammatical imperfections. The lack of resources for analyzing texts in a language other than English further complicates the involved tasks.

4.1   Domain and Dataset

We focused on Esophageal Achalasia (ORPHA:930), a rare disorder of the esophagus characterized by the inability of the lower esophageal sphincter (LES) to relax. Collaborating with *Associazione Malati Acalasia Esofagea (AMAE)*[34]—

---

[3] https://www.amae.it/.
[4] https://www.orpha.net/consor/cgi-bin/SupportGroup_Search.php?lng=EN&data_id=106412.

the main Italian patient organization for the disease under consideration—we downloaded anonymous text documents from the Facebook Group directly managed from it[5] (with ≈2000 current users and >10 years of history). The dataset consists of 6,917 posts and 61,692 first-level comments, published between 21/02/2009 and 05/08/2019.

The gold standards were defined by domain experts, categorized according to the type of correlation expressed (e.g., symptom ↔ drug, place ↔ doctor), and supported by scientific sources where possible. Overall, 178 known positive and 107 known negative medical correlations were defined.

4.2   POIROT Implementation

To cope with typical text distortions in social contexts, we included in the quality preprocessing step operations such as emote normalization, Internet slang translation, and word lengthening fixing. Moreover, we applied lemmatization during analysis preprocessing.

Considering the heterogeneity and specificity of the entity types mentioned by the patients, we implemented entity tagging with TextRazor[6], a commercial NLP system offering highly comprehensive NER and NEL systems. We obtained data for 88,782 entities, organized in fine-grained taxonomic types, and linked to Wikipedia, DBpedia, Wikidata, and Freebase.

Since the main phenomenon to be explained concerns the reasons why patients have a positive or negative opinion on various topics, the document classification phase corresponds to an opinion mining task [37]. We made use of a very simple algorithm based on *opinion word count* (Eq. 9) [31]. In particular, we adopted the opinion lexicon published by Hu and Liu[7] (containing 6800 positive and negative words), translated into Italian and extended with domain-specific terms.

$$score(d) = nMatches(d, pos\_words) - nMatches(d, neg\_words) \qquad (9)$$

We implemented the methodology with both LSA and LDA. In particular, for LSA we adopted Randomized SVD (RSVD) to perform a near-optimal low-rank approximation using randomized algorithms. By doing so, we experienced an average increase in calculation speed of 800%.

We publicly release the R and Python source code, along with the full term-document matrix and gold standards used for evaluation[8].

---

[5] https://www.facebook.com/groups/36705181245/.
[6] https://www.textrazor.com/.
[7] https://www.cs.uic.edu/~liub/FBS/sentiment-analysis.html#lexicon.
[8] https://github.com/disi-unibo-nlu/POIROT.

Algorithm 3. Phenomena Explanation.

PhenomenonExplanation $(U_K, \Sigma_K, Tls, Tksrs, Dls, DCs, C, SQ, Min,$
$MinNormP, NClosestP, MinPvalueP)$

$\quad TlsN \leftarrow \forall t \in \text{rows}(Tls) \, \|t\|_2;$
$\quad$ **if** $SQ \neq NULL$ **then**
$\quad\quad THN \leftarrow \text{GetT}(TlsN > MinNormP);$
$\quad\quad QCC \leftarrow \forall t \in THN \text{ QueryClassCorrelation}(t, \dots)$
$\quad\quad PExpl \leftarrow \text{Get } QCC \text{ with max Pvalue}$
$\quad$ **else**
$\quad\quad PExpl \leftarrow \text{QueryClassCorrelation}(SQ, \dots)$
$\quad$ **end if**
$\quad AnalysisFinished \leftarrow F;$
$\quad$ **while** $!AnalysisFinished$ **do**
$\quad\quad TRanking \leftarrow$
$\quad\quad\quad \forall t \in \{Tksrs - PExpl.Q.Text\}$
$\quad\quad\quad \text{CosSim}(t_{Min}, PExpl.Q.Dksrs_{Min}));$
$\quad\quad ClosestT \leftarrow \text{GetT}(\text{TopH}(TRanking, NClosestP))$
$\quad\quad \text{DecSortBy}(ClosestT, TlsN)$
$\quad\quad NextT \leftarrow NULL$
$\quad\quad i \leftarrow 1$
$\quad\quad$ **while** $NextT = NULL \wedge i < |ClosestT|$ **do**
$\quad\quad\quad Q \leftarrow \text{Concat}(PExpl, ClosestT[i])$
$\quad\quad\quad QCC \leftarrow \text{QueryClassCorrelation}(Q, \dots)$
$\quad\quad\quad$ **if** $QCC.Pvalue < MinPvalueP$ **then**
$\quad\quad\quad\quad NextT \leftarrow QCC.Q.Text$
$\quad\quad\quad i++$
$\quad\quad$ **end while**
$\quad\quad$ **if** $NextT = NULL$ **then**
$\quad\quad\quad AnalysisFinished \leftarrow T$
$\quad\quad$ **else**
$\quad\quad\quad PExpl \leftarrow Q$
$\quad\quad$ **end if**
$\quad$ **end while**
$\quad$ **return** $PExpl;$

4.3 Experiments

We made two types of experiments. Firstly, we assessed the quality of the correlations learned from POIROT with a global analysis (i.e., based on the whole corpus), using Achalasia gold standards as a reference. Secondly, through local analyzes (i.e., considering only a subset of the original documents), we researched the reasons behind the positive and negative opinions expressed by patients on the two main surgical treatments for Achalasia: Heller-Dor and POEM. The results of the experiments are shown below.

Gold Standard Evaluation. We applied POIROT on LSA and LDA models of various sizes: (50, 100, 200, 300, 500) and (10, 15, 20), respectively. For each of them, we calculated the F1 measure-score based on the selected knee point and several thresholds (i.e., $1 -$ p-value) for the recognition of positive and negative gold standards. The identification of the optimal parameters was carried out automatically through a dimensionality calibration phase, building a confusion matrix at each step.

- *TP*, number of known positive correlations correctly identified.
- *TN*, number of known negative correlations correctly identified.
- *FP*, number of known negative correlations that the method incorrectly considers above the acceptance threshold, and therefore as positive.
- *FN*, number of known positive correlations that the method incorrectly considers below the acceptance threshold, and therefore as negative.

We also repeated the experiments for various model configurations (i.e., with and without lemmatization, with and without term weighting).

Table 2 summarizes the best results obtained. Using LSA, entity tagging, and term weighting, we recognized medical correlations with an F1 score $\approx 79\%$ (details are shown in Fig. 8). The lemmatization led to a slightly lower score mainly due to the alteration of names of doctors and medical centers. The other data clearly show the importance of the term weighting step and the choice of the knee point for noise removal. The sparse Dirichlet prior and the consequential high precision in assigning the topic mixture makes LDA less effective in identifying correlations.

Table 2. Best results obtained by POIROT with various models through dimensionality calibration on Achalasia gold standards. ET = entity tagging, TW = term weighting, LE = lemmatization, K = model dimensionality, KP = selected knee point, PTH = $1 -$ p-value threshold.

Language model	Modules			Parameters			Indices (%)			
	ET	TW	LE	K	KP	PTH	ACC	PRE	TPR/FPR	F1
LSA	✓	✓	✓	100	5	0.9	72.98	79.19	2.35	78.06
	✓	✓	✗	100	5	0.8	74.39	80.35	2.46	**79.20**
	✓	✗	✓	500	15	0.7	70.52	77.98	2.11	75.72
	✓	✗	✗	200	13	0.8	65.26	71.86	2.40	69.57
LDA	✓	✓	✗	15	15	0.9	60.35	66.67	2.21	69.71

Phenomena Explanation. After identifying the best model, we automatically built explanations for the phenomena of interest, starting from the centroids of the recognized clusters. In Table 3, we propose the combination of some of the most interesting descriptions obtained, with p-value <0.01 (χ^2 test). By interpreting them, we can appreciate how the positive polarity is linked to names of doctors and medical centers, while the negative one is linked to symptoms or

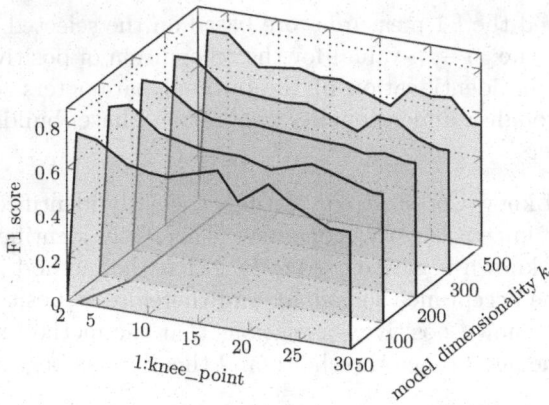

Fig. 8. The best F1 scores (i.e., with optimal p-value thresholds) for some predefined LM dimensions, as the selected knee point changes. The results are linked to the configuration with LSA, entity tagging, and term weighting. The absolute best F1 score is 0.792 with k = 100 and knee point = 5.

problems known in the literature. We also discovered new correlations such as "ppi" ↔ Negative opinion.

Table 3. Translated explanations returned by POIROT for positive and negative opinions about Achalasia treatments.

	Pos explanation	Neg explanation
Heller-Dor	Equipe, dr, costantini, salvador, padua, antireflux, plastic	Problems, drink, eat
POEM	Rome, prof, gemelli, costamagna, equipe, familiari	Reflux, inflammation, problems, liquid, pain, ppi, antacids

5   Conclusions

In this paper we presented POIROT, a novel unsupervised methodology of descriptive text mining to discover and achieve phenomena explanation from a corpus of unstructured and unlabeled texts. Specifically, POIROT first models relevant terms and documents in a latent semantic space, detecting statistically significant correlations between them. Next, unexpected concentration areas linked to the phenomenon of interest are investigated, and interpretable global textual explanations are constructed by iterative refining, accompanying the results with accurate probabilistic information.

POIROT is domain and language independent, as well as being modular in many of its component phases. One of the aspects that make POIROT so powerful is its ability to be used both in a human-driven and totally automatic way. In the first case, it allows to combine human skills and text analytics.

We conducted experiments on a medical case study focused on Esophageal Achalasia. Starting only from short and unlabeled social posts, POIROT automatically identified scientific correlations with 79% F1-measure score and provided valid explanations of patients' opinions on available surgical techniques. The methodology is applicable to any other target disease and in general to new domains, moreover it can be empowered with transfer learning approaches [16,38], which allow to leverage existing source learning models to overcome the lack of labeled data in new target domains [11,12,14,15].

We plan to add to the methodology polysemic neural language models and the capacity of detecting threads in conversational messages [19] moreover, we will address the representation of the extracted knowledge with description logics [2,5,24] and other approaches [43]. In this regard we will also explore the dynamic evolution of the knowledge in the form of knowledge graph with streaming techniques.

Acknowledgments. Gianluca Moro has developed this research and is the author of this methodology and its mathematical and algorithmic solutions, preliminarily reported also in [20,21], which are also included in his text mining course at the University of Bologna since the 2014/15 academic year and applied for the discovery of the reasons that contribute to cause aircraft accidents (https://unibodatascience.github.io/textmining/) from the raw textual reports collected by the US National Transportation Safety Board (NTSB).

Giacomo Frisoni has successfully applied this methodology to the real medical case study included in this work and in [20,21] and has contributed in this work to add the LDA and pLSA techniques and to apply and compare them in the case study.

We want to thank Cristina Lanni (https://www.researchgate.net/profile/Cristina_Lanni/research) (Researcher at the University of Pavia) and Celeste Napolitano (President of AMAE and National Secretary of the Italian Society of Narrative Medicine) for their precious help in building the dataset and participating in the realization of Achalasia gold standards.

References

1. Ahonen, H., Heinonen, O., Klemettinen, M., Verkamo, A.I.: Applying data mining techniques for descriptive phrase extraction in digital document collections. In: IEEE ADL 1998, pp. 2–11 (1998)
2. Baader, F., Calvanese, D., McGuinness, D.L., Nardi, D., Patel-Schneider, P.F. (eds.): The Description Logic Handbook: Theory, Implementation, and Applications. Cambridge University Press, New York (2003)
3. Blei, D.M., Ng, A.Y., Jordan, M.I.: Latent Dirichlet allocation. J. Mach. Learn. Res. **3**, 993–1022 (2003)
4. Bojanowski, P., Grave, E., Joulin, A., Mikolov, T.: Enriching word vectors with subword information. Trans. Assoc. Comput. Linguistics **5**, 135–146 (2017)
5. Bos, J.: A survey of computational semantics: Representation, inference and knowledge in wide-coverage text understanding. Lang. Linguistics Compass **5**(6), 336–366 (2011). https://doi.org/10.1111/j.1749-818X.2011.00284.x

6. Brown, T.B., et al.: Language models are few-shot learners. arXiv preprint arXiv:2005.14165 (2020)
7. Carbonaro, A.: Interlinking e-learning resources and the web of data for improving student experience. J. e-Learn. Knowl. Soc. **8**(2), 33–44 (2012)
8. Carbonaro, A., Piccinini, F., Reda, R.: Integrating heterogeneous data of healthcare devices to enable domain data management. J. e-Learn. Knowl. Soc. **14** (2018)
9. Datar, M., Immorlica, N., Indyk, P., Mirrokni, V.S.: Locality-sensitive hashing scheme based on p-stable distributions. In: Proceedings of the Twentieth Annual Symposium on Computational Geometry, pp. 253–262 (2004)
10. Devlin, J., Chang, M., Lee, K., Toutanova, K.: BERT: pre-training of deep bidirectional transformers for language understanding. CoRR abs/1810.04805 (2018). http://arxiv.org/abs/1810.04805
11. Domeniconi, G., Masseroli, M., Moro, G., Pinoli, P.: Discovering new gene functionalities from random perturbations of known gene ontological annotations. In: KDIR 2014 - Proceedings of the International Conference on Knowledge Discovery and Information Retrieval, Rome, Italy, pp. 107–116. SciTePress (2014). https://doi.org/10.5220/0005087801070116
12. Domeniconi, G., Masseroli, M., Moro, G., Pinoli, P.: Cross-organism learning method to discover new gene functionalities. Comput. Methods Programs Biomed. **126**, 20–34 (2016). https://doi.org/10.1016/j.cmpb.2015.12.002
13. Domeniconi, G., Moro, G., Pagliarani, A., Pasini, K., Pasolini, R.: Job recommendation from semantic similarity of linkedin users' skills. In: Marsico, M.D., di Baja, G.S., Fred, A.L.N. (eds.) Proceedings of the 5th International Conference on Pattern Recognition Applications and Methods, ICPRAM 2016, Rome, Italy, 24–26 February 2016, pp. 270–277. SciTePress (2016). https://doi.org/10.5220/0005702302700277
14. Domeniconi, G., Moro, G., Pagliarani, A., Pasolini, R.: On deep learning in cross-domain sentiment classification. In: Proceedings of the 9th International Joint Conference on Knowledge Discovery, Knowledge Engineering and Knowledge Management - (Volume 1), Funchal, Madeira, Portugal, 2017, pp. 50–60. SciTePress (2017). https://doi.org/10.5220/0006488100500060
15. Domeniconi, G., Moro, G., Pasolini, R., Sartori, C.: Cross-domain text classification through iterative refining of target categories representations. In: Fred, A.L.N., Filipe, J. (eds.) KDIR 2014 - Proceedings of the International Conference on Knowledge Discovery and Information Retrieval, Rome, Italy, 21–24 October 2014, pp. 31–42. SciTePress (2014). https://doi.org/10.5220/0005069400310042
16. Domeniconi, G., Moro, G., Pasolini, R., Sartori, C.: Iterative refining of category profiles for nearest centroid cross-domain text classification. In: Fred, A., Dietz, J.L.G., Aveiro, D., Liu, K., Filipe, J. (eds.) IC3K 2014. CCIS, vol. 553, pp. 50–67. Springer, Cham (2015). https://doi.org/10.1007/978-3-319-25840-9_4
17. Domeniconi, G., Moro, G., Pasolini, R., Sartori, C.: A comparison of term weighting schemes for text classification and sentiment analysis with a supervised variant of tf.idf. In: Helfert, M., Holzinger, A., Belo, O., Francalanci, C. (eds.) DATA 2015. CCIS, vol. 584, pp. 39–58. Springer, Cham (2016). https://doi.org/10.1007/978-3-319-30162-4_4
18. Domeniconi, G., Semertzidis, K., Lopez, V., Daly, E.M., Kotoulas, S., et al.: A novel method for unsupervised and supervised conversational message thread detection. In: DATA, pp. 43–54 (2016)

19. Domeniconi, G., Semertzidis, K., Moro, G., Lopez, V., Kotoulas, S., Daly, E.M.: Identifying conversational message threads by integrating classification and data clustering. In: Francalanci, C., Helfert, M. (eds.) DATA 2016. CCIS, vol. 737, pp. 25–46. Springer, Cham (2017). https://doi.org/10.1007/978-3-319-62911-7_2

20. Frisoni, G., Moro., G., Carbonaro, A.: Learning interpretable and statistically significant knowledge from unlabeled corpora of social text messages: a novel methodology of descriptive text mining. In: Proceedings of the 9th International Conference on Data Science, Technology and Applications - Volume 1: DATA, pp. 121–132. INSTICC, SciTePress (2020). https://doi.org/10.5220/0009892001210132

21. Frisoni, G., Moro., G., Carbonaro., A.: Unsupervised descriptive text mining for knowledge graph learning. In: Proceedings of the 12th International Joint Conference on Knowledge Discovery, Knowledge Engineering and Knowledge Management - Volume 1: KDIR, pp. 316–324. INSTICC, SciTePress (2020). https://doi.org/10.5220/0010153603160324

22. Girolami, M., Kabán, A.: On an equivalence between PLSI and LDA. In: Proceedings of the 26th Annual International ACM SIGIR Conference on Research and Development in Informaion Retrieval, pp. 433–434 (2003)

23. Gunning, D.: Explainable Artificial Intelligence (XAI). Defense Advanced Research Projects Agency (DARPA), nd Web 2 (2017)

24. Gyawali, B., Shimorina, A., Gardent, C., Cruz-Lara, S., Mahfoudh, M.: Mapping natural language to description logic. In: Blomqvist, E., Maynard, D., Gangemi, A., Hoekstra, R., Hitzler, P., Hartig, O. (eds.) ESWC 2017, Part I. LNCS, vol. 10249, pp. 273–288. Springer, Cham (2017). https://doi.org/10.1007/978-3-319-58068-5_17

25. Halko, N., Martinsson, P.G., Tropp, J.A.: Finding structure with randomness: probabilistic algorithms for constructing approximate matrix decompositions. SIAM Rev. 53(2), 217–288 (2011)

26. Hofmann, T.: Probabilistic latent semantic analysis. arXiv preprint arXiv:1301.6705 (2013)

27. Jia, R., Liang, P.: Adversarial examples for evaluating reading comprehension systems. arXiv:1707.07328 (2017)

28. Landauer, T.K., Dumais, S.T.: A solution to Plato's problem: the latent semantic analysis theory of acquisition, induction, and representation of knowledge. Psychol. Rev. 104(2), 211 (1997)

29. Landauer, T.K., Foltz, P.W., Laham, D.: An introduction to latent semantic analysis. Discourse Process. 25(2–3), 259–284 (1998)

30. Li, J., Sun, A., Han, J., et al.: A survey on deep learning for named entity recognition. IEEE Trans. Knowl. Data Eng. (2020)

31. Liu, B., Zhang, L.: A survey of opinion mining and sentiment analysis. In: Aggarwal, C., Zhai, C. (eds.) Mining Text Data, pp. 415–463. Springer, Boston (2012). https://doi.org/10.1007/978-1-4614-3223-4_13

32. Liu, H., Yin, Q., Wang, W.Y.: Towards explainable NLP: a generative explanation framework for text classification. arXiv:1811.00196 (2018)

33. Liu, T., Moore, A.W., Yang, K., Gray, A.G.: An investigation of practical approximate nearest neighbor algorithms. In: Advances in Neural Information Processing Systems, pp. 825–832 (2005)

34. Van der Maaten, L., Hinton, G.: Visualizing data using t-SNE. J. Mach. Learn. Res. 9, 2579–2605 (2008)

35. Mathews, S.M.: Explainable artificial intelligence applications in NLP, biomedical, and malware classification: a literature review. In: Arai, K., Bhatia, R., Kapoor, S. (eds.) CompCom 2019. AISC, vol. 998, pp. 1269–1292. Springer, Cham (2019). https://doi.org/10.1007/978-3-030-22868-2_90

36. Microsoft: Turing-NLG: A 17-billion parameter language model by Microsoft, February 2020

37. Moro, G., Pagliarani, A., Pasolini, R., Sartori, C.: Cross-domain & in-domain sentiment analysis with memory-based deep neural networks. In: Proceedings of the 10th International Joint Conference on Knowledge Discovery, Knowledge Engineering and Knowledge Management, IC3K 2018, vol. 1, pp. 125–136. KDIR, Seville (2018). https://doi.org/10.5220/0007239101270138

38. Pagliarani, A., Moro, G., Pasolini, R., Domeniconi, G.: Transfer learning in sentiment classification with deep neural networks. In: Fred, A., et al. (eds.) IC3K 2017. CCIS, vol. 976, pp. 3–25. Springer, Cham (2019). https://doi.org/10.1007/978-3-030-15640-4_1

39. Papernot, N., McDaniel, P., Jha, S., Fredrikson, M., Celik, Z.B., et al.: The limitations of deep learning in adversarial settings. In: EuroS&P, pp. 372–387 (2016)

40. Raffel, C., et al.: Exploring the limits of transfer learning with a unified text-to-text transformer. arXiv preprint arXiv:1910.10683 (2019)

41. Reimers, N., Gurevych, I.: Sentence-BERT: sentence embeddings using Siamese BERT-networks. arXiv:1908.10084 (2019)

42. Ren, X., He, W., Qu, M., et al.: AFET: automatic fine-grained entity typing by hierarchical partial-label embedding. In: Proceedings of the 2016 Conference on Empirical Methods in Natural Language Processing, pp. 1369–1378 (2016)

43. Riccucci, S., Carbonaro, A., Casadei, G.: Knowledge acquisition in intelligent tutoring system: a data mining approach. In: Gelbukh, A., Kuri Morales, Á.F. (eds.) MICAI 2007. LNCS (LNAI), vol. 4827, pp. 1195–1205. Springer, Heidelberg (2007). https://doi.org/10.1007/978-3-540-76631-5_114

44. Safavian, S.R., Landgrebe, D.A.: A survey of decision tree classifier methodology. IEEE Trans. Syst. Man Cybern. **21**, 660–674 (1991)

45. Sarlos, T.: Improved approximation algorithms for large matrices via random projections. In: 2006 47th Annual IEEE Symposium on Foundations of Computer Science (FOCS 2006), pp. 143–152. IEEE (2006)

46. Suzuki, R., Shimodaira, H.: Pvclust: an R package for assessing the uncertainty in hierarchical clustering. Bioinformatics **22**(12), 1540–1542 (2006)

47. Weiss, S.M., Indurkhya, N., Zhang, T.: Fundamentals of Predictive Text Mining. Springer, London (2015). https://doi.org/10.1007/978-1-4471-6750-1

Author Index